Privileged Populists

Privileged Populists

Populism in the Conservative and Libertarian Working Class

Micah J. Fleck

BLOOMSBURY ACADEMIC
LONDON • NEW YORK • OXFORD • NEW DELHI • SYDNEY

BLOOMSBURY ACADEMIC
Bloomsbury Publishing Plc
50 Bedford Square, London, WC1B 3DP, UK
1385 Broadway, New York, NY 10018, USA
29 Earlsfort Terrace, Dublin 2, Ireland

BLOOMSBURY, BLOOMSBURY ACADEMIC and the Diana logo
are trademarks of Bloomsbury Publishing Plc

First published in Great Britain 2022
This paperback edition published in 2023

A catalogue record for this book is available from the British Library.

Library of Congress Cataloging-in-Publication Data

Names: Fleck, Micah J., author.
Title: Privileged populists: populism in the conservative and libertarian
working class / Micah J. Fleck.
Description: London; New York: I.B. Tauris, 2022. |
Includes bibliographical references and index.
Identifiers: LCCN 2021036747 (print) | LCCN 2021036748 (ebook) |
ISBN 9780755627387 (hardback) | ISBN 9780755627394 (epub) |
ISBN 9780755627400 (pdf) | ISBN 9780755627417 (ebook other)
Subjects: LCSH: Populism. | Libertarianism. | Working class–Political activity. |
Social change–Political aspects. | Culture conflict–Political aspects.
Classification: LCC JC423 .F638 2022 (print) | LCC JC423 (ebook) |
DDC 320.56/62–dc23
LC record available at https://lccn .loc .gov /2021036747
LC ebook record available at https://lccn .loc .gov /2021036748

ISBN: HB: 978-0-7556-2738-7
PB: 978-0-7556-4637-1
ePDF: 978-0-7556-2740-0
eBook: 978-0-7556-2739-4

Typeset by Deanta Global Publishing Services, Chennai, India

To find out more about our authors and books visit
www.bloomsbury.com and sign up for our newsletters.

In loving memory of:
Peter J. Awn—a mentor.
&
David Graeber—an inspiration.

Contents

Figures

Preface

On December 16, 2007, a wave of grassroots supporters for the presidential campaign of the libertarian-minded Republican congressman Ron Paul held a twenty-four-hour record-breaking fundraiser to coincide with the 234th anniversary of the Boston Tea Party, one of the defining acts of protest that led to the American Revolution. The turnout was unprecedented, passionate, and most importantly, genuine. Its reverence for the revolutionary spirit of the eighteenth-century American colonists who felt wronged by the tyrannical British government was no farce—for all the bad press it would ultimately come to endure, the Tea Party movement of the early 2000s began as a very real call for liberation of working-class people.

But, liberation from what, exactly? If a group of people in this day and age are going to take rhetorical cues from the revolutionaries of their country's inception, it stands to reason they had better have a decent grasp on what it means to even be a "revolutionary" in the first place. From the perspectives of the Tea Party movement's founders, it was quite simple: to be a revolutionary in modern America was to hold deep skepticism of state power, disdain for collusion between government cronies and corporatist elites that edged out free enterprise, and loyalty to a sense of patriotism that was tethered not so much to one's geography but to the posited principles behind the country's very founding: autonomy for everyday people. Colloquially, this was referred to as the modern "liberty."

That broad sentiment finds its tangible political application in fights for more choices for workers, the ability to retain and live off the direct fruits of one's own labor, and a more decentralized, representative form of governance. The modern right's particular brand of revolutionary unrest is grounded in these same fights, not unlike any other form of radicalism throughout history that has called itself revolutionary. For this kind of unrest to even be present in the first place, of course, there must be held in common across the demographic experiencing it a set of genuine grievances with the given status quo. In the case of the originators of the modern Tea Party movement, those grievances were genuine because real, working-class people were those most enthusiastically supporting the Ron Paul campaign—not out of loyalty to the Republican Party or conservative tradition, but out of eagerness to create a better future for other workers much like themselves.

Only ten years later, in 2017, the self-described revolutionaries of the political right in America were no longer these same people holding the same ideas and principles mentioned earlier. Instead, a much broader sense of what it meant to be revolutionary and pro-liberty was growing increasingly prominent in this space, including reverence to geographical location, ethnic solidarity, and a united distrust against perceived enemies of different cultural values and lifestyles. It was as if the age-old bigotry of evangelical conservatism had somehow found a revival within the more radical wings of working-class conservatism, and that such a process had gone unchallenged due to it being rhetorically wrapped in the claimed cause of "liberty." Were the seemingly sincere libertarians still part of this movement? Yes. But alongside them, other stripes of revolutionary conservative were gaining prominence, and they held much more sinister sentiments along cultural lines. A little over three years after that shift had become the prominent driving force in the radicalized right, this broad subset of working-class conservatism and libertarianism finally attempted its long-craved revolution, and an armed march upon—and subsequent occupation of—the US Capitol building on January 6, 2021, occurred in an attempt by this group to stop what they believed was an illegitimate confirmation of a new US presidency that saw to end a four-year era of perceived populist representation of their most desperate plights in the form of the Donald Trump presidency.

At first blush, it might have been reasonable to assume that this shift had entirely originated from within the aforementioned Tea Party movement. After all, in only a matter of a few short years, that movement *had* significantly changed. No longer was it truly grassroots, instead infiltrated by corporate money and mainstream Republican politicians aiming to ride the wave of revolutionary unrest and use it to their own advantages. The movement was no longer genuinely guided by working-class conservatives, yet it still claimed to be. Unfortunately, many working-class conservatives themselves seemed to buy into that claim, continuing to participate despite the insincerity now prominent. However, this shift from truly bottom-up unrest with the present status quo to a veiled support of it was not exclusive to solely the Tea Party movement. That example can, however, serve as a microcosm of a more widespread process of distortion that this book's author contends to be a frequent occurrence within various conservative movements that consider themselves revolutionary.

To understand this, one has to dig much deeper into the history of revolutionary thought as a whole. When one does that, it becomes clear that all of these various flavors of outcry and government distrust from working-class people, conservative variants included, can all find their historical origins in *socialism*, not conservatism of any kind.

That is a position many readers may find difficult to believe if they have never encountered such a suggestion before. Indeed, if it is the revolutionary right wing under examination in this text, why wouldn't it be conservative principles driving the ground-level distrust of government? Isn't that what conservatives of all types claim is at the heart of their antiestablishment screeds? But the claim that socialism can give us the true insight to the rationale behind working-class revolutionary unrest as delineated earlier, even if a particular brand of said unrest exists on the right, is nevertheless a claim the author confidently stands by. In the following pages, the reasons for this will begin to become clear. For now, the summation can be understood as follows: socialism contains the authentic genesis of all antiestablishment unrest, while the right-wing anti-political manifestations that use similar rhetoric resulted from a distortion of that same unrest.

These conclusions were not initially intuitive to the author of this work. What now sits before the reader is the culmination of nearly two years of exhaustive research, philosophizing, corresponding with fellow scholars, revision, and, above all, a willingness on the author's part to unlearn what was assumed about what it means to be a revolutionary in the vein of those cited earlier. A brief overview of the specific questions and answers that cropped up over the course of the work is forthcoming, but at the outset, a handful of expectations for the reader.

First, the function of the book, and who it was written for. It should be made very clear right away that while this book is intended to be read by anyone who finds use in it, curious general readers stand to benefit the most from the information as it is laid out here (as opposed to strictly academics). The research and arguments within these covers can find some interest within academic circles as well, but the hope from the start of this project has been that those mindful everyday readers, who have taken interest in the topics of populism, political extremism, and working-class people's proclivity to being susceptible to falling into such spaces, can find here a definitive overview of the conditions and processes that lead to those ends. As such, the prose is put forth not assuming anything about readers' prior knowledge of the concepts and histories utilized to paint and frame the full picture of the book's thesis. Time is taken to define all of the most necessary terms for understanding the arguments along the way.

Over the course of this manuscript's revision process, it became clearer that the text needed more empirical grounding for the claims it was making about the thought processes and beliefs of the privileged populists under the microscope, here. Yes, the book always built up a strong enough argument in the more abstract world of theory, but it was found wanting in terms of tethering the theory to real-life subjects. An effort has therefore been made in the book's present form to lay out the thoughts and creeds of the people themselves at the outset of the book before the broader dissection of "movements" follows.

It is also worth clarifying right off the bat that when the author describes "libertarianism" at various points throughout the book, he isn't always referring to the same ideology or movement. Context plays a part in differentiating between the different forms of libertarianism explored here, but an effort has also been made in the revisions to more precisely label which libertarians are being talked about at any given moment. A point of confusion the author wishes to clarify right away, however, is that when a newfangled form of radical liberalism, infused with classically libertarian sentiment, is proposed as a possible path forward for misguided right-wing radicals in the book's final pages, it is not being suggested that the classical libertarianism of socialism gone by and the modern right-wing manifestation of libertarianism are the same thing—quite the contrary. Nor is the author trying to argue that the exact version of early libertarianism in the socialist tradition founded in the 1800s could possibly be revived without revision for modern political and economic times. Again, just the opposite is deemed true, and an effort has been made to better clarify this along the way. Those efforts, alongside the decision to introduce more tangible, empirical data concerning the real people within these movements at the book's outset, will hopefully make the reading much easier for readers who may otherwise struggle with the more theoretical elements of the books latter half.

The modern narrative surrounding self-claimed revolutionary philosophy of all political types is at times confounding, but this confusion is contrasted by how much more straightforward the reality is once one cuts through the decades of propaganda hoisted upon the working class—some of it intentional, and some of it organically occurring. But the result of this confusion in present-day discourse is that two people, claiming to hold completely opposing political ideologies, can in fact desire the same exact outcome for society and never realize that fact. The socioeconomic powers that be, as it turns out, are quite good at getting potential allies to talk past each other and for potential cooperation and organization against actual threats to break down. The presentation found in these pages hopes to lift the confusion and unite more people as a result of reading it.

Part of achieving this coherence has been contingent on this book reaching its own clarity on the matters at hand while still managing to parse out the tangled history with nuance and care. Many of the facts unearthed along the way are already known (and, indeed, there is no one piece of information in this book that taken on its own is particularly new), but a definitive volume that synthesized all of them together in a way that could put forth a cohesive argument, concerned primarily with distortion of genuine radical sentiment from within, had yet to be put forth. As such, this book serves the purpose of a tangible narrative as it pertains to the issue of working-class populism run amok in the hands of bad actors, and all the history and economic strife that has played into that (and will continue to play into it until our economic reality changes for the better).

The particular forms of this aforementioned process of distortion under examination here are those found within the movements of right-libertarianism (referred to by the left-libertarians as "vulgar libertarianism"), as well as "red-pilled" conservatism and other groups amounting to self-identified revolutionary movements on the right. Why focus on the right rather than the left? Because these movements on the right currently provide the most tumultuous examples of this distortion process being successful. In fact, said process has colored much of Western economic policy and social normativity for the past century. The pages ahead will lay out how and why this is the case. These radical rightists, despite their claims of genuine revolutionary unrest, often send their members down pro-authoritarian rabbit holes and get very *anti*-revolutionary reputations as a result.

The Alt-Right, the most extreme among these distorted manifestations in the present, is itself meant to be a normalization of fascism and nationalism on the main political stage. While the Alt-Right's function to make nationalism and racism appear sexy and "scientific" is clear, that quest would not have succeeded on its own had the other elements of political narrative examined in this text not already primed mainstream conservatism for this sort of exploitation.

Therefore, it stands reasonable enough that there are many still who do not realize that the larger problem is not necessarily the infiltration of the right-anarchist movement (itself an oxymoron, as this book will lay out) by fascism, but is instead the case of plasmic populist unrest allowing itself to willingly barter with extremism during liminal states that it increasingly inhabits.

I suppose I should briefly address the issue of whether or not there even *is* such a thing as a tangible "pipeline" leading the mainstream conservative groups I write about in the book into the Alt-Right, as this pipeline is referenced several times, and much of the book's entire thesis rests upon it being a real phenomenon. Many people in these groups, especially the modern right-libertarians, have pushed back on this claim quite often when I have presented it to them. On the other hand, many more have agreed. It will not take long upon a web search to find instances of the remaining sane voices in these groups decrying their fellow libertarians and conservatives for becoming more commonly brutal and fascistic. Among them, noted libertarian journalist Nick Gillespie, noted libertarian economist Steve Horwitz, all members of the socially progressive libertarian organization *Bleeding Heart Libertarians*, including moral philosophers Matt Zwolinski and Roderick T. Long (the latter of which is a leading scholar in the process of pursuing détournement—or utilitarian reconfiguration—of Austrian School economics' most salvageable elements), and many others who have taken a stand against this shift despite still wearing the label of "libertarian" for themselves. Not only should this demonstrate the internal acknowledgment of the reality of the aforementioned pipeline, but it should also serve as a list of very noble and admirable people who still remain within the movement. The purpose of this book is not to lump these actors in with everyone else around them in their movements, but it nevertheless makes clear where it seems that the movements themselves are still yet falling victim to false narratives.

Many of these narratives have been hoisted upon the younger generations within these movements through the newer forms of sharing information. The alternative media scene, a network of news sites, social media pages, online forums, and obscure think tanks that played a major role in crafting the outlooks of many of the young and active voters involved in the 2016 election discourse, has housed many self-labeled libertarians over the years who have also played apologetics for fascistic, crypto-fascistic, and nationalistic voices who shared common ground with them on certain socioeconomic topics. These figures include (but are not limited to) YouTube comedian Steven Crowder, libertarian journalist-turned-nationalist Lauren Southern, libertarian philosopher-turned-white nationalist sympathizer Stefan Molyneux, conspiracy theorist Alex Jones of *InfoWars* fame, libertarian podcaster-turned-white nationalist Christopher Cantwell, and so forth. In addition to these explicitly libertarian-identifying figures, many other supposedly revolutionary conservatives in the same intellectual circles who hold similar socioeconomic perspectives, including a large chunk of the online so-called skeptic community, have lent their collective hand toward legitimizing many of these more extreme transformations from right-libertarian to "identitarian" by either sharing or featuring the views held by these extremists within their own content as examples of critical thought and reasonable challenges to a supposedly oppressive cultural status quo.

In addition to this more relatively recent new wave of media personalities, more broadly respected, academic figures such as German economist Hans Herman-Hoppe and social scientist Charles Murray have for decades been laying the intellectual groundwork for making these conversations of race, nationality, and innate human worth based on surface-level differences more acceptable as academic points of interests for right-libertarians and other stripes of economic conservatives. Furthermore, they have done much to bring economic strife into the fold as a reasonable starting gun from which such conversations can take off in everyday discourse. These figures, as well as the newer, more youth-focused online personalities mentioned prior, bring with them scads of loyal readers, listeners, and viewers who themselves go on to influence the minds and hearts of their friends, families, and co-workers in the conversations they have related to the angst felt in their own lives. Of these who choose to become passionately politically active, most are doing so for noble reasons and in good faith. But they are acting on incomplete information that can lead to nationalism and fascism, as this book will demonstrate. They are numerous.

Certainly, it is the case that *every* political group has embarrassing elements that do not represent the whole. But in the case of right-libertarians and populist conservatives at large, something unique stands out about them. They claim at the outset to be in favor of revolutionary, antiestablishment ideas, but what they ultimately seem to fight for more often than not is the preservation of an economic system that oppresses them. This in effect aligns them fiscally with every other mainstream political group, despite their claims to the contrary. It is somewhere within this contradiction that I began to believe the answer to my question of how a revolutionary movement could behave like an oppressive one resided. "False consciousness," in the Marxist vernacular, had enveloped these movements.

There also needs to be a clarification here regarding what I intend to do by using the term "false consciousness" throughout this work. Historically, the term has been used in different ways for different intents, and not every case of its use has been particularly provable or mindful of ideological bias. I have no interest in resurrecting a frivolously applied, unempirical understanding of the concept, nor do I wish to retread the prior, arguably pretentious, ground of Marx himself when he used false consciousness to claim validity in his (in this author's view) broad-brush concept of the *lumpenproletariat*—essentially his way of saying that those who did not want to follow his brand of revolution were simply too uninformed to see the objective truth that he and his fellows already knew. Such imprecise and ideologically driven applications of this idea of false consciousness are ultimately unhelpful and stand to only confound the conversation further. Therefore, my aim with using the term in the context of this book is to tether it to provable, empirical realities of misguided populism that manifest first as deliberate insurgencies into working-class populist spaces and then ultimately induce an organic process of self-delusion couched in neoliberal hegemonic perspectives. The entire middle section of the book is at least adjacently dedicated to this endeavor.

So, in short, yes, there *is* a direct connection, and not just happenstantial infiltration, between these revolutionary conservative movements and their more nationalistic and fascistic forms. But it is important to note that the main thesis of the book is about how limited perspectives, due to intersectional privilege in certain working-class demographics, can unwittingly lend themselves to exploitation for the purposes of perpetuating class divides and wealth inequality. The fact that Alt-Right screeds have become normalized in conservative circles as a result of this process is important, but while it initially got me interested in this project, it is no longer the main focus. Trump, the Alt-Right, and other extremist right-wing manifestations finding footing in the present political climate is an externality of a much deeper and troubling problem. That problem is systemic, transcends this one snapshot of time, and stands to haunt us indefinitely if we do not face the economic and ideological realities that brought us here.

If there is any silver lining to be found at all in this complicated quagmire, it is the knowledge that through inquiries like this one, we might just determine how to truly jettison our extremist proclivities, see through the fog, and embrace working-class solidarity. That prospect, that hope, is ultimately why this book exists.

Introduction

Of Realizations and Distortions

We live in populist times. The 2016 presidential election in America solidified that reality if there was any remaining doubt. Despite this, many mainstream and well-regarded political analysts, reporters, publications, and television stations all failed to predict the outcome of said election. Even the polls that supposedly represented the voting public did not come close to accurately predicting what was to come. Everyone said Hillary Clinton was going to win by a landslide. Everyone claimed her opponent Donald Trump's rhetoric was too incendiary and his brand too offensive to ever get him the win in the general election. But something all of these analyses failed to take into account was the simple fact that Hillary Clinton, despite all of her credentialed experience as a politician (or perhaps because of it), came across too many working-class voters as fraudulent and tone-deaf to the general working people's perspectives and needs. In short, Hillary Clinton was not a populist candidate. She was a business-as-usual politician in a time when that branding no longer held the power it once did a few short decades before. But the mainstream political leadership of the DNC seemed unaware of this fact, as did many of the pundits and journalists who collectively got the election so wrong.

Four years later, when Joseph R. Biden, Jr. narrowly beat Trump to become the forty-sixth president of the United States, it was still clear due to the data surrounding actual support for Biden's proposed policies (only 46 percent of his voters)[1] that the Democratic Party still remained largely out-of-touch with the real working poor, opting instead for the typical centrist rhetoric that keeps fiscal elites comfortable.

None of this means that Donald Trump was what the working-class voters actually needed, but in these times of genuine cynicism and disillusionment with the establishment's status quo, there seemed no viable alternative—Bernie Sanders, another populist candidate like Trump in 2016, seemed to have a much more genuine and positive platform that was built upon compassion rather than antagonism, and his popularity during the Democratic primary race for the party's nomination was an organic and near-unstoppable force that also contradicted most of the mainstream analysts' narrative. But Sanders ultimately did not win the Democratic nomination, and what was left for the voting public to choose from was a run-of-the-mill politician with run-of-the-mill ideas in Hillary Clinton and a complete wildcard populist candidate who at least claimed to be against the political establishment in Donald Trump. The working-class voters organized in a way that had not been seen in decades, and they voted for the only option left in the election who at the very least stood a chance to shake up the system in a positive way.[2]

While that gamble ultimately did not pay off, and Donald Trump's presidency became mired by various scandals, investigations, and dropping citizen approval since the election, the reality is that without an equally populist candidate on the other side, the 2016 election in hindsight could not have gone any other way.[3] It seems that populist candidates, as extreme as they can often appear to centrist-minded observers, are tapping into something real and bubbling beneath the surface for an incredibly large number of working people who are sick of business as usual and long for a change to the system—a change with them, the forgotten working multitudes, in mind.

Working-class people of all political stripes are more aware than ever, for instance, of just how little they have to show for their arduous work in the marketplace. Hours are getting longer, wages are stagnating, the dollar stretches thinner and thinner, and daily life is becoming more stressful and anxiety-inducing for a growing number of folks.[4] Yet, even though the organic populist cry for a representative voice is legitimate, the growing populist masses on the political right have been given a slew of false explanations and boogeymen deemed responsible for their woes—explanations devoid of historical or economic accuracy, aiming to turn working-class people against one another rather than unite them in solidarity against the actual problem: the neoliberal economic system itself.[5] In America, these efforts have managed to misdirect what began as genuine populist frustration on the political right into anti-political paranoia and anger that blames manufactured antagonists on a cultural level for real-life problems on the economic level. These sinister and misdirecting elements, this book contends, are largely responsible for creating the intellectual climate on the populist right that made the Trump election (and everything adjacent to it) a reality.[6]

What this means is that false consciousness, a term traditionally used in Marxist theory to explain how institutions intentionally hypnotize people into accepting their own oppression,[7] has found an organic feedback loop within the conservative corners of the working class in which it can materialize from within populism as a naturally occurring logic—a logic full of genuine grievances and unrest with the state of affairs all working-class people now suffer through. The propaganda in these conservative populist arenas is no longer conscious or forced upon them from on high. Instead, actual revolutionary sentiment regarding real woes has emerged after generations of neoliberal normalization has denied commodious access to the facts regarding what the actual problem for said woes is. This is still false consciousness, but it is organic, self-imposed false consciousness that now runs like a well-oiled machine. Most recently, fellow anthropologist William Mazzarella corroborated this process by independently coming to this same conclusion, delineating the process as "an intensified insistence of collective forces that are no longer adequately organized by *formally* hegemonic social forms" but are instead an organic offshoot of past hegemony that acts as "a mattering-forth of the collective flesh."[8]

One of the biggest movements within this new populist conservatism, the Alt-Right, is not quite as straightforward or simplistic as a mere neo-Nazi resurgence (though this is often how it is framed). It is something much deeper: a normalization of extremist, nationalist views within mainstream conservative movements. This is done by tapping into deeply and broadly ingrained sentiments—at the hands of decades of neoliberal policy apologetics and anti-revolutionary propaganda—and merely bringing these sentiments' most ardent adherents to their extreme logical conclusions. If the free market is perfect and untouchable, this campaign proposes, then something else other than the economic system itself must be to blame for the aforementioned working-class turmoil. It is within this ubiquitous realm of ignorance and fear that nationalistic extremism has hidden in plain sight and proposed its own solutions to these yet-unanswered problems, and it is via neoliberalism's utter lack of substantive answers of its own that such extreme concepts have been allowed to flourish unchallenged.

Meanwhile, mainstream conservative movements such as modern right-libertarianism and the "red-pilled right" have been able to successfully masquerade as revolutionary initiatives designed to rope in honest seekers of change and veer them into unwittingly fighting to preserve the very system that has displaced them in the first place: capitalism. These two phenomena, capitalist apologetics and right-wing nationalism, are not consciously in cahoots with one another, but the failure of the former to provide satisfactory explanations for conservative working-class suffering had set the stage for the latter to decades ago infiltrate these spaces and fill in the gaps with their more extreme brand of populism. As social theorist Nicos Poulantzas once observed, "the rise of fascism corresponds to an ideological crisis of the working class, and to a significant crisis of the revolutionary organizations."[9] The same occurrence had happened in the history of the case in the United States examined in this book.

The 2016 Trump campaign, as well as similar right-wing populist movements in Europe, benefited from this perfect storm of a confounded working people's unrest, an inadequate status quo's empty promises, and a ruling class's desire to remain impenetrable. In the following pages, we will explore the entire storm and examine, among other things, how and why populism organically crops up within specific groups, how populism can be derailed and used for counterintuitive ends, why the present economic system has failed the conservative working class uniquely, how liberalism and socialism are interrelated throughout history (and how they have changed), and how even certain pockets of the economically failing working class can fear losing a sense of cultural privilege they once took for granted. Altogether, these circumstances create a sense of fear in said demographics, this book's main aim is to articulate how that fear can be exploited on the intellectual frontiers of faux-revolutionary conservatism.

These faux-revolutionaries of the right, whatever their specific self-labelings may amount to from group-to-group (and there are a few of them, all interrelated), claim they are the true arbiters of freedom. But what *is* freedom? Is it something that must be ubiquitous or merely personal in order to be tangibly realized? This is a debate that has raged for centuries, and yet the winning perspective often seems to be that freedom for *all* is the only genuine liberation human society can achieve. This was an idea that many would argue first took tangible shape as a governing prescription within the founding sentiments of the United States, yet it has spent centuries going unfulfilled in that very same country. In effect, universality of freedom has constantly been in a tug-of-war with the nation in which it was first perspicuously proposed, while said nation's populace has grown increasingly opaque to the irony.[10] Why?

Prior to 2016, the author of this work personally believed the best shorthand answer to this question was that the US government simply had too much power over the arena where personal opportunities to grow and succeed were most dominant: the market. While the pitfalls of corporate-government collusion are still acknowledged, such reductionist diagnoses have since been carved out to make room for the fact that there is another huge factor that perpetuates the unequal status quo: neoliberalism. To be more specific, the belief that a completely deregulated capitalist economy, under every circumstance, breeds true liberation for all people.[11] This is factually and historically incorrect, as this book will go on to explain, but that doesn't stop the most ideological of conservative populists from assuming that neoliberal policy and capitalistic social outlook are the only reasonable outcomes to shoot for.

This is by no means a revelation in and of itself—neoliberalism has been on the radars of many scholars who write on the issue of social inequality for many years. But there is still an element to this phenomenon that is rarely focused on, and that is the element in which genuinely noble classically liberal ideals, originating from the very first proponents of liberalism, are conflated with equally noble classical socialist rhetoric in an effort to recast these ideas as thought up by capitalists. This was done, in this book's view, to confound the populace and funnel the working class into embracing the present neoliberal reality—something that holds dear neither classical liberalism nor the earliest and truest forms of socialism. Instead, both sentiments are morphed into apologetics for the capitalistic status quo, which has historically existed to perpetuate class division and reawaken feudalist economic hierarchies.[12]

The existing literature on the topic of neoliberalism in particular will often describe classical liberalism and neoliberalism as being in essence the same thing, with neoliberalism merely being the modern manifestation of an ideology that always stood against the working class from the beginning; this book submits that this is not the case, and, furthermore, that what we might consider "classical liberalism" post-1830 is itself much different from the tone of the very first liberal thinkers' pronouncements from the previous century.[13] This distinction matters, because all of the variations and perspectives of liberalism appear similar enough in rhetoric in order that adherents to the concepts of its noblest concepts (liberation and free movement of people; opportunity for all) could quite easily end up protecting and justifying the effects of its more sinister distortions (class divide, division of labor, refusal of access to resources). This is precisely what has happened in American politics, and that is what this book will in large part set out to demonstrate.

The more dissected question of this manuscript, however, is whether or not the majority of right-wing populists in America are conscious perpetuators of the white nationalism and crypto-fascism now ever-present in the faux-revolutionary conservatism that elected Donald Trump as president.[14] To answer that, two key elements of said populism are examined: (1) anti-political populism as an organic phenomenon and how it, in particular, interacts with conservative idealism, and (2) a state of cultural and intellectual subjugation to the idea that true economic freedom must come at the expense of social equity. By looking at where these two elements intersect, how they interact, and what results from said interaction, we get a clearer picture of the current state of affairs in present-day America—something being referred to here and henceforth as neoliberal hegemony.[15]

Therefore, this book will investigate the genesis of the rhetoric and mindset of the populist working-class conservative. To do that, some historical and cultural context will be introduced periodically. However, in the interest of not losing its focus, this book does *not* aim to be an exhaustive history lesson on every form of oppression known to the American continent. The author simply intends to analyze how the process of normalization of inequality can take hold in ideologically narrow environs, and then apply that analysis to the current state of affairs in American conservatism and its populist forms.

The answer to the question of "are most conservative populists in America self-aware racists" is found in the following pages to be "no." While that much might be self-evident, it is also not where the concern should end. While it is certainly worth noting that most people helping validate the rhetoric of groups like the Alt-Right (and their "red-pilled" cousins often referred to as the alt-light) are not doing so consciously, this does not change the fact that the effects of a silent (or unwittingly compliant) majority cut just as deeply into the soft tissue of democracy regardless of said majority's initial intent.

But what are the tangible dangers of this, right from the outset? Why do these two aforementioned attributes of populist logic and neoliberal hegemony in particular go hand in hand the way that they do? Essentially, this marriage bleeds together two different kinds of populism: one that is found within a broader demographic of working-class American worker (long left behind by both major political parties and justifiably frustrated by this reality), and another, more sinister, populism—a privileged populism. One that perceives itself as similarly left behind, but for very different reasons—some of them economic, but many more of them cultural. It is on the cultural front where the economic elites and the working-class conservatives find their common ground. This privileged populism blames boogeymen for its woes, but it does such a good job of wrapping its rhetoric in classically liberal clothing that it has managed to assimilate into the broader, more understandable populism of the right-of-center working American. Again, whether this is a conscious effort or organic occurrence is not the point (it seems to be a bit of both, as the chapters ahead will lay out); the effect it is causing, however, *is* very much the point.

The project of pulling back the veil on these details is especially significant for this book's author, who is a former self-described libertarian. The "former" label came in the wake of the 2016 presidential election. What used to be infrequent instances of subdued nationalism and crypto-fascism among those within libertarian and conservative circles slowly became full-blown prejudicial screeds with insistent regularity. Said movements' adherents ended up sounding collectively less and less like John Locke, the supposed father of classical liberal idealism.[16] This ultimately culminated in the form of several fairly prominent right-libertarian figures suddenly arguing in favor of white genocide conspiracy theories, a fascistic transitional period, "blood and soil" (a Nazi dog whistle), and other similarly abhorrent ideas.[17] Empathetic libertarians who leaned left were greatly disturbed by this change and wanted to investigate how it happened—this author among them.

But things are, of course, more complex than a simple declaration of "Nazi!" against any given subject of analysis in this book can solely explain, lest we frivolously invoke

Godwin's law.[18] As Poulantzas correctly pointed out in his own work regarding the study of the subject, fascism "must be situated in the framework of a given stage of capitalist development," yet that stage in and of itself "is not enough to explain fascism."[19] In other words, while clear overlap with (and, at times, apologetics for) the nationalistic elements of right-wing populism are present more and more within the more mainstream working-class conservative spaces, that does not mean that every conservative working-class populist is innately a nationalist or a fascist. More is going on, here, as is always the case when fascism and nationalism rear their ugly ideological heads amidst socioeconomic crises.[20]

The conclusion arrived at in this particular investigation is disheartening, but sound: this is not a problem of bad apples spoiling an otherwise wholesome hoard within these particular populist spaces as the author originally thought; this problem is systemic, ideological, and driven by populism of an elitist, terrified kind that stretches across class and taps into an intersectional sense of cultural unrest: a populism that is privileged, not always economically, but socially and culturally. Simultaneously, the working-class half of the equation panics as it sees, like all other portions of the working class, the accelerating annihilation of fiscal security and sense of social purpose through work. Libertarianism in its modern, American form (i.e., the right-wing "vulgar libertarianism" mentioned earlier) is innately fashioned to make false promises to a populace presently coming up against the brutal shortcomings of late-stage capitalism and then offer no viable explanations in said shortcomings' wake. The end result is that present-day vulgar libertarianism, and faux-revolutionary conservatism at large, unwittingly aids and abets status quo ideals by appealing vacuously to the supposed classical liberalism of invisible hands and free markets—and has been for decades. As was alluded to earlier, this is something Marxist theorists call "false consciousness," and that term has been utilized in this book throughout to describe the organic phenomenon of mass self-delusion occurring within populist conservative spaces specifically. The author feels this is an appropriate classification, even if one is not a Marxist, because Marxist terminology is often the only etymological space to pull from when in need of describing various socioeconomic observations and function— the classical, neoclassical, and liberal scholarship simply does not trouble itself with understanding many of the same ideas and class-driven aspects of human action the Marxists have been aiming to unpack for the entirely of their scholarship.[21] This does not mean one must be a Marxist in order to understand and use the terminology— readers of this book who do not wish to make such a leap take heart.

All of this is to say that the 2016 election was not the beginning of the phenomena it embodied; it was the synthesis. Without a proper distinction made between the two perspectives of genuine and artificial anti-authoritarianism, one can bleed into the other. Celebrating individuality and simply fetishizing selfishness can become indistinguishable.

In his own way, the author hopes to identify and salvage what is left and worthwhile from the broader liberal tradition while laying bare the sinister hindrances of its remaining modern manifestation. It is also the intent of the author to reveal the reality of a sinister hijacking of classical anarchist and socialist rhetoric with the intent of repurposing it as populist sales pitches for the American capitalist platform.

Altogether, this deception, as well as the distortion of true liberal concepts and values (identified here as radical liberalism), has led to the present unrest and confusion within the political dialogue that served as the smokescreen for authoritarian ideals to win a generation of minds and hearts in a nonauthoritarian demographic. This work is the first major attempt by the author to shine the light on this grim reality.

* * *

In order to make this undeniably dense subject matter more easily digestible, the book has been divided into thematically focused parts that can function as both self-contained stand-alone entries and complimentary pieces of a larger whole. Having said this, the latter two parts of the book still build significantly on the more theoretical foundations laid in the first, so the author recommends every reader at least read the initial four chapters of the book first before venturing off into more nonlinear excavation of the latter material. It is also worthy of note that each chapter within the book parts takes its own approach to the dissection of the topic of focus, whether it be theoretical, anthropological, or historical. Each section has a summary here in the introduction to give the reader an idea of which approach will dominate the book part in question. All of this signposting is in place to help readers of all backgrounds and interests quickly find the best portions of the book for their own intellectual aims.

Part I of this work focuses on the basics of what populism is, what it looks like when it occurs within political confines, and what specific forms it can take. This is delineated by examining the definitions of populism, anti-politics, and other terms and citations that lend themselves to that end. Specific examples from human history and culture, including present-day examples of the common viewpoints of the very people populating the movements being examined, are then brought to bear on the subject. The author himself being once a prominent part of the right-libertarian movement in particular, much of this reporting comes from his own direct conversations with others in these spaces. In the cases where it was deemed necessary, names have been changed. But the data is still pulled from life. This is all done in an attempt to illustrate how this sort of thinking is not only not new but is in fact far more common than many everyday Americans might initially suspect. This also makes clear the fact that the phenomenon has materialized previously and elsewhere in the world, and that the results in these cases can be heeded by us in the States if we truly wish to liberate ourselves from the current state of affairs and avoid a similar end result. The empirical data is presented in Chapter 1 focusing on practice, while the more abstract theorizing on the how and why behind these views is present in Chapter 2.

These points are hit one by one as we first take populism as its own political logic into account, citing the work of eminent scholars on the subject such as Ernesto Laclau and Jens Rydgren, in an attempt to determine whether or not populism can be a good exercise under certain circumstances. Then, populism the reality is examined in contrast with populism as an ideal, and it is here in which historical instances of populism in action leading to the bolstering and validation of negative, antagonistic ideas are found. Conspiratorial anti-political populists are presented as the most topical examples for how populism can create both intentional and mental dictatorships and control the very populace that it claims to rally around.

The genesis of anti-politics and radical right-wing populism over the past several decades, tracing back to the public victories of the French Front National in the 1980s and then followed by the more covert metastasizing of nationalistic idealism through to the modern day, is synthesized into something manageable and ascribable for our purposes of understanding its semi-linear trajectory of growth. Here the book calls on existing groundwork laid within such theories of how populism manifests negatively, including the Ethnic Competition Hypothesis and Social Breakdown Theory. The work and perspectives of the late Nicos Poulantzas are also called upon to serve as a guiding force through these sorts of discussions.

Part II will start to delve more into how the populist phenomenon described in Part I can lead to organic false consciousness cropping up within the conservative working class. A big part of explaining that involves identifying the various revolutionary schools of thought that played their various parts in influencing both public consciousness and public policy over the centuries. Conservatives and modern libertarians claim to stand for classically liberal ideals. But what does that actually mean? Here, the questions "what is neoliberalism" and "what is libertarianism" are posed, followed by realistic, evidence-based answers that distinguish idealism from reality and ideology from history. The innate flaws within neoliberal philosophical postulations, as well as their policy-minded implementations, are discussed. It is also in this part of the book where the origins of libertarianism as a socialist and anarchistic philosophy that actually stood opposed to classical liberalism in many respects are identified.

First, neoliberalism and classical liberalism are defined individually; then the applicable similarities and differences between the two are specified. From there, neoliberalism's more ubiquitous elements are found to be present in much of modern conservatism's rhetoric, thereby adequately qualifying neoliberalism, and not "libertarianism" in the traditional sense, as the actual driving force behind the self-described revolutionary conservatives of today.

Some specific instances of cross-examination of modern conservatism and libertarianism are therefore included in this part—particularly when the elements under scrutiny are found to be viable candidates for having influenced and/or defended Alt-Right populist ideas in the American political conversation. Through this inquest, it is highlighted that liberalism, in both its classical and neoliberal forms, appears to, in the broad strokes, preserve the world of the privileged few—despite whether or not its most noble proponents claim the contrary (and they do). Examples are given, both philosophical and historical, of how liberalism fails to meet its claimed ideals in the real world and how its practical application and rhetoric lend themselves to validation and protection of some of the most toxic ideas in modern right-wing political thought.

Going back into the history of liberalism as a whole, a re-examination of the topical writings of John Locke, the father of classical liberalism (i.e., the philosophy modern libertarians and conservatives claim to be following), is undertaken in which it is determined what Locke *actually* wrote about versus what modern conservatives claim he believed on topics such as free markets and private ownership. This reveals some of the more sinister obfuscation that is afoot within the liberty movement today, especially when the issues of the social contract and property rights are discussed. Through a close reading of Locke, it is determined that he indeed advocated for a social contract of sorts, and that he postulated the concept that the land itself is a shared resource, and that people can remain equally free only if the need to share this resource is recognized and respected. This is, of course, the complete opposite of what the rhetoric from modern conservatives tainted by neoliberal ideology would suggest.

The focus then turns to libertarianism, whose origins are found to be socialism, not liberalism. The liberal contemporaries of the first socialists in the early 1800s are instead revealed to have misrepresented the libertarians of their day, appearing to align their own perspectives with that of the ruling class that stood to cripple, not liberate, the working people.

At the same time, certain aspects of the earliest classical liberals such as Locke and Smith are shown to overlap with the classical socialists, and the rhetorical arena in which such overlap still occurs today in the modern conversation is where this book finds the most potential for cultivation and salvaging for a reparative conversation moving forward.

Part III is where the issue of neoliberalism serving as an indirect normalizing smokescreen for nationalist extremism and crypto-fascism is finally addressed head-on. It delves deeper into how populism manifests itself within a very specific demographic of people in order to give rise to the support for Trump and what he stood for—to a certain degree, this means that the Alt-Right will be examined, but, more importantly, the book will unpack the way in which Alt-Right sympathies fill in the gaps of adjacent neoliberal political movements in order to synthesize all of the coalescing working-class anxiety that we have observed thus far into a tangible web of ideological influence and false consciousness takeover. What we learn in Part II of the book will help to even better frame the conditions under which such a transformation of outlook can occur largely organically within these saner overlapping groups.

The process observed over the course of these chapters can be summarized as follows: the contortion of liberating ideas into oppressive ones via the ideological allegiance to bourgeois policies and cultural promulgations that masquerade as pro-freedom. The thesis is that this process has given a validating voice to a specific sub-demographic of culturally privileged working-class people who nevertheless feel oppressed and forgotten. Their biases intact, and their ideology devoid of anything to challenge those biases, these scads of lost souls have found a means of *feeling* like revolutionaries against their perceived oppressors when in reality they are facing to give up nothing at all. Instead, they fight to preserve the status quo that makes them feel culturally secure—the only beacon of stability that can be seen in their paradoxically underprivileged economic situations. But this status quo does something else, as well. It perpetuates an uncaring economic system that is designed to deprive these privileged revolutionaries from what they ultimately want: complete autonomy. Thus, as they fight to preserve everything they know, they ensure their own deprivation from the world of success and prosperity they long for from afar.

To understand precisely how this confounding and counterintuitive storm kicks into form, we must begin our inquiry at the point that serves as its entire foundation: the organic and often misunderstood phenomenon of populism itself.

Part I

Populism in Theory and Practice

(Theoretical Frameworks)

1

Who Are the Privileged Populists?

The working class today correctly identifies that it is being shackled and exploited. The ways in which one's politics influence how one engages with this observation dictate whether or not reality becomes fiction when identifying what the actual driving force is behind said exploitation. Privileged populism, in this book's surmising, is what happens when an historically organic form of populism, the working class organizing upon fact-based grievances with their political system to change it, can be derailed into a distorted form of populism: a faux-revolutionary sentiment that walks and talks like its fellow revolutionary movements but in fact diffuses any actual striving for positive change. This form of populism has been diluted down to an almost exclusively economistic form of liberalism more concerned with celebrating "freedom" as a principled concept for a handful of preapproved demographics rather than a lived, ubiquitous reality for all. The most extreme form this can take (and has taken in the past) is fascism, but along the way toward that end, privileged populism can appear rather benign if still misguided. It is within such liminal states, between misguided and full-blown fascistic, where distorted populism does most of its handiwork—twisting and confounding the rhetoric of actual revolutionaries in order to woo certain privileged demographics into believing they are fighting the good fight without having to sacrifice anything about the comfortable way they currently already see the world around them.

The Movements of Interest

This chapter is concerned with identifying the specific movements within (or aimed at) the conservative working class at large that the author argues are currently undergoing these aforementioned distorting processes into privileged populism. It will be the observations laid out in this chapter that the more theoretical elements of the book should be connected to for reorientation when and if the reader deems it necessary to ground the theory and history in a present-day context. Without further ado, we are off to that end. It should be made clear that while these movements on their own were not large enough to have singlehandedly induced the 2016 US presidential election, each of them in their own respective ways played a part in turning the tide in favor of the faux-populist candidate of that election, Donald Trump.

Right-Libertarianism

One of the fastest-growing movements within the broader revolutionary right is the self-described "liberty movement," made up of those calling themselves "libertarians" and who consider themselves to be above the concepts of left versus right, despite most mainstream iterations of American libertarianism today holding much more in common with the right than anything else. While this movement in its present form has been around since the mid-1900s, it has been aided in its numbers significantly by a steady influx of young people in online and college spaces since the early 2000s. One of the most popular "libertarian" publications, *Being Libertarian*, went from having around 100,000 readers in 2014 to having over 900,000 readers in 2020.[1] Most of its readership is made up of young working-class men in the North American region.[2] Among some of its most popular content leading up to the 2016 election were posts and articles shaming trans people and accusing Black Lives Matter protestors of being terrorists.[3] This book's author worked at *Being Libertarian* as an editor and opinion writer during this same time and saw firsthand the spikes in viewers, readers, and ad revenue whenever these sorts of posts hit the front page.

One activist member of this movement (which for the purposes of proper distinction will be referred to as the "right-libertarian" movement moving forward) in an interview with the author stated that he was indeed a "revolutionary" and that the only real revolution that could make a difference for "the little guy" was the one started by Ron Paul and the modern Tea Party, which this activist saw as synonymous with the libertarians he also claimed.[4] Another member of the movement, who was also a top editor at a rival right-libertarian paper, said once in a personal conversation with the author that in order for true liberty to be reached, the country would have to "pass through the eye of fascism."[5] This claim would be repeated in 2018 on popular right-libertarian website *Radical Capitalist* in the article titled "Fascism is a Step towards Liberty."[6] In this article, the argument is put forth that (right-)libertarianism and the Alt-Right are the same movement in principle, and that it goes hand in hand with fascism, a label deemed by the author, libertarian and "anarcho-capitalist" Chase Rachels, as having been "abused and stigmatized to the point where [it] has become synonymous with pure evil" and subsequently lost much of its "discernible meaning."[7] The author goes further, claiming that fascism is in the same moral company as "nationalism, the nuclear family, monogamy, individualism, and capitalism."[8] All of these are equally moral and good, and any naysayers to this analysis are simply, according to Rachels, buying into "the Cultural Marxist agenda."[9] Rachels also makes it clear here that the goal of libertarians should be to "forge a union" with the Alt-Right, and that the principles held in common between the two groups include "libertarian principle," endorsement of private property, and a stance against "expansion of State power."[10]

This is not an uncommon view for the aforementioned young voting-age demographic that reads this sort of content. This author in particular wrote a book titled *White, Right, and Libertarian* that gained enough notice in the movement to gain an endorsement and foreword by prominent right-libertarian activist and writer Hans-Hermann Hoppe.[11] It should be noted also that the slogan for this popular website reads as follows: "Anti-State. Anti-Left. Pro-White." Notice the slogan does not claim to be pro-right, nor do the site's other various articles claim ownership of right-libertarianism. The site refers to itself simply as "libertarian," as does partner site *Liberty Hangout*, with the latter's whopping *one million followers*[12] exposed to almost exclusively right-wing–aligned content praising Donald Trump, bashing pro-minority movements, and arguing, once again, for abolishing the State.[13] Toward that latter point, this activist-run website, handled by real, everyday libertarians, genuinely does argue itself to be a place of revolutionary thought. The article "For a Peaceful Society, Privatize Everything and Abolish the State" begins its distorted call to populist sentiment by quoting historical leftist Max Weber's definition of the State as a monopoly on physical force, claiming him as a fellow voice in modern libertarianism's anti-government regulation cause.[14] Weber, a scholar whose work would go on to inform many revolutionary populist causes on the left throughout history, has just enough in common in his rhetoric with those on the working-class right who frame themselves as fellow against-the-man actors to make things fuzzy for someone already politically right-leaning who may recognize that the system they occupy is unfair and find the Weber quote to make a lot of sense. Divorced from context, Weber and the right-libertarian activists of today seem kindred spirits. These exemplary writings, interviews, and quotes thus far are only a portion representing the larger whole of the current state of the liberty movement today. The starting point is always economic and worker-oriented, and the stated sentiment up front is always one favoring a touted push toward freedom and liberation from oppressive forces.

Another common thread in the modern libertarian activist movement is the belief that private property and personal property are the same thing. T. J. Roberts, a young activist in the movement, says that self-ownership necessarily begets private property rights. In his words, "since you own yourself, you have the inherent right to acquire private property," adding that "private property is the foundation of a free society."[15] This book will go into detail later why private property is not at all what is being assumed here, but this assumption is common among modern libertarian activists and writers.

But despite the predominantly white and male makeup of the modern libertarian movement, there are exceptions to the rule. One young woman of color in the movement I interviewed, who we will call Bella, told me that despite being a member of a minority group herself, the only people who could actually make a lasting difference for the betterment of her demographic are the "conservatives and libertarians," because they "understand economics."[16] The implicit connection being made here, of course, is that since conservative and libertarian activism tends to concern itself a lot with economics-focused rhetoric and policy proposal, it helps these movements exude a more confident veneer of assuredness when it comes to liberating their fellow human beings. The argument is often made in right-leaning circles that the only way for true liberation to reach all people is for "economic freedom" to be reachable for every individual.[17] This is the official stance of not just the liberty movement loosely defined, but of its official political arm, the Libertarian Party.[18]

Another woman of color in the movement, who we will call Helen, told me that she actually considers herself to be a "social Darwinist" for similar reasons, citing how those who end up in poverty must have simply not worked hard enough to reach the same heights as their fellow humans, and that there was no self-assured action that couldn't overcome any racially based economic discrimination that might still be at play in our current economic system.[19]

Once again, this rhetoric exemplifies empirically the stance of the movement as a whole as well as its individual members, but it also illustrates how said stances can appear to be very pro-worker, pro-individual, anti-authority, and, yes, revolutionary. Rising up and taking one's place as a success in the face of a rigged system is still the broadly typed name of the game, here, but it fudges the details just enough to allow for narrowly economistic dogma to have final say. The claimed cause for these economically focused agendas is to liberate working people and give them the same freedoms as those who already achieved means of economic success. In spirit, that isn't too far removed from the leftist equivalent of giving all working people equal access to the means of production. But in application, it is very different. Instead of striving to change the rules of the game itself to open up pathways to self-sufficiency for workers immediately, the right-leaning variant of pro-worker sentiment strives to build ladders and staircases for those currently in economically dire straits to climb in order to play by the already-existing rules and not rock the boat. The problem here is that this has never been an achievable goal in the history of markets.[20] It is by design a pipe dream that still tickles all the same points on a right-leaning disgruntled worker as the historically organic populist voices tickle on their left-leaning equivalents. This is why the book argues that many participants in conservative populist activism likely believe themselves what they are claiming. Much of this is not a conscious conspiracy to hedge genuine revolutionary change once it reaches the working-class level. It is simply the case that many of these activists plainly do not know any better. This is not the same thing as lacking the ability to know better—it is simply an observation of fact, supported by the movement members' own words. The starting point is always solidarity on behalf of disgruntled working people against unjust authority, but where it goes from there can often be derailed, as the following chapters, focusing more on the theoretical side of this phenomenon, will show.

Another self-described member of the present-day libertarian activist movement is Lauren Southern, a former colleague of the author's when they both wrote for *The Libertarian Republic*, the publication founded and run by former Libertarian Party presidential candidate Austin Petersen. Southern's views, like many others in the movement, began as broadly pro-freedom for all people. In a move that was actually somewhat progressive at the time for right-libertarianism, Southern even publicly befriended and defended members of the trans community. But before long, her views on private property rights ended up evolving to their most extreme logical conclusions and she became a prominent supporter of closed borders—so much so that she ended up helping to popularize the pseudoscientific theory of the Great Replacement, which aligned her with white nationalism whether she wished it or not, as most proponents of that theory are not as concerned with preserving cultural sovereignty as they are with preserving what they perceive as pure races.[21] Here we see even more evidence of how a person's views in this movement can begin at an earnest place and end up aligning with something much more extreme somewhat organically. When the wrong vocabulary and obfuscated information serve as the foundation upon which one builds her political ideology, it becomes much harder to avoid these sorts of pitfalls. Young people make up the majority of this particular brand of privileged populism, and they act more at the behest of the privileged by passing on the talking points rather than always embodying privilege themselves.

Paleo-Conservatism

Even the more "mainstream" faces of modern right-wing populism show this same directional flow. Former congressman Ron Paul, the patron saint of many in the Republican Party who call themselves libertarians, or more precisely, "paleo-conservatives," fraternized with such controversial figures as Lew Rockwell, who it is said ghostwrote Dr. Paul's infamous 1990s newsletters full of anti-Black and anti-gay screeds in the name of personal liberty and freedom from big government oppression (i.e., racially sensitive holidays and anti-discrimination laws). Paul himself went on record time and again opposing the Civil Rights Act, once again arguing that it is government force and anti-freedom to force fair treatment of working people on business owners. Charles Murray, another libertarian figure who fights for seemingly noble, pro-liberty causes such as the school choice initiative and freedom of speech, co-wrote the grossly unscientific book *The Bell Curve*, which made the assumptions that "race" is a biologically definable concept (it isn't), and that IQ tests actually do empirically measure general intelligence (that claim is still hotly contested in the scientific community and has next to no empirical basis), in order to make the claim that Black Americans have lower intelligence on average than white Americans, and that this must be due to some innate genetic difference between the two demographics. Murray was, once again, acting on what he believed was sound science, but the wrong assumptions were made at the outset, making the findings and their implications worthless. Along the way, the pushback the book has gotten has given Murray another reason to fight for "freedom of speech" by presenting himself as something of a victim of unjust censorship.

The appeal of this brand of right-wing populism is for the older demographics of conservatives who still hold a more revolutionary urge within them compared to their fellow more straight-laced registered Republicans. The need to still rebel against a perceived oppressor is present here, but it manifests as more of a God-fearing, traditional values variant. The people in this movement call themselves libertarian, classically liberal, or traditionally conservative, but the movement itself is made up of both working-class Republican voters and upper-class Republican politicians and businessmen who have a lot of investments at stake. Once again, we see a propagation of ideals initially put forth by the privileged portion of this movement, espoused by the working-class members in an organic form that no longer seems to be directly connected to any intentional manipulation of perspective. By now, it has simply become accepted that the claims made for generations within this movement about the nature of such things as socialism, capitalism, and free markets are true.

Once Donald Trump was elected president, I saw everyday working people fitting this group's description attaching all of their feelings of anti-elitism onto him as if he were the very embodiment of that sentiment, despite being a member of an elite class himself.

When I was covering CPAC 2017 in my journalism days and I attended the Donald Trump speaking event there at the Gaylord hotel in the Virginia/DC area, I witnessed firsthand his knack for complete misrepresentation of the truth that early on—as well as the tendency for his followers to brush his fictions aside and still embrace him as one of their own regardless of what ridiculous claims he might make. "There are so many people here to see me today, they can't all fit into the hotel," claimed Trump that day. He then proceeded to describe a line of people that apparently stretched to outside the hotel and around the corner. This confounded me, as I had just been outside and seen no line. Nor had I run into any trouble navigating my way through the lobby and into the event room itself. Sure, there were enough attendees for some of us press people and audience members to flow out of our respective dedicated rooms and into an additional room with a viewing screen, one degree removed from the actual stage. But beyond that, there were no additional bodies in need of further spatial accommodation. Near where I happened to be sitting after hearing Trump make this baseless claim, I heard a couple of women laugh at its obvious untruth, and simply remark, "oh, he's a card!" Trump's dishonesty amused them; it did not worry them. As Trump continued to speak, once again invoking his faux-populist rhetoric and promising to drain the Washington, DC swamp of corrupt politicians and special-interest elites, an elderly gentleman directly to my right leaned over, jabbed me lightly with his elbow, and exclaimed, "he's so smart, isn't he? I'd wager he has a lot more in common with us than with them!"[22]

"Us." "Them." Once again, a very populist sentiment. This man, despite his clearly more traditional Republican background, was not referring to a left-vs.-right political divide. After further talking with him, I realized that he was referring to a working-class-versus-elitist social and financial divide.[23] He was buying into Trump's populist appeal and claims of being an outsider to the Washington machine, despite Trump's own lifelong status as an elite himself. To this man, and many others like him in the Trump camp, his love of paleo-conservative, so-called libertarian ideals meant that if he hated Democrats, he hated them for what he saw as an elitism intrinsic to their party that separated their perspective from understanding what he called "real people."[24] The "us" of his prior "us and them" distinction. He didn't dislike what he broadly called "the left" simply because they were liberals; he disliked liberals because he had grown to believe that liberals had completely lost touch with the real, lived-in plights of everyday working people.[25] Trump, for all his more ridiculous rhetorical qualities, nevertheless claimed to be the guy who was finally going to listen to people like my CPAC friend, here. To him, that was everything. Enough to induce him to describe Trump as having "more in common with us" than with the elites who had long forsaken the workers. Enough even, perhaps, to turn a blind eye when Trump would tell a lie or insight a bit of social unrest for unfamiliar minority demographics. Desperation to be heard and represented can lead to any number of compromises of one's own sense of consistency. It is that same desperation that tends to radicalize working people in the first place. This radicalization is not exclusive to Democrats and others further to their left; it affects those on the working-class right, as well. When more traditional conservatives are hit by that radicalization, a Donald Trump is precisely what they are looking for—someone who ultimately maintains the social status quo but promises to shake up its economic equivalent.

The Alt-Light ("Red-Pilled" Conservatism)

When the youthful appeal of right-libertarianism and the more blatantly traditionally conservative variety of paleo-conservatism meet, we get the alt-light movement, a push for a hip, punk-rock rebelliousness toward authority in its rhetoric while maintaining a reverence for the social and economic status quo of yesteryear in its actual policy underpinnings. It is out of this marriage of paleo-conservatism and conspiratorial anti-statism from whence the online conspiracy theory movement Qanon has also sprung, though this book does not focus on that particular phenomenon in depth.

The famous faces of this movement include the likes of since-disgraced political commentator Milo Yiannopoulos, who once again referred to himself as a "libertarian" (a common theme for all these variants of revolutionary conservatism) but who ultimately pushed for right-wing policy on the publication *Breitbart*, that publication's Steve Bannon, who went on to become a prominent cabinet member for Donald Trump's presidency, as well as a circle of prominent YouTube personalities, including Sargon of Akkad, Armoured Skeptic, Black Pidgeon Speaks, and Stefan Molyneux, the last of whom ultimately came out as a full-blown Alt-Right member and white supremacist.[26]

The typical gallop from this brand of faux-revolutionary conservatism involves claiming "skepticism" of any and all things socially progressive, claiming to take a "scientific" stance on things like trans issues, race, IQ, and immigration while in reality perpetuating outdated, bigoted positions in these areas that often, contrarily, ignores the latest science in order to hold fast to the already-existing outlooks on these matters held by establishment conservatives.[27]

Another main talking point of this subgroup is steadfast defense of, and belief in, so-called freedom of speech, which against amounts to a more distorted version of itself that aims to merely allow right-wing social perspectives to be trumpeted in public without much challenge[28]

One of my former friends from this movement at the ground, activist level demonstrates how despite these seemingly nefarious characteristics of the organization of this movement, those who organically fall into its ranks still often come from earnest beginnings. This friend of mine, a working-class person who formally supported Bernie Sanders for similar reasons, switched to supporting Trump for the 2016 presidential election due to resentment over the establishment Democrat's dishonest push to edge Sanders out of the primary running in order to make room for their more elitist candidate, Hillary Clinton. This woman's thinking, as was the thinking of many of her colleagues who also switched from Bernie to Trump, was that if the Democrats refused to truly hear the plights of the working people they claimed to care about and represent, then they deserved to lose to a more wild card–style candidate who at least claimed to shake up the status quo. That candidate was Donald J. Trump, whose famous tagline, "drain the swamp," was heard as music to the ears of many disgruntled working poor who had lost faith in the Democrats after several Democrat administrations and Congress majorities without any tangible improvement of their increasingly dire economic conditions.

This friend of mine in particular had been an advocate of LGBT rights, women's reproductive rights, and antiwar initiatives, but here was candidate Trump also promising to support all of these causes. He famously promised to protect LGBTQ people from violence, held up pride flags at rallies, and claimed to be against all the war waging being done at the hands of the US military industrial complex. At the time, this friend of mine told me that she did not feel ideologically compromised to support Trump under these circumstances, as he seemed the next-best choice to Sanders.[29] But once Trump had won and those promises of his, one by one, became forsaken, it was fascinating for me to see that this friend of mine, once a staunch supporter of these minority rights causes, ended up placing consistency in her support of Trump as a higher priority over her continued activism regarding said issues. It seemed that somewhere along the way, she too fell into the line of thinking that economic freedom was the main goal, and all of the subsequent social freedoms could be derived from that. Even when that seemed to not be Trump's plan, and he only further continued to explicitly target the freedoms of trans, gay, Black, and brown individuals by turning a blind eye to police brutality, supporting banning trans people from various spaces including athletics, public restrooms, and military service, and so on, this friend and her like-minded fellows only continue to unabashedly support Trump. Their reasoning? Because he was still more of an "anarchist" and "revolutionary" than the establishment Democrats.[30]

The urge, the need, for some kind of radical shakeup in the status quo is a common thread found across all these different subcategories of revolutionary conservative. All of these privileged populists, unwittingly or otherwise, are attempting to satisfy that revolutionary urge by fighting against perceived oppressors. It just so happens that their perception in this case is significantly compromised. While the aforementioned motivations for getting these various movements do appeal to the revolutionary urge of conservatives in more nefarious, dishonest ways, this book is arguing that the initial insurgencies to that end have already long been implemented, and that by this point the working-class members of each of these movements are genuinely and organically falling into their activism, unaware of the false qualities of the groups they proudly declare themselves members of. This does not mean that the end result of this move, from center-right conservativism, to right-libertarianism, to red-pilled "new" conservatism, cannot still lead many people into full-blown Alt-Right apologetics. In fact, that seems to be a common trajectory of many in each of these movements. But how they get there (from a misunderstood form of populism to full-blown fascism) is oftentimes missed by surface-level attempts to understand their motivations. The shift is driven oftentimes not by conscious hate, but by a genuine need for revolutionary change that ultimately cannot find true north. It is a misguided attempt to fight oppression and authoritarianism that remains blind to the systemic elements of present society that must be taken into account in order to properly identify the real enemy of freedom and liberty for working people.

In short: how the obfuscation action potential initially occurred was intentional and nefarious; how it has survived into the present moment in the hearts of the everyday people on the right who keep it alive is not. In the following chapters, we will explore and parse out just how that reality comes to be—in our own society, as well as others found in relevant pockets of populism's history.

Populist Logic and Anti-Politics

In the preface to his 2005 magnum opus *On Populist Reason*, the late political theorist Ernesto Laclau declares that he is interested in addressing "the nature and logics of the formation of collective identities," and explains that he has been dissatisfied thus far by what he perceives as a "too simple and uniform" approach by prior scholars to explain populist groups by way of connecting them to larger, utilitarian niches for them to fill.[1] Anthropologists for decades have still fallen back on the functionalist model of social analysis, postulated by the godfather of the field, Claude Lévi-Strauss, as a way of making sense of cultural phenomena that are otherwise elusive in their purpose and genesis. However, Lévi-Strauss's theories have by and large been carved out, refined, and outright jettisoned when newer, better explanations for social realities have come along. Over a decade ago, Laclau proceeded to seek out such explanations when it came to the concept of collective identity.

What he found was extraordinary and important: populism is not merely an example of the mass psychology theorized by scholars such as Freud, nor is it an externality of some bigger functional purpose. Instead, populism is simply its own self-contained phenomenon—a logic of representation that has echoes of democracy and noble solidarity within its confines.[2] This is achieved, according to Laclau, through populism's attempt to "grasp something crucially significant about the political and ideological realities to which it refers."[3] Populism on its own simply *is*. It can be used for good or for evil. More than that: it is a logical, relatable flow from idea to reality; individual to collective; voiceless to voiced.

But here is where populism can and does misstep: these aforementioned collective identities can be large, and therefore more truly representative of a genuine populace, or they can be quite small, in which case they would be far less so. In both cases, the formation is typically organic and internal, making the collectives with less merit in reality equally as sincere in their inception as their more grounded counterparts. All that really necessitates a movement to be populist in nature is the *belief* of the involved plebiscites that they do in fact represent the people; the reality of this belief varies from case to case. "In order to have the 'people' of populism," argues Laclau, "we need something more: we need a *plebs* who claims to be the only legitimate *populus*—that is, a partiality which wants to function as the totality of the community."[4] In this way, populist movements aren't always guaranteed to be serving functions necessary to their larger surrounding societies. They are instead serving their own goals, which *claim* to serve the populace at large even when that might in fact be an illusory perspective.

This understanding of populism differs a bit from the other more popular approach to populism known as the "ideational approach."[5] That approach to understanding populism simply boils down the conflict to being between "two homogeneous and antagonistic groups," such as "'the pure people' vs. 'the corrupt elite.'"[6] While this does successfully describe the surface-level observation of what is happening with group-on-group populist antagonism, it is found significantly wanting when it comes time to better dissect the more nuanced, multitiered forms of anti-political populism that can coexist in slightly different strains among single demographics of people. This is why Laclau's understanding of populism as an organic logic that builds up from within groups of people—even groups within the same on-paper demographics—serves us much better when attempting to explain the how and why behind the richness of populist anti-political dissent.

We might then ask, what does this have to do with fringe political movements? How can the argument of populism as a self-contained logic even be applied to such groups? Don't political movements by definition need to be directly tethered to the subsuming societies in which they occur?

This is where things get interesting, because we already have examples of what are referred to as "anti-political" phenomena throughout human history and across many societies. In general, these examples amount to movements, events, or entities that end up breeding a sense of distrust for the political status quo among the general populace of a given region or society. Put simply, to become anti-political one must first become disenfranchised with current political systems for one reason or another. The reasons can be anything from the words of a charismatic figure to a specific encounter with failed political action, and the rationale behind the choice to ultimately adopt a given anti-political narrative can range from the reasonable to the conspiratorial. No two anti-political phenomena are created equal. Yet, almost all of them lead to Laclauian collective identities of varying viability.

Let us take a look at a case study of one such collective forming under the aforementioned circumstances to better flesh out this process. In anthropologist James Ferguson's *The Anti-Politics Machine*, an examining eye is tilted toward the Kingdom of Lesotho in Africa in which several failed development projects took place from 1975 to 1984 for the purposes of bringing "development," with a positive connotation, to the third world.[7] This act was supposedly done in the best interest of the people, but in reality there seemed to be little to any positive change at all, which of course started stirring up distrust among the local people of the concept of "development agencies" in general, or even the supposedly "neutral" intermediaries of "state apparatus" present in Ferguson's case study who claim to represent the people themselves.[8]

This ties into what we can define as anti-politics in the form of a collective fantasy. A fantasy that takes two forms: first, the aforementioned distrust of intermediaries and the reverence for a Puritan, almost literally biblical, notion of the sweat of one's own brow (i.e., "honest work") being the only thing one can count on—this is almost purely anti-government as well as anti–status quo. The second form is more technocratic populist thinking, in which the anti-politics are informed by an awareness of the distinction between market rationality and mere private self-interest (the latter of which amounts more or less to the capitalism present in our own society). In Ferguson's study, we see a populace in Lesotho that first appears to exude the attitudes of the second form of anti-political thinking, but, over the course of the several-year period of multiple failed development attempts, seems to shift into the more hyper-skeptical and jaded view of the first.

One explicit example of how this process takes hold is found in the case of what Ferguson calls "The Decentralization Debacle," where once again we see intermediary forces claiming to have the best interest of the civilians at heart by claiming to merely be mechanisms of change rather than fashion tactics directly in interference with the common affairs of the people, yet ended up still embodying the latter.[9] The "District Development Committee (DDC), a body of elected and appointed representatives of 'the people,' was intended to provide a channel for communicating proper needs to the government," he writes.[10] Of course, that didn't really have the promised localized, decentralized effect, as Ferguson develops further: "The DDC was supposed to be 'advisory,' and was granted no executive authority, but it managed nonetheless to occupy a rather imposing position on the organizational charts."[11] Viewing these instances through the eyes of the locals, it is no wonder that they ultimately became more paranoid of all forms of government involvement in their lives.

This was a case in which the hyper-skeptical form of anti-political populism was completely justified, but it isn't hard to see how the same anti-government attitude could arise even without the undeniable stimuli experienced in Lesotho. It is natural to distrust entities in positions of authority; it is much harder to step outside of one's own vantage point and take all of the surrounding evidence into account. For every single case like that found in the Ferguson case study, there are dozens, if not hundreds, more in which the same hyper-skepticism is adopted by a collective, yet the evidence for justifying such an attitude is paltry. Not all instances of government involvement in a given society's affairs are created equal. Each case warrants contextualized investigation. Some are noble successes, others are noble disasters, and more still are quite possibly sinister attempts at social control. But without the proper context, determining which is not always intuitive. This lends itself to a perspective that moves beyond mere hyper-skepticism and flirts with the realm of outright paranoia, and it is within the anti-political movements which reside in this realm where we will find the spores of extreme right-wing populism that ultimately birthed and satiated the sentiments of the Alt-Right. Political theorist and democracy scholar Nadia Urbinati corroborates this motivation when she points out that populism often manifests as a "rescuing force" within a "'senile' democracy" whose representative institutions have "eroded their capacity of guaranteeing accountability, participation, and openness."[12]

Stepping away from the academic language for a moment, what all of this amounts to is actually pretty straightforward: populism can be anti-political while still applying to the more colloquial notion of what "political" movements are. This is because fringe political groups themselves are actually *anti*-political groups that oftentimes hold very little regard for actual politics, and instead argue for something that either transcends or does completely away with sociopolitical and government structures as we currently know them. The gray area arrives when we realize that this general sentiment of hoping to escape the entire system is one that is fairly widespread and relatable—shared not just with right-wing anti-politics movements, but with the first libertarians (e.g., anarcho-socialists in the tradition of Pierre-Joseph Proudhon and Mikhail Bakunin) and classical liberals (e.g., John Locke) as well.[13]

As will be explored later in the book, these groups can manifest themselves in both positive and negative ways—populism as a logic is morally agnostic when examined on its own self-contained merits. But for the case study we are undertaking, here— namely, the various distortions that have gone into mainstream matriculation of distorted revolutionary sentiment into the conservative working class—we will mostly be examining instances of the latter throughout the coming chapters. Here at the ovum of anti-political populism in the broad strokes, we shall begin to narrow our focus and observe some examples of how the negative forms of populism can exteriorize. Keeping with the examination of the hyper-skeptical form predominantly, we can see how the negative side of such thinking can come to fruition as collective paranoia and conspiratorial antagonism against an elusive *Other*.[14]

This is not a unique extrapolation on Laclau's foundations. As Glynos and Mondon have also articulated in preexisting literature regarding the discourse surrounding the theoretical approach to understanding populism as a logic, much of this initial outcropping results from what they refer to as "hype" that is built within already-existing populist unrest with a given status quo.[15] This right-wing variant is merely the most extreme distortion of this previously delineated pattern, as the remainder of the chapter will lay out.

*   *   *

When the 2017 documentary *Get Me Roger Stone* entered the homes of Netflix's 100 million+ subscribers, there was a collective gasp of shock and disgust. The same thought went through the minds of many who watched the film: How could something like this happen in twenty-first-century America? Here was a true event in which just a handful of people were able to tap into a brewing sense of anger and lack of representation in specific voter demographics, build a presidential campaign tailored to stoking those fires, and get said demographics' members to rally around a political figure who was a social elite posing as a spokesman for the common man. What a con. Seemingly one so obvious and transparent that no sound thinker could possibly have fallen for it. Yet, to the bewilderment of nearly every poll and televised political pundit, Donald J. Trump was elected the forty-fifth president of the United States in 2016.

Four years later, the establishment Democrat nominee Joseph R. Biden, only marginally more liked than Clinton, just barely beat the incumbent Trump, allowing for such narrow margins of victory in several key swing States that Trump's administration chose to demand recounts and take other legal actions in them to examine the possibility of incorrect vote tallying and possibly reverse the win projection. It was postulated by many political analysts on the left at the time that the only reason Biden ultimately did narrowly eke out a win was not due to Biden being all that well liked by the left, but rather due to Trump being so hated by liberals and leftists in general. The votes, therefore, could be seen not as passionate support for that Biden stood for but instead as a far less enthusiastic protest vote against Trump. In this sense, the Democrat establishment still lost the 2020 election. The polls once again incorrectly predicted a landslide win for Trump's challenger, and once again severely underrepresented the working poor.

So, why *did* the seemingly antiestablishment position of working-class voters only meagerly support Biden in 2020, and why did that same position actually win Trump the presidency in the previous election? On Trump's end of things, we now know more about the specific 2016 strategies that were used to spread the right kind of information and reach the right kind of demographics to give Trump the best competitive edge possible, thanks to the Cambridge Analytica scandal that has now become national news. It amounts to an incident in which Facebook user data was mined and sold for profit, and then said data was exploited for the purposes of aiding the Trump campaign in targeting its ideal demographics in a precise and (at the time) invisible manner.[16] Furthermore, as the Robert Mueller investigation that took place over the first two years of the Trump presidency unfolded and an increasing number of Trump's advisors, lawyers, business partners, campaign financers, and cabinet members continue to be found guilty of various dishonest and manipulative behavior, the reality of that election's methods for gaining the upper hand in terms of messaging and image control becomes clearer.

But this merely explains what avenues the campaign took in order to advertise itself the most efficiently; it does not explain how the targeted demographic of the Trump campaign came to exist in the first place. At best, this evidences a means of stoking an already-burning fire. What we should be equally and more importantly concerned with, however, especially for the purposes of this book's mission, is what caused the initial spark.

To those of us who study the subject of populism as something seen by its adherents as a logic rather than as an ideology, the mystery is much less prevalent. For one thing, the support for Trump largely came from the aforementioned first type of anti-politics populism—the type that compels the outright distrust of all forms of governmental status quo. The support also came in the form of less anti-political voters who still yet felt unrepresented by the current state of affairs in Washington, specifically.[17] Of the Trump voters who participated in exit polls on election night in 2016, only 19 percent of them said they felt satisfied with the present direction of government, while 46 percent of them said they were outright dissatisfied, and an even larger percentage of them, 74 percent, went so far as to say that they were *angry* with the government.[18] However, there is an interesting contrast to be found in another poll answer by this very same voter pool. When asked about their financial situations, the Trump voters overwhelmingly stated that they were worse off than they were four years prior—76 percent of them.[19] Despite this, their financial situations getting increasingly worse with time, these voters did not, on average, blame private business or the stifling financial strangleholds of capitalism. Instead, these voters placed the blame for their troubles primarily on the government, while endorsing a candidate whose platform promoted the idea of less regulation on the corporate world as a key factor in making the economy better.[20]

While it is an apparent contradiction to endorse further corporate unaccountability in the face of one's own financial despair (Trump voters also skewed largely poor in demographics even prior to their more recent fiscal downturns, according to a *Washington Post* study),[21] we will see over the course of the coming chapters that such a perspective is common among those who claim to subscribe to classically liberal ideology (which, being mostly conservatives and right-(vulgar)libertarians, the

Trump voters certainly did). Much of this exclusive focus on State hierarchies, and not market hierarchies, is once again predicated upon the conditions that give rise to anti-politics as identified by Ferguson, and many Trump supporters also voiced perspectives that fell perfectly in line with anti-political skepticism based on their socioeconomic positions and an expressed sense of the government having failed to represent them prior. According to a RAND Corporation survey conducted that year, the voters who agreed with the statement "people like me don't have any say about what the government does" were 86.5 percent more likely to prefer Donald Trump over any other presidential candidate.[22]

A particular attention should also be paid to the element of aforementioned anger that has accompanied the malcontent of many of these voters. It is an anger of a particular kind that has become a subculture in itself, and it exists across political persuasions. It isn't an anger of self-aware prejudice or active hatred; rather, it is a *reactive* anger to sociocultural milieus that affect certain demographics in a way that makes them feel restrained in their expression and cultural contentment, and it has been manifested at least since the early 2000s and the contentious political climate of the George W. Bush era.[23] Anthropologist Peter Wood identified this phenomenon at the time as "New Anger," and admonished both the right and the left for having embraced it.[24] For the left, there was a reactive anger in response to what was perceived as an unfair election of Bush as president (something else, incidentally, that Roger Stone takes credit for),[25] and for the right, there was a reactive anger toward what many conservatives considered to be a cultural erasure of their very identity. Wood notes that while conservatives had achieved "a measure of political power," they nevertheless felt a "marginalization by the arbiters of culture."[26] Most notably, the people within this demographic felt that their values were "ignored or derided," while they themselves felt "often caricaturized as racist, sexist, environmental-despoiling, militaristic jerks" and saw these attacks on them as "a looming danger to American rights and freedoms."[27]

While that fear itself takes on the rhetorical qualities of paranoia, it matches the general mindset characteristic of Ferguson's delineated anti-politics, albeit in more of a cultural space informed by politics rather than one political in itself.[28] Already, we see the general principles laid out at the top of this chapter manifesting in specific movements and demographics. It is also here where we can find Laclau's qualifier for the plebiscite mindset once again: a populace or a portion of a populace that feels utterly forgotten about, and feels representative of something larger (e.g., Wood's observation that the conservatives of the Bush era equivocated their own views to those representing the very freedom of America).[29],[30] If we are to accept Laclau's concept of populism as accurate, we need to find it occurring as an organic phenomenon in human culture. We should be able to see it initially forming from within, out of a collective need of a particular section of humanity to be heard; a logic of representation.[31] For Laclau, this process is how most populism, with the rare exception of completely manufactured narratives by fascist authoritarians, comes to be, which is a direct challenge to the very common claims to the contrary by his contemporaries.[32] But it seems to be very much the case with the rise of the typical Trump supporter that the unrest and dissatisfaction were indeed already present; Roger Stone and his ilk merely stoked the existing fires and put a face to the cause.

Why is this distinction important? Simply put: if populism is as organic and self-contained as the Laclauian interpretation suggests, then it is much more likely to be present anywhere, and to hold varying degrees of legitimacy. The rationale for populist actors, then, is on a spectrum that at times resides in such commonly occupied intellectual spaces that it is seen as relatable and even benign.

* * *

Populist Rationale Spectrum Theory's Competition

Often claimed to be explained by a concept known as "horseshoe theory," the tendency for working-class populist anger to bleed into itself across perceived political differences is much better explained, this book submits, by thinking of the rationale behind populism in general as existing on this aforementioned spectrum. Horseshoe theory's central thesis is as follows: if one goes far enough to the populist left, you meet the far-right populists ideologically, and if one does the reverse, one eventually meets the far left (Figure 2.1). It truly is as simple a notion as that. Why does this not

Horseshoe "Theory" Diagram

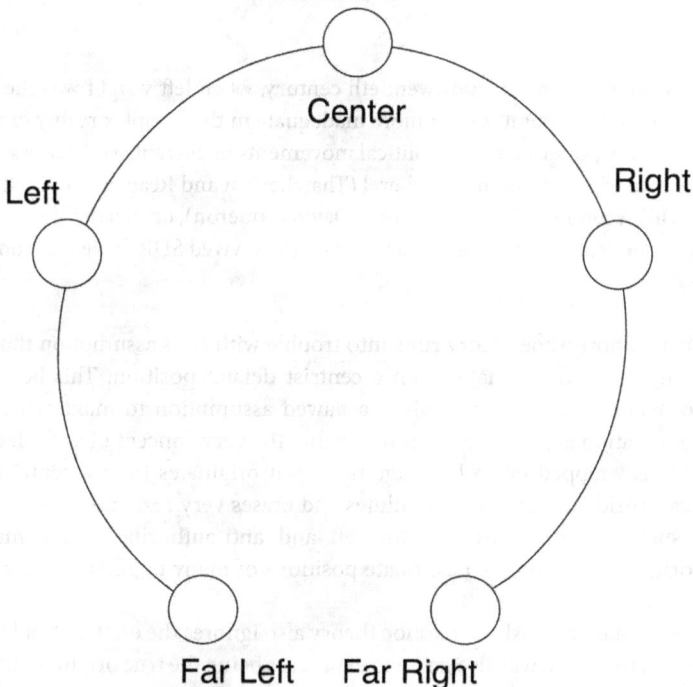

Center

Left

Right

Far Left   Far Right

Figure 2.1 Artist rendering of traditional horseshoe theory diagram.

adequately explain the phenomenon? For a number of reasons, but we shall lay out only the key among them.

First and foremost, horseshoe "theory" is not a theory. Theories should explain the function and process of observed facts, whereas horseshoe theory merely describes something observed and then makes a postulation as to its inner workings without ever really demonstrating, logically or empirically, why this is the case.

Second, horseshoe theory needlessly reduces complex political thought into a left-right paradigm that is unhelpful for unpacking the nuance clearly in play when we see left and right populism bleeding into each other in certain demographics and under certain cultural circumstances. It is reductionist to assume at the outset of a posited theory of something that all one can explore is a straight line of political divergence when even the most commonplace of modern political measurement, such as the Nolan chart for political positions, sees political ideology as having many more dimensions. Technically, horseshoe theory *does* add at least one other dimension to the left-right perspective by adding a curve to the line between left and right, it still presupposes political populism as being essentially linear, with "left" and "right" existing on a single plain of thought and practice. This, despite the fact that there has been demonstrated levels to both the left and right, where rich elites who call themselves of the left end up holding beliefs and carrying out actions that do not align much at all with working-class leftists, and it is much the same on the multileveled right.

One critic of horseshoe theory once framed its problems of oversimplification as follows:

> This was simplistic in the mid-twentieth century, when left v right was the main cleavage in politics, but it is even more inadequate in the complex reality of today. Contemporary politics is full of political movements or currents which are socially conservative while economically liberal (Thatcherism and Reaganism), or socially liberal while economically "right-wing" (David Cameron), or socially "right-wing" while economically "left-wing." (Blue Labour, the revived SDP, Steve Bannon, Neil Clarke)[33]

Something else horseshoe theory runs into trouble with is its assumption that politics can only be observed rationally from a centrist default position. This book will go more into detail later as to why this is a flawed assumption to make when dealing with populist rationale,[34] but suffice it to say that the very concept of a "far left" versus a "far right" is wrapped up in language that itself originates from a centrist view of the political world, and this in turn dilutes and erases very real and tangible populist concepts such as anti-fascism on the left and anti-authoritarianism, historically leftist in origin, rendering the passionate positions of many populists involving these concepts obfuscated.[35]

Perhaps most egregiously, horseshoe theory also ignores the existence of libertarian leftism, which this book will also go on to explain as being the true origins of libertarian philosophy. Ignoring this piece of populist history in particular sets any explanation of modern populism up for significant deficiencies.

Fish Hook "Theory" Diagram

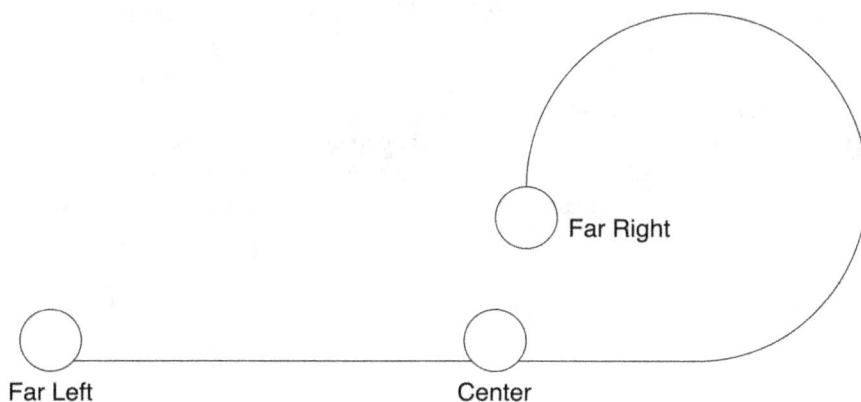

Figure 2.2 Artist rendering of typical fishhook theory diagram.

Why, then, is the posited populist rationale spectrum (PRS) described in this book any better for explaining precisely what is going on when we see populist anti-elitist sentiment drag working-class people from moderate conservatism into far-right extremism, left-to-right, and so forth? Because acknowledgment of this spectrum plain of existence allows for more organic shifts along populist lines that takes into account shared class-based experience as well as ideology, making the process of finding one's own populist positioning much more understandable within different contexts such as social surroundings, access (or lack of access) to certain information, and the varying levels of privilege one might find himself existing on depending on his specific demographic and history.

Certain proposed alternatives to horseshoe theory over the years have themselves often held onto the obfuscating centrist viewpoint that already plagues horseshoe theory (such is the case with fishhook theory, for instance, where the far right supposedly comes back around and becomes centrist after a time) (Figure 2.2), and are therefore no more useful. However, some alternatives have gotten much closer to taking into account all of the nuance this book aims to dissect in the populist world.

The Populist Rationale Spectrum in Summary

In summation, the PRS and its process can be briefly summarized in the steps outlined herein. Keep in mind that certain postulations within this model will be further elaborated on and explained in the subsequent pages and chapters of the book, and that the theory of the PRS in full has been fully delineated by the author elsewhere in the peer-reviewed literature.[36] What follows is merely meant as a reference point for the reader to return to while reading the rest of the book. The visualization of this process can be found in Figures 2.3 and 2.4.

(1) Organic populist unrest, comprising political philosophies ranging from what this book is dubbing "radical liberalism" (the earliest form of liberalism before even classical liberalism became the norm)[37] to the most classical forms of socialism, naturally forms across the working class in the face of exploitation by elite forces (Figures 2.3 and 2.4).
(2) These elite forces propagate a distortion, of populism's most basic conclusions about the surrounding political system's innately exploitative nature, obfuscating the true perpetrators and leading to a formation of information gaps along the

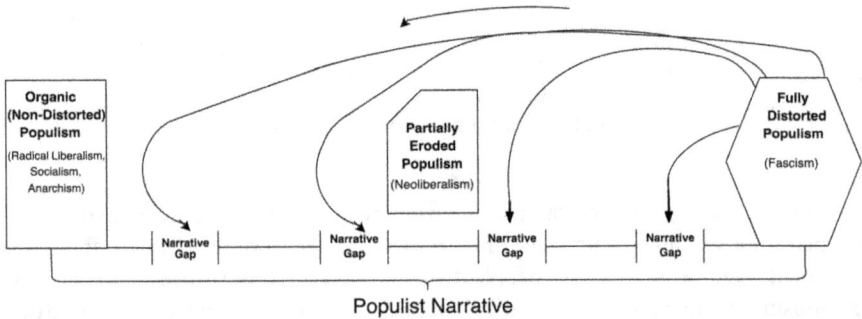

Figure 2.3 Visualization of the populist rationale spectrum's formation process. Distorted populist propaganda shoots out like tendrils and affects the gaps in the populist narrative leading all the way back to more organic forms of populist rhetoric. Originalsource: N. Berlatsky; revision: M. J. Fleck.

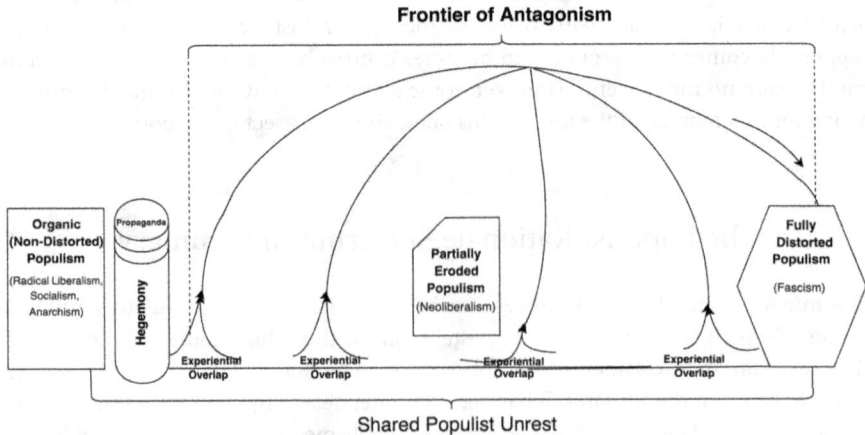

Figure 2.4 Artist rendering of subsequent organic migration within the populist rationale spectrum. Source: M. J. Fleck.

shared populist narrative while restructuring "liberalism" as a centrist, non-radical ideology (Figure 2.3).

(3) Neoliberal elitism (explained later in the book's Part II for the uninitiated) raises a wall of hegemonic obfuscation in order to perpetuate complacency with the present economic system and redirect populist unrest away from the more anti-capitalist solutions it naturally gravitates toward (Figures 2.3 and 2.4).

(4) At the same time, the faux-populist narrative, ranging from center-right to full-on fascist, sends out tendrils of propaganda insurgences, containing rhetoric that still sounds revolutionary, in order to fill the aforementioned narrative gaps with revisionist histories and manufactured antagonists (Figure 2.3). The revolutionary urge present within the working-class populists is then given something to aim at, while the actual economic and political system is spared from having any truly revolutionary action taken against it, thus preserving the elitist status quo.

(5) Those in the working class who still lean politically left tend to break through the hegemonic barrier and correctly identify the real systemic problems, while the working-class members who lean right are successfully redirected by the aforementioned obfuscation efforts.

(6) From these newly filled sections of revisionist revolutionary rhetoric, working-class conservatives are successfully radicalized, find experiential overlap, form solidarity around a frontier of antagonism, and move back toward the source of the propaganda, this time all on their own and without any further inducing from any top-down elitist forces (Figure 2.4). Along the way, they fall into any one of the aforementioned subcategories of revolutionary conservative listed in Chapter 1, with some of them going all the way into fascist beliefs (*Ibid.*).

PRS Theory's Promise for Better Visualization

Now that we have seen a succinct layout of the formation and function of the PRS, we will dig deeper into how this process was delineated and what models are used to visualize it.

For starters, Laclau's own description of what he called a "chain of equivalence" building process, in which movements can comprise allied groups with shared interests in seeing major shifts in power relations, even if their initial push for said goals differ at the outset, dictated much of what populist rationale theory's basic trajectory of movement was delineated as.

From there, the "rationale" portion of the framework needed to be better theorized. In other words, how does the populist distortion reach as far as it does, even so far as more self-described centrist and moderate political circles under neoliberal social systems?

A fellow scholar dissatisfied with the present explanations of populist phenomena, Noah Berlatsky of the *Pacific Standard*, in 2018, proposed an alternative to the aforementioned horseshoe and fishhook theories that he called "tendril theory." Under tendril theory, it is described how fascism bifurcates away (leftward) from the extreme populist right and swings back around to fill in various gaps in the narrative found across all other areas of the spectrum of populist thought, co-opting historically leftist language and anti-elitist sentiment along the way.

I have built upon Berlatsky's initial idea and further refined an illustration of this process (Figure 2.3).[38]

The PRS proposed by this book, therefore, aims to delineate the other side of this coin as well by exploring and understanding the organic reasoning that leads to the process of everyday working-class populists falling victim to the more extremist view of the so-called revolutionary right (Figure 2.4). Once the narrative gaps described in tendril theory are filled with propaganda, the naturally occurring populist unrest shared by all working-class people finds areas of experiential overlap. From there, revolutionary sentiment builds and seeks solidarity for action, just as Laclau describes. Blocked from moving back into populism's organic roots due to an obfuscating force known as hegemony (explored further in Chapter 4), this solidarity latches instead onto the concept of the aforementioned abstract *Other* as its enemy, forming a frontier of manufactured antagonism (explored further in the next chapter), and being ultimately funneled, little by little, into the "folksier" side of fascist ideology— something this book proposes is the ultimate distortion of populist sentiment.

Evidence of PRS Theory's Veracity

As touched upon earlier in the book, the process described by PRS theory was being independently corroborated by fellow anthropologist William Mazzarella during the course of this book's writing, where he described the organic bottom-up form of false consciousness this book observes in these working-class spaces as resulting from a less conventional hegemonic residue—a "mattering-forth" of the collective flesh."[39] In addition, the process also aligns consistently with a 2017 study by anthropologists Dinorah Azpuru, Mary Fran T. Malone, and Orlando J. Perez, where they dissected the circumstances under which citizen embrace of undemocratic leaders (referred to in the paper as "strongmen") in times of economic crisis—even in the face of contrary ideology adherence—is rationalized as a radical necessity. In this study, the scientists laid out seven potential hypotheses:[40]

H1. Respondents who are more willing to limit the opposition will be more likely to vote for a strongman.
H2. As negative evaluations of personal and national economic conditions increase, respondents will be more likely to vote for a strongman.
H3. As respondents' fear for their personal safety increases, they will be more likely to vote for a strongman.
H4. Respondents with more negative perceptions of out-groups are more likely to vote for strongmen.

H5. As trust in political institutions decreases, respondents are more likely to vote for strongmen.
H6. Respondents who evaluate democracy more negatively will be more likely to vote for a strongman.
H7. As levels of nationalism increase, respondents are more likely to vote for a strongman.

To test these hypotheses, the team examined both the 2016 American National Election Studies (ANES) Post-Election Survey and the 2012 Latin American Public Opinion Project (LAPOP) "Americas Barometer" survey to see if this trend of organic false consciousness and radical rationalization was consistent with both US voters and voters in Latin American countries who have a history with the authoritarian figure there known as the *caudillo*. Like Trump, the caudillos of old tended to tap into already-existing populist unrest and frame themselves as the only viable alternative to the existing state of affairs, calling upon the revolutionary sentiments within otherwise-democratic voters to justify their authoritarian methods.[41]

The researchers matched each LAPOP question with a similar question in ANES. In addition to including independent variables to test the hypotheses, the team also followed standard practice in survey research and included variables to control for socioeconomic status (SES) and other characteristics that typically shape political attitudes and behaviors. The hypothesis test methodology utilized cross-sectional analyses with binary logistic regressions for each country. For the Latin American analysis, the LAPOP's 2012 survey was relied upon; for the analysis of the United States, the ANES.

To measure the dependent variable (vote for strongmen) in Latin America, the researchers relied upon a LAPOP question that asked respondents, "Which candidate did you vote for in the last presidential election?" They then recoded the question into a dichotomous variable: (1) "Strongman" and (0) "other candidates." For the ANES survey, similar recoding was done to map a vote for Trump as a (1) variable and a vote for any other candidate as a (0) variable.[42]

The results were telling. In Latin America, the eight caudillos cited in the survey ended up appealing ideologically to many working-class voters on the left despite the equivalent economic factors in the ANES survey ending up appealing to the Trump voters on the right.[43] The rationale ended up finding parallels between the caudillo voters and Trump voters as well, with the most recurring supported hypotheses being H1 and H2. None of the other hypotheses were found to be consistently true across all voters and regions. Across both Latin American and US models, the study found that these two variables could be explained in plain English as follows: Support for a strong leader who will bend the rules or limit the voice of the opposition to the perceived sociopolitical liberation of the voters was deemed worth it among the strongest supporters of both Trump and the caudillos.

Those supporters also were shown to be the most in favor of democracy. Indeed, the results of this study showed that satisfaction with democracy is in fact an important variable for understanding why voters are willing to endorse strongmen. In the case of Latin American caudillos, those countries that are satisfied with the democratic process are curiously *more* willing to elect strongmen who champion their disrespect for the democratic process. The researchers determined in this study that this was rationalized in the minds of the caudillo's supports "in order to save the country from peril."[44] Similarly, the US survey respondents claimed they chose Trump in spite of anything else because they believed the country needed a forceful enough leader to take "us in the right path."[45] The ideology of the Latin American voters being leftward while that of the US voters being rightward is yet more evidence that some sort of distortion has taken place in the States, with historically leftist concepts of pro-worker, anti-elitist politics becoming wrapped up somehow in conservative and right-libertarian sentiment for American political types.[46]

This process as described earlier is arguably the best explanation yet of what is actually going on with right-wing populist distortion, as it has historical merit in actual right-wing populist infiltration strategies of the past, most notably among them something called the *Querfront*, German for "transversal front." First identified in Germany (hence its German title), *Querfront* has been described as "a recurrent motif in far-right thought over the past century" in which populist reactionaries, "craving the legitimacy that an alliance with progressive forces can provide," exploit "ostensibly shared positions, chief amongst them opposition to corrupt elites, to create the impression that progressives could benefit from making common cause with them."[47]

It should be noted that tendril theory on its own, by tapping into this historical precedent, only explains the *intentional* qualities of this phenomenon while still leaving the organic process of broadly populist people falling into unwitting susceptibility to right-wing ideology unaccounted for. This is why the theory of a PRS, which delineates both the initial infiltration and the subsequent organic response from within these movements themselves, serves as a holistic framework. PRS uses tendril theory as a foundational plane of operations for a visualized point of reference, but it also builds upon a set of ideas first put forth by moral philosopher Jonathan Haidt in 2012, which states that collaboration between unlikely political ideologies at the populist level is fostered through moral psychological overlap borne out of shared unjust experience.[48]

Haidt's concept itself was building upon Moral Foundations Theory, which argues that when faced with these said shared unjust experiences, broken down into five main areas of populist concern (loyalty, authority, sanctity, fairness, and care), both the populists on the political left and the political right put equal emphasis on three out of those five areas (care, fairness, and loyalty), therefore bringing about organic solidarity on matters of principle that transcend typical political divide.[49] From there, the aforementioned frontier of antagonism is formed, and perceived common enemies are identified. This can, especially when alternative perspectives are obfuscated by hegemonic forces, lead to mass misunderstandings of what causes these injustices, which can be exploited and veered into a perverted form of populist activism (such as "folksy" fascism and other populist-pandering authoritarianism and statism).[50] This ties into the false consciousness of many working-class people identified by the Marxists without using the term pejoratively, since empirical investigation of the real history and stated motivations behind the phenomenon is what the book pursues.

The working-class Trump voter is therefore a perfect example of this PRS in action: the same individual could hold parallel social perspectives to the everyday working-class American *as well as* absolutely abhorrent views that still fall into the person's internal narrative without the latter ever seeing the light of day in many interactions with other people. This is precisely how so many apologetics for Republican voter support during the 2016 election came to be taken seriously.

It is also true that the kind of solidarity found within these specific kinds of populist spaces on the right mirrors the same sentiments as the solidarity of the Jacobins. Indeed, "Jacobinism" is a term that originated from the Jacobin movement during the French Revolution that rose up against the royal leaders of the day to overthrow theocracy and declare independence on behalf of the common people. There was legitimate class struggle in that case that was legitimately identified for what it truly was, which is arguably one of the reasons it was so bloody. "Jacobinism" has lived on in revolutionary vernacular beyond its initial etymology and has been applied to similarly minded movements elsewhere in the world, with its embodiment being more than evidenced in the right-wing populism of America, as cited above.

It is arguable that Jacobinism in and of itself was largely responsible for setting the groundwork for how all populist movements have subsequently behaved, and as such should be seen as an origin point for much of what modern populism, in any region, appears as today.[51] Succinctly, Jacobinism can be described for our purposes as, in the words of anthropologist Dr. Claudio Lomnitz, a "fantasy of unmediated popular power; the will of 'the people' embedded in the law."[52]

* * *

Limited, Yet Specific Working-Class Support Made the Difference in 2016

"Desperation" is the word many of us likely think of when the possible motives for overlooking Trump's worst qualities and heading out on voting night roll through our minds. As cited earlier, most Trump voters expressed feeling like they had less economic and social influence than before. But this does not necessarily mean that all of these voters were members of the working-class themselves. The reality is that only a very specific demographic within the entire working class on average ended up voting for Trump in the numbers needed to have a tangible effect on the election. That demographic? Predominantly white, predominantly male, and predominantly politically conservative—not a small portion, by any means, but also not the entire working class.[53] Beyond that focused chunk of the working class, Trump's other supporters, donors, and voters were more typically affluent people from higher economic brackets.[54] In that sense, it was business as usual in November 2016, as another bourgeoisie elitist got support from those who had vested interests in seeing him as president—albeit an elitist from the corporate side of the machine rather than the governmental. Trump is nothing, if not a successful chameleon, managing to reinvent himself more than once depending on what campaign (marketing or political) he has been engaged in at a given time.[55] Once a Democrat who claimed to care about minority rights, then an obscure third-party contender for president of the United States back in 2000 when he was the Reform Party's nominee, then finally a Republican working-class hero figure with a streak of xenophobia for his 2016 campaign, the only thing consistent about Trump throughout all of those persona shifts (more simulacra than simulation) was that he was a millionaire real estate and business mogul who lived a perpetual life of elitism far removed from any real working-class experience.[56]

This is arguably why there still were just as many, if not more, members of the ruling class supporting Trump's opponent that election cycle as were supporting Hillary Clinton. But Clinton ultimately didn't win. Thanks to the number of red States in support of Trump, as well as the amount of swing States affecting the decision of the electoral college, Donald Trump narrowly claimed his victory. Yes, he was still largely supported by non-working-class voters, but the working-class voters who *did* show up to support Trump that night did so from a place of deep and passionate conviction. To them, Trump was the working-class hero they had been waiting for. It is also the case that many of the working-class voters who did not vote for Trump also did not vote for Clinton, as Clinton's campaign was seen by many as fraudulent in its attempts to assuage working-class voters in a non-populist, centrist manner.[57] Even among the higher earners who voted Trump, they too clearly felt, as the data earlier indicates, that they were losing social and economic ground in their own way. Because of this, the real overlap between the working-class Trump voter and the more affluent Trump voter seems to be a shared fear of loss of social, cultural, *and* economic influence—far more complex than just the working poor worried about their next paycheck. This was a cultural anti-political populism from the beginning that stood hand in hand with legitimate working-class fears as a means of legitimizing and strengthening its actual concerns. Many of these Trump voters, fancying themselves the true voices of whichever demographics they belonged to, whether it be the working people, or the people of social influence, or both, *did* likely vote the way they did out of a desperate attempt to finally be represented—just as Laclau being correct in his understanding of populism would predict. But what, exactly, was that representation expected to manifest as in this case?

On the surface, the collective desire of the most sane-sounding Trump supporters was to simply shake up what was perceived as an overbearing government unconcerned with the plights of the "true" Americans. But what constitutes a "true" American? The common working man, or something much more specific and ostracizing? Going by the common denominator pulled from the voter data, it would seem like the latter, though presenting publicly as the former. Digging beneath the surface quickly shifts the tone of the conversation and, thus, the aforementioned rationale spectrum as well. Because what motivated one mainstream Trump supporter might not have motivated another ten white nationalists who also supported the president. For those ten white nationalists, the vaguely fascistic and xenophobic rhetoric spewing from the Trump presidential campaign might have been the more powerful impetus.

But here is the most important part of all of this: it doesn't matter what specific populist logic motivates the dozen extremists in a given sample; all that matters is what drives the single mainstream Trump fan. Why? Because the moment the needle on the PRS hits the "normal" range, even for a split second, and one relatable reason for supporting a cause or figure can be found in evidence, it becomes much easier for a given populace to legitimize illegitimate ideas that might be adjacent to the more relatable ones. To turn blind eyes and deaf ears of the general members of a populist movement toward the cancerous concepts of an ideology while only acknowledging the handful of salvageable ideas that can establish common ground. Again, when the broader desire of a given collective identity is simply to be heard, the potentially detrimental details are frankly seen to be of less immediate consequence. After all, through the eyes of the hyper-skeptical, anti-political plebiscite, there is a common enemy out there on the horizon worth uniting against. An enemy that threatens not just economic stability for the everyman but also the kind of cultural capital both the affluent and the working-class white demographics share. Depending on which ideological bent is enacted in a given hyper-skeptical collective, the common enemy can take on any number of potential labels: "the elite"; "big government"; "political correctness"; "cultural Marxism"; whatever broad brushstroke is used to depict this seemingly monolithic *Other*, it is seen in the same way: as a direct threat to the way of life of the (perceived) common people, of which the populist collective of the hyper-skeptic has appointed itself the sole representative.

But if it's all so cut-and-dry in these aforementioned ways, why is it that this perpetual state of antagonism hasn't been identified within populism at large long ago as something that holds the kernel of nationalism (e.g., in the case of the hyper-skeptics of this book's focus ultimately leading to the legitimization of the Alt-Right)? The answer is simple: populism and nationalism are simply not one and the same. The Alt-Right in and of itself is not nationalism or fascism in its totality; rather, it is a populist echo of the anger and paranoia that can ultimately add credence to said ideologies. Urbinati, in her book *Democracy Disfigured*, builds on the findings of Laclau to determine that "populism is the longing for a totalizing unity of society, but without its achievement," and is therefore not the same thing as a full-blown successful social takeover of a single ideology—it is merely the fight for being heard.[58] However, it is key to note that Urbinati seems to differ slightly from Laclau in her skepticism toward the stance that populism is always benign at its outset—though she too notes in her book *Me the People* that populism can still often take nonauthoritarian forms.[59] Turning briefly back to Laclau himself, we can see this contrasting difference embodied within his example of the politics in Ataturk, which succeeded in literally extinguishing certain demographics in Turkey.[60] Politics of this sort Laclau clearly defines as non-populist in nature for this very reason: the outcome did not simply give voice to one group; it also silenced others. Once populism achieves its goals, it ceases to be populism and becomes policy. The most sinister of populist strains, then, intends to ultimately lead to policy as well, albeit policy of the sort that exiles a specific group of *Others*—or worse (the following chapter will dissect how these *Others* are conjured within pockets of populist unrest).

But this isn't meant to make one wary of populism altogether; on the contrary, this is again all intended to simply make clear once and for all that populism in and of itself is not inherently bad, nor is it the direct culprit of the state of affairs examined within these pages. It is, however, at times prone to hijacking at the hands of those who might desire that their world play out much more closely to the nationalism of Ataturk than the basic cultural conservatism of, say, the hyper-skeptical and anti-political Trump voter. It is through this dissection of this particular brand of populism, one tainted and morphed by neoliberal ideas (which will be laid out in the following chapters), that we discover the fact that within its antagonistic and broad-brush rhetoric resides the untapped potential for nationalism and fascism apologetics. This means that while populism as a whole should be understood on its own terms, each instance of its emanation should be individually examined to better determine if it is of the political or anti-political sort—and if the latter, whether *that* amounts to the more reasonable technocratic strain *a la* what was observed by Ferguson, or if it in fact veers into the hyper-skeptical, identity-tethered world discussed by Wood.[61] The neoliberal populism of the privileged plebiscite, which this book argues is the main convoy from mainstream conservatism to faux-populist radicalism, is decidedly the latter.

The Manufactured Antagonist

As anthropologists have continued to uncover our species' past, humanity at large has gotten a better understanding of just what it is that seems to make us tick—across cultures, space, and time. Trends crop up, familiar behaviors take various adjacent forms, and it becomes easier to predict outcomes of a given society's actions based on circumstance and cultural attitudes held at a given time. While there are no guarantees, there are probable directions whole groups of people may move into that are either directly or indirectly informed by their social circumstance and zeitgeist. The first "societies," the archaeological evidence suggests, were nothing more than nomadic family units who didn't typically number more than fifty people at a time.[1] It becomes easier, then, to understand why humans evolved to cherish a joint sense of society and family in a way that is oftentimes emotionally entangled. What's more, these early societies, when encountering other families and tribes, would often feel the need to protect themselves from these *Others* lest a threat to their survival and way of life be considered impending—this can then be seen growing and shifting into the next logical manifestations of said protections as societies grew and became stalwart nations (China's Great Wall, the towers of the Incas, the Roman gates, etc.).[2]

This touches upon the often-conflated concepts of the "other" (small-O), which is a broad type of antagonist manufacturing common within far-right ideologies, and the (large-O) *Other*, which is more of a survival-based concept found in nativism, as demonstrated earlier. Why, then, is this book seemingly attempting to further conflate these different approaches at the concept of otherness?

It needs to be made clear straight away that there is no illusion on this author's part that somehow the most extreme forms of right-wing ideological (i.e., distorted) populism are in any way genuine in their concepts of otherness, or that they arrived at such concepts through any actual need for survival. What is clear, however, is that the justification for these ideological extremes from within these movements often walks and talks like nativism specifically and not just broadly bigoted. What this means is that, in order to fully understand at what point along one's movement of the populist rationale spectrum one begins to find one's organic (leftist) populism distorted, we need to theoretically approach both forms of otherness, nativist and populist, as if they are both variant forms of "large-O" *Other* manufacture—not in reality, but in ideology and personal rationale.

This sense of togetherness and protectiveness, altogether human and seemingly evolved within us prior to our migrations out of Africa and subsequent dispersal across the planet, cannot help but play a role in how we behave when thrown into situations that bring us face-to-face with more *Others*. The concept itself of holding solidarity in the face of something foreign still makes sense as an evolutionary remnant,[3] but when it clashes against the relatively recent idea that individuality somehow must trump the community, it stands to distort these once-noble ideas of comradery into an unaware collectivism in which one's individuality is celebrated by others of the same mind, and in which one's shared cultural outlook with his fellows becomes an unwitting replacement for true shared interest for survival—arguably an evolved-in necessity.[4]

The reality is that even so-called individualism is not immune to socialization, and we can demonstrate that. On the individualized scale, then snowballing toward manifested collectives, the same principle is in play: homophily, a mathematically measured social phenomenon in which social contact between two people of similar traits is predictively more likely than between people who have opposed or dissimilar traits. Much of this is self-selecting, as we might imagine, but it is interesting to keep in mind that it is not always conscious action such as congregating that brings such associations about. Things such as similar physical characteristics, as long as they are visible and socially meaningful in some way, also predict contact, which demonstrates that even when we think we are individuals with no intentional collectivizing in mind, collectives of similar people on various meaningful social levels, conscious and otherwise, still occur. This author submits that the aforementioned tribal survival clustering is therefore playing a part within these "individualists" of the modern right even when they deny collectivist traits and claim to merely be mutually celebrating just how individualist they truly are.

In his book *Human Behavior and the Principle of Least Effort*,[5] philologist George Zipf devised the following equation to demonstrate how homophily of location, for instance, works:

$$P = G \cdot \text{Pop1} \cdot \text{Pop2} / (\text{D12})^2$$

Breaking this down, it goes as follows: Population (P) equals whatever socially malleable similarity that serves as a constant (G) multiplied by the populations of one community (Pop1) and another community (Pop2) divided by the distance between these communities squared. Through this formula, Zipf was able to delineate the behavior of peoples interacting within these communities as to predict the circumstances under which their social paths are more likely to cross. Zipf is arguing that if we observe two population clusters, and said clusters (cities, countries, sub-communities within these larger bodies, etc.) have large populations, the likelihood that members from each of them will interact will be higher due to the sheer number of people in both. However, by this same token, as the distance between these clusters becomes greater, likelihood of interaction will go down.

Applying this more broadly to worldview, it can give us an insight to how similar or dissimilar two geographically distinct populations are. Honing in on this book's main occupation with right-wing sentiments bleeding into fascism, this implies that not only will ideologically similar groups be more likely to gravitate together, but that on greater distance scales, what a specific version of right-wing sentiment looks like in one place might wear a different face elsewhere, making it harder to identify if one has only ever had a more distant example to go by. The right-wing populists in the United States, for instance, tend to think of Nazi Germany's version of fascism as the only face fascism can wear. Meanwhile, the Alt-Right pushes a narrative latching onto socioeconomically homophilic specifics based on particulars of American working class and cultural strife, and it becomes more difficult for the target audience to see through the deception. In whatever case homophily is seen in play, however, the result is still the same: socially affecting traits we come to possess pull us together whether we choose to be affected or not.

Historian Robert O. Paxton writes in his 2004 book *The Anatomy of Fascism* that there should be a delineated distinction between upper-case "Fascism" and lower-case "fascism," with the latter being of a folksier, seemingly everyman approach to the ideology compared to the transparently statist form of the former.[6] Paxton's thesis is also couched in the realization that there are more organic, internal elements to the growth of movements that ultimately turn fascist that are often overlooked by analysts due to being overshadowed by the more obvious top-down, *external* elements. Paxton points out that the name itself actually is derived from the Italian fascismo, which Mussolini chose to "describe the mood of the little band of nationalist . . . pro-war revolutionaries that he was gathering around himself," indicating the plebiscite comradery already in play that Mussolini was simply exploiting.[7] It is also notable that the term might have also been used due to its similarity to the term *fascio*, which "remained in general use for activist groups of various political hues," according to Paxton.[8]

There is biological evidence as well to support the group over the individual as the more viable mode of human propagation. Thought initially to be put to bed in the 1960s and 1970s within the evolutionary conversation by the work of biologists George Williams and William Hamilton, the concept of group selection as a means of evolutionary impetus has in recent years seen a rebirth.[9] Altruism, demonstrably a hindrance at the individual level when surrounded by selfish actors, has actually been shown to flip into becoming advantageous once it graduates to the level of a shared trait within groups.

To summarize the gathered data on these dynamics thus far: if a giving and pacifistic person is pitted against another individual who is an aggressor, the aggressor is much more likely to win and therefore pass on his or her genes to subsequent generations.[10] Furthermore, if we graduate to the level of groups and the giving and pacifistic person exists within a *community* of selfish aggressors, then that person once again loses— taken advantage of and exploited by others.[11] If we stay at the group level but flip that dynamic, and a selfish person is dropped into a group of altruists, then we still see selfishness appear to win the day. This is observed as what is commonly referred to in anthropology as the free-rider problem, in which the selfish individual once again wins in his own right by not having his bloodline stamped out due to a lack of resources for survival. Why? Because this selfish individual can simply kick back and enjoy the benefits of all of the altruists around him giving and sharing the means to survive without him needing to alter anything about his own selfish proclivities.[12] In summation, while it seems as if group cooperation should work for human survival, it appears as if that force is weaker than one might think due to the fact that group cooperation still seems to lead to the cohabitation with—and survival of—narcissistic self-preservation (or exclusive kin selection, in evolutionary biology lingo). This is, in a nutshell, the reason why it seemed for many years as if kin selection on a more individualistic level was the far stronger element at play within the natural selection.[13]

However, there is still yet one other dynamic that needs to be considered: homogeneous group comparison. What happens when an entire group of exclusively altruistic actors is compared against an entire group of exclusively aggressive and self-centered actors? This should hypothetically demonstrate the advantageous or disadvantageous qualities of self-interest versus group cooperation in their purest and most innate forms when operating at the community level. This is important to determine, because even if kin selection is the stronger evolutionary force, what cannot be denied is that individuals interact within groups almost always. Which means communities and groups must be acknowledged as the most common backdrop upon which natural selection takes place. This fact must be taken into account in order to truly demonstrate which force, group selection or kin selection, truly gives the advantage for propagation within the real world.

Thus, when we compare homogeneously altruistic groups against clusters of homogeneously self-interested individuals, something very interesting happens: with no altruistic stragglers within the selfish group to feed off of, the selfish group eats its own in a dog-eat-dog existence and ultimately dwindles its numbers by adding stress, anxiety, cutthroat competition, and more violence into the mix.[14] Contrary-wise, the purely altruistic groups induce more fertility, more happiness, less stress, and ultimately greater numbers of offspring.[15] This occurs with *or* without the so-called free riders identified by Hamilton and Williams being part of the mix. This suggests that even when selfish individuals take advantage of altruistic groups, said groups *still* provide the greater net benefit to everyone and are therefore the most effective for further propagation of the species. Of course, if everyone in the group is altruistic, it is much the same outcome. What evolution functioning more effectively at the level of groups would suggest, then, is that altruism is the more advantageous trait, and that the level of groups is indeed the more affecting level at which natural selection operates.

Neuroendocrinologist Robert Sapolsky once argued it like this: while it is true that $A > B$, it is just as true that $AA < BB$. In other words, *individual* A might have a trait that dominates the trait of individual B, but *groups* of people possessing the trait of A can be demonstrated as being dominated by the trait of B when B is also operating at the group level.[16] Since creatures interact with each other at the group and community level the vast majority of the time, it is that group level that ultimately ends up dictating a great deal of circumstances that affect the natural selection process of the species in question. David Sloan Wilson, arguably the leading proponent of group selection in the early twenty-first century, has been famously quoted as saying that "selfishness beats altruism within groups. Altruistic groups beat selfish groups. Everything else is commentary."[17]

How does this apply to us humans and our cultural interactions? Well, the homophily phenomenon laid out earlier can demonstrate how exclusionary mindsets are simply yet another manifestation of this strength-through-groups mechanism, albeit with said mechanism being misunderstood or ignored and therefore the manifestation unwitting. Even when clusters of people identify with each other more than they identify across groups, group dynamics are still ultimately in play. In other words, our naturally selected circumstances have given us an innate desire for fellowship with our fellow humans, and it manifests as an itch in need of scratching, even when a particular cultural outlook insists the contrary. This still is usually for a sense of survival for us, just as it was for our roaming ancestors.

The most current understanding of group selection really amounts to something much more nuanced referred to as multilevel selection. Within this framework, it is possible for the individualists to be more or less correct at the individual level, but to fall short in their claims about individualism being the only viable perspective when forced to acknowledge the reality of the overarching level of groups and collectives being the foundation upon which all individualist philosophizing occurs. The hard-nosed individualists are therefore making a mistake in the sense that they assume they cannot be pulled into collectivist thinking. In reality, they are just in need of comradery as anyone else. As science writer Matt Ridley puts it, "selfishness is almost the definition of vice," and, by contrast, "virtue is, almost by definition, the greater good of the group."[18]

What then happens when this communal outlook is denied is an individually minded substitution, described by social researchers and psychologists in what is called social breakdown theory.[19] Instead of locking arms with our fellow human beings for genuine needs (such as propagation of the species through basic survival), a newer, artificial collectivism that masquerades as a mere mutual celebration of individual genius and earned privilege is primed to take the stage. It promises to give purpose in an existence that feels purposeless; confidence in an existence that feels humiliating; direction in a state of mind that feels confounded. What this looks like in the flesh is indeed populism—just as laid out in the prior chapter, and just as genuine. But when the focus of one's persecution—perceived or real—is one's near-exclusive individuality, and when *that* focus is wrapped up in one's sense of accomplishment, purpose, and value, then this particular populism becomes one of privilege rather than survival. What one can earn and opulently present is what makes one's identity, and when the ability to do so is stymied, the sense of loss is very real for the person being affected, albeit perhaps not truly warranting of the populist cry that typically echoes from the more impoverished corners of society.

This is *not* to suggest that anyone who feels financially or socially threatened within these aforementioned intellectual confines must be someone who comes from *economic* privilege (many of the people who would ultimately vote for Trump were blue-collar working-class people who could never be called so); rather, he need only reside within a place of *cultural* or *intellectual* privilege. If a person feels like he at the very least has a handle on understanding and somewhat affecting his cultural and social surroundings, he can subsequently predict those surroundings. That provides a sense of security and control within at least one plain of daily existence, and when one cannot control his work circumstances as easily, control of any sort is a precious commodity.[20] If and when the tides turn in this regard, however, and this same person starts to feel less capable of predicting and navigating the local spaces and people around him, he is more likely to feel threatened in this arena, which is arguably just as frightening in its own right as being threatened in one's ability to financially manage his life. For many of the right-wing populists who voted for Trump, the threat (or perceived threat) was often twofold: finances *and* cultural controllability were put into doubt.[21]

Some readers, especially those who might be coming from the blue-collar white American perspective just outlined, might still not be convinced that one can still be privileged without financial security. But the aforementioned sense of cultural and philosophical privilege is very capable of existing without its economic equivalent. This is because much of our societal structure is intersectional—it exists within multiple overlapping power dynamics that all come to bear on how the sustainability of the system as a whole is informed by social dynamics of all demographics of people. In 1989, feminist and social theorist Kimberlé Crenshaw coined the term "intersectionality" to describe how within these intersectional power dynamics, people of different racial, gender, and economic demographics can experience varying levels of oppression and privilege in relation to one another.[22] This complex and nuanced overlap of social experience is often lampooned in both conservative and mainstream liberal circles for supposedly amounting to an "Oppression Olympics" that merely aims to compete for special treatment and societal pacification based on how many layers of oppression one claims to endure.[23] The argument goes that if we spend all this time focusing on who is more oppressed than the next person, we may lose sight of real plights of real people on an individual, here-and-now level. However, while this argument isn't entirely unsound, it is important to realize that most proponents of intersectional analysis are not asking for participation in said Olympics; they are merely pointing out the reality that the complex and overlapping power structures in societies are reflected in said societies' citizens. This is a fact that can explain the apparent contradiction cited earlier in which certain groups of economically poor workers experience financial oppression while simultaneously benefiting from cultural privilege because they still belong to a demographic that has historically held more social capital: straight white men. This does not negate their financial woes, yet it goes a long way toward explaining their long-felt sense of influence and foresight regarding their immediate cultural surroundings.

How do we know for certain that this specific white and male demographic within the working class has consistently looked anti-political and populist even outside the confines of the Trump votership? How do we know this identitarian sentiment has been so long-brewing?[24] Because we have already done the research to determine what these anti-political populists in conservative working-class spaces look like. In a 2013 study by the Public Religion Research Institute dedicated to determining various demographics within populist conservatives who call themselves "libertarian," it was demonstrated that "nearly all libertarians are non-Hispanic whites (94%), more than two-thirds (68%) are men, and more than 6-in-10 (62%) are under the age of 50."[25] For context, 63.7 percent of *all* Americans are classified as non-Hispanic and white.[26] This means that these self-described libertarians and their red-pilled cousins (which this book will go on to demonstrate as being mostly faux-revolutionary conservatives experiencing an organic false consciousness) underrepresent racial minority groups by a 6-to-1 margin. This is a significant indicator that the anti-political populists we find within the conservative working class are primarily the origin pool for most of these more esoteric revolutionary types on the right who are also working class. It also indicates that there is plenty of room for lack of context or perspective in these movements for anything outside of the white male daily experience in America, just as the intersectional analysis prior predicts would be the case.

We have spent the past chapter establishing what populism is and what it is not, as well as how a negative ideology can utilize populist logic as its vehicle for growth and support. This is an important line to draw, because the mainstream concept of what populism is, even among some in the modern left, tends to conflate it with ideology. What is wrong with the current state of affairs? Well, in the mind of the modern well-meaning centrist, it's those pesky CEOs hijacking an otherwise efficient system (capitalism) for their own greedy desires—if they would simply play fair, everything would function beautifully when truly left alone. Likewise, the average American voter would likely argue that populism is intrinsically hive-minded, therefore rendering the concept of populism as a potentially noble concept inconceivable.[27]

But if Laclau is correct, and populism is merely the *process*, or logic, by which unrepresented collectives unite and fortify, then neoliberalism is not singlehandedly the cause of the larger problem; it is a symptom. It is merely one ideology among many that utilizes populist logic (a morally neutral vehicle) to try and veer the existing system into its adherents' collective favor. What if the flaws of the status quo are intrinsic to what is, for all intents and purposes, the capitalism of today? How would a particular collective, with a particular perspective favoring capitalism, choose to respond to the evidence making this case? Would the response be one of reason and empiricism? Or would it be one of hostility and paranoia?

This is what separates the broader base of anti-political populism and the specific right-wing, Trump-favoring camp housed within. The average Trump voter and the Alt-Right have one major thing in common through which their populist ties could be made: cognitive dissonance. Neoliberalism—the doctrine of "free markets" and the failure to acknowledge that power corrupts just as absolutely in the corporate world as it does in governments—has informed and constructed the present system in which the societies of the West function. From the highest corporate skyscrapers down to quite literally our shoes, the neoliberal concept of preconceived commerce possesses us. Yet, the expectations set by such a system increasingly do not square with the reality that the average working-class American experiences on a daily basis.[28]

This is because poverty, contrary to the popular neoliberal gallop, is not decreasing from the perspective of everyday life for many, many people. It is in fact rising.[29] This is due to the fact that poverty itself is now spreading into different demographics that previously did not have to experience it, such as the more affluent regions of the white working class, and even more interesting, suburbia.[30] All told, poverty in these regions has more than doubled in the past twenty-five years, according to Scott W. Allard in his 2017 book *Places in Need: The Changing Geography of Poverty*.[31] Since the 1990s, poverty has increased by 50 percent, contributing to this spread into these new social class frontiers.[32]

The aforementioned principle of homophily works sometimes outside of preference and is just as likely to be in play due to constraint. Financial constraint, for instance, is a means of homophily coloring our interpersonal interactions with one another based on having no other fiscal means of changing our locations, jobs, living situations, and how often we interact with our already-existing social circle. In these ways, it is once again more than fair to argue that much of the sub-demographics within the broader working class find their own brands of populism due to this constraint—and white conservative working-class people are no exception.

What is meant by the earlier-postulated "preconceived commerce" is one that is manufactured. The greatest thinkers across the past several centuries, holding varied political views and ranging from John Locke to Paulo Freire to Michel Foucault, all found agreement on one key point: the most important form of human commerce is the one of collaborated ideas. While the current representatives of clashing ideologies debate in the modern lecture hall whether human societies comprise individuals or collectives, these earlier titans of intellect were already uncovering the more nuanced truth. Russian philosopher and anarchist Mikhail Bakunin once wrote with cutting precision about just what one should take into account to be a true individualist rather than merely an observer without grasp of the individual's surrounding influencers:

> The real individual is from the moment of his gestation in his mother's womb already predetermined and particularized by a confluence of geographic, climatic, ethnographic, hygienic, and economic influences, which constitute the nature of his family, his class, his nation, his race. He is shaped in accordance with his aptitudes by the combination of all these exterior and physical influences. What is more, thanks to the relatively superior organization of the human brain, every individual inherits at birth, in different degrees, not ideas and innate sentiments, as the idealists claim, but only the capacity to feel, to will, to think, and to speak. There are rudimentary faculties without any content. Whence comes their content? From society . . . impressions, facts, and events coalesced into patterns of thought, right or wrong, are transmitted from one individual to another. These are modified, expanded, mutually complimented and integrated by all the individual members and groups of society into a unique system, which finally constitutes the common consciousness, the collective thought of a society. All this, transmitted by tradition from one generation to another, developed and enlarged by the intellectual labors of centuries, constitutes the intellectual and moral patrimony of a nation, a class, and a society.[33]

What Bakunin observed two centuries ago is something that many present-day self-described revolutionaries on the right, who claim to be exemplary individualists, still fail to grasp. Yet it remains a true observation in the fields most concerned with relationships between individuals and their societies. Anthropologist Clifford Geertz would echo Bakunin's sentiments in the 1970s with his memorable declaration: "Without men, no culture, certainly; but equally, and more significantly, without culture, no men."[34] Even more recently, education researchers Hervé Varenne and Ray McDermott similarly argued that "there is no humanity to single human beings except through interaction with other human beings—even if the interaction is indirect, painful, and most of the relevant others are dead," adding that "agency is always limited in its initial conditions and process, and the restrictions are always particular to a time and place. They are historical, constructed, 'cultural' in our sense."[35] (Social constructs, a concept often made enemy number one of present-day conservatism at large, was actually first put forth as a means of explaining various social phenomena by a sociologist who was a conservative, himself: Peter Berger, in his 1966 book *The Social Construction of Reality*.[36] Objective reality cares little for political or ideological bias, and it is simply a fact that many concepts we consider axioms are merely socially or culturally conceptualized.)

What each and all of these thinkers and researchers are getting at is the formulation of an argument that appeals to one of the deepest-rooted realities of humanity: we are individuals *within* collectives, not one or the other. Each interacting element of human experience informs the next, and the sum total is nothing without the integers that comprise it. Foucault, for instance, argued that a society held up via a network of shared knowledge among its peoples was the means by which true power was established. Through discourse, knowledge informs social perceptions which in turn normalize and inform conduct consistent with said perceptions. This therefore comes full circle and re-informs the larger social conversation, further solidifying the perspectives of the knowledge network as a whole.

This concept, when taken on its face, runs the risk of seeming too obvious or even cliché. Of *course*, "knowledge is power." But what does that actually mean? Taking into account the communal nature of Foucault's observation, it means that the sort of hyper-individualized perspective pawned off as liberating by neoliberalism is nothing of the kind, but instead a means of isolating its adherents and instigating division and antagonism. But this also means that in order for intellectual commerce to truly be beneficial to free societies, it needs to operate by respecting the shared nature of its most organic forms. Michel de Certeau tapped into this same idea in *The Practice of Everyday Life* when he identified two distinct categories of social participant: the strategist and the tactician. The former category comprised "producers"—politicians, lawmakers, businessmen, advertisers, and so on—while the latter made up the consumers. But the tactics of the consumers, de Certeau found, were just as integral to the direction of a society as the strategies of the producers. In this way, society (especially one with democratic elements) stands to almost never be explicitly controlled from a top-down system.[37] Unless, of course, this organic process of democratically discerned cultural value is replaced with an artificial one.

Neoliberalism is just such a replacement. It distorts actual intellectual commerce and peddles pre-packaged, artificially limiting, avenues in its stead. It demands that in order for us to succeed as individuals, we must turn ourselves into consumable commodities—"personal branding," "marketing," "demographics," "human resources," and so on. The fiscal nature of this rhetoric is present even outside of topics directly involving business and profits. It is now ubiquitous in the very words we speak to describe intellectual ambition and self-worth. We as individuals are not worthy of success, according to the neoliberal sentiment, unless we can meet the particular expectations of the existing market that will not only make us money to take care of basic living expenses but also give us the profit margins to reap a more opulent daily existence. If these hurdles are not cleared, we are deemed failures as individual human beings. The value of our ideas, the value of our personhood, is directly tethered to our profitability as marketable goods in a frozen system of perpetual capital.

Political theorist Wendy Brown sums up her thoughts on the matter as follows:

> Neoliberalism . . . is best understood not simply as economic policy, but as a governing rationality that disseminates market values and metrics to every sphere of life and construes the human itself exclusively as *homo oeconomicus*. Neoliberalism thus does not merely privatize—turn over to the market for individual production and consumption—what was formerly publicly supported and valued. Rather, it formulates everything, everywhere, in terms of capital investment and appreciation, including and especially humans themselves.[38]

This pathway to conformity placed at our feet is not one which is all that conducive to the American Dream as it is described. After all, when one's self-worth is tied up in one's ability (or inability) to fall in line and operate according to profit margins rather than social and personal enrichment, the standard for what counts as a success becomes more and more alien to the average person. Despite this, the neoliberal narrative that currently dominates the West continues to advocate for self-made greatness in the style of the revolutionary while simultaneously (and ironically) arguing for the preservation of a social system that protects the most privileged of said society almost exclusively, which in turn puts superfluous limitations on the very working-class demographic it claims to be championing.[39] Therefore, when the everyday conservative or right-libertarian in America, who believes in the promises of a "free market" and "land of opportunity," finds himself either working incredibly hard yet gaining no ground or, worse, unable to find work at all, he will not immediately question the veracity of the world he's been sold; instead, he will turn to other possible explanations for why and how his due success has yet to find him.[40] It is, after all, easier to question the outside world than one's own echo chamber when expectations are not met.[41]

We return, then, to the concept established in the previous chapter of the hyper-skeptical, anti-political brand of populism. The one that results from populist logic being put in the hands of the disgruntled and the weary. More specifically, the means by which said populist tends to identify his enemy: the concept of the *Other*. The demographic described earlier, which, again, includes predominantly white, conservative working-class men, has grown very weary and disgruntled indeed with the status quo.[42] When the expectations set up by the American Dream are not fulfilled, despite members of this group going through the motions and fighting for an honest living, the blame gets projected onto the monolith. Why this projection gets normalized is simple: it is relatable, even outside the particular echo chamber of the disillusioned American right. The monolith is not exclusive to the Trump voter; it is present in almost all antagonistic ideologies. Philosopher and political theorist Slavoj Žižek touched upon this concept with his consideration of the purpose of the shark in the 1975 Steven Spielberg film *Jaws*. Žižek postulates in his own film, *The Pervert's Guide to Ideology*, that while the interpretations of the symbolic purpose of the shark tend to contradict each other depending on which political perspective is present in the critic of the moment, all of said critiques are both correct and incorrect simultaneously:

> On the one hand, some critics claim that, obviously, the shark stands for the foreign threat to ordinary Americans. The shark is a metaphor for either natural disaster—storms—or immigrants threatening United States citizens, and so on. On the other hand, it's interesting to note that Fidel Castro, who loves the film, once said that for him it was obvious that Jaws is kind of a leftist/Marxist film and that the shark is a metaphor for brutal, big, capital exploiting ordinary Americans. So, which is the right answer? I claim: none of them and, at the same time, all of them. Ordinary Americans, as ordinary people in all countries, have a multitude of fears. . . . We fear, maybe, immigrants, or people who we perceive as lower than ourselves, attacking us, robbing us. . . . We fear natural disasters, tornados, earthquakes, tsunamis. . . . Corrupted politicians . . . . Big companies, which can basically do with us whatever they want. The function of the shark is to unite all these fears so that we can in a way trade all of these fears for one fear alone. In this way, our experience of reality becomes much simpler.[43]

We will revisit Žižek a bit later for a deeper dive into the utility of this sort of broad boogeyman creation process as it applies specifically to the populist right wing, but for now, let us consider just this initial point alone. The external threat being something broadly defined and possessing something of a multiple-choice criterion (which makes its label something anthropologists call a "floating signifier") lends itself to a hazy identification that is fairly ubiquitously applicable. This is a problem on multiple levels because, in the first place, such a broad brush when identifying a perceived problem on the horizon means that oversimplifications and consolidations *a la* Žižek's analysis occurs both in everyday life *and* within esoteric groups, meaning that both the average Joe and the hyper-skeptic could potentially find solidarity over the same oversimplified, hypothetical foe.

It also veers collective perspectives into territory susceptible to ethnocentrism, something anthropologists in particular find troublesome—mainly because our own field fell victim to such thinking in its initial incarnations. The earliest anthropologists tended to be glorified explorers with journals, observing surface-level differences of skin color and cultural norms and declaring that these differences proved the existence of independent trajectories of objective "progress" tethered to specific regions and races. Evolutionary anthropology dispelled the latter assumption, while Johannes Fabian's quintessential work *Time and the Other* obliterated the former.[44] Yet the assumptions on both fronts remain far too commonplace in the world of the layman. This, too, works toward the potential bolstering of exclusionary and fear-laden narratives, namely, those that blame an enemy of dissimilar comportment for all the common woes of a given demographic.

Distilled into a single identifiable phenomenon, a sort of frontier of manufactured antagonism, this attitude operates as follows: for populism to take hold and move forward in utility, especially within an anti-political context, there *needs* to be a perceived enemy on the horizon of a given society that "the people" feel the need to rally against, lest they risk losing their collective ability to bargain and subdue said enemy's reach. Again, Laclau makes clear that the plebiscites in question need not actually represent the populace at large; they need only *perceive* themselves as doing so. As Roger Stone and his ilk also correctly identified during the Trump campaign, hatred and fear are much more effective meeting points for the reactionary than are love or empathy. If one is driven to fear and/or hate a perceived antagonist, there is virtually no telling how far one will go to "win" the fight (for a more detailed unpacking of how this phenomenon manifests in relation to economic realities, see Chapters 4 and 5).[45]

While the anti-political type of populism lends itself well to this mindset taking hold, there are some pretty significant flaws innate to its vague and onlooking focus. This is exemplified in the social condition surrounding the passage of Proposition 13 in California in 1978, which amended the State constitution and required that property taxes be fixed at their then-present valuation, increasing only to account for natural instances of inflation over the following years. This marked a division of sorts between different demographics within the local populace; between the pro-infrastructure crowd and the generation of the disgruntled and less confident in regard to the effectiveness and value of public services.[46] Once again, we can find the anti-political seeds being sown.

But the plebiscite voting power in particular during this time (post-1911) gave "the people" of California a reason to frame their local government according to their own concept of the manufactured antagonist and keep it in line with checks and balances and, essentially, civilian-level veto power.[47] The problem with this, however, is that such thinking can ironically be exploited by the sort of antagonism the populist movement in question still believes to be accounted for and anticipated. Special-interest groups, for instance (e.g., "well-organized political and economic entities"), can pose as the plebs' representatives and exude relatable purpose in order to ingratiate support from the very people they end up exploiting.[48] In other words, the manufactured antagonist is a vague and imprecise distraction; a preoccupation with the *Other*, on which general fears and paranoias get projected, and which is counterintuitive to the purported self-beneficial goal of populist movements.

Something else that puts populist thinking of this sort once again alongside conspiratorial groupthink, in line with the previously established hyper-skeptic identified in Chapter 2, is what has been exemplified earlier—putting more emphasis on imagined enemies on the horizon rather than real enemies right within a group's midst. The division of California via Prop 13 was not even close to the only historical example of this. For another, we can turn to the very real and documented threats of Nazi and other authoritarian regimes at various points in time, and how the conspiracy theorists of the day ignored said threats, instead opting to fear more abstract and illusory enemies perceived as approaching from the distance.[49]

In the current context, the hyper-skeptical brand of the anti-political populist can obviously find parallels with the modern Trump supporter. Likewise, we can also make connections between the imagined enemies of the past hyper-skeptics and the present cultural "threats" the mainstream conservatives claim to be taking a stand against. We have already explicated the ways in which manufactured antagonism applies to Trump's rhetoric via the prior examples already given thus far, but what about specific conspiracy theories, that can clearly be identified as such, of Trump's own making? Daniel Pipes defines conspiracy theories in his book *Conspiracy* as "fears of nonexistent conspiracies."[50] Trump built up such a conspiracy in the past that plays once again into his own brand of manufactured antagonism—his own concept of the *Other*: inherent distrust of Muslims, which actually taps into the appeal to anti-immigrant and white nationalist sentiments present in the most extremist right-wing populism, and that will be explored later in the book.[51]

Before he ran for president, Trump had promulgated another manufactured anti-Muslim boogeyman in the idea that President Barack Obama was not actually born in the United States and was in fact a Muslim himself.[52] This grew the "birther movement," as it is called, into a monstrosity that unfortunately showed just how many American citizens still seemed to distrust non-Christians, as well as just how gullible people were when Donald Trump spoke. The match was arguably lit at this point, and it was clear to anyone paying attention even back then that Trump had populist appeal.

Using said appeal, Trump pressed his luck again when confronted during his campaign about his starting the birther movement. Finally admitting that Obama was indeed a US citizen, Trump then made the claim that the birther conspiracy theory was actually started by Trump's 2016 opponent, Hillary Clinton, all along.[53] This too would be shown to be untrue, but once again, Trump's populist followers were already too swept up in his "seduction" (*a la* Trujillo) to care. Trump's followers, like Trujillo's, seemed to see their populist hero as possessing a kind of "preternatural omnipotence," and, as such, they were willing to believe anything he said.[54]

Trump's rhetoric also stands out as fairly Jacobinistic, which again ties into the definitions we have drawn elsewhere in Chapter 2. But Trump's Jacobinism certainly seems to embody more of an anti-political type rather than the more reasonable, technocratic form. He seems to echo everything his supporters hate about the current system and claims to stand for a complete overhaul of the status quo. In other words, Trump sold the narrative that making America "great again" would be possible only through his plebiscites' collective will becoming embedded, as Lomnitz qualifies, in the law.[55] Thinking that immigrants might be the reason for one's economic woes? Trump promised to build a wall.[56] Afraid of Muslims eroding Western culture? Trump tried to mark and/or deport them.[57]

All of this was accepted by Trump's plebs despite him having a very big government, big spending ideas in his platform that directly clashed with claimed conservative values (as well as his own promises to do things like cut taxes and shrink government). Appealing again to Žižek, his explanation of the process of normalizing anti-Semitism as a means of explaining the lower-class woes is a neoliberalized system is telling, and a good way of explaining the general xenophobic manufactured antagonism the conservative anti-political populists were willing to forgive in Trump.

"The fantasmatic figure of the Jew in anti-Semitism," Žižek offers, "obfuscates the class antagonism by way of projecting it onto the 'Jew,' the external cause that disturbs an otherwise harmonious social edifice."[58] In other words, when the problems that befall an individual of a certain economic class are systemic in origin, but the affected person in question holds an ideology informed by neoliberal hegemony, the blame will be put upon an external phantom menace in lieu of admitting the reality of a rigged game. This is one such avenue through which both the Alt-Right and the average American conservative in the early twenty-first century can reach a shared rallying point. It needn't be obviously anti-Semitic; it need only be nationalistic.

Ironically, the nationalism of populists-turned-fanatics often stems from a place of the populists themselves feeling like the outsiders. The feeling of need of representation brings with it an implicit belief in the genuineness of one's paranoid sense of ostracization. In his classic work analyzing how populists become fanatics, entitled *The True Believer*, American moral philosopher Eric Hoffer states that "within a minority bent on assimilation, the least *and* most successful (economically and culturally) are likely to be more frustrated than those in between" (emphasis mine).[59]

Notice the specifics of this observation. Both the least successful *and* the most successful of people tend to be the most frustrated, and with that measure of success and existing on multiple dimensions involving both economic and cultural influence. This is arguably not much different from the Kimberlé Crenshaw postulation of intersectional existence covered at the beginning of the chapter.[60] Both Crenshaw and Hoffer seem to recognize that one can have a level of influence on multiple plains, and that cultural influence and economic influence are both equally valid levels of influence that one can hold. What is most interesting about this, however, is not that two thoughtful scholars arrived at similar conclusions, but that Hoffer's observation of this reality came several decades before the concept of intersectionality would be widely accepted—back in 1951. Much like Berger, Hoffer was simply a good scholar and followed the data where it led in order to make note of the objective facts. The rightist outcry about these sociological concepts, actually quite sophisticated, being somehow pulled from thin air by brainless drones for the left is therefore farcical.

Concepts such as intersectional oppression or influence, then, or even the ability to find privilege on one of these plains of influence depending on one's cultural or economic demographic, are not recent inventions by supposed leftist fanatics like the modern right-wing narrative supposes. Instead, these concepts stem from observations of the facts of society that have been put forth by people for decades long past—the general public simply wasn't listening then. For an even more modern insight on this, we can turn to anarchist thinker and historian Lucien van der Walt, who has articulated that there are two major types of elite and not just one: the economic elites and the cultural elites.[61]

Hoffer's point that even the privileged minorities can feel like outsiders is a very important one, and it goes a long way toward explaining why something like pro-capitalist rhetoric can successfully present itself as simultaneously pro–working class, since both the influential businessman and the white working-class populist can find overlap in perspective on issues regarding proposed shakeups to the present economic system and subsequent threats to the American Dream.[62] For the businessman, a shakeup to the current system might threaten his financial empire, but for the working-class person who happens to belong to a more culturally privileged demographic, a shakeup to the system might make it even tougher for him to find work than it already is—and putting food on the table for his family is oftentimes as far as he can look ahead (and it isn't hard to understand why).[63] Both parties might differ in motivations for maintaining the status quo, but they genuinely believe in the principles they fight for.

Returning to Paxton, he states that while fascist rule once already in power appears monolithic, the reality is much more the result of cross-demographic cooperation, arguing that fascist governments are "neither monolithic nor static," and that "no dictator rules by himself. He must obtain the cooperation, or at least the acquiescence, of the decisive agencies of rule—the military, the police, the judiciary, senior civil servants—and of powerful social and economic forces."[64] But Paxton goes a step further and argues that fascism's version of these alliances is a "special case" whose "power sharing with the preexisting conservative establishment" made it "fundamentally different" in origin and practice from Stalinism.[65]

Paxton called this sort of acquiescence a "dual state."[66] Greek-French sociologist Nicos Poulantzas had his own name for it, while also pointing out how similar partnerships can also be made between the disillusioned working-class person of privilege and the influential corporatist needing a new foothold for his own influence: a localized version of the "power bloc."[67] In Poulantzas's words, it is described as follows:

> The power bloc, like every other alliance, does not generally consist of classes and factions of "equal importance," sharing the crumbs of power among themselves. It can only function on a regular basis in so far as the dominant class or faction of a class imposes its own particular domination on the other members of the alliance . . . in so far as it succeeds in imposing its [influence] and cementing [the other factions] together under its leadership.[68]

While Poulantzas carries implicit with his descriptions of power blocs a charge of intent on behalf of the dominant faction, this book sets out to argue that all involved parties are capable of self-motivation without conscious malice or desire to deceive. There really is enough lived-in rationale, even (and perhaps especially) for corporatists, under late capitalism to do everything people do within power blocs as a means of sheer survival. In the case of the working-class person in this equation, he is at an economic disadvantage but still culturally privileged. Meaning he can relate to preservation of the *cultural* status quo while still desiring to change the *economic* status quo. For the businessman, the cultural status quo is of minor concern, while economically, things need to run pretty much as they always have in order for him to feel secure in his position. None of this means that the businessman is trying to be sinister. The desire to keep himself financially secure is a desire we can all relate to—it is just that his particular position as a *successful* minority who exists on the plain of economic influence, per Hoffer's qualification, means that his perspective is necessarily not going to benefit the working man at the expense of his own position being maintained. More of the how and why behind this dynamic's ultimate translation to pseudo-revolutionary rhetoric within mainstream economic policy will be explored in Chapters 5 and 6.

In the end, all of these apparitions are the same—the ethnocentric *Other*, the manufactured antagonist, Žižek's *Jaws* shark, and so on, and all of these are instances in which collectives of people utilize populism as a political logic to bolster *anti*-political sentiments and ultimately act on ideological grounds. The starting point for many is one of honest desire for solidarity, but the end result can manifest in any number of forms, including those that are dangerous and counterintuitive to the growth of a free and open society for all. In the following chapter, we will examine how collectives like these have historically served as havens for some of the most extreme groups ever known to ride the populist vehicle into relevance—and what implications these instances may hold for the present day.

4

When Populism Meets Ideology

We have examined the bedrock of what anti-political populism is built upon. We have also investigated how paranoia and distrust bred from such a thought environment can lead to a frontier of antagonism in which districts within larger political groups can perceive themselves as the true plebs in need of a cultural voice. Power blocs can form where intersectional overlap of privilege occurs, and economic privilege can become less distinguishable from cultural privilege inside rhetoric and narrative aimed at ingratiating certain susceptible pockets within the working class. Examples have been briefly touched upon in the broad strokes of how this sort of thing *can* occur in various anti-political circles, but it behooves us to better connect what we are seeing in America, in which the economic system itself breeds organic unrest that then falls victim to a mainstreaming of fascist and nationalistic ideas, to specific prior occurrences elsewhere in history.

This sort of analysis has already been under way in European countries well before America had even seen the current public explosion of Alt-Right sympathies we are now enduring. In the 1970s, Nicos Poulantzas focused specifically on the issue of fascism as a power structure borne out of class struggle and gave the scholarly world arguably one of the most integral works on the subject in *Fascism and Dictatorship: The Third International and the Problem of Fascism*.[1] Poulantzas's focus in that volume was on Italy and Germany's transitions into fascism, but the insight he gives within those case studies still applies fairly ubiquitously to how class struggle and obfuscation can lead to similar outcomes anywhere.

For Poulantzas, the mainstreaming of fascism from the very start correlates to crises of influence within the dominant classes—without their typical ability to mass-hypnotize the general public to buy into their dominating worldview (something Marxist theorist Antonio Gramsci called "cultural hegemony"),[2] the ruling classes need additional tactics for reclaiming this influence, lest they stand to lose their economic dominance. This is often internally justified and organically occurring within these classes, and it does not on its own bear the earmark of pro-fascistic attitudes.[3] However, when the prevailing economic system hits a crisis and faces upheaval, collapse, or otherwise irreversible transformation, the desperate may in fact cling to any means of alliance to maintain the status quo currently benefiting them.

The term itself is derived from the Greek *hegemon*, which refers to dominant factions using State force to influence the cultural outlook of the general population of a given society. Specific instances of this happening all the way back to the city-states of antiquity, such as with the Spartan hegemony and the Theban hegemony, demonstrate that this is something that has been happening throughout human history long before Gramsci gave it a name.[4] While back then it took the form of more obvious militarized force and control,[5] the *hegemon* of today, Gramsci's cultural hegemony, occurs much more subtly on the zeitgeist level—thanks in no small part to the rampant occurrence of corporate-government collusion on everything from monopolistic marketplace regulations to advertising campaigns and corporate twenty-four-hour news commentary.[6]

The everyday hegemonic normalizing process described earlier, articulated by Gramsci as "the political aim of transferring hegemony to the urban element,"[7] is in practice the cross-class power bloc described by Poulantzas and highlighted at the end of the previous chapter.[8] These initial power blocs are formed, as analyzed by Poulantzas in his case studies, when the working class begins to veer from its actually revolutionary ideas and tactics into a more complacent crusade for abstract cultural ideals and economic pacification.[9] In the absence of a full-blown revolutionary change to the status quo, working-class suffering does not go away. Thus, the next-best course of action to at least *feel* like progress of a sort is happening is to latch onto causes that feel more immediately achievable.[10]

But this can only last for so long, as the promises made on behalf of the ruling class and their cronies in the State cannot fully deliver the true equality working-class people want—if they did, they would cease to be in power. Thus, there occurs a "fraying" between the working-class people and their petty bourgeois spokesman (e.g., union leaders, compassionate capitalist proponents, and other mediary figures with influence who straddle the line between the working-class and the corporatists and politicians), resulting in what Poulantzas refers to as a transition between "formal" power and "real" power.[11] In the real power dynamic, a new power bloc is formed exclusively between the dominant class and the State, excising any pretending to care about the common man's strife that might have once been the veneer—this state of affairs is something he calls "big monopoly capital,"[12] and it is always characteristic of "the stabilization of fascism" (i.e., legally and culturally legitimized fascist rule).[13]

The initial phase of hegemonic dispersion among the susceptible pockets of the working class outlined earlier is arguably the phase America sees itself approaching right now, if it isn't already occurred. Once the first power bloc between these parties is formed based on a *seeming* overlap of cultural and economic unrest (even though the ruling class parties in the bloc are not actually concerned with significant changes economically), the society in question, according to the observed trends, is approaching "the point of no return" in the words of Poulantzas.[14] From there, Poulantzas argues that the full-blown rise of fascism is inevitable, but prior to crossing that threshold, there is still a chance for a given society to turn back, seeing as how much of the power bloc construction is only due to steps being taken by both the working class and those in power out of desperation for survival in the face of economic insecurity—in the case of those in power, these steps are "offensive," and in the case of the everyday working man who becomes anti-political, the steps are "defensive."[15]

There is an incredible irony to be found here, in which both parties are forming this alliance for entirely different reasons, and yet the cause can appear common when both parties' motivations occur organically inside the feedback loops and along the populist rationale spectrum that will be delineated in the forthcoming chapters. While those in power and those in need form a clumsy alliance within the desperate death throes of late capitalism (the economy pushed to its very limits of usefulness and dividends), and while this occurs largely organically and without directly evil intent on the part of the former party, truly evil ideas are then free to take advantage of this confusion and "invade the void" made in the wake "the retreat" of genuinely revolutionary ideas.[16]

In other words, according to Poulantzas's observation, a society experiencing a crisis of its economic system's promise has one of two choices: it can either move toward genuinely revolutionary change to that system, or it can cling to the system as it presently exists, with the latter choice bringing with it great risk of the powers that would be ultimately falling, unwittingly or otherwise, into company with fascist rule. This latter process is characterized by three intertwined hegemonic developments: one being the consistent descent of the working class as it slowly leaves its revolutionary aims and becomes complacent with the surface-level pacification of slightly tweaked economic policy, the second being the rise of Poulantzas's identified "big monopoly capital" from corporate self-interest to State tyranny, and the third being a parabolic journey of the aforementioned petty bourgeois mediators as they initially enjoy the benefits of the first power bloc but ultimately lose their influence once the second power bloc is formed and the State no longer needs to pretend to represent the interests of any party but its own.[17]

Together, all three of these paths of hegemonic development cross the point of no return simultaneously, after which point they collectively and organically snowball into the next threshold: State seizure of power.[18] At that point, the populism of the agitated workers falls away, and as Urbinati qualifies, the moment State power takes hold of the supposed cause, there is no longer a mere "longing" for a "totalizing unity of society"; there is an actual means of totalizing unity of society—by force, the only means by which such a cause could ever be made a reality.[19]

But, how do we know that Poulantzas's delineations are accurate and reliable? Do they have predictive qualities to them? Can we see the trends he identified occurring elsewhere in time and place? Indeed, we can. For one thing, Poulantzas identified these trends in not just one case study, but two. As he dissected the rise of fascism in both Germany and Italy, he was able to find common threads of behavior and ideas in both. Looking even beyond Poulantzas's own scholarship, others have discovered the same course of events occurring well into the present. Again and again, in various countries, we observe disenfranchised pockets of the working class, lacking economic privilege but clinging to cultural privilege, making deals with petty corporatists and buying into toxic exclusionary anti-politics as a means of rationalizing their circumstances without needing to let go of their desperate desires to still believe in liberal economic ideals— ideals such as liberation through capitalism, a concept that is on its face oxymoronic, as Chapters 5 and 6 will work in tandem to demonstrate.[20]

While we now understand "populism" to reflect movements that behave similarly to what Poulantzas identified in the working classes of crisis-laden Italy and Germany, it should be noted that the term itself is American-derived, and the movements that outwardly identified in Europe as populist did not fully emerge until the 1970s.[21] Nevertheless, what we now understand to qualify as populist in mindset and behavior does indeed trace back to earlier history, despite not donning the label contemporaneously, and Poulantzas certainly made a good case for how and why it occurred in Germany and Italy for his case studies.

In the case of Italy in particular, there are some very interesting dynamics present that can give us insight into how faux-revolutionary populism can emerge on the right in late capitalist America. A divide between two different kinds of elitist class existed in Italy leading into its respective economic crisis: the feudal lords in the form of landowners and self-made businessmen "outside the process of industrialization," and the newfangled factory owners benefiting from the new capitalist system borne almost entirely out of industry and automation.[22] Not unlike elsewhere the industry boom had touched, Italy managed to not be entirely taken over by it in the beginning, with the southern landowners seeing themselves as perhaps more legitimately entitled to their financial returns than the bourgeois manufacturers in the north.[23]

While this wasn't completely exclusive to Italy (after all, the United States had fought a civil war over similar divides once the right of States to use literal slave labor to maintain southern landowner's ability to compete with the speed of northern automation was legally threatened), Poulantzas does seem to feel that this dynamic leading to the growth of fascism makes Italy's crisis-to-fascism path different from that of Germany's. He refers to this divide in Italy as a "contradiction" of self-interest, pointing out that the southern landowners and self-made businessmen (the General Confederation of Agriculture), while still economically privileged, were "opposed to the fiscal policy of the State," as said policy stood to potentially threaten their feudalist chokehold on the laboring poor who worked under them.[24] The State also "favored industry exclusively," willing to collude with the manufacturing class in the north (the General Confederation of Industry) and giving the factory owners all of the benefits of regulating markets in a way that benefited and subsidized them—at the expense of the southern farmers and landowners, who as a result of this tipping of the scales were suffering increasing deficits of budget and overhead.[25]

In 1919, Sicilian priest Luigi Sturzo founded the Popular Party, a seemingly pro–working-class party that stood against the northern manufacturers and argued for "liberty" on behalf of the farmers and landowners who still operated under more feudalist economic dynamics.[26] In a sense, this was simply one form of elitism battling another, but in an explicitly anti-State manner that appealed to the anti-political sensibilities of the farmers who were aligned with the landowners ideologically. The most telling part of the Popular Party's intent to masquerade as pro-worker can be found in the fact that it became colloquially known as the "peasant party."[27] Nevertheless, it became quite popular quite quickly, and it did, despite its flaws, serve to better represent the skepticism of the State-corporate collusion going on at the time better than any other political party around. It demonstrates something that is very apparent in twentieth-century and early twenty-first-century America: the ability for privileged business owners and working-class people to both be anti-political and form alliances rather organically when it comes to issues of an intrusive State. It is within these areas of overlap of perspective that faux-revolutionary movements on the right, such as modern American libertarianism and even the more extreme red-pilled right, are forged without any conscious sense of irony. Ultimately, of course, the second power bloc predicted by Poulantzas did indeed form in Italy as well, and, as the fascists rose to power, they banned all political parties, forcing the PPI leaders, who were by then serving as a kind of functioning petty bourgeoisie, into exile.[28]

In Germany, of course, things were a bit more typical in that the feudal lords simply became the capitalists of the new industrial age, joining forces with the manufacturers and factory owners to collectively gain exclusive ownership of all forms of resources for production—whether they be natural resources or machinery. In the face of this, a German workers' revolution was attempted. The most memorable element to this push for revolution was the Spartacist uprising in 1919.[29] Said uprising was a major step along the larger German Revolution in the post–First World War German corporatist economy that supposedly led to a generally successful outcome: the replacement of the German federal constitutional monarchy (remnants of Germany's feudalist structure) with a democratic parliamentary system called the Weimer Republic. In August 1919, the Weimer Constitution was adopted, bringing with it a sense of complacency for the working-class revolutionaries who played a part. After all, they had "won." Now, they could enjoy the benefits their new democratic government would give them.

The problem with this narrative is that the genuine revolutionary attempts of the Spartacist uprising failed, with the militants of that uprising being defeated rather quickly by superior government firepower.[30] Beyond that, no other revolutionary attempt succeeded in bringing about an actual free market, pro-worker repositioning of the economy except in the case of the self-proclaimed "Soviet Republic" in Bavaria.[31] While unfortunately named, the Soviet Republic of Bavaria was genuinely pro-worker, unlike the Soviet Union. It declared independence from the newly formed Weimar Republic, and it stood to be one of the few shining examples of what an actual anarchist society might look like—until, of course, German *Freikorps* (military volunteers working at the behest of the Weimar Republic) overthrew it in less than a month.[32] While broadly trained to carry out military hits on behalf of the government more generally,[33] the *Freikorps* would end up acting essentially as hitmen against any potential uprising against the Weimar Republic moving forward.[34] A truly free republic with a non-intrusive government, this was not. What it was instead was an elitist power bloc takeover that tickled the ears of the workers and claimed it would play nice. This lasted for less than a decade.

Shortly after the Soviet Republic of Bavaria was overtaken, thousands of anarchists from the region were executed, thereby wiping out what was left of the briefly free anarchist republic.[35] The region had been subsumed by force, and it was ironically renamed the "Free State of Bavaria" within the Weimar Republic, all the while bearing the markings of a right-wing totalitarian State.[36]

But once the government of the Weimar Republic got what it wanted, it actually did make good on its surface-level promises to pass policy that at least appeared to be pro-worker. It never actually shook up its hierarchical structure, of course, but it at least tried to pacify the once hostile and violent unrest within the working class. If further revolts and subsequent military action could be avoided, then of course that would be the preferred direction to go in.

Because the government in the Weimar Republic still felt that the maintaining of power depended on public support, it can be argued that Germany had still not crossed its point of no return yet, even despite the violence it had unleashed to initially claim said power. With a pro-worker image to uphold, the following decade was filled with attempts by the Weimar Republic to maintain its "counter-revolution," in the words of Poulantzas.[37] It still saw small bursts of pushback along the way, with groups like the United Committee of Independent Anarchists (USPD) and a reborn strain of Spartacists (KPD) fighting to create recognized workers parties through the appropriate parliamentary channels (so as to not be considered traitorous and therefore worthy of military assassination).[38]

Then in 1921, another attempt at armed insurrection occurred at the hands of several members of the KPD, resulting in the government severely limiting the legal representation and power of the KPD at large, and causing a mass disillusionment from within that cost the KPD over half of its 350,000 membership.[39] In 1923, something Poulantzas calls "the great turn" occurred, wherein another counter-revolutionary power bloc alliance was offered by the Weimar Government, offering the slogan "workers governments" as a means of bringing in the remaining numbers within the KPD.[40] It worked. The KPD ultimately sacrificed its initial call for a workers' united front in trade for what was seen as necessary "alliance with the petty bourgeoisie" and the social democrats who at the time held more political sway.[41] This was the first identified instance of the aforementioned *Querfront* introduced in Chapter 2.[42] It is also notable that an even more extremist power bloc formed during the Weimar Republic, the fascistic Black Front, is the earliest recorded instance of horseshoe theory rhetoric and imagery—and it was used by pro-Black Fronters to promote said power bloc's sinister tactics of common cause working-class overlap.[43] This further supports the notion that the Berlatsky model of tendril theory infiltration is the more tangible reality of what horseshoe theory attempts to delineate.[44] Thus, Poulantzas' identified trends were found once again, and before the end of the decade, a new group that claimed to stand for true worker revolution, the National Socialists, had begun to gain influence.[45]

By 1930, Heinrich Brüning became the chancellor of Germany during the Weimar Republic, acting to further liberalize the policies in a way that would keep this merry alliance of working-class movements and the ruling class alive. But he also believed that Germany would be able to steer itself clear of the lingering financial unrest without the need for appealing to full-blown worker takeover. This ultimately proved unsustainable, and worker unrest continued to grow once again. Leading into the fall of the Brüning government in 1932, essentially the end of what had been a string of watered-down social democracy policy inspired by the slow fizzling out of once-revolutionary working-class demands, serves in Poulantzas's timeline as Germany's point of no return.[46]

The evolution to this point is fairly straightforward when one steps back from all the chaos. Once the assuaging of the German working poor took place with surface-level policies that claimed to have working-class best interests at heart, the pacification and complacency became clear. Alliances were formed between the workers and elite mediators claiming to represent the workers, all with the corporatists and their big government cronies continuing to benefit.

Yet another country thrown into economic crisis after capitalist promises failed to deliver to both corporatists *and* workers, Germany was facing the same "contradictions" of "factions of classes in power" that, in whatever form they take, are always "characteristic of the transition to monopoly capitalism," in the words of Poulantzas.[47] That is to say, Germany attempted to ingratiate its working class by pushing liberal policy that claimed to give workers what they needed while actually maintaining the economic status quo relatively untouched. Once that model was no longer sustainable and late-stage capitalism found its limits, the workers, having traded in their initial revolutionary proclivities for complacency with incremental change for so long, needed a revolutionary resurgence. Once the Brüning government fell and large gaps in worker need were left in its wake, working-class unrest once found itself at an all-time high.

To fill in those gaps, the Nazis weaved their narrative about how the economic strife could be accounted for largely through social Darwinist explanations about those who are superior having their opportunities for success being gobbled up by those who are "inferior." It is here that the Nazi form of fascism got around to building its own frontier of anti-political populist antagonism—to constructing its own concept of the *Other* (as identified in the previous chapter) in the form of the anti-Semitic caricature of "the Jew."[48] This caricature served as a scapegoat for all of the economic system's problems to be hoisted upon, with the added quality of wrapping up economic strife with cultural identity. That marriage of cultural and economic perspective has gone on to color many right-wing populist movements ever since.

In 2005, social scientist Jens Rydgren edited a volume entitled *Movements of Exclusion*, in which he and several other experts on right-wing populism pointed to several right-wing populist movements across Europe, including Denmark, Norway, France, and Sweden, and found common threads in rhetoric and mission statement across all of them—namely involving the fear of the aforementioned manufactured antagonist from Chapter 3, paired with a set goal of preserving one's own economy *and* culture by eradicating said threat.[49] This synthesized thesis has come to be known in academic circles as the Ethnic Competition Hypothesis.[50]

This did not arrive out of the blue. Financial crises abound within economic hierarchies of the sort found across most of the Western world. During the boom years of these aforementioned countries, labor was seeing a shortage.[51] In an attempt to kick-start their accumulation of capital, said nations began actively encouraging immigration to their borders in order to gain guest workers. By 1966, West Germany had gained over 1.3 million new laborers through immigration.[52] In 1970 France, there were over 2 million—bringing in tow nearly 700,000 more in dependents.[53] Similar numbers had accumulated by the same time in Denmark, Great Britain, the Netherlands, Switzerland, Norway, Sweden, and Belgium.[54] In many cases, the influx was so rampant because the countries in question had opened up their borders entirely for literally anyone willing to work, no other questions asked.[55]

At the time, the hope was that with more hands to take part in the economy, the overall strain would lessen. But as this book will go on to lay out in later chapters, the number of workers alone cannot solve the problem itself, which is systemically hierarchical and exploitative to most working-class people.[56] Suffice it to say that when the economic system itself is anti-worker by design, the crisis of strained labor will ultimately return in one form or another. In the case of these countries seeking foreign laborers, the crisis took the form of the bosses of the economy desiring more production and the workers needing some relief from their strained workload; in the case of what happened with the rise of populism in these same spaces in the 1970s, the crisis had returned for the workers, in that they no longer made the same income they once did. This is a result of a difference of motivation between the corporatists running the workplaces and the laborers *within* the workplaces. For the corporatist bosses, the desire was to have more hands on deck in order that more products and services could be produced at a faster rate. For the workers, of course, the desire was to keep earning livable incomes while also being freer to enjoy their lives outside of work.

The bosses got what they wanted while the workers, ultimately, did not. This is because the prevailing economic system in the West is designed to accumulate as much capital (profit that turns more profit) as possible for people who own enterprises by funneling profits upward first. From there, the people in charge of the companies and workplaces decide, sometimes arbitrarily and sometimes with company costs in mind, what the value of the workers down below is truly worth to them. Hourly wages, fixed salaries, and so forth cannot end up putting the business owners in the red—*and this is not the fault of the business owners*; it is simply the way the system itself is designed to operate. But because of this, when more workers join the force, the profit margins for the companies usually stay the same. This is done by any number of means, but mainly it is done, through whatever roundabout form is feasible, by ensuring that the existing wage pie is kept its current size and simply cut into more pieces to account for the workforce numbers' increase. Whether or not this is a "moral" act is subjective; the objective reality is that the system is designed to operate in this manner. If workers (rightly) want to genuinely gain more autonomy and livable conditions, the system itself has to change. The alliances outlined by Poulantzas made between the workers and the bosses, as well as the trust put in liberal legislation to pass "fair" policy that favors workers, are misguided. Thus, it came to pass across the West that by the 1970s, these alliances were proving themselves of little consequence when it came to the livability of daily life for the working people.[57]

But instead of questioning the marketplace itself, these workers looked for other explanations for why their gods had forsaken them. As it seems to occur quite often, the first strain of populist outcry in these spaces was of the anti-political stripe articulated in the prior two chapters. It does make sense—when one's own labor has the potential to bring financial security and autonomy, the responsibility for the reality being a contradiction of that likelihood must fall squarely in the laps of those who are perceived as calling the shots: the monetary law makers. Of course, these law makers are oftentimes merely the cronies of corporatists who initiate a collusive relationship between the two parties, but nevertheless, the anti-political hyper-skepticism toward the powers that be was understandable in Europe amidst this new crisis, as it was in Italy and Germany specifically in their prior crises, or in America in the present one it faces post–Great Recession.

But what evidence was apparent to explain the how and why behind this new sense of livable wage loss? Why, all of the foreigners who were occupying the jobs and hours the "native-born" (itself an anthropologically demonstrable incorrect concept) could otherwise be taking advantage of, of course! Indeed, this is not only what the anti-political populism in post-1970s Europe began to latch onto; it is also what informed the ultimate politics of said populism.[58] As journalist John B. Judis points out:

> The first European [populist] parties were rightwing . . . They accused the elites of coddling communists, welfare recipients, or immigrants. As a result, the term "populist" in Europe became used pejoratively by leftwing and centrist politicians and academics. . . . The main difference between American and European populists is that while American parties and campaigns come and go quickly, some European populist parties have been around for decades.[59]

And, so it is. Across Europe, decades of brewing right-wing populism of the anti-political stripe has exploded into movements that genuinely see themselves as revolutionary and against the establishment, all the while keeping its focus on other working-class people who simply were not born in the same geographical spot on the globe. Part of the appeal rightward rather than leftward, according to Urbinati, is the right-wing populists' ability to tap into the existing hegemony and accuse the emptiness of contemporary liberal policy appeal as being due to some intrinsic failure of leftism at large to help working people.[60] This incorrectly conflates modern liberalism with historical leftism and ignores the true problem behind why these economic crises continue to return again and again. Need we be reminded that the same or similar economic strife that was being felt in pre-fascist Italy and Germany was not accompanied by rampant immigration, but it happened anyway. As it always does, and always will, as long as the system itself continues to operate in an artificially hierarchical fashion.

Yet, the proposed solutions from these populist groups, many of them stronger than ever, is to undo the very thing their working-class demographic once wanted and close the borders to their countries, isolating anyone else considered foreign and threatening to the economy from entering. In short: the desire is to unite society across ethnic and geographic lines. The cry for populist action began with tangible economic woes, but a lack of adequate change ultimately led it into xenophobic antagonism against, once again, a perceived *Other*.

This kind of repeated misunderstanding of the real problem on behalf of workers can perhaps be more precisely understood through a dialectical approach of examination. In Hegel's dialectic, one thing comes together with another thing to produce something tangibly new, despite obvious external contradictions—nothing exists in isolation from the other. The synthesis that does occur between these different things and what form it takes is determined by the qualities of the things themselves. In this way, some syntheses through contradiction are benign. If one feeds a pet, that pet will grow, but if one puts food into couch cushions, one will simply be left with a mess to clean up. With any given thing in life, the cause of what comes next through interaction lies partly within that thing itself (internal contradiction) while everything else is informed by outside forces (external contradiction). While a product of a contradiction might seem to originate from its own external contradiction, there will always be internal factors at play as well that give the contradiction's parts their respective qualities.

In the hierarchical marketplace as it functions today, the bosses must find any means they can of maintaining their profits. This results in both internal and external contradictions: bosses and workers have completely different interests in mind when they interact, but the outward synthesis of that is that the boss-worker dynamic is visibly hierarchical yet appears necessary. But the internal problems are often glossed over while the external contradictions are seen as needing the primary focus when considering solutions. Therefore, rather than open up genuine competition between non-hierarchical co-ops (which would be addressing the internal, systemic problem of hierarchy), the proposed fix to worker unrest instead usually amounts to something like minimum wage raises (which only looks at the synthesis of worker unhappiness as being a product of its own external contradiction of worker-boss relations).

This can also be thought of as benign versus antagonistic in additional to internal versus external. If something's internal contradiction with another thing is not antagonistic but merely incongruent within the given material conditions of the moment, then the synthesis that comes from these two things can be benign and therefore addressed in a way that operates more at the external level should it end up being seen as in need of changing or improving. But if the synthesis between two things comes from antagonistic internal conflicts, then it will be fundamentally incompatible with a benign interpretation or a merely surface-level fix. Yet within neoliberal hegemony, the worker-boss dynamic is seen as being a result of a benign contradiction rather than an antagonistic one, meaning that people tend to only operate on the surface level rather than question the internal contradictions going on at the foundations. When that happens, the anger and unrest felt by workers who also buy into the neoliberal narrative becomes deflected under the delusion that both bosses and workers have the same interests in mind: fair workplaces.

We will revisit Hegel in the next section of the book. But for now, let us go back to the beginning of *this* section of the book and Urbinati's qualification that genuine, unaltered populism is a "longing for a totalizing unity of society, but without its achievement," we can safely assume that whatever exclusionary ideologies have taken hold in these various aforementioned spaces amount to rhetoric and likely have little grounding in anything demonstrable that could actually sway a legislative arm— unless, of course, members of these populist pockets themselves win elected offices *a la* the Latin American caudillos.[61] Nevertheless, this persistent cry of one's culture being eroded is still objectively unfounded.[62] So, why does it even take hold within any substantially numbered populist group at all? The answer is actually fairly simple: ethnocentrism. The belief that one's own culture is somehow uniquely valuable, or even innately superior to others, stems from the limited perspective of someone who has never experienced—or chooses not to experience—the world from any point of view other than his own. In this mindset, it is very easy to find oneself assuming that one's own way of life is the only preferred way of life. In many ways, Western culture at large has buried this line of thinking deep into its subconscious due to its own ugly history with violent militarism and colonization of other regions on the globe. Many of us here in America, for instance, are at risk for assuming "primitive" qualities of other people who look, speak, and behave differently than we do—even if we consciously do not hold such beliefs. There have even been studies done in which it appears that something as consciously trivial as skin color difference can induce a subconscious lack of empathy for fellow human beings across racial lines.[63]

With proclivities like these already brewing beneath the cultural surface, it only takes certain circumstances to ignite them amidst the distrust and anger that anti-political plebs already endure. As we observed in Chapter 2 via the writings of Dr. Ferguson, the disruption of daily life that can lead to the anti-political brand of distrust need not be rational; it need only induce a reaction common enough to be shared and internalized within a collective.

In the case of something like the European right-wing populist movements, different and varied and spread out as they may be at first blush, their cultural perspectives are shockingly uniform. Rydgren lays it out succinctly as follows:

> These parties have in common that they are movements of exclusion: their conception of "the people" is narrower than for other parties within respective party system. Immigration should be stopped or radically reduced, and immigrants already living in the country should assimilate. The idea and practice of multiculturalism is the principal enemy and the conception of cultural diversity—as it is conventionally understood—is denounced. Instead an alternative conception of diversity is presented: that ethnic mixing leads to cultural extinction and must be avoided in order to safeguard the existence of different cultures and ethnicities in the world (and the majority culture in each country from annihilation). Radical nationalism (and hence ethnic homogeneity in each country) is thus presented as a necessary condition for maintaining ethnic diversity on an international scale.[64]

In addition to this broader qualifier, which arguably makes the same points about self-partitioning plebs as Laclau, Rydgren also points out the same anti-political qualities cited by Ferguson. Rydgren writes about the "anti-establishment populism" of his observed right-wing groups, and of how they see themselves "as distinct alternatives outside the 'political class', clean-hands alternatives, which want to give the power back to the people."[65]

So here we have the first piece that is arguably the most ubiquitous and integral for all populist movements of this kind: the manufactured antagonist as necessitated by the most extreme forms of anti-political paranoia. In this regard, we're right on track to simply bolster the previously cited claims of the likes of Žižek and Ferguson.

But Rydgren's next observation inculcates the second component needed for the specific strain of right-wing populism that fuels the likes of the present state of American conservatism: an appeal to fiscal normalcy and faux economic concern as a justification for arguing against indiscriminate liberty and the mixing of cultures.

Rydgren continues:

> The so-called welfare chauvinist frame has become increasingly important lately: the real or allegedly costs of immigration is seen as a threat to the generous welfare programs of Western societies. Immigrants are commonly depicted as

"economic refugees" or "social welfare tourists" that have come in order to live good parasite lives on state subsidies. In a similar vein, immigration is played out against real or perceived defects in public health care and education, etc. With the same logic, that is, to present immigrants as illegitimate competitors over scarce resources, radical right-wing populist parties often claim that immigrants take jobs for natives, and that immigration is a major cause of unemployment. Finally, immigration is presented as a cause of insecurity and unrest: immigrants do not understand the culture of the West, and do not behave according to "our" norms and laws.[66]

This is an attitude being exuded more and more amidst self-proclaimed conservatives and libertarians in the West. In America particularly, such an attitude takes shape in the form of so-called fiscally responsible capitalism. It is not bigoted to be against immigrants, claim the anti-immigration crowd, nor is it classist to argue against social equity even among natural-born citizens; it is just "fiscally conservative." By framing their position in a way that is presented as one of hard numbers-driven realism, these voices effectively shield their more hateful ideas, hiding them amidst traditionally conservative rhetoric. This process is helped along considerably by the general public's willingness to buy into a larger narrative: that the economic status quo is the only realistic or noble form a modern society can take. To suggest otherwise, it is argued, is an attack on America's culture.

But how can a society's money flow be so synonymous with its cultural identity in the minds of those who argue against social equity? The conservatism we see today is full of adherents who have grown to associate economic equity with communism, and communism with immorality.[67] This conveniently plays into the hands of those who wish to argue that one's culture is being threatened whenever talk of socioeconomic change crops up. What better way to shut down any and all challenges to the bourgeois status quo than to associate economic shift with cultural corrosion? If we make it easier for people to legally immigrate here, we will have to share our jobs with them. If we guarantee a certain economic class of people a minimum income every month for bare necessities, we will have to redistribute some of our collective wealth. These ideas are frightening to many on the conservative right who have grown to truly believe that the very concept of economic change threatens to upheave everything that is great about American life.

I still remember when I first heard the term "cultural Marxism" uttered within my former right-libertarian circles. I found it obnoxious from the start, but I took heed of the fact that this was a popular accusation for conservatives (and libertarians who leaned conservative) to hurl at people. So, I set out to find out why. What I ultimately discovered was that most people using the term could not even agree among themselves as to what it actually meant. Some people say that cultural Marxism is synonymous with political postmodernism, but this is absurd, because postmodernism materialized out of a desire to bring the cultural conversation outside the bounds of strict metanarratives, Marxism included.[68] Others argue that cultural Marxism is an ideology first promulgated by the critical theorists of the Frankfurt School and is now championed by the "SJW" (social justice warrior) crowd.[69] But this, too, is an imprecise definition, since critical theory is not strictly tied to Marxism in its application, nor is every person in favor of social justice a communist of any stripe.[70]

What "cultural Marxism" actually seems to be, then, is nothing more than a snarl word—a pejorative to shut down dissenting voices from a right-leaning perspective.[71] Its etymological roots actually trace back to Nazi propaganda literature, wherein supposed "Cultural Bolshevists" were scathed and abused for daring to hold opinions contrary to fascism.[72] While it would be unfair to accuse modern users of the term to themselves be full-blown Nazis, it is still important to put into perspective where the rhetoric came from, what attitudes originally spawned it, and how seemingly unaware of these innate weaknesses in the position its current adherents seem to be.

The use of this term is largely nothing more than popularity through ignorance— ignorance of its origins, but popular nonetheless due to the confirmation bias it lends to so many conservative Americans. The perpetuation of these attitudes is not a conscious and deliberate conspiracy; it is an organic phenomenon. A phenomenon identified here as neoliberal hegemony. Neoliberalism, as already outlined, is itself a doctrine that perpetuates evils such as militarism and wealth disparity under the guise of classically liberal principles. Neoliberal hegemony, therefore, is evidenced as an entire cultural takeover by a mindset that apologizes for the systemic cruelties associated with said evils. But this hegemony would not have been able to take hold had it not also managed to tap into the anger and anti-political populism outlined in the prior chapters of this book. In this way, both elements, neoliberalism and anti-political populism, are equal postulators of the version of American conservatism growing more visible by the day.

* * *

One of the most predominant qualities within all of these right-wing populist movements is their common claim of being revolutionary. At the bare bones, "revolution" is typically defined as the overthrow of a governmental or social order with the intent of implementing a new system. All of the prominent revolutions throughout history that have been successful have resulted in this outcome. By extension, any movement that has yet to lead to an actual revolution is still in its pre-unification of society phase, making it populist.[73] In this way, we can think of any movement that genuinely sees itself as a beacon of change as not only populist but also Jacobinistic according to the terms set in Chapter 2.[74] Even if a given group bases its stated aims on misinformation or paranoia, as long as the group members themselves truly believe it, the group is for all intents and purpose a genuine revolutionary group of the Jacobinistic type. This book has made references to these right-wing groups as "faux-Revolutionary," but from the eyes of those working-class people acting within the movements, they are truly wanting revolution just as much as any other populist group in similar economic circumstances. Understanding that most people in these spaces genuinely believe in their causes is important to understanding how they can perhaps be reached and veered into a clearer understanding of what is actually happening to them—assuming right away that they are all hateful bigots to the core who aren't interested in real liberation for working people is, in this author's view, premature and unhelpful. Chapter 9 will better demonstrate why this is the case, but suffice it to say that many of the disenfranchised who happen to land in intersectionally privileged spaces are still very *under*privileged economically, which makes their everyday outlook as workers just as grim and endless as anybody else to share their economic bracket.[75]

So, what *is* a step toward leading the misguided-yet-earnest actors within these more culturally privileged pockets of the working class out of their present tunnel vision? For starters, one must understand that while internally these groups might genuinely see themselves as revolutions, it can be deciphered independently what the marks of revolutions anchored on reality are versus "revolutions" that are anchored on the kind of anti-populist paranoia we've already made significant headway toward unmasking. To demonstrate, we can compare two case studies of similar *claimed* purpose, from the same point in history, but facing opposed realities: the 1980s civil war in El Salvador between the grassroots Farabundo Martí National Liberation Front (FMLN) and the US-backed El Salvadorian government being one, and the French Front National's (FN) efforts in the same decade to unite various nationalist factions in order to fight claimed enemies of French economic and cultural sovereignty being the other.

In the case of the first examination, it is important to note that rebellions were something of a tradition in El Salvador by the time of the Salvadorian Civil War— going all the way back to the violent resistance to the *conquistadores* in the 1520s by the indigenous Pipil.[76] This made the contemporary Salvadorians at the time more primed to accurately decipher real threats to their sovereignty. The threat in this case was the Salvadorian government itself, and while that might at first seem like a domestic threat rather than a foreign one, the reality is that the right-wing regime running El Salvador at the time was being financially supported and militarily armed and trained by the Reagan administration.[77] The rationale given for this amounted to the typical appeals to the spreading of democracy and "liberation" to other places on the Earth, with the United States claiming to be fighting the good fight against "communism," which by this point had become the personal monolithic *Other* of the US government.[78]

While it was definitely true that the FMLN was a socialist coalition of various rebel groups, this fact does not on its own serve as condemnation of the umbrella's moral stances; nor does it excuse the intervention of the US government and the artificial tipping of the scales in favor of the oppressive Salvadorian government in the conflict that resulted from said meddling. In actual fact, while the FMLN was publicly labeled as a Marxist-Leninist outfit in an attempt to scare Westerners into supporting the US involvement, the reality (ultimately revealed through the release of private Salvadorian resistance documents) was that the FMLN's actual economic outlook was much closer to a market-oriented socialist system like mutualism or syndicalism—certainly more progressive than the command economies of the *actual* Marxist-Leninist–controlled countries or, for that matter, the economy El Salvador currently had.[79]

The Salvadorian resistance groups' motivations to unite under the FMLN banner in the first place is similar to the motivations of the extremist right-wingers in the West to unite with the right-of-center moderates: to grow numbers and forge solidarity for the cause at hand. But unlike the right-wingers, there was no appeal to an abstract boogeyman concept like imminent "cultural erosion" or "demographic replacement." Instead, there was the urgent need to fight back against a clear and present oppressive government that had already begun to join forces with the elite economic classes of the time and dig its clutches into the exploited laborers. Political assassinations of vocal dissenters against the status quo were occurring at the hands of the Salvadorian government at least as far back as the 1970s, and yet, many tenant farmers (*campesinos*) and workers still chose to take public stands for better wages and more humane working conditions, ultimately going on strike in 1979.[80] When that happened, the National Guard was brought in to violently end the resistance.[81] All that did was spread awareness into the more residential areas of El Salvador, giving way to a populist explosion—but one grounded in undeniable reality rather than anti-political paranoia. Various already-formed working-class guerrilla groups, including the Popular Forces of Liberation (FPL) and the Revolutionary Army of the People (ERP), then chose to merge into the FMLN as a coalition of resistance fighters for a common cause.[82] But they were not, as depicted by the governments oppressing them, violent and rabid by nature; they were pushed to this place of violent pushback because their government, backed by a foreign government of vested ideological interest, struck first.

The war lasted twelve years, with the Salvadorian president in 1992 finally pushing for a negotiation with the FMLN to end the violence—but it was too little, too late by then to reverse the carnage that had ravaged the country for the past more than a decade. In the end, the death toll was over 75,000, missing people totaled nearly 18,000, and over two million more were evenly divided between being homeless and exiled.[83] It was one of the most bloody and unnecessary atrocities the US government has ever had on its hands, yet in the name of ideological, anti-communist rhetoric, the Reagan administration justified every killing it had a hand in. Many obfuscations and outright lies tied to the FMLN were pushed into the Western zeitgeist, with Reagan claiming that "leftist propaganda" was to blame for the accurate reports of Salvadorian government death squads racking up body counts in the tens of thousands, or saying that the FMLN was fully armed and unstoppable, despite the fact that in reality the resistance groups were nearly wiped out of weaponry completely several times.[84] If this was not a legitimate revolutionary populist revolt, then what could possibly count as being one?

In the case of the second case examination, things aren't as grounded in reality for the populists in question; although the origins of the unrest behind the National Front's inception in France *did* originate in actual fiscal strife for the working masses. By 1981, 1.5 million people had become unemployed and inflation had skyrocketed.[85] And while a seemingly pro-worker campaign helped get François Mitterrand elected president of the French Republic that same year, the realities of his policies over the next couple of years amounted to liberal welfare measures and context-deprived redistributions that merely aimed to pacify working people's financial fears and bailed out businesses that may have made bad investments.[86] In short, it was once again the furthest thing from an actual revolutionary economic shift it could have been despite its pro–working-class rhetoric, and it stood to simply balance a maintaining of the status quo with making nice with voters through shallow aesthetic changes to issues of income and worker livability. The hierarchies remained, and the workers still felt the financial limits of barely being able to live off their own labor.

This lack of genuine change to the systemic dynamics themselves led more typically center-right movements in France, such as the Rally for the Republic (RPR) and the

Union for French Democracy (UDF), to join forces with the FN out of desperation and desire for stronger numbers (if this sounds similar to how center-rightists in the United States allowed the Alt-Right and the alt-light to infiltrate *their* own spaces for similar reasons, it is because said similarities are indicative of how the similar cycles in both countries' economies led their respective privileged populists to do similar things under similar pressures—albeit in different decades).[87]

It did not seem to matter enough to these center-right parties that the FN's founder, Jean-Marie Le Pen, was a documented anti-Semite who downplayed the Holocaust as a mere "detail" of the Second World War, hired full-blown Holocaust deniers as top members of his party, and publicly held various other xenophobic and prejudiced views.[88] What mattered more, it appears, was the need to build a strong united front against whatever the perceived cause of the ongoing economic strife was. In the case of the FN, it was yet another unempirical concept of the *Other*—foreign and non-European workers were held as prime suspects in the growing trial-by-populism to determine why things were not getting substantially better (though this view was made less public), as were communists and anyone perceived as communists.[89]

This synthesis of extreme right and moderate right movements had long been a part of Le Pen's plan, as he wanted what he called "total fusion" on the issues as a means of finding solidarity against the *Others* he named his enemies.[90] Here yet again we find Urbinati's qualification for populism in the FN's desire for total unification without its result, but the FN has certainly attempted many times to still yet achieve that goal.[91] Le Pen's daughter and later president of the FN, Marine Le Pen, ran for parliamentary positions in France many times over the years attempting to make the FN's positions even more mainstream. In 2017, she ran her second presidential campaign (her first was in 2011–12) in the French 2017 presidential election, losing to her opponent Emmanuel Macron. Since her political runs began, Marine Le Pen attempted to rebrand the FN in order to distance it from the anti-Semitism of her father.[92] The shift, however, went from anti-communist and anti-Jewish rhetoric to a more strictly anti-immigrant—and more specifically, anti-Muslim immigrant—platform that bled into her subsequent political campaigns.[93] Going into the twenty-first century, the FN's ideas still connect working-class strife to xenophobic perceptions of threatening *Others* rather than to the systemic problem of hierarchical economies. These views on immigrants, much like that of the Jews and communists held by the FN's prior incarnation, are demonstrably unfounded (Chapter 5).

* * *

So, here we are with two instances of populist unrest reaching levels of violent revolutionary quality. Both movements under scrutiny with the word "National" in their names, and both claiming to stand for the populist needs of an oppressed people. But while the FMLN was founded to take back national sovereignty, a state of being, the FN was formed to promote national*ism*, an ideology.

There is also more to this distinction than concepts, seeing as how the demonstrable evidence also favors one scenario significantly over the other. For the FMLN, there was a documented and provable connection between the outrage of the populist movement in question and the perceived threat—the US government really was meddling in El Salvador's affairs by backing their government and attempting to overthrow genuinely grassroots liberation movements on ideological grounds. For these reasons, it is fair to argue that El Salvador's revolutionary movement from this period was genuine both in its conviction and in its cause. As far as the cause goes, the same legitimacy cannot be granted in the case of the FN in France during the same set of years. The "revolutionary" movements in that case amounted to one extremist group laden with unsubstantiated paranoia about perceived foreign boogeymen working to slowly recruit more mainstream adjacent groups by focusing on more mainstream overlapping concerns between the parties. No real measurable threat matched the extreme descriptions given by the FN, therefore rendering *its* revolution empirically bankrupt.[94]

However, in terms of conviction, it could be argued that both the FN and the FMLN are equally genuine (founders' possible ulterior motives notwithstanding, of course). Because once the ball starts rolling on any particular cause grounded in at least a kernel of truth, many subsequent adherents are honestly looking for real solutions to their completely real strife. The populist rationale spectrum, as it is being described here, allows for these sorts of overlaps of causes across class and ideology, with sometimes the only initially visible point of agreement being the most mainstream and recognizable one.

In intersectional spaces, a white European, for instance, can share many views in common with another white European and join forces along these lines well before the more extremist viewpoints become tangible. From the outside looking in, a claimed revolutionary cause on behalf of everyday working people would seem appealing to anyone, and if one lacks the cultural or social perspective needed to fully grasp the daily plights of non-whites, the certain terminologies and pet social theories of the extremists associated with racial or ethnic prejudice may not be visible at all. Dubbed "dog whistles," these are certain strategic phrasings and terms that seem to be designed as a means of appealing to other like-minded extremists without giving away their positions to everyday people who might still serve as numbers-growing allies.[95] These can come in different forms and appeal to different extremist groups, such as fascists or racists (the appeals to the latter being called "strategic racism" by law expert Ian Haney López), but as long as they appear alongside other more mainstream populist views, the everyday working voter with a bone to pick with the social or governmental elites of the day has a much higher chance of joining the perceived cause.[96]

The aforementioned "cultural Marxism" accusation that gets hurled quite frequently at various liberals and leftists by any number of conservatives, even mainstream ones, therefore counts as a dog whistle. The origins of the term coming from Nazism means that by tweaking it just enough to sound different, it can appeal to mainstream conservatives while still being familiar enough to modern fascists that it serves to also build a more sinister solidarity. Does this mean every person who uses the term is consciously perpetuating fascist ideas? Of course, not. As pointed out earlier, the term is often used by people who themselves don't understand its etymology or application. But this does not change the fact that the term itself, and many others like it, are serving this purpose whether the general public is aware of it or not. As a result, well-meaning people in the political center-right can forge alliances with those whose views overall are far more extreme than the moderate right-populists would have ever promulgated on their own. Nevertheless, once the alliances are forged, it is much tougher to undo them.

Indeed, the populist rationale spectrum, running the gamut from more sensible populist unrest to its extremist poles, can allow extremists to woo and recruit the unwitting moderate by appealing to the middle of this spectrum with their upfront stated platforms and causes. From there, solidarity has already formed between the two parties, making it much harder for them to separate later—even in the face of the extremism of the wooing parties slowly becoming more obvious.[97] At that point, homophily has set in, and the relatable causes (e.g., financial stability and/or a sense of cultural worth) have become the main uniting force between the moderates and the extremists of similar demographic.[98]

It is here in the perspective-overlapping middle of the spectrum that economic and cultural anxiety in non-minority working-class groups can find its validation—and, in spite of its empirical unsoundness, its perpetuation.

* * *

Something few in America seem to dispute is the reality that the fiscal state of a given society and that same society's cultural state are related. Whether it be the ultimate decline of the once-mighty ancient Egypt, the collapse of the Roman empire, or even the more recent events in Venezuela, economic mismanagement and drastic wealth inequality tend to play at least some integral part in cultural turmoil. But this does not mean that every instance of fiscal action is the direct cause of something culturally phenotypical. Oftentimes it is the opposite, and a cultural movement or social action then leads to fiscally tangible results. This is because culture is much more complex and interwoven with the functional bedrock of its surroundings than it may first appear—especially if one is inclined to only give credence to the study of economies and not a more holistic understanding of their corresponding civilizations (a tendency many on the modern right exude with increasing regularity). Context matters, and circumstances are intertwined. The key difference when it comes to right-wing populists, however, is that they tend to view this connection as a one-directional flow: fiscal mechanisms come first, then culture follows. As such, the mantra of many conservatives and libertarians now amounts to focusing on fiscal policy first and foremost, and not having as much concern for an understanding of culture beyond the elementary level.

The reality is, of course, much more interesting than what the anti-political conservative view would have us believe. Sometimes, culture comes first and fiscal reality follows. Sometimes, the cultural and historical backgrounds of a given society or public present a unique context that requires an exception be made to conventional wisdom regarding how a given marketplace should be regulated. These broad brushstrokes that beg for economies to be either completely regulated or completely unregulated miss the finer details necessary to best navigate a given societal canvas.

In the minds of typical American conservatives, a truly fair society is one in which everyone is taxed the same exact amount, regulations are applied to everyone equally, and personal responsibility is recognized in every individual's given situation. That's a wonderful ideal. If human societies existed in historical and cultural vacuums, it would even be correct. The problem, however, is when these ideals come up against the real world and these cut-and-dry sentiments become multilayered. Yes, it is the most ideal situation for everyone to start at an equal level of opportunity so that all successes and failures in life happen on fair terms. The successful actors would then all deserve celebration, and the failures would all have nobody to blame for their misfortune but themselves. But this is not how human societies actually work. Everything is constantly in flux, and norms are always changing. It was once considered normal, for instance, for Black people in America to be legally separated from their fellow countrymen and given second-class treatment. Before that, of course, it was considered normal for them to legally be treated as property. What led to the civil rights movement that ultimately lifted these absurdities from the legal mores of America? Was it a loosening of regulations on a place of business? Or was it a cultural revolution that welled up from within? All other things being equal, the innate ability and drive of an individual person would indeed be the deciding factor in societal success or failure. All other things being equal. However, all other things are not equal.

This is where the anti-political populists come in. They utilize that same culturally revolutionary mindset and apply it to a *maintaining* of the status quo rather than a challenge to it. Because cultural conservativism has historically been so unfamiliar with how to properly contextualize social phenomena in general, its proclivity for ethnocentrism and general tone deafness toward minority plights is on full display, here. The aforementioned civil rights movement, of course, did not bring an end to discrimination with a mere stroke of a pen; it began as a public awareness that continues to spread to this very day. Yet, remnants of this darker time still remain in certain pillars of American life. The now infamous Southern Strategy, for instance, aimed to lead southern working-class voters into political action based on validating preexisting prejudices around the social concept of race through false narratives. This is government-officiated racism, plain and simple. The justice system is still arresting and sentencing Black Americans at disproportionately high rates, all the while leveling harsher sentences at them for similar crimes compared to whites.[99] Between 2010 and 2012, 52 percent of New Yorkers stopped and frisked were Black and 32 percent were Hispanic, while only 9 percent were white.[100] This is despite whites making up 44 percent of New Yorkers,[101] and the fact that whites were found more often to actually be in possession of weapons or drugs.[102] But none of this seems to sway the minds of those who have already decided that the problem is about external threats to the American Dream rather than systemic ones.

Economist and former secretary of labor Robert Reich once said in a rousing speech before the Democratic Leadership Council (before quitting his position in the Bill Clinton administration out of frustration) that the working American's "anger and disillusionment" can be "easily manipulated," and that "once unbottled, mass resentment can poison the very fabric of society . . . replacing ambition with envy, replacing tolerance with hate."[103] Dr. Reich was referring to the swelling of fresh anger at the current establishment he was beginning to witness in the American middle class— the same anger that ultimately would birth the right-wing anti-political populism under dissection in these pages. He went on to make a very chilling observation: "Today, the targets of that rage are immigrants, and welfare mothers, and government officials, and gays, and an ill-defined counterculture. But as the middle class continues to erode, who will be the targets tomorrow?"[104]

Who, indeed? As it has come to pass, the antagonists of the anti-political right are now depicted more in broad strokes than ever. In the eyes of the right-wing anti-political plebiscite, everyone who isn't completely on board with the extreme nationalistic language of a Donald Trump is a communist, a socialist, or otherwise "anti-American." With such imprecise classifications for who to hate and such narrow criteria for how to join the club, it should come as no surprise that the plebs of populist American conservatism are finding their enemies in more and wider spaces by the day.

This is how organic hatred of the *Other* as a concept can and does materialize. It is how anti-politics can grow from within, all without the need of external imposition. To suggest that much of this phenomenon is all a conscious conspiracy is itself somewhat of a frontier of antagonism, and it also tends to neglect how ideology works. So, while the claim being made here is not that right-wing anti-political populism is a full-blown scheme of the elite class from its inception, there *are* compelling reasons to suggest that this organic hatred is stoked and perpetuated by certain members of said class for their own advantages.

Rydgren described what he observed in the earlier quoted passage as "anti-establishment populism," but for his purposes, antiestablishment and anti-politics might as well be seen as interchangeable synonyms of each other. For our purposes, however—when we have need of a different application between Ferguson's anti-politics and the more rational distrust of *all* hierarchical systems, capitalism included—these terms should be seen as distinct. As Dr. Noam Chomsky has pointed out many times, both the government *and* big corporations are key offenders when it comes to the harsh realities many anti-political types face, but out of the two of them, only one of these entities is designed to operate at least somewhat democratically. Therefore, to focus solely on government (anti-politics) and not on both government and corporate collusion (antiestablishment) in one's populist outcry is to attack the shadow and not the beast. That is likely just the way certain entities who stand to benefit from such misdirection would prefer it.

But as this book has made clear up to now, the argument is not that the false consciousness found within the conservative working-class populists is still yet being perpetrated by conscious bad actors in the upper echelon of economic class and privilege; the argument is that the false consciousness in these groups is by this point organic and self-maintained. Everyone in these circles seems to genuinely believe the narrative they are perpetuating, and the fight they see themselves as being a part of is one that truly feels to them like a fight for working-class liberty. In this way, their revolution is a real one, albeit one that to objective investigation has counter-revolutionary results. Despite this, however, there *is* a history to be found of deliberate hijackings of causes, redefinitions of terms, and ingratiating public policies that all converged on the same purpose of misdirecting working-class people into the false consciousness they now self-perpetuate.

In other words, what is now an organic occurrence within present-day conservative populism was indeed *initially* an artificial construction of a narrative that aimed to preserve the economic privilege and control held by those already in power. It is to the creation of that narrative, and the distortion of broadly revolutionary causes in the process, that we will now turn.

Part II

Inducing an Organic False Consciousness

(Historical Contexts)

5

From Radical to Classical to Neo

The Great Liberal Distortion

In Book IV, Chapter II of his 1776 defining work *The Wealth of Nations*, economist and moral philosopher Adam Smith posits the following argument regarding the rationale for why domestic benefit will still prevail in a globally trading marketplace:

> As every individual, therefore, endeavors as much as he can both to employ his capital in the support of domestic industry, and so to direct that industry that its produce may be of the greatest value; every individual necessarily labors to render the annual revenue of the society as great as he can. He generally, indeed, neither intends to promote the public interest, nor knows how much he is promoting it. By preferring the support of domestic to that of foreign industry, he intends only his own security; and by directing that industry in such a manner as its produce may be of the greatest value, he intends only his own gain, and he is in this, as in many other cases, led by an invisible hand to promote an end which was no part of his intention. Nor is it always the worse for the society that it was no part of it. By pursuing his own interest he frequently promotes that of the society more effectually than when he really intends to promote it.[1]

This explanation of how one's short-term self-interests can result in a communally beneficial outcome was one of the first observations of its kind. It was not a moral declaration or behavioral prescription; rather, it was simply a discovery of how human nature can unwittingly work toward a greater good—even in potentially sinister systems of self-interest and unregulated markets of trade and exchange (notice that once again we observe seeming evidence of group selection mechanics occurring despite selfish motivation aiming to win the day).[2] This is also the only reference that Adam Smith makes in the entirety of *Wealth of Nations* to the so-called invisible hand. Simply because Smith uses this term to describe a process of unintentional positive outcome does not in itself mean anything beyond what was put to paper on the topic in 1776. It certainly doesn't prove that Smith was upholding complete self-interest as a moral good. On the contrary, Smith seems to find localized mutual benefit within societies to be the preferred outcome of a deafeningly imperfect situation. He even goes on to state that he finds intentionally calling for altruistic action to be less effective due to the selfish state of society.

In other words, to best direct the tides of a self-centered market, it seems one could utilize self-centered motivations as a means to an end rather than go against the grain. One can argue whether or not this is a completely accurate or noble course of action, but what is less arguable is the accuracy of the observation. Adam Smith is not arguing that it is therefore moral to be self-centered, but rather that it is not entirely hopeless for domestic market survival despite the self-centered nature of the beast. He does promote elsewhere in his book the ideal systematic benefit of freer markets, but he also acknowledges his present realities. This is a quality that is largely missing from the rhetoric of many modern so-called free-market advocates. Instead of speaking of self-interested action as a necessary evil, the more common refrain from present-day conservatives and libertarians is to praise this kind of selfishness as a noble, virtuous personality trait. It is excused away as benign or even beneficial to free society because, as these new bannermen of supposedly liberal thought declare, the free market is magic, and the invisible hand will provide. In other words, the prescription is as follows: don't worry about being proactively giving or communal; just look out for yourself and be happy with the knowledge that this vague concept of "the market" will take care of any real problems.

Except, as the prior chapter touched upon, this isn't how the market actually works. We do not actually have a free market. We have a considerably rigged market. It is rigged in favor of those in the corporate world who have the means and connections to collude with regulatory forces in government in order to maintain the wealth inequality and exploitative nature of the workforce that makes up the present reality. The fact that free-market advocates who lean right tend to speak from both sides of their mouths on this issue has not slipped past those in the socialist and anarchist movements who still believe in what actual libertarianism, in the broader, baggage-free sense, stands for (i.e., anti-authoritarianism).[3]

Case-in-point: the self-described "free-market anti-capitalist" and mutualist author Kevin Carson coined the term "vulgar libertarianism" to describe the present outbreak of supposedly freedom-centric right-leaning libertarianism that seems to argue America's current market is truly free only about half of the time. The other half, this same crowd, admits that free markets do not exist and that working-class people are suffering:

> Vulgar libertarian apologists for capitalism use the term "free market" in an equivocal sense: they seem to have trouble remembering, from one moment to the next, whether they're defending actually existing capitalism or free market principles. So we get the standard boilerplate article arguing that the rich can't get rich at the expense of the poor, because "that's not how the free market works"— implicitly assuming that this is a free market. When prodded, they'll grudgingly admit that the present system is not a free market, and that it includes a lot of state intervention on behalf of the rich. But as soon as they think they can get away with it, they go right back to defending the wealth of existing corporations on the basis of "free market principles."[4]

Dan Sullivan of the Georgist movement also has a thing or two to say about this inconsistency, ultimately identifying it as a movement of privileged, pseudo-revolutionary thought he refers to as "royal libertarianism."[5]

The political types that are still libertarian in its truest historical sense (more on how we can determine that distinction in the next chapter) arguably *are* the mutualists and the Georgists, since they still delineate a distinction between personal property and private property, as well as recognize the argument that property upon which a person lives cannot extend beyond one's own labor (and therefore cannot extend to the notion of closed borders and other nationalistic ideas now adopted by right-libertarians). This was, in fact, an argument similarly proposed by the cited father of classical liberalism, John Locke, though at the time Locke was writing anonymously in his *Two Treatises of Government* (1690).[6]

Within Chapter V of his *Second Treatise*, Locke presents his conditions for how truly free peoples can homestead in relation to how they interact with the land itself—a shared resource. This is a level of nuance and care that is rarely continued by those today who claim to advocate for classically liberal concepts regarding ownership and property. The very fact that Lock exercises it at all is enough reason to doubt the legitimacy of these imprecise current adherents to his words. But what Locke specifically writes on this issue is even more damning to the supposed libertarianism of the present.

What Locke essentially argues is that the land, being a shared resource, is in fact not property in and of itself. By extension, we can conclude that property rights are therefore *not* innate in the same way other natural rights are described as being by Locke. Instead, they are conditional and their boundaries are determined by their encapsulating scenarios as dictated by interactions with other free people. This is to ensure that all involved parties' liberties are not compromised.

That may sound like a tall order, and, of course, intent can be interpreted and read into words more so than what is perhaps actually there, so let us actually cite Locke's words themselves to be sure that we are not taking away from them more than what is actually there:

> But this being supposed, it seems to some a very great difficulty, how any one should ever come to have a property in any thing: I will not content myself to answer, that if it be difficult to make out property, upon a supposition that God gave the world to Adam, and his posterity in common, it is impossible that any man, but one universal monarch, should have any property upon a supposition, that God gave the world to Adam, and his heirs in succession, exclusive of all the rest of his posterity. But I shall endeavour to shew, how men might come to have a property in several parts of that which God gave to mankind in common, and that without any express compact of all the commoners.[7]

From the start, Locke is acknowledging that the earth itself is a resource intended to be shared by what he refers to as Adam's heirs but what can be more ubiquitously applied to any and all free moving people who will utilize the earth for their betterment. This is important to make note of, because what Locke is about to do next is lay out his exceptions to the rule, but what the rule is itself often gets swept under the rug by those who do not wish to see the land as a shared resource, and therefore not property in and of itself. There is no mistaking here, however, that Locke himself absolutely recognizes and respects this view.

Locke continues, stating that individual people can *earn* personal ownership of a specific portion of the land by "mixing their labour" with it and building a homestead, but brings along with that requirement a set of other conditions.[8] Namely, that the act of acquiring property through this mixing of toil and soil does not necessarily infringe on another free person's right to do the same. For Locke, claiming a portion of a shared, unowned resource for yourself was essentially an act of appropriation, and therefore it was only ethical if said appropriation did not come at the expense of another free person, or, in Locke's words, in the form of "any prejudice to any other man."[9] To meet this condition, one needed to leave behind "enough, and as good, in common for others" so that by tapping into a shared resource such as the land, one would not be impeding the ability of another from still benefiting from said resource.[10] This condition has been posthumously referred to as the Lockean proviso.

Unsurprisingly, this particular aspect to Locke's argument for recognition of natural rights has all but been disposed of in the present discourse. The vulgar libertarian gallop of today tends to ultimately get around to the war cry of "property rights!" This is especially the case when the wing of libertarianism infatuated with closed borders rears its head. The general line of thinking seems to be that, when followed to its logical conclusion, the natural right to personal ownership of property applies to the American border. If one can own the land itself, and America is by and for "the people," then it is in fact the people who collectively have the right to close off the portion of the land declared to belong to America if it is being invaded, so-called, by immigrants and other scary threats to American life. That is the position, in a nutshell. It is claimed to stand on the merits of true classical liberal tradition. This is, of course, incorrect right from the outset in the face of a correct contextualization of Locke, as the prior close reading of the Lockean proviso preemptively demonstrated, but this is of little concern to the most populist among the closed-border libertarians and conservatives. Those adherents have already chosen to believe in the frontier of antagonism they and their peers have constructed. In their minds, the immigrants are a threat—one of many—to the so-called American way perceived by the "New Anger" anti-political conservatives identified in Chapter 2.[11]

Proponents of this idea that became more numerous in the 2010s were the Internet personalities on the right who presented themselves as "skeptics" as a means of bolstering their neoliberal casuistries as axiomatic truths. Benefiting financially through donations and ad revenue from big corporations to continue spinning reality in their favor on unsound empirical grounds, all while presenting themselves as critical thinkers speaking on behalf of everyday people, these figures can be thought of, perhaps, as intellectual petty bourgeois actors *a la* those identified by Poulantzas as being characteristic of the first power blocs that are formed in the lead up to the point of no return of societies that find themselves in the midst of financial crises.[12]

One such proponent of this idea, only one particular manifestation of the manufactured antagonist among scads within present-day populist conservatism, was self-described libertarian writer (she denied being Alt-Right), online personality and former Libertarian Party candidate in the Canadian federal election Lauren Southern (who was also, as an aside, a former colleague of mine while we both wrote for a prominent libertarian news and opinion outlet in the years leading up to the

2016 election), who had on more than one occasion actively and violently fought to keep refugees from crossing into Western territory and boasted about it.[13] While as of this writing, Southern has all but dropped out of the public eye after receiving widespread backlash over her accused influence on a right-wing terrorist's ideological stances (more on that in Chapter 10), she was fairly influential as part of the alternative media in the years leading up to the 2016 election. She had also gone on racist rants about non-white immigrants in general on television, but her fan base claimed she was more genuinely libertarian than these moments might have made her appear and that she simply had the objective facts on her side.[14] But did she?

A Canadian, Southern still appealed to the alt-light and vulgar libertarian movements in the United States because her perspective and rhetoric gave a legitimizing voice to their common concerns regarding threats to their fiscal security. She also appealed to the more extreme Alt-Right and the UK-based Generation Identity movements because *their* economic concerns, mirroring the more mainstream populist conservative groups, had already long gone a step further and pinned said woes on a supposedly impending foreign threat to their Western way of life and soundness of their culture, as the previous chapter recalled.[15]

In one of her more infamous videos, "The Great Replacement," Southern had made the argument that mass immigration to North American and European countries from non-Western territories threatens to lead to a complete takeover of Western cultural values and a replacement of "one people" currently in the West with a "different people" originating from elsewhere.[16] Of course, Western culture is simply assumed as being superior to all others in the outset of the argument. Accompanying her commentary in the video, imagery of clean-looking white Westerners in an old-timey conservative setting is suddenly replaced through a jump cut with an image of Muslims looking unhappy and gruff during rush hour moving through a modern marketplace.[17] The implication of this juxtaposition, of course, is that the "one people" being replaced are happy, wholesome, white conservatives, and the "different people" doing the replacing are hectic, numerous hordes of scary foreigners—*Others*.

Watching the video, the fallacious, manipulative quality of this visual framing of Southern's argument should be apparent, but she includes cited sources that, upon a surface-level cogitation, seem to bolster her claims and add legitimacy to the general cry of cultural takeover via mass immigration. But upon closer inspection, it becomes pretty clear pretty quickly that Southern is desperately reaching.

To start off, Southern gives credit to French writer Renaud Camus for coining the term "The Great Replacement" and cites his ideas as resonating within "nationalist" and "identitarian" movements across various regions of Europe (a signal of solidarity toward Generation Identity and the Alt-Right)—as if these are positive, legitimizing things to point out.[18] Of course, the reality of the situation is that Camus's claims about a threatened cultural takeover due to Muslim immigration to Europe were found to be factually unsubstantiated, yet he still defended "any call for violence" in the name of fighting against this phantom menace, and he was convicted of incitement of racial hatred by French authorities in 2014 as a result.[19] Lauren Southern conveniently chose to omit that little detail of Camus's past in her video where she cited him as a credible source.

Things only get shakier from there, as Southern's included sources continue to contradict what she claims they support. For instance, Southern makes the claim at one point in her video that people of "primarily Indian, Pakistani, or African background" have flocked to the UK since 2004's EU expansion and "drastic shifts in immigration policy" to culminate in a supposedly scary statistic of 13.5 percent of the population that is foreign-born.[20] The glaring problem with this claim, however, is that the very source she uses to support this claim, University of Oxford's Migration Observatory, actually shows the claim to be factually incorrect. The vast majority of these foreign-born migrants, according to Southern's own source from The Migration Observatory, are from Poland—not India, Pakistan, or Africa. In fact, no African countries of any kind are represented in this data, even when we get as low as single-digit percentages.[21] We do see the aforementioned Indian and Pakistani migrants represented, but they are only around 6 percent and 3 percent of the total incoming migrants, respectively; all the rest (i.e., the vast majority) come from countries with predominantly white populations.[22] Southern's claims (and the similar claims of her identitarian populist peers) are outright untruths.

It is also worth pointing out that, even if most of the foreign workers *were* from non-white countries, the perspective of seeing foreign workers of any kind as a threat in Europe is something that itself seems to be dictated more by cultural climate than by economic reality for "native-born" people, indicating that nothing tangibly threatening to "native-born" fiscal security is measurable. For decades, going all the way back to the 1970s, foreign-born workers in various European countries were in the millions, yet this had been a result, as the previous chapter showed, of calls *in favor* of worker immigration, and only when the already-existing economic strains in these places failed to be alleviated did the attitudes begin to change.[23] In that decade alone there had already accumulated in Switzerland 1 million foreign-born workers; in France, 3.4 million; in Germany, 4.1 million, and the list goes on—yet no found links between foreign worker presence and economic unrest.[24] Propaganda is a powerful thing.

Suffice it to say that demonstrated in Southern's list of sources is an utter lack of concrete foundation upon which her narrative is built. Indeed, if these are the best sources she could find, then the credibility of her argument as a whole should be seen as just as lacking in verifiable evidence. She is not the only prominent right-libertarian figure in the online alternative media to make these same claims. Another among the growing numbers of like minds on this front is Stefan Molyneux, a self-described philosopher and libertarian who famously frames all of his positions as coruscating examples of empiricism and logic. "Not an argument," his catchphrase, has become something of a meme in the online circles that look up to him—unsurprisingly, once again predominantly the right-libertarian and alt-light demographic, which is, again, predominantly white, young, and male.[25]

Molyneux, who claimed for years to not be a white nationalist, has nonetheless parroted white nationalist and identitarian talking points when it comes to his own means of explaining the loss of economic ground for the white working class—one of his videos going so far as to depict him being brought to tears of joy while attending a white pride parade in Poland. His rationale? Nationalist voices and cultural pride have been "scrubbed from the language of the West" by social justice warriors, and this was a sign of said voices being able to "rightly" declare their white pride in the open and without fear of further oppression.[26] "I'm not a white nationalist, but I am an empiricist," Molyneux claimed after the event, quick to point out that he has been "skeptical if not hostile to collectivism as a whole" in the past.[27] But upon seeing the demonstration, Molyneux claimed to feel something had "broken in two" inside of him, causing him to recall Aristotle's declaration that in order to live alone, one but be either an animal or a god.[28] The postulation we, his audience, are supposed to swallow here is that Molyneux once was a staunch individualist, but upon putting those beliefs "to the test" like a good critical thinker, he has come to realize that he was mistaken, and changed his mind—and Aristotle agrees with him; therefore, it is implicit that there is wisdom to be found in this realization.[29]

Aside from the fact that this is a misquote of Aristotle in the first place, the interpretation of the quotation as presented is still wrong. As the Bakunin discovery and subsequent modern equivalents in anthropological literature from Chapter 3 beautifully explain, the real power of individuality comes from the informed ideas and behavior the individual subsumes from the other individuals he interacts with. Without collectives to exist within, individuality has no shape or distinct identity. This does not negate the importance of individuality as a concept; it merely renders said concept in three dimensions and demonstrates all of the complex nuances of human interaction that contribute to the concept's impact.

Molyneux, with his misrepresentation of Aristotle in tow, falls victim to the false dichotomy fallacy when he assumes, wrongly, that we can only give importance to collectives or individuals. This is why both exclusionary individualism and groupthink collectivism are detrimental to the human condition: they both divorce themselves from key elements that give their own concepts real meaning and utility. Collectives work most effectively when diversity is involved because it forces multiple perspectives to converge and multiply their possible outcomes through collaboration. Likewise, individuality is truly valuable only if one is free to act as an individual within a society that offers many options and avenues for human interaction and intellectual stimulation. Echo chambers, by contrast, have the exact opposite effect, and as a result do not push the human condition forward. It stymies human acquisition of the knowledge and collaboration necessary for survival and transcendence of present conditions. Many of his other videos and arguments are full of similarly fallacious logical leaps and context-less assumptions, and yet this man has managed to assuage significant chunks of these majority white and male populist groups within the conservative working class because his explanations for their woes do not tread upon the illusion that the economic system is a free market and that the American Dream is a truly attainable goal. These explanations, like those of Southern, Camus, Generation Identity, and other similar figures and causes, allow the young and impressionable of more privileged demographics to have the confidence of well-read philosophers while changing very little of their already-entrenched beliefs.

What's more is that the arguments pawned off to these young white working-class men as cutting-edge revelations are nothing more than long-existing prejudices repurposed. The claim itself of Europe specifically being threatened by immigrants from countries populated predominately by brown people, for instance, might have been given a new moniker in the form of Camus, Southern, Molyneux, et al.'s "Replacement," but ideologically and rhetorically it is indistinguishable from a much older white genocide conspiracy theory labeled with the portmanteau "Eurabia"— coined over a decade ago by author Gisèle Littman in her book of the same name. The blame for this process of supposed cultural erosion within the Eurabia movement is given to any number of different manufactured antagonists, including the media, universities, and, somehow, both fascists and communists simultaneously.[30] Yet again, the anti-political paranoia and frontier of antagonism is found in evidence, and not much else, as further confirmed by Dr. Nasar Meer in his study of the Eurabian conspiracy, "Racialization and Religion," wherein he likens the growing prejudice and generalization of *all* Muslims to one such as anti-Semitism, which is itself couched in an odd suffusing of race and religious heritage.[31]

In other words, all this "Great Replacement" theorizing is just run-of-the-mill racism wrapped in academic garb, in much the same way that other extremist concepts regarding supposed cultural erosion are various other forms of baseless prejudice wrapped in neoliberal rhetoric and purpose. Remember, Southern and her ilk's appeal to reason amidst the racist dog whistling is that the arguments are merely referencing "data."[32] Data can't be racist, right? It is through such appeals to broader purported causes and ideals, through seemingly indifferent data and statistics, that we find the bridge from the misguided but well-meaning majority within neoliberal hegemony to the malicious and precise extremists in the Alt-Right and white nationalist crowd.

So, we have identified and demonstrated how neoliberal hegemony can lend the existing neoliberal zeitgeist to becoming warped and derailed into more extremist culture wars territory in the supposed name of economic stability, but this is found merely at the end of a slower process that theorists like Mark Fisher have called "the overvaluing of belief" that occurs within capitalistic ideologies.[33] That process itself needs to have first occurred before the common person moving through everyday life can even be conditioned to accept crossing the aforementioned bridges built by the Lauren Southerns of the world. How does said process unfold? How does neoliberal hegemony take hold in the first place?

* * *

Dr. Stephanie L. Mudge's book *Leftism Reinvented: Western Parties from Socialism to Neoliberalism* serves as a comparative history between American Democrats and their European contemporaries (such as the German and Swedish Social Democrats and the British Labour Party) in which she explains how the broader liberal landscape, once headed in a more outwardly socialist and labor-centric direction, shifted alongside the influential economics schools accompanying them. In the 1900s, presents Mudge, these parties across Sweden, Germany, and Britain had "appointed people with strikingly similar priorities to the top economic posts of their respective administrations," which at the time meant the policies were more sympathetic to socialist causes since these figures often grew up inside of "mass socialist parties."[34] However, such figures were simply part of "a new elite" in which erudition and journalistic work from within the socioeconomic spaces they once inhabited stood in for the stuffy academic credentials that were up to then seen as most befitting of a policy maker.[35] One can surely already see the parallels with the same sort of populist climate present with these figures as with the aforementioned Latin American caudillos from earlier in the book—it isn't enough that the policies might be sound; the person proposing them must be both a common man from the very displaced group he's representing and an intellectual, charismatic figure holding a certain level of prestige making him stand out from the rest.

But does this "new elitism" square with the kind of common person solidarity the representatives actually need? If the society in question still craves that elitist quality to their political causes, is there really a guarantee that the next person to come into socioeconomic influence won't be just another elitist of the more typical kind?

According to the century-long history laid out by Mudge, this is essentially what ended up happening as the broader liberal ideals of Locke and Smith began to narrow and favor a policy narrative more favorable to the elite class as a whole—all still while claiming to be working on behalf of the autonomy of working people.[36] Classical liberalism ultimately eroded and became much more similar to what we now think of as "liberal" in colloquial conversation, starting in the 1830s and culminating in their most extreme forms by the time we arrived in the latter half of the previous century. What began as a genuine call for freedom of movement and opportunity for all people ultimately became a call for freedom of movement and opportunity for companies and other powerful entities at the *expense* of people. Economist and philosopher Roderick T. Long has referred to this, in a similar manner as Robert O. Paxton, as the "folksiness" quality of elitist power bloc alliances in which private interests don a populist mask to appear pro-worker while actually keeping their own exclusive private ownership artificially enclosed.[37] As the trend predicts, it was indeed a new breed of elites who again ingratiated the masses into accepting this dynamic as reasonable in the new century.

When Milton Friedman, one of the most influential economists who ever lived, published his book *Capitalism and Freedom* in 1962, people understandably sat up and took notice. Friedman's was a voice that carried much weight and authority not just in the academic world, but in the everyday lives of the laypeople who read his works and attended his high-profile public appearances. By all accounts, much of Friedman's renown was rightly deserved. This was a man who was proposing concepts like the basic income, better school access for low-income and minority students, and data-based economic policy decades before these approaches and policies had become ubiquitously embraced. But while much of Friedman's intentions and scholarship were clearly noble and honest, the fact remains that he also served as one of the mainstream legitimizing voices of neoliberal ideas while claiming to espouse classically liberal principles. As a result, liberalism began to covertly shift into neoliberalism in plain sight.

In *Capitalism and Freedom*, there is a passage dedicated to the debate surrounding the integration of schools. The book was being written in the decade following the *Brown v. Board of Education* Supreme Court decision in the United States, and many States were still restructuring in its wake. Dr. Friedman examines in this passage the moral merits of integration and segregation, coming to a startlingly incorrect conclusion:

that both integration *and* segregation are "evils."[38] Right there, in black-and-white, Friedman commits a false equivalency. Now, it's important to note that the evidence does not support the idea that Friedman himself was a conscious racist—the bulk of Freidman's work suggests the contrary, if one were to ask this author—but the fact that Friedman was so ostentatiously tone-deaf to the immediate cultural and societal needs of specific issues that didn't directly deal with economic perspectives serves as a rhetorical microcosm of the narrowed perspective of the liberalized zeitgeist at large during his day. Whether one called oneself a classical liberal or not, the assumption was already in place that figures like Friedman had managed to boil much of society's ills down to numbers and statistics, and that doing so was not at all incompatible with liberal ideals of freedom and liberation. It all reads as very scientific and objective, as well, since it is dealing with collected data.

The problem, of course, is that merely looking at raw numbers does not give us the full picture of predominately social issues. Data on its own and through a narrow lens of number-crunching cannot tell us about the cultural or historical environments surrounding said issues, nor how large or miniscule said environments' effects might be having on human action and circumstance. What data *can* do is determine whether there is a long-term net benefit to society through certain human action and circumstance, and indeed, it is when Friedman implements his data in this way that he is at his most brilliant. However, in this case, his argument is counterproductive to that end. The framing of the problem in Friedman's book is such that the reader is expected to accept as axiomatic the postulation that integration and segregation are somehow equally bad, and that it is only a shift in perspective that determines which side a thinking person might fall on. We will explore Dr. Friedman's reasons for taking this position a little further along in the chapter, but for now, let us examine the position itself on its own merits, divorced of any political or ideological habituation.

The claim: that integration and segregation are both evils. The reality: segregation, and not familiarity, is the true breeder of contempt. How do we know this? From any number of peer-reviewed studies and experiments on the subject of cultural and economic diversity, but some stand-out pieces worth citing in here include the following: a recent exploration of economic class diversity within Delhi schools in India by Harvard economics professor Gautam Rao, which concluded that the rich students who actively interacted with their poorer counterparts were "more prosocial, generous and egalitarian; and less likely to discriminate against poor students, and more willing to socialize with them."[39] Notice that in this scenario, the choice to interact or not is still very much at play; nobody is forced to interact with people they don't wish to. That will become important a bit later when we dive into Dr. Friedman's rationale behind his equivalency.

That example, while powerful, wasn't carried out in the United States, so one might want to argue that its results are therefore not applicable to an argument about US policy specifically. In that case, we can turn to another major study that takes the form of a full book by diversity expert Dr. Scott Page, *The Difference: How the Power of Diversity Creates Better Groups, Firms, Schools, and Societies.* "Societies," plural. Indeed, in his book, Dr. Page demonstrates how this principle of diversity breeding intellectual growth and tangible progress is ubiquitously applicable across all humanity, not just certain cultural pockets of it.[40] Specifically, Dr. Page has this to say as to why this is the case: "The best problem solvers tend to be similar; therefore, a collection of the best problem solvers performs little better than any one of them individually. A collection of random, but intelligent, problem solvers tends to be diverse. This diversity allows them to be collectively better. Or to put it more provocatively: *diversity trumps ability*."[41] Conversely, Page also delineates why lack of communication between differing focuses on the same observation can be lacking in scope of vision:

> Two people can use the same perspective but create different categories within that common perspective. One person may identify birds by their colors. Another may identify them by their songs. For any perspective that creates multiple dimensions, any subset of those dimensions could be an interpretation. In this way, one person may fail to distinguish between two things that another person sees as importantly different.[42]

Finally, Dr. Page acknowledges that entirely differing points of view altogether are even more likely to bring about wildly different approaches and understandings to a single topic or interaction. "In addition, two people may use different perspectives," he states. "If so, the interpretations based on those perspectives are bound to differ as well."[43]

In other words, both intellectual growth and conceptual multiplicity can, and do, result from diversity of perspectives and their accompanying interpretations, and the end result is that empathy goes up, and problems get addressed with even more statistical likelihood of being solved—all thanks to embracing diversity and cross-perspective interaction rather than fighting against it. That is a tangible and undeniable net benefit to society at large, without the need for additional input from sociocultural circumstance. Yet in this case, notoriously data-based Milton Friedman seems incapable of simply admitting that.

Of course, once one *does* choose to also factor in the sociocultural contexts surrounding many educational issues, it becomes even more clear that segregation has only gone to senselessly cripple otherwise capable children from reaching the same opportunities and successes as their upper-class counterparts. An individual's SES (socioeconomic status), for instance, has been shown to predetermine a higher risk for low academic and language performance, largely due to lack of access to the resources and lower-stress environs as individuals who have grown up in more affluent regions— and said shortcomings have been proven ameliorable through social-conscious educational interventions with neuroscientific grounding.[44] Just as the previously cited studies have gone to show, diversity in perspective is not only beneficial in schools themselves, but is absolutely necessary in the academic study of schools in order to accurately determine what is best for growth across the board. This merging of different fields and approaches to both properly identify and prescribe solutions to sociocultural problems is a practice becoming more prominent in recent years, but unfortunately remained neglected for far too long. As a result, brilliant experts in their respective fields have run the risk of only ever seeing a one-dimensional solution to very three-dimensional societal puzzles over decades of influential literature. Dr. Friedman, in this aforementioned passage of *Capitalism and Freedom*, is found to be no exception.

Again, we must not make the mistake of assuming that Friedman's shortcomings here are racist in nature. It needlessly complicates the issue and shifts the burden of proof toward the naysayers of neoliberal philosophies when such accusations are made without evidence. It is also ridiculously unfair to Friedman as a person as well as to his larger legacy of promoting very pro-diversity and pro-liberation policy. What we *can* do, however, is look at the words themselves in the passage in question and decipher what brought Friedman to his conclusion that both segregation and integration in schools are somehow equally evil.

The passage in question, with the header "Segregation in Schools," has Dr. Friedman prefacing his thoughts on the topic with an acknowledgment that he, like many others, believes "color of skin is an irrelevant characteristic" and that it is "desirable for all to recognize this."[45] He does not, however, argue that this is anything more than a personal opinion. He outlines the non-racist view with the qualifier, "those of us who believe," and makes no attempt to argue with any real ferocity or appeals to objective biological facts that believing skin color to be anything *other* than phenotypical variation is factually incorrect.[46] Friedman continues with the following: "If one must choose between the evils of enforced segregation or enforced integration, I myself would find it impossible not to choose integration," but then quickly lays out what he sees as "the appropriate solution that permits the avoidance of both evils"—"to eliminate government operation of the schools and permit parents to choose the kind of school they want their children to attend."[47]

This is where much consternation toward genuinely noble school choice legislative initiatives comes from—there is a clear gray area in this conversation where the kind of anti-politics delineated in Chapter 2 rears its head and leads otherwise reasonable people to prioritize poorly and make decisions without consideration of cultural condition and objective well-being for intellectual and interpersonal growth in society. Yes, it is true that overreaching government intervention has been the culprit behind many localized societal ills, but it is also true that government intervention has often been necessary for protecting the liberties, rights, and free movement of citizens who would have otherwise not had the privilege under the existing social paradigms of a given place and time. One need only glance at the state of air quality in the major cities of the United States both before and after the creation of the Environmental Protection Agency, for instance, to see how federal measures can supersede localized governments when necessary to improve overall quality of life for citizens nationwide.[48] More specifically, the Clean Air Act's effects on the country "prevented more than 200,000 premature deaths, and almost 700,000 cases of chronic bronchitis" within its first twenty years of implementation, according to data gathered by the EPA.[49]

Once again, this is numbers-based data of the sort scholars like Friedman happily engaged in and cited when the arguments being made were purely economic in nature. But the moment a sociocultural issue was in the spotlight, Friedman and many of his fellow self-described classical liberals fell back on the anti-political assumption that "government" was synonymous with "bad," and "privatization" was synonymous with "good"—regardless of context or nuance. Whether it be to clean the air and prevent deaths of blameless multitudes or to enforce integration of public schools as a means of beginning the slow process of liberating an oppressed minority, State action was unshakingly depicted as an affront to so-called liberty because of the entity that stood to enforce such social changes. This reductive dichotomy was pointed out as faulty by a figure within the ranks in Alan Milchman in the 1960s, arguing that the government is not a "mystical entity" but is instead comprised itself of private individuals, and private organization among the few who stand to benefit from exploitative tactics will do so within or without the government apparatus.[50] It is within these margins of cultural tone deafness that neoliberal hegemony hid in the open and normalized anti-politics paranoia—to the point where the morality of blanket market unaccountability became an assumed axiom amidst the postulations of mainstream conservative and vulgar libertarian thought. That trend would only continue into the remainder of the century with increasing commonality. If one wishes to propose a means of escaping the State for humanitarian reasons, then one must also propose a means of constructing viable alternatives that can still promise equitable legal protections prior to such a transition. Otherwise, the call for ending *all* State involvement across the board tomorrow comes across as coldly unconcerned for social justice.

Friedman's positive reputation as a thinker, whether one believes it deserved or not, would go on to further legitimize the aforementioned dilution of classical liberal concepts into neoliberal policy across much of the West and Western-influenced world. The oft-celebrated "Miracle of Chile," for instance, which drastically reformed much of Latin America's economy (and saw significant per capita gains in GDP as a result), is something many people credit to Friedman's effort to academically introduce more free market-focused economic concepts in the region.[51] Likewise, the UK had also become much more obsessed with en masse deregulation after the election of Margaret Thatcher, herself very much influenced by a very heavy-handed approach to anti-political economic policy.[52]

What was less popular to the narrative of economic growth via staunchly anti-political policies was the fact that this all-or-nothing approach to State involvement in socioeconomic matters led to inconsistent results. Depending on which country's economy, culture, and situational subsets thereof were being affected by this laissez-faire approach, the long-term benefits could vary dramatically. Returning to Freidman's "Miracle," it has actually been shown to have been demonstrably less of a success initially, failing to fully account for the Latin American debt crisis of 1982, and only seeing long-term stability upon the implementation of a more issue-by-issue approach to its economic handling that took reasonable regulation into account.[53] [54]

Likewise, Thatcher put forth sweeping deregulation and privatization across various services in her own country to similarly uneven results. While the more innately exchange-based aspects of the marketplace in Britain seemed to thrive well enough (at least for a time), there were other areas where Thatcher's neoliberal policies simply created problems that did not need to be.[55] British railways, for instance, along with many other sectors of the economy that were originally part of public ownership, including British Airways, British Telecom, British Aerospace, and the providers of water, fossil fuels, and bus transportation, became privatized all in the name of "progress" through competition.[56] The problem was that these types of services did not have, nor did they need, competition to keep them in line, since they were not designed while part of the private marketplace to begin with. To simply divorce something from the public service arena without any systemic alterations to account for such a shift is to fundamentally misunderstand what the real benefits or functions of genuinely freed markets stand to be. Suffice it to say that railways in particular faced a conundrum when they found themselves split into various fragments of capitalist ownership—the railcars themselves were now owned by what were called "rolling stock companies," which leased out their "products" to the companies that operated the railways.

These added choices, however, were illusory, as the different operating companies each had very specific structures, speed capacities, voltages, and clientele, meaning that the specific companies that made specific types of train cars had no choice at all but to lease out their machines only to the specific railways that could make use of them. There was no boom of variation, competition, or choice; there was only privatization and superfluous complication with the added feature of less public accountability. As a result, the private railways in the region have perpetuated the national debt with hidden subsidies amounting in the billions and a complete lack of the private investment one would expect from a so-called liberated free market.[57] In addition, these unaccountable single provider companies have gone on to *increase* prices for customers rather than lower them many times over the years, with the most recent instances of this being a 3.9 percent increase in travel fare in 2013,[58] and an additional increase of 3.4 percent more in 2018.[59]

Thatcher's unregulated approach at privatizing the entire market, including areas of public service, proved to be a disaster. Yet, the policies that led to said conditions were initially able to see public acceptance and implementation due to a disgruntled zeitgeist informed by anti-politics, and the normalization of the proposed solutions had already been in process thanks to the growing acceptance of neoliberalism as a rhetorical scalpel against the perceived inadequacies of then-present economic systems. Dubbed "mixed economies," these existing systems were present among much of the West and Western-influenced world.[60] They aimed to merge the salvageable elements of both State and "market" economies that, as was argued by social scientists Charles Lindblom and Robert Dahl in 1953, had failed to sustain in their base forms.[61] More specifically, these supposed base forms were communism and capitalism, respectively, and with this framing came an assertion that would go on to color the political conversation for decades to come: that "true" communism amounted to State authoritarianism, and that "true" capitalism amounted to complete freedom.

But is that assertion true? The typical answer in the West from the 1930s up to and all throughout the 1980s was considered a self-evident "yes," due in no small part to the fact that the Soviet Union and Mao's China had already attempted so-called State socialism and failed, with their respective governments quickly devolving into authoritarianism and totalitarianism and accruing a suggested maximum body count by its harshest critics of nearly 100 million, often called the most prolific number of deaths under a single ideology in history.[62] However, was it the supposed socialist ideology that logically led to such outcomes? It must be noted that despite the claims of these regimes that what they were implementing in their countries was "socialism," most non-Marxist-Leninist socialists condemned these governments as being the antithesis of what actual socialist thought promulgated. Notably among the dissenters to the Soviets in particular was Russian revolutionary Leon Trotsky, who, despite being a key player in the revolution and initial appointment of the Soviet government, came to be disenchanted with the Soviet Union in the 1920s and 1930s and was subsequently banished from the Communist Party and written out of history under Stalin's rule. Such behavior from a government that is supposedly built upon the concept of less hierarchical structures and more democratic control over resources by the working class (which is all socialism essentially is, as will be demonstrated in the following chapter) should send up a red flag for anyone being sold the notion that such a government is actually living up to its ideological claims.[63] Nevertheless, the propaganda machine of the Soviet Union, whose slogans kept depicting its government functions as shining examples of socialism in action, was a force too strong to overcome in the pre–Internet age.[64] Similar realities exist regarding Mao's China and its respective propaganda as well in the form of the "Mass Line," the "from the masses, to the masses" process through which the Chinese Communist Party's government *claims* to form its public policy around the will of the everyday population via elite-to-non-elite communication, but whose reality often amounts much more to mere rhetorical pandering and little action.[65] This of course is a form of the State ingratiating the people, which simply took its cues from the established Marxist-Leninism of the Soviets (and as such was an ideologically genealogical continuation of it).[66]

Despite the former information being a clue for those of us who remain skeptical regarding whether or not the aforementioned dictatorships were actual examples of socialist implementation, the damage had already been done—"communism" was seen as an ideological form of government that led to human suffering when not reined in, and "capitalism" was depicted as runaway freedom with its own unsustainable qualities (thanks to the historically incorrect newfangled definition the word was given by the laissez-faire economists of the early twentieth century).[67] Thus, Dahl and Lindblom's mixed economies had become the standard model as a means of striking a pseudo balance between these perceived poles. What this manifested as by the 1960s was a version of capitalism heavily informed by the economic ideas of John Maynard Keynes, but this "Keynesian compromise," initially popular, had failed by the following decade to ultimately put an end to the exploitative hierarchies and lack of social mobility for the working class.[68]

By the late 1970s, the red-scared general population of the West also bought in quite easily to the postulation that the slowly returning dip in working-class autonomy was somehow caused by failures of the Carter administration to properly manage the economy.[69] In reality, the hierarchical nature of the system was still the ultimate culprit, resulting in wage stagnation and further unchecked exploitation at the hands of bosses. As a result of the general population's refusal to recognize this reality, however, it was Keynesianism that was blamed for supposedly having intrinsic qualities about it that led to these failures. So, the rationale behind the neoliberal policies of both Thatcher and newly elected US president Ronald Reagan was that Keynesianism was too heavy on socialist influence and that its supposed opposite, the "free market," was the antidote.[70] It also did not hurt that Reagan in particular, who took office in 1981, had already gone fully fundamental conservative in his prior career as governor, and relied on appeals to arguably racist tropes such as "black militants" and neoliberal boogeymen like "communism," the "welfare state," and "big government" (which he seemed to have lumped together as equal degeneracies)[71] to serve as the accused enemies of American greatness that he would aim to shut down through his policy rollouts.[72]

Notice the pendulous quality of the public policy rhetoric over the course of this handful of decades; rather than reconsider the colloquial definitions of capitalism and socialism, and rather than apply nuance to the issues, the political gallop was to assume a false dichotomy utilizing already familiar concepts that the masses could immediately recognize, and then within these confines pick one extreme interpretation over another for as long as it lasted, then rinse and repeat. This pendulum, if we can visualize it, represents the rhetoric that colors our modern political conversation. It hangs beneath the clock's face, innocuously swinging to-and-fro as anyone would expect. Beyond the pendulum, however, just behind the premium stained wood that exudes expert craftsmanship (this, of course, represents the normalized and positively depicted status quo), is the clockwork itself. Unlike the pendulum, whose job is to always maintain its back-and-forth momentum, this clockwork moves in one direction—the same direction, always, without exception: forward. The gears and cogs spin the same way, every day, hour, minute, and second, as the clock face follows the onward march of time. In our metaphor, the clockwork represents capitalism itself and the State- and privately funded system of privileges keeping it in its momentum. If one were to look at our clock and somehow manage to lack any prior knowledge of what a clock is or what utility it serves, there stands a good chance that this person might mistake the pendulum as its primary function, and not the clock face. In our world of neoliberal markets and hegemonic fallout, it can be observed that most of us are ignorantly paying too much heed to the political rhetoric at the expense of fully comprehending the inner workings of the system itself—we are mistaking the pendulum for the clockwork.

This much was certainly the case when the general public accepted Keynesianism as socialism. Make no mistake: the Keynesian model, while noble in intent, was and is still *capitalistic* in nature, which means that the same systemic deadfalls as any other capitalist economy were still present and in play. The hierarchies were still there, and the workers still had little to no control over their own livelihoods. These so-called mixed economies were little more than repurposed versions of those that had already existed, and, thus, the call to completely abandon socialist elements was premature and unjustified, since the Keynesian model was not truly socialist by any real measure.

What came from this dishonest characterization of both socialist and capitalist realities was an illusion of progress. To the layperson, the UK and American governments had made a good-faith effort to consider the best elements of all possible economic structures, only to arrive at the conclusion that largely deregulated capitalism with few exceptions was the definitive model. To the ruling classes in these countries, that illusion was precisely the point and likely intentional. The pendulum did swing on the surface, rhetorical level, but inside, the clockwork ran smoothly like always without a hitch. The United States and the United Kingdom (and the many countries they interfered in) never did try out real mixed economies; instead, they reupholstered capitalism several times over and sold it back to their citizens with different labels each time, tweaking the inner workings only slightly. Further, the reason why neoliberalism at the global scale materializes as imperialism might not at first be obvious, but as French revolutionary Frantz Fanon pointed out, the

Western campaign of colonization was framed in much the same way as the local economic debate: there is a perceived struggle between "capitalism versus socialism" that is actually masking the reality, "colonialism versus anti-colonialism."[73] If anti-colonialism is seen as "socialism" (or at least the mischaracterized version of it), then the noble cause must be its opposite. Both locally and globally, then, the elites remained the owners of capital, and the workers remained exploited automatons. But under the guise of experimentation and alternate model consideration, the public was sold a false narrative whose conclusion was that unaccountable capitalism was the empirically proven "free-market" panacea to the working-class woes that were growing increasingly visible.

The irony is that by selling its citizens this myth, the American government–corporate machine was having an effect not very dissimilar from that of the Soviet propaganda it so fervently admonished. Neoliberals were, in the words of Mark Fisher, "more Leninist than the Leninists, using think-tanks as the intellectual vanguard to create the ideological climate in which capitalist realism can flourish."[74] By "capitalist realism," Fisher means both a normalization of the daily life experience within the status quo and a conscious argument for perpetuation of said experience into the future.[75] If one comes to accept life as it is within the present capitalistic world of hierarchies and commodity overload, then one tends to embrace even the less desirable aspects of said world as necessary externalities for the greater good. In this case, that good amounts to what the government–corporate machine has sold its citizenry as freedom— freedom of choice, freedom of expression, and freedom of opportunity. Capitalism, it is said time and again, is the only way to achieve these freedoms lest we fall into capitalism's supposed antipode, the "communism" of Stalin and his ilk. Through the aforementioned repurposing of capitalism, which masqueraded as genuine attempts at varying degrees of socialist economies, the State can justify its stance that this pro-capitalism view is moral and correct. We tried the other way, or so we are told, and that way failed. Onward to private enterprise!

Capitalist realism is therefore, in substantiation, neoliberal hegemony in the rearview—a type of false consciousness that fancies itself intellectually skeptical and empirical. It is the result of decades of normative subsuming of self-centered economic planning, domination by the owners of capital, and State-assisted market rigging. It ties into our dissection of populism as an organic, bottom-up manifestation in the previous section of the book in that it appeals to the frontier of antagonism built up by populist narratives in crisis. When the problems one is facing are systemic, but the system itself is what is being defended, then a scapegoat is needed in order to explain the origins of the turmoil without the need for self-reflection. In this way, the government–corporate machine in the West, and especially in the United States, intentionally or unwittingly, provided the perfect boogeyman to explain why the American Dream was deteriorating: communism, Marxism, socialism, or any other (misunderstood) variant thereof. The Keynesian approach at more controlled markets was framed as a socialist economic construct, and despite that not being true, the red scare rhetoric was so effective that it hardly mattered.[76] Socialism was ideologically bankrupt in the eyes of everyday American citizens, and this meant that the country's policy makers could prescribe neoliberalism as the cure with almost no pushback whatsoever.[77]

But since these changes really only amounted to more extreme versions of the same hierarchical market structure, the problems facing working-class Americans persisted. Keeping within the populist framing, what remained on the frontier of antagonism to blame for these continued economic woes? What enemy to American freedom remained to be manufactured? Anything but capitalism; anything but systemic weaknesses in the present framework. It is from this position that the anti-politics of the right-wing populists in America form. Without the normalization of neoliberal ideas, without the distortion of classical liberal concepts on human interaction, these populists would have far less of a rhetorical arsenal—and a far more transparently false cultural perspective. As it stands now, the hegemonic nature of neoliberal experience has made flush an otherwise staggered bookshelf of varying grievances toward overreaching authority and control. The anti-politics on the right has been given a validation it has not intellectually earned amidst the scads of other perspectives solely because the anti-political narrative most closely matches that of neoliberalism—the narrative that it is solely outside forces (government regulation, welfare collectors, invading job-takers, etc.) encroaching on capitalism that is the problem, rather than capitalism itself.

Returning to Laclau, he describes a similar process when delineating the general trend of populist bolstering through hegemony, stating that "in a hegemonic relation, one particular difference assumes the representation of a totality that exceeds it. This gives clear centrality to a particular figure within the arsenal of classical rhetoric: synecdoche (the part representing the whole)."[78] A little further into this same observation, Laclau qualifies a specific process that characterizes this trend regarding the eroding individuality of demands of specific demographics the longer said demands go unsatisfied. "If the demand is satisfied," Laclau posits,

> that is the end of the matter; but if it is not, people can start to perceive that their neighbors have other, equally unsatisfied demands. . . . If the situation remains unchanged for some time, there is an accumulation of unfulfilled demands and an increasing inability of the institutional system to absorb them in a *differential* way (each in isolation from the others), and an *equivalential* relation is established between them.[79]

That process, warns Laclau, can further widen the gap "separating the institutional system from the people."[80]

The aforementioned populist rationale spectrum, as understood and delineated earlier in this book, abides according to this process as outlined by Laclau.[81] What it results as is a manifestation of something Slavoj Žižek might refer to as an unreal specter; an abstract, vague, immaterial, unmeasurable concept that nevertheless marries with and dictates many aspects of "the Real"; Žižek describes the process of such specters coming to us as "illusory appearances" that "arise out of the world."[82] In a somewhat Kantian understanding of our concept of reality, one might assume that we should not bother to properly identify what we have yet to empirically measure and determine as being "real"; on the other hand, taking a page from Hegel (as Žižek often does), this divide is more than just between the known and the unknowable, but is rather a difference between what is real for us as we experience it, and what reality is in itself. In this sense, the world outside of our present full understanding is perhaps still within our imagination, and as such, we can still identify it, albeit through a means of finding the closest representations of it that are already familiar to us from the known world.[83] The result, the thing for us rather than the thing itself, can therefore inform societal norms in a way that the Kantian realists would consider to be unearned due to the lack of empiricism involved. Yet, as a culture, we gravitate toward this method of reality construction far more often than not. Therefore, to not give credence to the existence of the unknown as a "real" thing in and of itself is to allow for ourselves a glaring blind spot in regard to how the populist rationale spectrum finds its own narratives within our present known realities. In Žižek's terminology, the belief that capitalism is the only achievable norm, and therefore one's social woes must be caused by something divorced from neoliberal policy, is an example of how reality "is never directly 'itself'," and instead "has the structure of a fiction in that it is symbolically (or, as some sociologists put it, 'socially') constructed."[84]

Fisher's concept of realism, then, is in utility the Hegelian "thing as what it means for us," while neoliberalism is the Kantian reality that can be measured and empirically demonstrated.[85] The greater reality beyond neoliberalism, by this same Kantian token, is thus rendered unknowable, and therefore unworthy of further investigation. The everyday person belonging to the working class who resides in a neoliberal economy is subsequently far more likely to identify her understanding of her daily experience (the thing for her) by pulling from the nearest point of reference for its rationale she has in her known material reality: economic liberalism. Despite the fact that neoliberalism has distorted liberalism's most radical aspirations in actuality, this working-class citizen still must make sense of things with the knowledge her present known reality has to offer in the face of no "realistic" alternative. Even if capitalism *is* exploitation, even if neoliberalism *does* justify said exploitation, this everyday person is told she must either accept her reality as the only one we can know or strive for a new one that has yet to be fully and thoroughly demonstrated. This alternative, articulated from a more Hegelian perspective, is still worthy of acknowledging as being much more than "unknowable." People will still strive to know it even before evidence of its existence has fully materialized, or else they will abdicate their positions as seekers and simply accept their present world as the only one they can ever know or experience. In the latter case, many of these people, resigned to this rather reductionist position, justify the imperfect reality of the neoliberal market by appealing to what they perceive as classical liberalism as its ideological justification. Thus, the cycle continues.

If we remain strictly Kantians in our approach to understanding and indeed solving the problem of this process of liberal distortion, we will at best be stuck perpetually circling the already carved-out ontological discussion on this front, and at worst, we may never fully comprehend its epistemological counterpart. In the case of the modern so-called classical liberal wing of libertarianism in America, this choice to follow a more Kantian path toward squaring their ambitions with their present realities has apparently been made, and the unquestioning embrace of neoliberalism as liberalism's only "real" and "knowable" form has ensued.[86] From there, we find more unreal specters in the Žižek tradition within the everyday interactions of those who accept liberalized markets (i.e., capitalism) as the norm (such as those who are willing to accept exploitation, wage labor, hierarchical structures, etc. in the name of "liberty").[87] In the words of Professor Robert W. McChesney in his forward to Noam Chomsky's *Profit over People*, "neoliberalism's loudest message is that there is no alternative to the status quo, and that humanity has reached its highest level."[88] Over the course of this chapter, we have been shown how and why such a grim trend has come to pass. Whether or not it continues depends on if enough of us wake up and speak out against liberal distortion to break the spell.

* * *

As asserted at the start of this book, the on-the-ground everyday citizens are not consciously weaving lies, and therefore it is not fair to characterize every anti-political right-wing populist as an active racist or propagandist; however, the initial twisting of traditionally accepted liberal ideas into neoliberal realities, as well as the defamation of any alternative market system to the one we currently have in the United States, is quite obviously an intentional move—not to turn everyone into crypto-fascists or white nationalists, but to perpetuate capital and bolster the bourgeoisie class as long as possible.[89] Keeping the machinery running because it's proven a good thing for yourself and your financial backers is not the same thing as consciously aiming to rip the country apart at the ideological seams. We should not subscribe to the notion that every wealthy business owner is full of hateful ideology. In fact, it is very likely that many people in the elite classes themselves are also very sincere in their collective belief that what they are fighting to maintain is truly the best way forward for everyone.

Nevertheless, that fight to maintain the status quo has led to the normalization of all aspects of capitalist society—including the more negative aspects that affect the working class with increasing regularity. As automation continues to make life more convenient, a contradiction to neoliberal dogma emerges: the inability for everyday people to justify their value to society through work.[90] Entry-level jobs continue to disappear, being replaced by the market, yes, but with jobs that often require specialized skillsets and technological knowledge only obtainable through vocational training or university degrees, which themselves require mountains of money and time that both out-of-work and overworked Americans typically do not have.[91] Capitalism is often praised for being the bringer of innovation, but what happens when that innovation reaches such a level of sophistication that it stands to undermine the very system that birthed it? Will we march *through* capitalism into the next economic iteration, as Marx predicted? Or will we cling to the present structure with a death grip and continue to claim that our current system is the most viable and realistic system we can conceptualize?

If we continue to choose the latter option (which we have been doing for decades), we will only perpetuate the confusion and alienation of more and more demographics of American citizens as the tent poles of late capitalism continue to wane.

The Original Libertarianism versus Right-Libertarianism

While this book is aiming to explain the mindsets of those involved in various forms of conservative and right-wing faux-revolutionary movements, a common thread tying all of said movements together (regardless of their respective labels) is a near-ubiquitous claim of philosophical adherence to what is referred to as "libertarianism." More specifically, classical liberalism, which is often used as a synonym for the type of libertarianism held by these groups. Everyone from the paleo-conservatives like Ron Paul, to the alt-light figures such as Milo Yiannopoulos, to Internet pseudo-skeptics like Stefan Molyneux, to identitarian activists like Lauren Southern, to straightforward Republican politicians like Ted Cruz, to people who went on to become full-blown fascists like Chris Cantwell, have all at one point or another appealed to a more radical, "hipper" audience for their messages by claiming to be philosophically aligned with "libertarianism."[1]

But what do these people and their connected movements truly mean by the word "libertarian"? Well, as evidenced by their other political alignments, their libertarianism is of a specific kind that was only invented within the past century: right-libertarianism. In order to understand what *that* amounts to, we need to examine the tangled history of how libertarianism and classical liberalism relate to each other.

Over the past several decades, classically liberal concepts have been slowly distorted into neoliberal realities surrounded by reductionist normativity, as the previous chapter was concerned with demonstrating. In equal measure, however, classical liberalism has also become known as having been the precursor (and, in many respects, the very philosophical bedrock) of libertarianism (and free-market nobility as a whole). This claim is a falsehood. While it is true that classical liberalism sprang to rhetorical life prior to libertarianism, it is not true at all that libertarianism then naturally grew out of liberalism. If present-day right-libertarians claim to be the arbiters of classical liberal philosophy (and they do),[2] then we must explore and examine why it is that the label itself, "libertarian," came to be seen as synonymous with liberalism, as well as what libertarianism has *actually* amounted to—both historically and ideologically—over the course of its centuries-long existence. This chapter aims to do just that. To that end, let us begin by turning to 1857, and a fateful letter that was written within the French socialist circles of the day.

Then-exiled Joseph Déjacque was writing from New Orleans to fellow anarchist thinker Pierre-Joseph Proudhon in response to something the former had read regarding the latter's view of women—more specifically, the way in which Proudhon described women as being dependent on the male intellect for their own emancipation:

> But, old boar who is only a pig, if it is true what you say that the woman cannot give birth to brains like belly without the help of the man . . . it is conversely just as true that man cannot produce by the flesh as by the intelligence without the help of the woman. It is logic, and good logic, Master-Madelon-Proudhon, that a pupil who has always been a disobedient subject can tear you out of his hands and throw you in the face. The emancipation or non-emancipation of women, the emancipation or non-emancipation of man: what is it to say? Are there rights for one that are not rights for the other? Is the being-human not the human-being in the plural as in the singular, in the feminine as in the masculine? Is it changing its nature to split the sexes? Likewise, are the drops of rain that fall from the cloud less raindrops, that these drops pass through the air in small numbers or in large numbers, that their shape has such dimension or such other, such configuration male or such configuration female?[3]

Looking past the obvious fiery passion in which Déjacque chastises Proudhon, something very specific about his perspective on human beings shows through—he sees them as equal. Equally deserving of the same freedoms and cooperative interactions—regardless of gender. Noble. Does he extend this same courtesy of equal judgment to other minority groups? As it turns out, he does. "The man called free," he states at one point in the letter, "in the present society, the proletarian, produces much better and much more than the man called Negro, the slave. What would happen if men were truly and *universally* free? The production would be a hundredfold" (emphasis mine).[4] Here, Déjacque not only states with utmost certainty that the enslaved Blacks he observes in the United States would be just as capable of anything their white counterparts could do under an emancipated state of affairs, but he also continues on to advocate for a kind of equitable liberation that even many of the classical liberals of the day would not have echoed.

"On this terrain of true anarchy, of absolute freedom," Déjacque continues, "there would undoubtedly be as much diversity among people as there are people in society, diversity of age, sex, aptitudes: *equality is not uniformity*. And this diversity of all beings and all instants is precisely what makes any government, constitution or contra, impossible" (emphasis mine).[5] In essence, Déjacque is presenting a view of the world that recognizes and celebrates diversity from an equitable standpoint. Yes, we are all very different; no, this does not have to result in unequal treatment. In order for any unjust hierarchical system to exist, be it government, capitalism, or any other structure of similar constitution, it must artificially choose winners and losers to stay viable. To illustrate this point, Déjacque accuses Proudhon of demonstrating a hypocritical favoring of hierarchical structure in his version of sex-tiered anarchism, telling Proudhon the following:

A half-measure anarchist, liberal and not libertarian, you want free trade for cotton and candle, yet you advocate protective systems of man against woman in the circulation of human passions; you cry against the high barons of capital, yet you want to rebuild the high barony of the male on the female vassal; a logician with spectacles, you see the man by the telescope which magnifies the objects, and the woman by the glass which diminishes them.⁶

Another declaration of advocacy for true liberation for all, regardless of factors such as gender, but also, the first time in recorded history that the term "libertarian" is used to describe oneself in a strictly political and activist sense. For Déjacque, libertarianism is *beyond* mere liberalism; it is total liberation of the individual, regardless of present social status or innate differences from the presently ruling sex, gender, orientation, or race.

Furthermore, the inconsistency of trying to separate gender divides from class divides in principle is also highlighted in the letter, with Déjacque postulating that "to put the question of the emancipation of women in line with the question of the emancipation of the proletarian . . . that is understandable and revolutionary; but to put it in view of privilege, oh! Then, from the point of view of social progress, it is meaningless, it is reactionary."⁷ Déjacque's liberty is indeed one of total consideration; not just economic. He summarizes his thoughts on this cultural versus economic divide as follows: "to pose [our position] thus is to solve [the confusion]: the human being, in his rotations every day, gravitates from revolution to revolution towards his ideal of perfectibility: Liberty."⁸

In other words, it is a desire for total liberation—not just from class divide (though that is clearly a key element to it), but also from cultural norms and their subsequent social expectations—that constitutes the libertarianism of true anarchists and socialists. At least, this should be the case according to Déjacque. This attitude would be further reflected in his choice to name his own socialist advocacy paper *The Libertarian*.⁹

We will revisit this fateful publication in a moment, as it helps tell the story of how libertarianism as a philosophy and movement ultimately made it to the United States and got distorted into the capitalism apologetics it largely functions as today. But before we even get to that, we need to establish the clear distinctions between the classical socialists of this time period (such as Déjacque and his fellows) and the classical liberals who served as their contemporaries. This is perhaps one of the most fascinating aspects of libertarianism's tangled history, the fact that the *actual* libertarians of old coexisted alongside of the classical liberals who are solely credited these days as the noble proto-libertarians (who were supposedly the mavericks of free markets, democracy, and voluntaryist cooperation). The reality is quite different, in that it was the libertarians (anarcho-socialists) of this period, not the classical liberals, who were much more consistently promulgating these concepts.

While Déjacque and Proudhon were duking it out via written correspondence about whether or not social hierarchies should join State and economic hierarchies as undesirable to true human freedom, classical liberal luminary Frederic Bastiat was writing his famous work *The Law*, published in the same decade as the aforementioned correspondence between Déjacque and Proudhon, which to this day is still considered by modern right-libertarians to be one of the most important and influential so-called libertarian writings in history. In it, Bastiat recalls a debate he had regarding the nobility and validity of the viewpoint of socialists (aka the first libertarians). One of the key points he seems to be very proud of making in this exchange is the supposed fact that socialism is itself a form of "plunder" in which "property is violated" by way of "organized justice" that, in Bastiat's view, amounts to force propagated at the hands of the law itself—the government.[10]

Right away, we can see that Bastiat is misrepresenting the socialists of his time when we contrast his depiction of them with their actual words as cited earlier. Whether this is an intentional deception or genuine misunderstanding is not clear, but what is undeniable is the fact that Bastiat seems to be making two major errors: first, he appears to assume that socialism is somehow synonymous with or at least tantamount to government force through narrow-minded legislation. This can likely be explained by simply acknowledging that the classical liberal gallop by this point in history was to apply a false dichotomy to the government–private sector dynamic. In the eyes of the classical liberals of Bastiat's time and onward, government is unequivocally bad and evil and stands to limit the prospect of free people, while a hands-off approach to private accruing of capital is seen as wholesome, noble, and the only means of providing free people with pathways to liberation and success.

While Bastiat himself might not have admitted or even been aware of it, this was actually a somewhat recent development for classical liberalism during his time as a thinker in the movement. Prior to this, as the previous chapter highlights, the original liberal tradition was much broader in its understanding of what avenues can lead to true liberation for all people. Noam Chomsky has defined anarchism in the past as being part of this broader liberal tradition; and indeed, the areas of overlap, few as they were, between the original 1800s libertarians and their liberal contemporaries are certainly visible. But as Déjacque made clear in his harshly worded letter to Proudhon, liberalism by this time had become merely a half-hearted, half-measure form of anarchism—liberalism was becoming narrower, despite its promising origins within the larger conversation of access to commons and free movement of people. Indeed, Bastiat and his fellows in the French liberal economic tradition blooming at that time (including other luminaries such as Gustave de Molinari) seemed sincere enough, as they took very seriously the Smithian critique of feudalist mercantilism as being a convoy for concentrated business enclosure, even aiming to radicalize it further by applying it to their contemporary economies.[11] Yet in spite of this sincerity, the elitism and favor toward the hierarchical structure of the academy that stood to benefit figures like Bastiat, Molinari, and their peers won out and economic policy proposals took on a liberal veneer while slowly losing the true radicalness of liberalism's origins—origins whose sentiments were now being carried on almost exclusively by the anarcho-socialists of the nineteenth-century working class.

This reality is further bolstered by the facts found in the history accounting of Dr. Mudge, who points out that "socialism had an organizational and practical terrain" in areas such as publicly accessible speeches and lectures, journalist activism, and clubs, while their liberal peers had become more of an imposed, bourgeois substitution that appealed to working-class fears rhetorically but elite class preservation in actual practice.[12]

Mudge, Chomsky, and Déjacque are not the only voices in this chorus about liberal distortion's rather early occurrence. As economic historian Karl Polanyi also makes note of in his history of markets *The Great Transformation*, "not until the 1830s did economic liberalism burst forth as a crusading passion and laissez-faire become a militant creed."[13] The reason for this shift in liberal thought, according to Polanyi, was that around this same time, an amendment was being proposed to the Tudor-era English "Poor Laws" from the 1600s that aimed to perpetuate their original workhouse conditions into the new century with severe limits on allowances for official recognition of an industrial age working class (and a subsequent "free labor market").[14]

The original Poor Laws, already reinterpreted by this point as what became known as the Old Poor Laws, dictated terms, conditions, and limitations of poor relief systems at the time—a kind of proto-welfare program. The Poor Law Amendment Act, which was indeed passed in 1834, set out to limit the scope in which such poor relief could be applied. Under this new amendment, which in actuality was essentially a complete replacement of the prior system, no able-bodied worker was eligible to receive any form of relief outside the confines of grueling workhouses for the destitute.[15] If a recipient *was* able-bodied, he or she would be required to forfeit all personal belongings first before then joining said workhouses as both occupation and home.[16] This meant that most working-class people, initially able to benefit from base-level support and therefore have the ability to make demands for better work conditions, lost their bargaining abilities and were relegated to depending on whatever pay they received from their workplace employers as their sole means of survival. The New Poor Laws were thus born, and this otherwise organic growth of the market into something that stood to give more power of organization to the workers was curtailed. In addition, industrial invention itself was seen as a threat to "the manufacturing class" of the time.[17] This was largely due to the fact that up until this point, workers were still setting their own hours and working at their own pace, and access to these new rapid manufacturing means stood to empower them even more.[18] It was in these early years of industry that the eight-hour work schedule was demanded (and won) by workers.[19]

Economist David Harvey, citing Marx's thoughts at the time and applying them to modern analysis, points out:

> The autonomy of the worker was taken away by the factory system; the skilled worker was in control of their tools—they could put them down. If they didn't want to work in a particular way, they didn't do it. So, they had a certain power simply by virtue of the fact that their contribution to production was their skill in using a particular tool. This was, in one respect, a free gift of labor to capital, but on the other hand, it was . . . a bit of a poison chalice. Because once that capital accepts it, it has to accept the fact that the laborer is autonomous and has a skill. But what happens with the machine is that the skill is located inside of the machine, and the autonomy, in terms of the speed of the process, is now located outside the purview of the laborer.[20]

In other words, it was not the development of new technology and industry itself that characterized capitalism and built the hierarchies; it was the way in which the manufacturing class chose to structure and run the factories that used this technology. Initially, workers were still able to continue utilizing *themselves* as the needed skills as long as they had access to the machinery itself. Thus, the classical liberals, supposedly "disciples of Adam Smith," acted contrarily to the Smithian tradition and began pushing on behalf of this manufacturing class for the Poor Law Amendment Act in tandem with new divisions of labor in the factories in an attempt to shut down this development.[21] After all, without the ability to maintain class divides and keep workers in their place as essentially cogs in the machine of developing industry, the aforementioned manufacturers might not have remained in their lucrative positions for long. Without poor relief to fall back on, under new harsher (and unregulated) work conditions, and deprived of unabridged operational know-how of new technology thanks to division of labor, workers collectively lost their potential to dictate their own destinies and became locked into a subservient class not unlike its feudalistic predecessor.

So, this explains how the aforementioned class division was first locked into place at the emergence of capitalism, but the logistical reality of *maintaining* this divide, beyond merely the philosophical support of the sentiment found in the contemporary liberal literature, was for the manufacturing class to use its entrenched power to effectively separate all property from labor.[22] Famously, transcendentalist thinker John Stuart Mill once lamented how advancement in automation, intuitively something that should have lighted the laborious load and liberated workers, ended up having even more oppressive effects on them instead.[23] This was indeed done with calculation and intent, as observed by Marx, in a process he and Engels referred to as "primitive accumulation."[24] This term was a reworking of a prior term, "accumulation of stock," first coined by Smith, but then later reworked by subsequent classical economists as "original accumulation"—the claim that capital over time accumulates in the hands of a ruling class separate from the workers for completely justified and organic reasons.[25] Marx obviously disagreed, portraying the identified concept in a new light. The fact that this process is artificial yet is portrayed by its supporters as organic (much like capitalism itself) does not bode well for the sincerity of those who at least initially wrote on these matters from the classical liberal perspective.

So, this might very well account for the first stages of the process the previous chapter identified as the slow distortion of liberalism. It's hard to imagine Adam Smith, as we have previously clarified him, being fully in favor of such a shift in priority. The same can be said by any number of his contemporaries, including French economist Jean-Baptiste Say, one of the first to promulgate the market mechanism as a natural result of innate human qualities upon interaction.[26] Say argued in favor of less government meddling with these market forces, but he did so from a place of genuine trust in communal mutual benefit and fair, non-exploitative exchange of labor for products and income—he was not arguing for the freedom for bosses and owners to divorce workers from the fruits of their own labor.[27]

Yet, those who were considered the intellectual descendants of these initial liberal economic thinkers were going along with the new narrative of supposedly "hands-off" markets that were themselves benefiting in reality from other forms of government meddling, such as the Poor Law amendments, and as a result, it wasn't long before *their* intellectual descendants, Bastiat included, were parroting these ideas against any form of regulatory influence on the market that stood to undo the prior preservation of the manufacturing class's power. The irony here is the fact that it was regulation that granted that power's artificial perpetuation in the first place, which is itself evidence of how all regulation is not created equal, and it arrives in both good and bad forms depending on what influence is behind it. The socialists of Bastiat's era were keenly aware of this nuance, hence their suspicion of *all* forms of unjust hierarchy in both government and private enterprise alike. By comparison, Bastiat and his ilk by this time were perpetuating a sloppy, needlessly one-dimensional view that seems to have been birthed out of the need by an elite ruling class to maintain class divides and keep feudalist dynamics in the marketplace alive well after the boom of industry might very well have organically done away with them.[28]

The second error Bastiat makes in his attempted sizing up of socialists in *The Law* is in the form of his understanding of "property."[29] There is no attempt whatsoever on Bastiat's part to distinguish between personal property and private property—it is simply "property," and as a result, socialism is accused here of using force to strip men of the very things that make them men—"their personality, their liberty, their property."[30] This assumes, of course, that property is property no matter how it manifests, and that it always amounts to personal belongings of a person. If that were in fact true, then Bastiat's fears of a socialist economy might be warranted—after all, who *doesn't* wish to keep ahold of his or her own goods that were worked for and purchased? Who *wouldn't* want to ensure that his or her personal stuff, including his or her house, remained untouchable by would-be thieves guided by a State-enforced mandated sharing initiative? Unfortunately for Bastiat and everyone else who followed after him, this was not what socialists meant when they spoke or wrote about private property. As is often the case, the reality of the situation is much more nuanced than supposed.

Private property, in the traditional socialist and anarchist vernacular, *is* the means of production that socialists want all working people to have equal access to. By contrast, personal property is all the material stuff a person buys for herself. In other words, private property produces a person's smartphone, while personal property *is* the smartphone. While this is certainly a very base-level understanding and is simplified for purposes of introductory success to a potentially new concept, it is in essence the correct framing for us to grasp what it is that socialists actually mean when they use the term "private property." In the days of Marx, Bakunin, and Kropotkin, private property would have amounted to the factories by which all major goods post-industrial boom were mass produced. Today, the equivalent of the factory on a smaller scale might be a 3D printer, a computer program used for creating content, a professional studio in which such programs are put to use, etc. These things, of course, are themselves sold or rented as products or services, which means they are technically potentially private *or* personal property. It depends on how they are used and how they are acquired. But this muddying of the delineation between "personal" and "private" property is merely the result of prior meddling with an otherwise straightforward and organic distinction between the two. Before we could sell factories-in-a-box, we relied on the large factories (and all the natural resources they utilized, such as forests and mountains) to produce all mass-marketed goods and then dole them out to us for a profit. As such, the more black-and-white understanding of private versus personal property present in classical socialist writings is far more forgivable.

By present-day standards, of course, such a distinction is arguably imprecise and unhelpful. Which is why certain voices in socialist thought today tend to now veer into different modes of categorization as a means of identifying what we are seeing now— "alternative economies" is one such category that has been put forth as a more localized replacement for the manufacturing big business economy.[31] It may be that the term "personal empire" might be a much better descriptor for private property by today's standards, as that serves to be a bit all-encompassing and takes the aforementioned alternative economies and homebrew manufacturing into account. Nevertheless, the broader concept itself is still sound: *everyone* should have equal access to this opportunity. The opportunity to build. The opportunity to create. The opportunity to directly benefit from one's own labor.

Such a concept is not at all controversial when stated in the more modern reframing of the former. Yet, thanks to an outdated term (that admittedly many modern socialists still refuse to update), as well as a misrepresentation in liberal literature (which would go on to dominate the economic conversation by the early twentieth century), the general public's perception of what socialism aims to seize is distorted. When John Lennon earnestly wrote "imagine no possessions" in the lyrics to his brilliant song "Imagine," he was unwittingly perpetuating a misunderstanding of what it meant to be a genuine socialist in a genuine reality.

Despite this distinction between types of property being very straightforward for the period it was coined in, we can see evidence of (classical) liberal thinkers misrepresenting the libertarian (socialist) thinkers of the time in an attempt to sway opinion and support the economic system that stood to uphold the already-existing divide between the elites and the craftsmen—the manufacturer and the laborer. This separation of the work from the product, Marx's "primitive accumulation," became the prevailing axiom within the economic conversation of the elites from then on.[32]

But this manufactured narrative, which amounted in practice to class divide being seen as indicative of organically successful markets, did not remain free of its detractors. Indeed, the "libertarian socialists" (a term officially recognized and adopted by French anarchist congress in the 1880s) who served as post-industrial boom, newfangled classical liberalism's initial foes followed the liberal narrative into the early twentieth century for the purposes of continuing to challenge it whenever possible. Déjacque's own political magazine, *The Libertarian (Le Libertaire)*, had been circulating European political spaces since Déjacque's self-declaration as a libertarian, and had become wildly popular. But in addition to its European circulation, *The Libertarian* was being consumed by American readers, as well, thanks to its very first publication actually appearing in New York (remember, Déjacque was an exile to America during this time).[33] The New York anarchist activist group known as the Locofocos took cues from it. By the early 1900s, both American *and* European working-class citizens were consuming libertarian socialist literature and challenging the status quo's depiction of class divide and primitive accumulation as necessary for/indicative of successful economies.

The previous chapter talked about how liberalism itself has slowly been distorted over time, even as early as the 1800s. So far, we have seen evidence of that early turn taking place, and how the anarchists and socialists came along to define what *actual* liberation for people would continue to look like post-industrial boom. The distortion continued, and the liberal-against-libertarian divide would color the policy conversation for generations. Political parties in both Europe and the United States had begun to swing more toward anarchist and socialist sentiments thanks to the presence of actual socialists and anarchists in influential positions.[34] But as also pointed out in the previous chapter, these influential positions came part and parcel with the elitism implicit for such figures, which meant that it was only a matter of time before said elitism marched to the bourgeois tune of popular economic narratives and the genuine revolutionary solidarity slipped away to be replaced by disingenuous liberal pandering. Returning to the historical recounting of Dr. Mudge cited previously, she states that socialist expertise in this time was "party-dependent" and "distinctive from labor movements" despite claiming otherwise.[35] The liberal parties acted during these tug-of-war platform days as the "main competitors" to the labor parties of socialist and anarchist populist outcry, demonstrating yet again that liberal distortion played its part in confounding the economic narrative on national stages for the general public to interpret.[36]

Anthropologist Johanna Bockman further corroborates this claim in her book *Markets in the Name of Socialism: The Left-Wing Origins of Neoliberalism*, in which she also clarifies how many of the public policy initiatives claiming to care about working people were actually just liberal distortions acting on behest of elites in Eastern Europe and other parts of the West.[37] One example of this can be found in the mid- to late 1800s when libertarian socialist unrest threatened to undermine the authority of Otto von Bismarck, founder and chancellor of the German Empire and a major actor in the economic affairs of Europe at large beginning in 1860.

Bismarck's initial response to the worker outcry against State-backed capitalism was to institute "anti-socialist laws" in the late 1870s in an attempt to arrest and silence dissenters. Libertarian meetings and literature were effectively banned during this time, marring Bismarck's rule with tyranny.[38] When he realized far too many dissenting voices were continuing to emerge, Bismarck changed tactics in the following decade and developed what is often referred to as the first modern welfare State as a means of pacifying the dissenters and keeping them loyal and under control.[39] This welfare State amounted to a series of programs that provided what we might think of as proto-social security, yet his biggest critics at this time were the local Marxist advocates for worker autonomy, arguing that this was all an insincere attempt to keep the working class oppressed.[40] Despite this pushback, Bismarck ultimately succeeded, as those hopeful worker uprisings never happened, once again beating back the unrest and keeping it at bay.

But this motivation for State-implemented social welfare was not limited to just the nineteenth century when worker awareness was still fresh and passions still hot. Indeed, as relatively recently as the early twentieth century, socialism was still a semi-regular facet of neoclassical economics, largely because many socialists (still calling themselves libertarians) were themselves becoming actual members of the leading parties at the time, once again demonstrating Mudge's point that as long as the elites were themselves members of a represented demographic, said demographic would have at least some influence. One of the most important figures in the marginal revolution, for example, was Leon Walras, a socialist himself who was also a supporter of "free competition."[41] This form of market-oriented socialism was less controversial for the entirety of its adherents' time in these elitist and influential spaces.[42] During this time, non-ideological neoclassical economists were less concerned with how markets worked as they were with how value could be pulled from said markets.[43] The ever-narrowing liberal window was continuing to close in, however, and the elites became more and more exclusively liberal as time went on. Once the liberal presence tipped the scales, the party alignment outshouted actual worker concerns yet again.

The ultimately tone-deaf nature of these party-tethered economic policies became too much for those who saw through them across all of the liberalized West regions. In America in the 1920s, prior to the Great Depression, workers were on the verge of a socialist revolution, but their representatives in the New York assembly were expelled, which further lessened the Socialist Party of America's power and influence in the big political arenas.[44] That same decade, the first globally recognized successful socialist revolution in Russia had been devolving into a twisting of socialist sentiment into totalitarian degenerated workers State economy and political dictatorship under the Soviet leadership of Vladimir Lenin and, later, Joseph Stalin.[45] In these economies, workers had no autonomy or control over their circumstances or the means of production. There was no free market, and classically socialist horizontal organization was nowhere to be found—only top-down control by the elite (a "rotten edifice," in the words of Noam Chomsky).[46] This, nevertheless and understandably, scared many outside supporters of socialism into second-guessing the effectiveness or nobility of socialist philosophy and economic planning—perhaps something was innately present within socialism that inevitably led to such atrocities?[47] Such worries further contributed to the slow weakening of influence of libertarianism in the everyday political conversation in the West.

The following decade, during the Great Depression, there was a brief resurgence in the belief that perhaps a more worker-concerned and worker-controlled economy was noble and justified. Until the New Deal, as crafted and implemented by the administration of Franklin Delano Roosevelt. The New Deal was, much like Bismarck's welfare measures, a means of keeping working-class people pacified and ultimately complacent so that they would not revolt. The false consciousness had not yet taken hold everywhere, but the perceived immediate benefits of playing along with the ruling class's economic desires became increasingly difficult to withstand.

Yet again, we see here in actuality a following of the trends predicted by Poulantzas, where he demonstrated through his case study work in Germany and Italy that the initial alliances made between the bourgeois class and the working class comes as a means of filling in the gaps left by the fleeing of genuine revolutionary ideals, and aiming to try and explain the reasons for working-class strife in a way that still perpetuates the given economic state of affairs.[48] This ultimately fails, and even more extreme explanations (e.g., nationalism and/or fascism) follow. But before things reach that apex, the means by which the corporatist-controlled State tries to initially ingratiate the working-class people willing to listen comes in the form of things such as, in the words of Poulantzas, "trade unionism and reformism."[49] In other words, neoliberal welfare offerings. The New Deal is a perfect example of such an offering, but it is still often credited by liberals even to this day as a wonderful economic policy that "saved" the economy and got us out of the Great Depression. In reality, the financial hole working-class people were in was made longer and deeper by the policy.

In an August 2004 *Journal of Political Economy* article, UCLA economists Cole and Ohanian pointed out that the supposed recovery from the New Deal was "very weak," and that work hours were at 27 percent below trend in 1933 and 21 percent below trend in 1939.[50] By 1939, unemployment was still at a dismal 17.2 percent despite seven years of so-called economic salvation.[51]

According to neoclassical economic model building, the initial downturn and subsequent large economic shocks *did* go up by 1933.[52] So, on paper, the economic reality should have followed. But it didn't. Because the conversely positive economic shocks, injected into the economy by the government, simply increased the monetary base by 100+ percent; it didn't address the true problem: the system itself. It built infrastructure and doled out welfare programs. But it didn't actually give the working class any more power.

The government could (and arguably should) have liquidated the monstrous corporations that were feeding off the working class to excess and becoming overcapitalized. Instead, it turned these companies and industries into effective cartels through rigged pricing and output reductions, which many economists estimate accounted for about 60 percent of the difference between actual output and trend output.

This prolonged the Depression and made things even worse for the working class. Taxes, originally conceived to *only* tax corporations' excess capital, ultimately went to the incomes of working people—the people who could afford parting with any portion of their income the least. Yes, there were indeed excess profit taxes and the like put upon business, but as economic historian Jim Powell argues: "The most important source of New Deal revenue were excise taxes levied on alcoholic beverages, cigarettes, matches, candy, chewing gum, margarine, fruit juice, soft drinks, cars, tires (including tires on wheelchairs), telephone calls, movie tickets, playing cards, electricity, radios."[53]

So, in order to eat, get to work, keep the lights and heat on, and then try and enjoy one's free time with recreation (essentially every aspect of life from top-to-bottom), working-class people had to part with what little money they *were* making as a means of helping fund the cause. The primary funders of the New Deal were therefore effectively the working class and poor—the very people it was supposed to save.

Or, the government could have simply liquidated those companies, made the corporate taxes broader and deeper, held big business more accountable, and not rigged prices against output, etc. Perhaps we would have gotten out of the Depression sooner. Instead, people were kept complacent by seeing returns on their taxes, such as more infrastructure and welfare programs. On the surface, it appeared like a great thing. But it also served the purpose of simultaneously taking chunks of working-class income away through excise tax and urging working-class people themselves to become reliant on the State to take care of them when their remaining finances weren't quite enough to get by. This is a form of control, not liberation. In addition, it was yet another measure to keep capitalism artificially alive and discourage working-class revolt. To that end, it worked.

Poulantzas's thoughts on this sort of deal-making with State power were similarly grim, and he characterized such dynamics as examples of the power bloc previously covered in Chapter 4—oppressed classes forming an "alliance" with their oppressors as a means of feeling represented when in reality, the result was a contradictory class position that stood to fragment or even outright erase the concept of class division as a relevant framing of socioeconomic strife.[54] Indeed, a detailed examination of the New Deal by Rhonda Levine and inspired by Poulantzas was summarized as the State, having conceded to certain demands from laborers, forging an alliance *a la* Poulantzas's outlined process with certain slices of the working class willing to buy into the American Dream mythos and let down its guard.[55]

Combined with the hysteria in response to the Soviet Union's sins, liberal policy that threw crumbs at working people gave an illusory impression of security and reliability to many. If the system as it existed could always pacify the working class, the argument went, then perhaps it could stay—unjust hierarchies and exclusive accumulation of wealth for the few notwithstanding. After all, went the narrative, the alternative was "communism," a boogeyman version of socialism that depicted all forms of socialism as being coterminous with the aforementioned atrocious Marxist-Leninist regimes.[56]

The aforementioned example is yet another step along the trail of both liberal distortion and neoliberal normalization. If it can be presented to the public as having their best interests at heart while also being the only viable option, then neoliberal policy combined with post-Bastiat classical liberal sentiment can survive well beyond the threshold for working-class patience. The New Deal, Keynesian "mixed economies," and so forth, are but bandages upon a gaping wound that perpetuates the problem of stifled worker autonomy and obfuscated opportunity for actual free markets—free for workers themselves, and not for the owners and bosses exclusively.

Still, there remained that original libertarian appeal. It persisted in spite of the ever-swinging pendulum giving the general public the illusion of progress and debate. As late as 1954, there were still people daring to peer beyond the pendulum and name the system for what it truly was: capitalism in the flesh; not simply a perversion of a so-called real capitalism that has never actually existed. A group of largely anarcho-syndicalist (a school of market socialism thought) workers had formed *The Libertarian League* in the United States.[57] Those who bothered to look could always return to the rational and empowering libertarian literature by the socialists of old in Déjacque and Proudhon's tradition. It was precisely that connection between the working class and other would-be revolutionary types to libertarian sentiment that would color the decisions of the next group of liberal apologists to come onto the scene.

* * *

"Libertarianism." That word carries with it a promise of being something more than merely liberal (a term that by the time the anarchist-minded socialists split off from the liberals had become synonymous with favoring the manufacturing class and justifying the division of labor from labor's result). Something that speaks to everyday working people directly. Something that promises to dramatically change the system to something completely anti-authoritarian. Something that is truly revolutionary.

These promises, though prone to compromise when they tangle with reality like any political aspiration must, once rang true within the libertarian movement as it was originally conceptualized. The classical socialists who coined and proudly donned the label all wanted some version of a worker-controlled market that would tap into functions such as mutual benefit, free trade, and true voluntary exchange of one's labor for some form of direct, self-sustaining benefit. Bakunin believed in the power of the individual but didn't do so at the expense of recognizing the equal importance of community.[58] Proudhon was the one who postulated the definition of anarchy as "order without power," which itself dictated the insignia of anarchism as the self-contained and self-sustaining "A."[59] Déjacque, a fierce believer in true equality for all, urged his fellow socialists to turn a skeptical eye to *all* forms of hierarchy, and not just those found in government or private economic enterprises.[60] Pyotr Kropotkin, a scientist and the founder of the anarcho-communism school of socialist thought, wrote extensively about the biological basis for mutual benefit and communal aid being something innately present and even desirable within humans for the purpose of survival and propagation of our species.[61] All of these ideas broadly promote the two key notions that humanity can survive without an overbearing government and that the hierarchical structures of the existing social order would collapse without said government colluding with the manufacturing class (or simply "capitalists," in socialist terminology).

It does not escape the author that all anarchists are not created equal and that those listed previously belonged to different sub-movements of socialism. Indeed, it has long been debated whether or not more individualist anarchists like Proudhon and more collectivist anarchists like Kropotkin ever really found enough common ground to reach complete solidarity across the board on the more nuanced issues. This book is, decidedly, not a place where that debate is going to be continued for the simple fact that socialism and anarchism as a whole did stand in solidarity on the two aforementioned key notions of State and hierarchical socioeconomic structures as equally prominent threats to true worker autonomy. For our purposes in this volume of tracing the distortion and usurping of their broadly agreed-upon views, we need only acknowledge the fact that said actions against those views were done by the opposing liberal voices acting on behalf of elitist interests. The claims that hierarchy and wealth division must happen naturally have always been hollow—the initial opposing voices to these claims, the first libertarians, were simply obfuscated by the powerful.

In other words, the largely vertical institutions that presently saturate the marketplace are, in the eyes of the original anarchists and libertarians, artificially propped up through State-corporate cooperation. In the eyes of present-day vulgar libertarians and self-described "anarcho-capitalists," these structures are organic and would remain in place even with the abolition of government collusion with corporations (an end said groups still claim to support). As we have uncovered in the previous section of this chapter, however, the evidence suggests that such structures are in fact not organic, and that they were instead engineered by a powerful upper class that wanted to maintain its exclusive access to resources and products while the laborers remained artificially partitioned from the same luxury. Without this process, observed by Marx as primitive accumulation, the vertical corporate structures of today might not be nearly as numerous. Yet, the narrative of present-day right-libertarians holds steadfast to the notion that such structures are legitimate and necessary for a thriving economy—just like how the classical liberal economists of the 1830s spoke in favor of wealth accumulation's organic veritableness. Why does this insistence of the legitimacy of a status quo that has been historically demonstrated to be illegitimate prevail? And in prominent wings of a political movement like modern libertarianism, no less? The movement that at its outset held the exact opposite position?

The answers to this question can begin to be uncovered when we take a look at some key shifts in the political conversation and general public perception of what it meant to be a "revolutionary" that occurred in the twentieth century. Some of these changes have already been highlighted, including aforementioned liberal takeovers in working-class-pandering economic policy spaces across Europe and America, the collapse of publicly visible so-called socialist governments such as the Soviet Union, as well as general anti-communist propaganda doled out by the US government toward its own citizens to coincide with the aforementioned foreign regime's implosion. Coinciding with those happenings and carrying the anti-revolutionary sentiment well into the 1980s in the West was, of course, the neoliberal economic campaigns detailed in the previous chapter aimed at propagandizing the general public into believing that the only alternatives to the status quo have been tried and failed, and therefore, the only system we can possibly have is the one we currently inhabit.[62] All of these factors certainly played a part in pushing back the working-class thirst for true revolutionary change, whether it be out of fear of communist State tyranny or simply belief that capitalism was the empirically proven superior system, and yet even all of this was not quite enough to fully stamp out the seemingly innate quality of working people to intuitively identify their place on the socioeconomic totem pole as one of artificially limited perspicacity.

In short, everyday people know when something is amiss. While the completely destitute and people of color tend to historically be the people who realize this much sooner, the limits of late capitalism are finally beginning to catch up to what has been perceived for decades as "middle class" (arguably a mythic concept in itself, as Chapter 10 will explain), predominantly white people with no reason to fear economic hardships. This is the case today, just as it was the case during the years leading up to and during the Great Depression. FDR's New Deal policies led to a calming of the latter storm, but going into the mid-twentieth century, these more compassionate public welfare initiatives were beginning to become more visible to the highest earners of the day.

Indeed, between the years 1950 and 1980 in the United States, the marginal tax rates on highest income earners ranged anywhere between 70 percent and 90 percent.[63] But from 1950 to 1960, the marginal tax rates were the highest, and rising—from a little under 80 percent to nearly a full 90 percent on the top income bracket, Bracket V, which constituted the very richest people in the country.[64] This entire stretch of time from 1950 to 1980 at large, even with the disillusionment with Keynesianism in the 1970s highlighted in the previous chapter taken into account, is often hailed as being one of the most economically prosperous periods in the country's history.[65] Vulgar libertarians and conservatives today will certainly admit that much (they aren't *complete* historical revisionists), but a main argument given from those camps as to why this occurred is that, despite the higher taxes on the richest American citizens, federal government spending on the whole dropped significantly after the war, and therefore the tax money that was being used was free to go toward more noble things— initiatives such as medical services prior to Medicare and Medicaid.[66] This is a point that doesn't necessarily bode as well for the laissez-faire promulgators as they perhaps think, seeing as how this scenario is one that many on the political left in America surely would prefer over the present unaffordable reality. While things certainly are different now from how they were then economically speaking, the fact of the matter is that if the major differences amounted to *how* the tax money was utilized rather than the amount that was spent, it seems feasible that a similar initiative to spend the money in a similar fashion could be recreated even today. If one wishes to combat that approach, one must devise an alternative that is compassionate and accessible to all on equal grounds.

The reality is that during this aforementioned stretch of time, the United States managed to utilize the extra money, taken at *marginal* rates (e.g., only starting above the ten-millionth dollar earned in a given year)[67] from the highest earners, in ways that benefited everyone of *all* economic brackets far more efficiently and directly than the current hands-off economic system does. During this time, the United States had one of the most prosperous periods for working-class people in history—everyday people could afford to buy homes, grow their families, have more free time for recreation, and live much closer to (albeit of course still not fully embodying) the promise of directly benefiting from the fruits of their own labor. We put men on the moon, cleaned up our air, solidified our place as a manufacturing giant, and expanded businesses domestically so that even more long-term (i.e., not just shovel-ready) job opportunities opened up for working-class people. It was still capitalism, but it was a capitalism with more checks and balances on the powerful than we currently have today, and a capitalism that cared more about sustainability for all participants than just for the elite class exclusively. In other words, it was a system dangerously close to bringing about the same kind of worker autonomy the classical liberal economists and the manufacturing class of the 1830s pushed a narrative to discourage. After all, with more prosperity to go around to everyone, in every earning bracket, there is more chance that workers themselves will have more free time, more savings, and more opportunities to stop, think, and reconsider how well their present work conditions are truly treating them. Just like in the days of the pre-amendment Poor Laws in 1800s England, working people in 1950s–1980s America were poised to have access to something very empowering: the leverage to bargain and demand.

How does one in a position of power, therefore, put a stop to this when everything else has failed to completely stamp out the revolutionary spirit within everyday people? Yes, the fall of the Soviet Union (and subsequent authoritarian, faux-socialism modeling similar to the Soviets' appearing in other places such as Mao's China and Cuba) helped sway people's opinions away from socialism in the West, as did the propaganda designed to exploit that fear and perpetuate distrust of any alternative economic offerings.[68] But once all of that has been stretched as far as it can go, and the populous *still* hasn't quite let go of socialism, what then can head off those proto-revolutionary voices that remain?

The answer might be so simple it could be seen as blatantly obvious, and yet huge pockets of politicos on the right have apparently gone decades oblivious to it: turn a would-be revolution into a counter-revolution. This is an old tactic, yet a very effective one, if history is any indicator. It is what the Nazis did leading into the Second World War when they appealed to their own working-class fellows by calling themselves "national socialists" (and thereby hijacking the rhetoric of the cause of the working class in order to veer potential revolutionaries into support of the nationalist cause).[69] It is what the rise of fascism in Italy was aided by when entrepreneurial celebration was injected into the holes left by past failed attempts at working-class representation.[70] It is what the Bolsheviks did when they too claimed to hold the mantle of true working-class unrest before ultimately shifting their movement into a dictatorship.[71] It is what Mao's China, Chavez's Venezuela, and Castro's Cuba also unloaded upon their respective populist masses to gain *their* leaders' holds on power.[72] It is even what has occurred in the United States—according to Bernard E. Harcourt, author of *The Counterrevolution: How Our Government Went to War Against Its Own Citizens*, counter-revolution occurs when a small group of propagandists takes aim at another small group of actual revolutionaries, while the vast majority of people in-between, ignorant and docile, are the intended target of the propaganda as a means of swaying majority opinion.[73] Suffice it to say, when false consciousness is evident in these sorts of spaces, conscious counter-revolution efforts are a fair bet to have played some part in it.

While counter-revolution has been found in evidence throughout history, as exemplified earlier, it should be noted that the phenomenon we are seeing at present in the late capitalism-defined West (and, even more specifically, in the United States) is something slightly more surreptitious. Instead of the obvious propaganda tactics of old simply being repackaged by conscious bad actors, there seems to be a growing number of activists, pundits, and intellectuals in populist right circles who earnestly fight for their counterintuitive causes completely devoid of deliberate dishonesty.[74] Instead, all of the economic, historical, and cultural circumstances laid out thus far in this book seem to have set the stage for a new generation of honest activists who genuinely see themselves as revolutionaries fighting against perceived evils in such monolithic boogeymen as "the State," "immigration," "cultural erosion," and others. Even something as seemingly straightforward as the aforementioned Southern Strategy of Goldwater, Nixon, and co.[75] has its own populist interpretation dubbed the "Suburban Strategy" in which an alternative, bottom-up motivation is said by some historians to have taken more influence in the more economically charged zeitgeist shifts in the post–civil rights movement South than the top-down racialized propaganda that also clearly played a part.[76] The claim in this case isn't that said propaganda wasn't present, but that it was simply playing a part in further bolstering an already-existing organic anti-political pushback to perceived forced socioeconomic limitations (such as de facto segregation, misapplied affirmative action measures leading to faux-diversity quotas in workplaces and on school campuses, and other such ubiquitous conservative grievances that seem to have sprung up naturally amidst working-class frustrations related to increasing lack of access to work).[77]

These pseudo-revolutionaries are revolutionaries of privilege—not always of economic privilege (although they do end up fighting on behalf of those who do possess such privilege), but of philosophical and cultural privilege within intersectional social spaces, as was touched upon already in Chapter 3. In the face of very real financial strain and less returns for labor, the American Dream is found to be empty. This is already anxiety-inducing in everyday life for most people living beneath a certain economic bracket, but in the face of such uncertainty of one's own financial future, a person belonging to an historically privileged demographic can at least find solace in the knowledge that he has everything figured out on a cultural level.

In the mind of the white, socially anxious, and blue-collar laborer, believing that you have a complete handle on the sociocultural rhythm of your own society (a society that has historically gone according to the whims of those who look like you) is emotionally tantamount to being ensured that up will still be up tomorrow, and that two plus two will still equal four. Even if your entire economic future hangs in the balance, at least you can feel assured in believing that you are still smart and capable enough to ensure some level of personal success. At least not *everything* is falling apart—some consistency can still be found for refuge. This not only plays into the systemically privilege-led nature of the West's governmental and economic functionality; it also makes turning a blind eye to true injustice and inequality in other demographics that much easier. If oppressed people speaking out against the system itself can simply be recast as entitled little snowflakes, then a person wholly invested in worshipping said system as if it is perfect and untouchable can continue to do so—as long as the system continues to not affect the person doing the worshipping.

At certain points in working-class history, that very eventuality has cropped up, as we have seen. When this happens, additional steps must be taken by propagandists in order to scoop up the remaining dissenters to the system who previously might not have been forced to see the reality of class divide in their own personal existences. But the uniqueness of the present-day right-wing populism this book is occupied in understanding comes from the fact that most of its adherents, even those in the positions that would historically poise them to be deliberate propagandists, seem to be true believers. In this case, the counter-revolution insurgencies outlined earlier by Harcourt seem to be unconscious and put forth by people who have grown to completely believe in the cause and claims of their own pseudo-revolutionary movements.[78] This reality is obvious to those who are active everyday participants in said movements, namely modern Americanized libertarianism and the less extreme Alt-Right counterparts dubbed the "alt-light."[79] Yet despite this earnestness from within, many opposing voices on the liberal and so-called SJW left continue to frame every instance of anti-political populism gone organically awry as every bit as consciously conspiratorial as the aforementioned counter-revolution insurgencies of old.[80] This does not square with the lived-in realities of many right-libertarians and red-pilled conservatives, and it was one of the reasons why I kept the label of "libertarian" for myself for so long; I could not quite reconcile the realities of what I observed in the real world with the sometimes-conspiratorial rhetoric coming from many liberal voices.

Yes, there is wealth inequality; no, the boogeyman-of-the-week CEO is not always an evil racist mastermind pulling the strings to intentionally harm people. Having one's own self-interest upheld is a common desire in all classes within this neoliberalized construct, as we have seen, and it just so happens that being a CEO of a major corporation tends to align one's self-interest with that of the capitalistic status quo. Grasping this, as well as trusting that most people in mainstream center-right political spaces fell into acceptance of Alt-Right rhetoric from a place of earnest ignorance, is key in better understanding the how and why behind the spread and normalization of nationalism in these arenas. The counter-revolutionary influence in this present state of affairs was indeed at play, but the insurgency for this particular strain of thought influence had already taken place decades before, leaving most present-day adherents to trust the sincerity of the narrative they are now fed.

Enter Murray Rothbard, who in the early to mid-twentieth century played a key role, perhaps unwittingly, in said insurgency. The Austrian School of economics, made popular by such academic giants as Ludwig von Mises and F. A. Hayek, had long been promoting a view of economies and markets that held up capitalism as an organic truism rather than an artificial construction by the time Rothbard, initially something of a left-market anarchist before forging alliances with the right wing for claimed strategic reasons, himself promoted the Austrian School as an alternative to more restrained Keynesian models.[81] While we have already demonstrated good reasons, both historical and economic, to doubt the claim that capitalism is naturally occurring, it is important to note that it was a very mainstream idea that had caught on in every somewhat popular avenue of economic thought throughout the West by this point, largely thanks to said Austrian School economists. Historian Clarence B. Carson observed upon inspecting the new use of the word "capitalism" on the right that it "does not have a commonly accepted meaning, proponents of it to the contrary notwithstanding. As matters stand, it cannot be used with precision in discourse. And it is loaded with connotations which make it value-laden."[82]

This reality was not going to stand in the way of the Austrians, however. They went ahead and misused the term despite the lack of historical precedent, which confounded Carson and his fellow economic historians. Going further, he stated that "indeed, it is most difficult for those who use it from whatever side not to use it simply as an 'angel' or 'devil' word, i.e., to signify something approved or disapproved. Meanwhile, what that something is goes largely unspecified because it is hidden beneath a blunderbuss word."[83] Keynesian economic policies, then, while mischaracterized as socialist by the true believers in complete hands-off economies, were nevertheless just as pro-capitalism as the promulgations of any other mainstream school of economic thought. The main distinguishing characteristic about Austrian School economics, however, is that it attempts to promote a narrative approach to understanding human action within economies in lieu of being tethered exclusively to raw data gathering and statistical analysis. This approach is referred to as "praxeology."[84] It is largely considered a heterodox approach at analyzing human and market behavior considering its critics' claims that it holds anti-empiricist sentiments, and the Austrian School has indeed made claims often considered difficult, if not impossible, to verify as a result (and even certain Austrian School economists themselves have previously admitted this).[85]

So, why even keep such an approach to economics alive if it offers no empirical certitude? Well, because the claims that the most popularized form of praxeology makes, such as that human beings are rational actors operating within a naturally occurring free market that stands to liberate them (provided it be allowed to operate unconstrained), validate the same kind of liberal apologetics for unrestricted capitalism that the classical economists in the 1830s were peddling. Except neoliberalism, the modern resurgence of these ideas, stands to appear all the more unshakeable if academics and self-described scientists can promote the entire system itself as reverent to rational human action (regardless of how little proof might actually exist for such a claim).

This is not to say that Austrian economics is itself a pseudoscience. There are aspects to said field that stand to have utility in the modern socioeconomic conversation, including its tendency to be critical of other economic schools of thought for bringing insufficient and out-of-context sociological observations to bear on their raw data gatherings. In this sense, the other schools of economic thought are also aiming to understand human behavior in much the same way praxeology is. There are even some strides being made in left-anarchist circles to perform a kind of détournement upon the field by holding onto and synthesizing its most useful elements.[86] But many of the Austrian School's most empirically barren claims are still often presented as scientific in nature despite the lack of empirical data behind said claims that would normally be required by any truly scientific standard. This veneer of unshakeable certainty, perpetuated into the remainder of the twentieth century by Rothbard, went a long way toward giving many capitalistic ideas an unearned sense of reverence and self-assuredness that curtailed any potential criticisms that might have been taken more seriously had Rothbardian praxeology's shortcomings been more publicly laid bare.

It is important to note here that praxeology, despite its bad rap among modern critics of capitalism, predates both Austrian economics and capitalism itself. Its first principles were actually discovered by the Greek philosophers, who in turn utilized it as a foundation for eudaimonism, the Aristotelian philosophy that posits correct human action as that which leads to well-being, and which often occurs through practicing virtues found in everyday life and practical wisdom.[87] In other words, praxeology is not, in its truest form, a replacement for scientific analysis of human behavior but is rather, at its best and when properly applied, a companion to it, serving as a means of delineating how human beings within localized cultural contexts choose to arrive at decisions, and how those decisions are often rationalized as being for the good. This does not mean said actions always *are* for the good, nor does it mean that praxeological analysis of human action should singlehandedly determine whether or not a given socioeconomic system is actually conducive to well-being in an empirically demonstrable sense.

It should be then put forth that the earliest Austrian School interpretation of praxeology, which Rothbard promulgated, was arguably not entirely in line with praxeology's actual historical application and would have likely benefited from further refinement in order to parse out the distinctions between contextual human behavior and empirically demonstrable human nature in economic analysis. Alas, that was not a step Rothbard and his contemporaries seemed to take, and as he continued to veer further politically right, praxeology as a claimed axiom of human rationality prevailed, playing its own role in the aforementioned counter-revolutionary shift toward reframing capitalism as a free market and worker decisions in said market as natural and beneficial. This shift was arguably necessary for putting neoliberal ideas convincingly into the minds of working-class people who would otherwise never swallow the pill that workplace hierarchy and limiting top-down division of labor were somehow *pro*-worker. After all, if one can present the idea that capitalism is organic, pro-worker, and empirically justified in its existence, then it becomes much more difficult to be antagonistic toward it. And indeed, in his work *Praxeology: The Methodology of Austrian Economics*, Rothbard depicts praxeology as an application of deductive reasoning that uses "unquestionable" axioms as its base.[88]

One such axiom that is apparently so self-evident it need not be questioned is the "fundamental axiom of action," which states that "individual human beings act."[89] This is true enough on the surface, but is it really so clear that mere action is exclusive to human beings? Is it not also true that machines also act? What about other animals that are not humans? To be fair, this is a point of contention that Rothbard attempts to give credence to when he clarifies that he means "human beings take conscious action toward chosen goals," but all this really does is multiply one vague assertion into two vague assertions.[90] Certainly, action can be conscious, but that still doesn't make conscious action exclusive to human beings, and the whole "individual human beings" part of his claim (presumably as opposed to collectives) has already been demonstrated by the likes of Bakunin, Geertz, and so on back in Chapter 3 to be deficient of proper understanding of how the context of social interaction dictates much of what individuals ultimately do and why.[91] A leftist student of praxeology, the previously cited Dr. Roderick Long, has likewise argued that it behooves free people to see knowledge as a collective, collaborative project, demonstrating that one does not have to present hard individualism in the way Rothbard ultimately came to do in order to successfully take cues from praxeology as a logical insight.[92]

And what of the second part of Rothbard's attempted clarification? "Conscious action toward chosen goals" reads as potentially oxymoronic, since choice itself already implies conscious action.[93] But perhaps Rothbard did see a distinction between conscious action and choice, thereby rendering "goals" as something of a product of the two.[94] The problem is that we cannot know for sure because Rothbard's other work has at times seemed to contradict itself depending on the topic at hand in regards to human action and individuality, and his writings on praxeology do not clearly express anything more about a potential distinction between choosing and acting—the supposedly rock-solid logic of this observation, as phrased by Rothbard, seems to rely much more on *verbal* analysis rather than proper formal analysis in order to make its point. But if that is the case, then "individual human beings act" is not an axiom.[95] Or at the very least, we cannot demonstrate it ubiquitously as being one. Too many remaining points in need of clarification keep it from being as self-evident as Rothbard claims that it is. This largely comes from the fact that Rothbard's version of praxeology is framing initial observation of *presumed* natural behavior as evidence in and of itself—a full-fledged theory rather than a hypothesis. The observation has not yet been tested against models or predictions that can validate it in more controlled environs.

But scholarship from the likes of more left-market anarchist supporters of praxeological analysis, such as the aforementioned Dr. Long, suggests that this approach is not necessary to the true foundational utility of praxeology itself. One need not treat praxeology as a science (or its equivalent) but rather as a logical analysis of aspects of human behavior that can be grasped *a priori*—the conceptual implications of things such as choice, preference, and the relationship between means and ends.[96] If one is going to claim that human beings are rational actors, and therefore the results one sees when people make choices in the present economy are fair and the circumstances natural, one needs to test such a claim devoid of the specific context these actions already occur in and instead look at human behavior in spaces and scenarios outside of the socioeconomic influence the upfront claims of pro-capitalist scholars is trying to validate. Anything short of this approach can simply be chalked up to confirmation that these behaviors occur organically from inside said spaces—not that they are innately evident in human nature.

Thus, Rothbard and Mises's interpretation of praxeology's biggest selling point to the pro-capitalist narrative is not so much what it actually does in reality, but what it posits to account for. To that point, it should be made clear that the biggest appeal to the so-called scientific and empirical crowd today of laissez-faire economics is that out of the many times praxeology itself has been suggested as a science, it is suggested as such for the purpose of filling in perceived gaps in our understanding of human interaction in economies. One of Austrian economics' biggest aforementioned strengths has unfortunately also contributed to, in this author's view, one of its biggest weaknesses in typical praxeology: because it doubts the accuracy of the methods of the more socially concerned schools of economic thought elsewhere, it aims to provide its own answers to these perceived gaps regarding voluntary human action. Rothbardian praxeology claims that involuntary action is simply physiology—a hard science. By contrast, voluntary action, the thing praxeology claims to explain, is everything outside of hard science's limits for delineating human behavior. But this gap is already filled in the sense that there are other social science fields working on the question of what factors into the influencing of human choices. Yes, it may be true that other economic schools sometimes utilize these adjacent fields much too liberally at times to answer more strictly economic questions. But this does not mean that an inadequately demonstrated substitute for these already-existing fields is the answer. It simply suggests that a more ontological integration of the relevant fields for specific complex riddles of human behavior may be needed—an approach that anthropologists have already been utilizing themselves to great effect.[97] Economics does not always need to be the sole academic field leading the charge on answering questions about human action—sometimes, it is okay and even recommended that other qualified fields bring their own expertise to bear on such questions.

Nevertheless, the faux-empiricism needed to make Rothbard's brand of human liberation convincing has had great influence despite it being shown to be found wanting, and we must keep in mind that it played a huge role in convincing everyday people of the validity of neoliberalism's claimed axiomatic nature. But this wasn't the only factor in persuading more and more working-class people into supporting neoliberal policy. Perhaps the even more important step Rothbard took in pulling off this funneling of would-be revolutionaries into full-blown support for the capitalistic status quo was his decision to consciously hijack the terms "libertarian" and "anarchist" from the socialists who coined them.[98] By doing so, he effectively relabeled capitalism, the man-made construct designed to perpetuate worker exploitation and unjust class divides, as an ideal free market that the working class may utilize to reach the sort of hierarchy-free liberation that the likes of Proudhan and Déjacque advocated for at libertarianism's inception. This might sound contradictory, considering what we have explored thus far regarding capitalism's hierarchical design, but the sentiment working-class people of all demographics share regarding a feeling of limitation and curtailed personal opportunity can be easily diverted by red herrings, it seems. It came to pass that the very system designed to keep working-class people stifled was recast as their liberation. Rothbard was a conscious actor in this misrepresentation.

How do we know this? Because Rothbard himself admitted to co-opting the names and terminology from the actual libertarians and anarchists (and even celebrated it) in his own words:

> One gratifying aspect of our rise to some prominence is that, for the first time in my memory, we, "our side," had captured a crucial word from the enemy. . . . "Libertarians" . . . had long been simply a polite word for left-wing anarchists, that is for anti-private property anarchists, either of the communist or syndicalist variety. But now we had taken it over, and more properly from the view of etymology; since we were proponents of individual liberty and therefore of the individual's right to his property.[99]

Thus, we see the tradition of misrepresenting what the original libertarians (i.e., socialists and left-anarchists) meant by "property," started by the likes of Bastiat, carried on into the twentieth century. If "property" can encompass both the means of production *and* personal belongings, as Rothbard and his ilk seemed to have misunderstood it to do, then, of course, it would be noble to push back against any intellectual initiative that calls for the abolishment of such a sloppy and broad understanding of what property is. Unfortunately for Rothbard and the other post-1830s classical liberals, that is not what the original libertarians, socialists, and anarchists meant by the term.

It is also important to note that Rothbard sees real libertarianism as "the enemy," and that he admits who the actual libertarians were "long" before he chose to use the label for his own ends (nearly a hundred years prior to this right-wing laissez-faire appropriation).[100] Whether or not Rothbard's assertion about property meaning something it doesn't is ignorance or a conscious strategy to reach the right is not clear, here. But what *is* clear is Rothbard's intention on wrangling away the term "libertarian" from actual libertarians in order to frame capitalists as the true "proponents of individual liberty," which he tethers exclusively to the concept of owning property.[101] He might have truly believed that this *should* be the case, but he also knew that it was not the reality. Utilizing the term "libertarian" for his own ends was therefore a deliberate distortion.

Another seemingly intentional mislead for the working class was Rothbard's decision to recast anarchism, as well. Though the actual anarchists are (and always have been) socialists, the term "left-wing anarchists," in Rothbard's words, implies that right-wing anarchism is an equally valid movement—it wasn't at any point in history up to the point that Rothbard decided to claim otherwise.[102] As we laid out earlier in this very chapter, anarchism was a socialist movement from the very beginning, and took umbrage with capitalism and the artificial limitations it put on worker mobility and freedom. Indeed, Rothbard himself admitted in an unpublished bit of writing that "we are not anarchists, and that those who call us anarchists are not on firm etymological ground, *and are being completely unhistorical*" (emphasis mine).[103] Despite acknowledging this truth, Rothbard would ultimately come to call his band of capitalist propagandists and private property apologists "anarcho-capitalists," a knowingly oxymoronic perversion of what anarchism has always historically stood for: freedom and liberty for all, and not exclusively for the manufacturing class and rigged markets (like capitalism) that benefit said class.

There is a reason why Rothbard was the first major Austrian economist to call himself an anarchist: the notion of being both things simultaneously *is* oxymoronic. Anarchism at its roots is philosophically incompatible with capitalism. Anarchism, despite its capitalist usurpers' claims to the contrary, is about skepticism toward *all* forms of unjust hierarchy, not just of the federal government. Its earliest proponents were very clear about this, its insignia was visually inspired by this, and the anarchists around today on the political left still maintain this nondiscriminatory ire toward any construct that could oppress autonomous people. To say anarchism is only against the government is to disregard everything fundamental about it. Therefore, the only conclusion we can come to while remaining intellectually honest is that the synthesis of anarchist thought and capitalism worship is, and always was, a disingenuous farce.

In order to frame capitalism as a system designed to help rather than restrict working-class people, one needs to completely take leave of history. Rothbard, it seems, knew this, considering his own acknowledgement of the "unhistorical" nature of the anarchist-capitalist conversation.[104] But to the public, he chose to use the label of anarchist, anyway. His published works served as prescriptions for capitalist apologists who wished to bring anarchism and libertarianism into conservative intellectual spaces.

To what end? This is where the aforementioned remaining would-be revolutionary types come in. After the failure of the Soviet Union and the subsequent growth of all the anti-socialist propaganda, arguably most everyday people in the West, even if they had issues with their present economic situations, let go of any ideas of libertarian revolution against the capitalist system. The alternative, it was perceived, was too risky and could lead to another Soviet Union. Thus, most people left behind their hopes for true revolution and began to accept more pacifying policy shifts that would make daily existence within the machine more incrementally bearable (more social programs and welfare initiatives from both major parties within an otherwise unmoving capitalistic structure—our illusory swinging pendulum effect from the previous chapter). But there remained a handful of socialist types who still wanted a truly revolutionary cause to fight in, hence the existence of the aforementioned *Libertarian League* and the small-but-passionate initiatives to get socialist representation in local government bodies. What to do with them? Well, tell them they are fighting for a revolution while funneling them back into support of the status quo, of course. The result ultimately manifests as a mass delusion in which oppressed people unknowingly bolster and celebrate their oppressors in the name of reason—false consciousness.

Recasting libertarianism and anarchism, originally socialist initiatives, as pro-capitalism (and, furthermore, recasting capitalism itself as a "free market") serves this purpose perfectly. If the revolutionary spirit cannot be fully extinguished, then manipulate the revolutionaries into becoming unwitting supporters of the very system that has enslaved them in the first place. While most present-day libertarians and anarcho-capitalists seem genuine in their beliefs, it is harder to know for certain how deliberate Rothbard's misrepresentations were. He may have genuinely believed the new definitions of libertarianism and anarchism to be noble postulations for what he honestly believed were necessary political alliances, but there nevertheless seems to be an intentional decision to recast these terms as a means of broadening the banner of libertarianism and veering it rightward—aside from the intentions of Rothbard, whose writings during his left-anarchist years remain arguably some of the most brilliant political philosophy ever put to paper, the end result was somewhat of a foil to true working-class solidarity against the elite classes based on an historically literate grasp of economic history.

Part of this foiling process resulted from this newly forged libertarian–conservative alliance rhetorically building up the American Dream as an attainable reality within the system as it already exists. Another part of it was this same crowd making the working-class believe that a self-centered system like capitalism was designed to be on its side from the start. Therefore, the more culturally privileged among working-class people—white males with historically precedented proclivity for public recognition and higher social capital, for instance—were by happenstance the most likely demographic to be successfully fooled by such propaganda. If one's daily existence is not bombarded with the same kind of systemic discrimination as the daily existence of a person of color, for example, it might be more believable to said person that the present socioeconomic system is truly nondiscriminatory. In this author's estimation, the fact that the majority of the right-wing anti-political populists who would ultimately normalize and overlap with the Alt-Right fall into the white male demographic *is* purely happenstance. Because the neoliberal empty promise of the American Dream is most appealing to those who have not seen as much evidence of its *systemic* futility firsthand, so too would those same experientially deprived people more frequently buy into the manufactured antagonists offered by fascist and nationalist propaganda to populate the narrative gaps that neoliberalism is unable to fill. Everyday working-class people are suffering. White working-class people suffer in a daily existence that deprives them of the full context regarding minority mistreatment. Therefore, when propaganda like the American Dream was blended with historically anarchistic class commentary and delivered to the masses by the likes of Rothbard, it was the white working-class people who bought into such propaganda far more easily.

This does not indicate a conscious racist effort on behalf of the Rothbards of the world, nor does it intend to unjustifiably paint Rothbard as wholly detrimental to libertarianism (on the contrary, as cited earlier, in his left-anarchist years Rothbard's was some of the most poignant commentary to be found on topics such as means of production, homesteading, and corporatist serfdom). These facts simply indicate a systemic reality that dictated which demographics of working-class people were predisposed to believe the American Dream the longest. It just so happens that said people, many of which were Rothbardians by happenstance, belonged to the same demographic that nationalistic and fascistic ideology infiltrates in America. When neoliberal economics fails to explain why the American Dream has not come through for white workers in particular, these more sinister ideological movements are there to potentially pick up the slack. The coordinated effort on the neoliberal side of things is not to fan the flames of racism or xenophobia, but to protect the exclusive access to capital the manufacturing class has granted itself through the distortion of liberal ideas since the 1830s. The Alt-Right's current hold on many anti-political neoliberal adherents on the right is simply a dark coincidence, though its ability to successfully infiltrate mainstream conservative populist spaces such as post-Rothbard libertarianism and anarcho-capitalism is testament to just how much neoliberalism has failed at providing adequate solutions to an ever-expanding working-class problem: poverty despite hard work and belief in oneself.

It is also the case that Rothbard's ultimate alliance with the right came after what seemed like an organic separation on his part from what became known as the New Left, not unlike what happened when F. A. Hayek drifted from the left out of dislike for what he saw as more tribal, alienating tactics.[105] Even after his shift to the right was already underway, Rothbard still retained for many years some of his leftist roots, in one case actually making one of the most brilliant nuanced critiques of his fellow right-libertarians' reductionist distinction between government and privatization by stating that "what we libertarians object to . . . is not government per se but crime, what we object to is unjust or criminal property titles; what we are for is not 'private' property per se but just, innocent, non-criminal private property. It is justice vs. injustice, innocence vs. criminality that must be our major libertarian focus."[106]

In this way, Rothbard's shift to the right can be seen as sincere, but his conscious decision to bring libertarianism rightward with him still arguably led to much needless confusion of fundamentally incompatible ideas. His new flavor of right-libertarianism was solidified over the years and easily legitimized due to his personal political evolution occurring amidst his visibility and impact on libertarian thought as a whole. It should also be pointed out that Rothbard's fellow left-anarchist thinker, Karl Hess, remained largely on the left after Rothbard began to shift, later becoming even more radicalized into the 1970s and writing that he had "turn[ed] from the religion of capitalism" and that he "resist[s] the capitalist nation-state."[107] Not all of Rothbard's contemporaries, it would seem, were as quick to adopt capitalistic vernacular and buddy up with the right as was Rothbard himself.

So, regardless of one's own thoughts on Rothbard, good or bad, his part to play in libertarianism's co-opting from socialist thought must be recognized as undeniably significant. The tactics he used to ingratiate revolutionary types were somewhat successful—but typically only in those demographics who would stand to keep benefiting from the existing status quo. For white working-class people, that prospect was at least still feasible, while for working-class minority groups the Dream had long died.

Yet, even the white working class is now starting to hit the barriers of late capitalism and its ever-shrinking promises of financial stability for everyday people (for details on just how dire the financial situation currently is for working-class America, see Chapter 8). The current youth is more statistically prone to take into consideration the plights of those less fortunate than themselves. Therefore, Rothbard's appeal to a certainty on par with scientific empiricism in praxeology is more important than ever for those who wish to keep neoliberalism's influence hanging on into future generations. But there are other key elements at play, as well. One being the appeal to selfishness as an edgy, appealing, and noble mindset, and the other being the initiative to make ignorance of other perspectives a seemingly intellectual venture that can appeal to a growing group of aspiring critical thinkers and skeptics within the neoliberal wheelhouse. The following chapter briefly deals with the former tactic, and the following section of the book will unpack the latter.

While everything this chapter has looked at proves that the term "libertarian" has been repurposed by the right, does this in and of itself prove that modern right-libertarianism still holds within it an underlying socialist spirit? No. But what *is* very clear was the right's outlook that it needed to take socialist, radical rhetoric for itself in order to tap into the already-existing populist unrest present in all corners of the working-class—including those with conservative histories. The argument here is not that modern libertarianism can be fully rescued and brought back to a socialist outlook. The argument is that those who are attracted to libertarian rhetoric of any kind, right or left, already have within *them* a radical sentiment that houses the potential for working-class solidarity. It was that sentiment that modern vulgar libertarianism aimed to seduce in the first place, and it is that same sentiment wherein the possibility for a less fragmented working-class activist future still exists.

Selfishness

Making Noble a Sinister Concept

Knowing now how actual revolutionary anarchist movements in the socialist tradition came to be misrepresented on behalf of right-facing capitalists and their true believers, we are starting to veer into understanding the process by which such misdirection is cemented into the political conversation for the purposes of enduring long past its initial insurgency date.

As has been pointed out many times throughout this work so far, most of the people perpetuating the myth of neoliberalism as liberation (and privileged social frustration as noble populism) truly seem to believe the propaganda, therefore making this faux-revolutionary ideology an *actual* revolutionary ideology in the minds and hearts of its adherents by the time we catch up to them spreading their gospel in present-day America. The false consciousness they display is one induced out of organic means through populist frustration and then diverted in its antagonism away from real solutions thanks to neoliberalism's hegemonic hold. By this point, the process is not conscious. Those who are more culturally and historically privileged but who still belong to the working class themselves are more prone to be blind to the plights of those less fortunate than themselves and to normalize the cultural anxiety around their peers who fear cultural erasure from foreign workers and domestic minorities asking for more legal and fiscal power of their own. Understanding why this is the case has been briefly revisited throughout the book up to now, but a final exploration of the phenomenon will be laid out in Chapter 9.

For now, we take a slight sidestep into the world of enduring self-validation that keeps the initial propaganda of the 1830s liberals, Rothbard and co., and modern neoliberal policy rationale alive and well into the foreseeable future—even within younger demographics of conservatives that fancy themselves to be open-minded critical thinkers.

In order for such a perpetuation to be carried out by said self-fancied intellectuals, certain innate proclivities need to be tapped into and exploited for the purposes of normalizing elements of the status quo that keep feudalist class divides framed as natural occurrences. Austrian economics and neoliberal hegemony, as we have already seen, set the stage for a very convincing backdrop. But if you are a young, thoughtful person attempting to reach intellectual breakthroughs and feel as if you are a rebellious maverick on a revolutionary frontier, then you must have the existing status quo repurposed and sold back to you in an ingratiating package that promises to set you apart from "mere" conservatives—after all, your grandparents were conservatives, and you are a new breed of thinker who will charge into the future and revolutionize political discussion. Or, at least, so you think.

This aforementioned repurposing of old right-wing ideas comes about in different ways, one of which being the very obvious and loud abandonment of religious right rhetoric and the declaration of oneself as a true "skeptic" in the face of religious absence. Prior to this, the sort of extreme conservatism that more obviously had the potential to lead to fascism had religious fundamentalism as one of its key ingredients. In 2006, ten years before the libertarian-to-Alt-Right shift took full hold and helped get Donald Trump's brand of nationalistic populism into the White House, scholars were still observing how coterminous religious fundamentalism and right-wing extremism really were, as observed in the Chris Hedges book *American Fascists: The Christian Right and the War on America*. In those pages, Hedges wrote about how such religious extremism (at the time in full political swing) was legitimized by the following faux syllogism: communism is the enemy of freedom; secular humanism is the new communism; therefore, secular humanism must be destroyed. Hedges, of course, pointed out in his book that this was nothing more than an "effective scare tactic" designed to shift "the objects of fundamentalist hatred" to align with the times.[1] In reality, secular humanism at the time had been incredibly miniscule in its numbers and social influence. Christy Macy and Barbara Parker of the Norman Lear–founded advocacy group People for the American Way wrote at the time that "these humanists rank with militant vegetarians and agrarian anarchists, and were about as well known—until the Religious Right set out to make them famous."[2]

And famous they did become—so much so that a new brand of edgy intellectual rebel emerged from secular humanism to become a sort of cultural rock star in the early 2000s: the New Atheist. Suddenly, questioning religion was sexy and cool, and empiricism and trust in science (or, at least, New Atheism's conception of science) was a sign that a person was intellectually superior to others who did not have as much reverence for or knowledge of such elements. Public figures such as journalist Christopher Hitchens, scientist Richard Dawkins, philosopher Daniel Dennett, and neuroscientist Sam Harris were lauded as the titans of this movement and collectively formed a cult of personality around them. Dubbed the four horsemen of the atheist apocalypse, these men would go on to influence the young and impressionable minds of many of these aforementioned seekers and self-labeled critical thinkers. In many ways, it was a perfect marriage between earnest desire for truth and a more self-conscious desire for a sense of societal belonging and confidence—things many young people today severely lack due to the crushing economic realities they now face.[3]

This climate has proven to be a perfect breeding ground for a new kind of conservative. A conservative that gets to claim superior intellect by simply casting aside his religiosity while still clinging to other socially conservative beliefs, albeit reframed as objective, empirical positions that only the unscientific and unempirical would dare disagree with. This in actuality is not a scientifically literate view of the world and is instead a means of masking confirmation bias for preconceived notions. Scientism, a misunderstanding of "science" as a be-all-end-all declaration of an unshakeable reality, functions itself like a religion in which the adherents to "science" must stick forever to the present narrative rather than remain open to new information that could alter or amend one's present understanding of a given concept.[4] While this is arguably not what the secular humanists or the initial New Atheist scholars at large were pushing for, it is nevertheless the sort of mindset that began to take hold in the minds of many conservative working-class youth who discovered the New Atheist movement.[5] Ironically, it was by shedding the religious fundamentalist branding that this newfangled right-wing ideology got away with masquerading as somehow more rational than the prior proto-fascism described by Hedges. In reality, it functions in much the same way.

By pushing back against religious fundamentalism, these new right-wingers get to claim that they are a new breed of thinkers, with facts on their side, and therefore whatever new declarations they make should be trusted as being grounded in scientific empiricism rather than "primitive" religiosity. Of course, everything else about their brand of right-wing rhetoric is essentially the same in principle as the religious version of it. Except now, the peddlers of the same old proto-fascistic anti-immigrant, anti-LGBT, anti-diversity, anti-feminist, and anti–social justice talking points pose as "woke" intellectuals who get their positions from empirical data rather than empty prejudice. As we have seen with the examples of so-called empiricism of Southern, Molyneux, et al. from the previous section of the book, said empirical data is often not empirical at all and merely feigns to be.[6] Most adherents to new right ideology don't care, however, because their confirmation bias is served regardless. The claims that immigration erodes Western culture or that selfish marketplace hierarchy is organic and beneficial do not actually have to be empirically or scientifically verifiable—they merely need to *appear* to be so.

"Facts don't care about your feelings" has as of late become a mantra among many age groups on the modern right, but it began as a chant from the faux-skeptical youth who hid among secular humanists and New Atheism in an effort to validate old right-wing prejudices by way of redressing them as empirical declarations of fact.[7] It is simply easier to sleep at night if you believe that science can back up your personal demographic's privileged place in the social hierarchy as legitimate and natural instead of artificial. Chapters 5 and 6 have demonstrated the process by which our present economic reality has indeed been constructed artificially, however, and so in order to truly be empirical, one must divorce preconceived notions from whatever research one does on any given topic. The right-wingers who often frame their positions as grounded in unbiased empiricism are in fact clinging to their already-existing beliefs and looking for data to validate them.[8]

This is not science, nor is it objective, and yet, it gets away with posing as both things because it taps into the growing anti-political angst already present in the very demographics of working-class people that prior generations have primed to buy into empty neoliberal promises about the American Dream, as the previous chapter explained. A recent study conducted by the University of Alabama and published by the University of Virginia's Institute for Family Studies confirms that eleven million white Americans think like the Alt-Right on many culturally aligned issues, even if they themselves do not personally identify as being part of the Alt-Right.[9] That figure should frighten anyone who believes that working-class people who lean conservative are just as primed to correctly identify the problems befalling them as other working-class people who are members of non-white and non-male demographics. Again, the cultural inertia caused by living inside a bubble of social and philosophical privilege for generations often gets in the way of reality— the study of intersectional existence within complex and interconnected power structures predicts it (as seen in Chapter 3), and the numbers here prove it.[10]

Noted libertarian journalist Nick Gillespie has also been quoted as admitting that his own movement's wing of revolutionary conservatism has also fallen victim to fascistic thinking. "There is no question," Gillespie stated, "that some elements in the broadly defined libertarian movement articulate policy positions almost indistinguishable from those of the alt-right and Donald Trump."[11] Although he does qualify that despite the initial libertarian label, the people in his movement who turn fascist "are the antithesis of everything that the libertarian project stands for."[12] That is true, philosophically speaking; Chapter 6 of this book has laid out the real intellectual and moral intentions behind the first strains of libertarianism, and these do indeed clash quite heavily with the crypto-fascism many on the right are flirting with today.

But right-libertarianism is a much bigger influence on mainstream conservative thought than it realizes, with celebrated moral psychologist Jonathan Haidt demonstrating in his book *The Righteous Mind* that this form of libertarianism is one of the three major political groups in America today (with the other two being modern conservatism and modern liberalism).[13] Historically speaking, this is largely thanks to the Rothbardian project of finding solidarity between historically libertarian (i.e., genuinely revolutionary) ideals and modern conservatism for the purpose of growing numbers that has already been cited elsewhere in this book.[14]

In her book *Democracy in Chains*, author Nancy MacLean does a good job actually laying out the less-than-principled end result of the corporate right's collusion with radical rhetoric and how it has simply led to the same elitist influence of narrative and policy masquerading successfully as the underdog, citing hard-hitting political figures of the 1950s such as Harry Byrd and T. Coleman Andrews as being poster boys of this new alliance, framing their so-called libertarianism as a radical fight against their recast elites: the socially concerned leftist libertarianism framed by them as "collectivism and slavery," contrasting in a false dichotomy with "capitalism and freedom."[15] This led to the rhetoric surrounding issues such as "states' rights," "liberty," and "libertarianism" becoming synonymous in the general voting public with a specific type of radical conservatism that stood to stand up to perceived authoritarian bullies of the common person—all the while still serving the interests of the corporatists actually holding much of the political power.[16] MacLean refers to this mindset in her book as the "Marxism of the master class," which is in effect the purpose this specific kind of hegemony aims to have: riling up the populists on the right by appealing to the same revolutionary urges that the Marxists and other classical socialists did, while actually aiming to achieve an end result favorable to the masters, not the workers.[17]

While MacLean's book is cutting in its investigation of the modern manifestation of the libertarian right's far-reaching influence and is therefore a recommended read for that reason alone, this author must nevertheless stress that MacLean, like most of her contemporaries, still makes the gross error of assuming that libertarianism is a relatively recent invention and that it has always represented the political right[18]—two assumptions already shown in this book as being as far from the truth as is fathomable. Making this error gives far too much ground to those responsible for that distortion of terms in the first place, and therefore misses some fundamental elements of why right-libertarianism (and radical conservatism at large) is still so successful at ingratiating its target audience. Gillespie and his ilk are arguably just as much part of that ingratiated audience as anyone, and therefore they are quite possibly unaware that their own form of libertarianism is one that has long been foiled by incompatible contradiction a la Hegel's dialectic long ago.[19] Not acknowledging this fact is arguably disingenuous and potentially harmful for the longevity of the larger liberty project (i.e., the one that began with the libertarian socialists and individualist anarchists), which Gillespie and his moral colleagues inside the movement today claim to care so much about.

There is, however, no seemingly conscious effort on behalf of the average white male conservative in the working class to harm or exploit others; rather, the already-existing biases and historical ignorance imbued within said demographic are simply tapped into and given a verifying voice that masquerades as scientific empiricism in order that the people in said demographic are never given a scenario in which they need to challenge their preconceived notions about the culture and society they have always known.[20] The Alt-Right actors know what they are doing, and the initial hijackers of anarchist rhetoric on behalf of the ruling class knew what they were doing; everyday working people, by contrast, are simply trying to survive and make sense of the system that seems to be crumbling around them—all while trudging through grueling forty-hour work weeks that physically exhaust and creatively incapacitate them.[21] They are just as much victims in this grand distortion of terms and ideologies as anyone else. Many of them also happen to belong to a racial and gender demographic that stands to benefit from their existing worldview prevailing, which makes them particularly susceptible to the brand of propaganda that the aforementioned groups put forth. "Useful idiots" may not be the right term to use, since I do not believe ignorance and idiocy to be the same thing. However, usefully ignorant is certainly what this demographic effectively turns out to be when a ruling economic class and a conscious group of fascist propagandists mingle together in said demographic for their own ends—and continue to do so unchallenged because their surface-level proclamations of cultural erosion and white male persecution play into the already-existing cultural panic and economic unrest present in the white working class.[22]

But again, this infiltration of well-meaning (albeit historically ignorant) conservative revolutionary spaces is further legitimized when a veil of empiricism and objectivity is thrown on top of it to validate the already-existing biases. One major bias in conservative spaces, of course, is the belief that capitalism is the most ideal economic system because it benefits from human selfishness. Though Chapter 5 has already addressed the misquote of Adam Smith regarding the invisible hand and its supposed nobility, the claim marches onward that selfishness can somehow lead to the benefit of everyone if capitalism is simply allowed to work its magic. But, *what* magic, exactly? Well, to believe the most ardent true believers of capitalism as a free market, capitalism is able to serve as a mechanism that converts selfish opportunism into altruistic results. The argument goes that since the only way a businessman can make money is through offering a good or service that makes customers happy, said businessman has no choice but to do his best to provide the best product at the fairest price, lest he risk the informed consumer walking out of the store in protest and patronize a fairer competitor.[23] This is, of course, not the reality, as we have laid out by now the fact that capitalism strong-arms competition out of business through stated power by design, but it still amounts to the general economically conservative gallop: selfishness is fine because it is actually, in a roundabout way, altruism. Because "the market," like a stage magician, waves its misdirection of free-market principles (not realities) and wins the day. This is perhaps not the most generous depiction of the ideology, but to present the typical pro-capitalist argument in this way would not be diluting it by very much in actual practice. An adherence to principle over practicality, and a favoring of apologetics for the current system rather than truly radical alternatives for a new one, ensure that selfishness within the marketplace, even in the eyes of the most caring and altruistic right-libertarian or conservative, is at best forgiven and at worst celebrated.

To begin to understand how the now-ubiquitous fetishization of self-centered action found in modern mainstream conservative movements like American libertarianism and the "red-pilled right" (alt-light) came to be embraced by the same faux-empiricists and pseudo-skeptics mentioned earlier, we need to take one final detour into the sinister world of Objectivism, a movement that claims to be a philosophy but more often than not operates more like a rabid cult of personality surrounding one very polarizing intellectual figure: Russian novelist Ayn Rand.

Rand's personal history with the Bolshevik perversion of socialism (a perversion itself predicted by Bakunin in the prior century when he stated how he feared statist takeover of socialist principles) goes a long way toward explaining why she had such disdain for socialism as a whole. Born in Petrograd, Russia (which would become Leningrad and, eventually, St. Petersburg), Rand's entire family was nearly starved to death after the Bolshevik revolution when Lenin confiscated their home and finances.[24] Rand grew up Jewish in a time when being Jewish in Russia was not looked upon very favorably, and her parents were considered to be part of the bourgeoisie class, which (for no direct fault of her own) meant that she herself nearly lost all access to her in-progress education at Petrograd State University.[25] By way of the serf system, a major precipitator of statist communism in Russia, these actions against Rand's family were deemed justified.[26] This treatment was inhumane and beyond doubt damaging to young Rand, and it makes sense that after escaping such conditions that a system calling itself socialism put her in (which she did escape, but not with her family), she would be somewhat triggered and wary at the suggestion that socialist systems hold any good in them at all.

Nevertheless, for someone who devised the label "Objectivist" for herself, Ayn Rand certainly seemed to ironically celebrate remaining within the limited subjective vision of her own biases. There is no better example of this in play than in Rand's own willingness to buy into Soviet and US propaganda about socialism (see Chapter 5) rather than do her due diligence to look objectively at the evidence—a near-century of socialist literature contradicts the statist twisting of so-called socialist values promulgated by the Bolsheviks for their own ends, and yet, due to paranoia and fear, the West allowed its next generation of intellectuals to carry on the tradition of elitist pandering toward the working poor—part of the newest set of propagandizing tools in the elitist liberal wheelhouse was to defame socialism as big government overreach and collusion with the powerful.[27] The ironic reality, however, is that while neoliberalism began to take over the mainstream economic conversation for the next generation, the founders of the Neo-Marxist Frankfurt School, Horkheimer and Adorno, were demonstrating that big government collusion with corporatists was in fact a natural evolution of capitalism into *fascism*, not socialism.[28]

According to Kevin Carson:

> Owners of the corporate economy operate directly through the State, as in feudalism or Asiatic mode, to exploit population at large through entirely political means. Some members of the Frankfurt School saw fascism as an attempt to do just that. According to Horkheimer and Adorno, Neumann, and Pollock, Nazism reflected an evolution in which capitalists increasingly acted through the State. They speculated that such a society might, in future, altogether abandon commodity production and the law of value. At some point, in that scenario, the market would be superseded by state administration, and the capitalists would extract a surplus from labor directly through the State. When that point was reached, the market would have been completely into a state-owned and state-managed economy, and the capitalists would no longer be capitalists. Instead, they would be owners of the state economy by virtue of their control of the State.[29]

This process described earlier by the Frankfurt Schoolers, which is described in a very unfavorable way, evidencing Marxist repulsion at the idea of authoritarian States (yet another direct contradiction to the Randian and broadly conservative narrative of socialism as being pro-big government), explains the process the Soviets went through to achieve their economic control of the Soviet Union. Many socialists and anarchists today describe the Soviet Union and its copycats as being examples of "state capitalism." But Adorno and Horkheimer, and others are right—this is not technically capitalism because it is no longer private ownership of the means of production, per se. It is completely State-owned property instead. Which, according to Trotsky, is more of a "degenerated workers state" than it is a capitalist State.[30] But one thing is for certain across the vast majority of socialist and Marxist literature on the matter: Soviet Union economic planning wasn't socialism.

What socialism actually is in application, especially when taking into account the classical definitions tracing back to the very inception of the idea and then moving into the "American radicals" strand of the movement, according to socialist moral philosopher Dr. Gary Chartier, is a "project of building a society free from the privileges secured by the State," exhibiting "obvious affinities with classical liberal and libertarian thought."[31] Of course, Dr. Chartier refers to the pre-industrial boom version of classical liberalism highlighted in Chapter 5, and to the libertarianism of the classical socialists who first coined the term. This is clear when Dr. Chartier makes it a point to argue that the system he promulgates "unequivocally repudiates the affirmation of corporate power and statist privilege too many classical liberals and libertarians seem inclined to offer."[32]

Suffice it to say that most socialists, including Trotskyists, Marxists, members of the Frankfurt School, mutualists, syndicalists, and other variants of anarchist—past and present—are against the kind of big government tyranny present in the Soviet Union and other Marxist-Leninist empires. But these objective facts were, ironically, rejected by the Objectivists, and Rand embraced capitalism if for no other reason than the simple fact that it was perceived to be the complete opposite of socialism. Again, her personal experience gives context to why she agreed with the Western consensus at the time on what socialism was, but this fact doesn't excuse her own brand of selfishness fetishization that was to become her trademark.

Unlike many of those on the right who argued (and still argue) that capitalism somehow leads to altruistic and generous outcomes for everyone, Rand argued (rightly) that capitalism is selfish by design. In her book *Capitalism: The Unknown Ideal*, she put forth the now nearly ubiquitous argument within conservatism that free-market capitalism *is* the true form of capitalism, but since that version of capitalism is merely an ideal, the version we currently have is still the most moral economic system we can hope to achieve.[33] This is now a very common talking point among conservative intellectuals who attempt to excuse the violent systemic aspects of capitalism. The trade-off for Rand, according to the book, is that while capitalism is indeed self-centered, the benefits one gets from participating in it are individualized in nature, which for Rand implies autonomy, as opposed to collectivism, which implies central planning and loss of identity. Thus, Rand declares in the book that capitalism "is the only system geared to the life of a rational being and the only moral politico-economic system in history" (emphasis hers).[34]

We have already laid out in Chapters 3 and 5 of this work all the various reasons, philosophical, economic, and biological, why it is unfounded to consider individualism and collectives as separate concepts, and why it is much more empirically sound and arguably moral to consider individuals within collectives the greater priority. The evolutionary benefits of group selection, as well, are not easily ignored (though it was in this same decade of Rand's writing that self-interest and extreme individualism was permeating throughout various academic fields, including biology, as was pointed out earlier in the book).[35] Nevertheless, Rand's philosophy of Objectivism held up capitalism as the only moral economic system yet devised by human kind, and since this was a movement that fancied itself, not unlike praxeology, to be somehow more certain than empiricism itself, the sex appeal of it grew and enticed the young minds of aspirational entrepreneurs who also fancied themselves to be intellectuals and philosophers of a new, more hip stripe.

Something of a precursor to the right-wing scientism of the early twenty-first century, Objectivism became a means of adhering to economically liberal, privileged ideology without needing to bring along with it the outdated Christian fundamentalism that, as often happens, was beginning to lose its hold on the youth of that era. Rand stood apart from typical conservative public figures in that she rejected religion, calling it "blind belief; belief unsupported by, or contrary to, the facts of reality and the conclusions of reason."[36] Again, Rand argued for facts, reason, and evidence while simultaneously perpetuating unfounded myths about capitalism and socialism in their barest forms—and without displaying any hint that she was aware of the irony.

The parallels between Objectivism, then, and other forms of pseudo-woke conservatism such as post-Rothbard libertarianism should be obvious by now. Yet, one of the more amusing facts about Ayn Rand is that she hated libertarians in life, lambasting them as "hippies" of the right for claiming that altruism was good and that capitalism was a means of reaching it—she saw this as empty "superficial political action which is bound to fail" (and, to her credit, that much is correct).[37]

This meant that Rand's Objectivism would not be subsumed by right-libertarianism until after her death, at which point various aspects of it were essentially canonized within vulgar libertarian philosophy as unshakeable creeds. The most notable among these is the Non-Aggression Principle (NAP), a concept that is—once again, ironically—incredibly subjective to the degree that it is essentially not useful in any tangible sense of application.[38] Presenting itself as axiomatic, the NAP argues that all one has to do to ensure she doesn't violate the true liberty of her fellow human beings is to simply not "aggress" against them. The problem with this actually being applicable as a self-evident principle should be apparent, but let us nevertheless unpack it for a moment. If person X believes that secondhand smoke is aggression, and person Y is smoking right next to them, then per NAP logic, the NAP has been violated from person X's perspective. But if person Y does not share person X's belief that secondhand smoke qualifies as aggression, then person Y can continue to smoke and remain ideologically consistent with her own subjective understanding of what constitutes aggressive behavior.

The point here is that the NAP cannot apply equitably to every conceivable interaction between two or more equally autonomous people. Far too many variables come into play, not the least of which being the undeniable reality that everyone is not going to share the same opinion on what counts as something as vague as "aggression." Let us graduate this point to the level of ecosystems. Depending on one's opinion on the truth of the adverse effects of climate change, pollution may or may not be considered aggression. A consensus on this is not even close to forthcoming. What about in social justice debates? Can language be violent? If so, does it count as aggression? How do we enforce consistent behavior accordingly? Do we pass more laws? The reality is that the only way something as vague as the NAP could ever be successfully applied is if every single free person on Earth were able to reach a consensus on every single potential act of aggression. In other words, successfully applying the NAP is impossible. In this author's opinion, it is merely a half-hearted attempt to make Objectivism appear somehow less heartless against everyone but oneself than it actually is. But it cannot be denied that its founder saw compassion as a weakness, writing an entire book of essays entitled *The Virtue of Selfishness*,[39] and stating that she also believed "very few" people in society deserved things like compassion, love, and generosity, calling most human beings "weak."[40]

Not only does this declaration contradict the evolutionary evidence laid out earlier in the book about the net benefits of altruistic collectives over selfish collectives, it also gives power to the exclusionary mindsets that take hold and grow within the most toxic forms of culturally ignorant working-class populist unrest. If someone already thinks like this and greatly reveres the likes of Rand as moral and empirical, then graduating into thought spaces adjacent to concepts such as xenophobia and fascism isn't entirely out of the question—especially if this person is already frustrated that the capitalistic American Dream has failed to deliver on its promises and is desperate for an *Other* to pin this failing on.[41]

Also like Rothbardian praxeology, Rand's Objectivism charges the social sciences with being inadequate in their explanations of human behavior and motivation, stating that "in psychology, one may observe the attempt to study human behavior without reference to the fact that man is conscious," and that "in political economy, one may observe the attempt to study and to devise social systems without reference to *man*" (emphasis hers).[42] This is a misrepresentation of the social sciences, as the previous chapter points out, but it is nevertheless the prevailing view of both Objectivists and the typical anarcho-capitalists in the Rothbardian tradition, with Rand's Objectivist prognosis about the supposed "collapse of science" claiming to be derived from evidence of the contemporary academic scholarship having "accepted as its axioms the fundamental tenets of collectivism."[43] Rand argues that this has been done "implicitly, uncritically, and by default," and that her new philosophy of Objectivism stands to offer a "process of thought" to truly unpack the "how" behind man's actions in order to veer humanity back on track with a newfound appreciation of individual autonomy as the true mechanism of freedom.[44]

It is once again no wonder why post-Rothbard libertarianism ultimately made nice with this viewpoint, despite the fact that Rothbard and Rand had significant disagreements and clashes of perspective prior to their ideologies colluding. It is also notable that Rand's assumptions here about collectivism being exclusively subscribed to by scientific scholarship is wrong for several reasons, the biggest one being that the fields she cites to supposedly prove this claim are not sciences but humanities, and the second biggest one being the fact that Rand seems to be unaware of the more nuanced individualism of the socialists and anarchists in the Bakunin and Kropotkin tradition, in which collectives are seen as mutually uplifting and celebratory pools within which individuals can succeed.[45] She certainly doesn't seem aware of the science—in both biology and neuroscience—that backs this notion up.[46] Devoid of any real grounding in the most empirically backed philosophizing of the individual-to-group dynamic, Rand's philosophy went on to prescribe a fetishized self-centeredness that fancied itself to be "a new concept of egoism" while retaining and understanding none of the nuance present in Max Stirner's original philosophy it was supposedly built upon.[47]

Stirner's egoism, ironically anarchist and communist in nature, was not one of selfishness so much as it was one of self-determination—self-determination that can, provided everyone involved voluntarily wills it, be celebrated and mutually supported within what Stirner called the Union of egoists, first proposed properly in writing in his 1844 work *The Ego and Its Own*.[48] The Union itself is delineated by Stirner as a non-systematic association, meant to serve as a superior alternative to collective dealings in contradistinction to the forceful top-down systems of the State.[49] These associations of egoists are themselves still based on support through an act of will, and if someone in this union is suffering but puts on a front without always being conscious and present within his own will, then the union has degenerated into something less than what Stirner's egoism is supposed to be about.[50] Ayn Rand's version of egoism is such a degradation, since its primary concern is the self at the *expense* of union with others, and considering that its outward representation is one of unwavering strength and lack of empathy for suffering. Indeed, as Rand wrote in her book *For the New Intellectual,* we should only associate with our fellow men whose values we deem make them worthy, and suffering itself "is not a value."[51] In fact, according to Rand, the strong are the only truly deserving precisely because "only man's fight against suffering" is, in her mind, a worthy virtue.[52]

None of Rand's claims of the necessity of selfishness change the fact that Stirner still managed to be against the State and pro-individualism without needing to divorce himself from the concept of mutually beneficial unions. None of his egoism was eroded in this way, and his ideas were not at odds with the larger anarchism and socialism organically bubbling up from within the working class of his time. Rand's belief in capitalism as the most ideal form of economic order we could ever hope to achieve brought with it the same typical blind spots and misunderstandings that fell upon any other traditional adherent to capitalist ideology. Yet another area in which Stirner's version of egoism was already miles ahead of Rand's in its sophistication was its ability to distinguish between private and public property just like any other anarchist of old. While his own take on property was a bit more dystopian than his fellow anarchists (he saw it as something that came through might), it nevertheless existed within the understanding that private ownership of the means of production is different from individual ownership of personal goods.[53]

"I do not step shyly back from your property, but look upon it always as my property, in which I respect nothing," famously declared Stirner. "What I have in my power, that is my own. So long as I assert myself as holder, I am the proprietor of the thing," he continued, clarifying that "Whoever knows how to take, to defend, the thing, to him belongs property."[54] Truly individualistic in its rhetoric, yet still understanding that personal property is one's own, while private property is an invalid idea because use of the commons is simply open to whoever is accessing it at the time. In this sense, Stirner is arguably lending credence to a very *un*selfish idea: sharing.

Despite Rand's inability to make these same distinctions, and despite her apparent lack of knowledge regarding what both social and natural sciences actually have to say on matters of human action and interaction, she continued to present her own version of egoism, and her philosophy of Objectivism, as lighting the only empirical way forward for anyone concerned about freedom and self-liberation. Once again, we see faux-empiricism masquerading as objective reality, wrapped up in an appeal to intellectualism and superiority.

Of course, this does not mean that everyone who finds utility in Ayn Rand's work is necessarily prey to these same pitfalls of her exclusive narrative. In fact, certain leftist scholars such as the aforementioned Dr. Long have argued that it is indeed possible to pull from Rand's work meaningful insight in spite of Rand's own blind spots. One argument of Long's is that while Rand claimed to be a follower of Aristotle, she herself departs greatly from him in her answer to the question of what the nature of human well-being is.[55] Replacing Aristotle's approach of shared experience and testimony epistemology with her claimed foundationalist empiricism means, in Long's view, that Objectivism is left vulnerable to what he calls a "corrosive skepticism," much like the type we are beginning to delineate here in this book.[56] What this amounts to lies in Rand's misapplication of her philosophical aspiration. According to Long:

> Rand unfortunately adopts a Platonic rather than Aristotelian conception of theoretical rationality; that in turn leads her to adopt a Humean rather than an Aristotelian conception of practical rationality; and that this leads her to adopt a Hobbesian rather than an Aristotelian conception of the relation between self-interest and morality—all of which tends to undermine her basically Aristotelian inclinations and sentiments. Hence, I would maintain, Rand's admirers may still have something important to learn from their teacher's first teacher.[57]

In regard to the Humean quality of Rand's approach to practical rationality, Long opines that this is contrary to Rand's claim of skepticism because Hume is "not in the end a skeptic, either in theoretical or in practical matters," and that he instead argues that "reason cannot provide us with true premises, and in fact is more likely to lead us astray."[58] It is therefore prudent, according to Long, for students of Rand to consider studying Aristotle themselves so as to better understand Rand's posited inclinations rather than the more tangled and sometimes problematic application of her isolated writings, which can and does lead at times to a kind of fetishization of self-centeredness.[59] Long calls this approach, which I observe to amount to a détournement of Randian philosophy, "the Aristotelian alternative."[60] A true Aristotelian application of Rand's claimed principles would likely look nothing like Objectivism as we know it today. The reason why is because of Aristotle's concept of the *endoxa*, the reputable belief.[61] It is achieved, observed Aristotle, through collective gathering of knowledge rather than a selfish or isolated origin point.

Long articulates it as follows:

> So far, I have spoken as though the Aristotelian strategy—whether we call it negative coherentism or neoclassical broad foundationalism—simply starts from one's *own* belief system, whatever it may be. But Aristotle speaks of starting from the *endoxa*, or reputable beliefs; and the reputability of a belief is determined, as we have seen, be a) the number of its adherents, and b) the wisdom of its adherents. So if something I do not believe is nevertheless believed by the majority, by the wise (or by the majority of the wise, or the wisest among the majority, and so forth), that, according to Aristotle, gives me some (prima facie, defeasible) reason to believe it myself. Why this appeal to collective belief? Why can I not simply start from my own beliefs and work out from there, rather than including everybody else's beliefs too? Well, it is ultimately from my own *endoxa* that I will reach whatever conclusion I reach. . . . The pursuit of knowledge is a collective endeavor, and will be more successful if everyone is allowed to make a contribution.[62]

Despite the ability to utilize Rand's work soundly when keeping these pitfalls in mind, the reality is that most Randian conservatives seem to swallow whole the entirety of Rand's postulations without regard to nuance, and it makes sense as to why—those who have already bought into the American Dream myth and economically liberal propaganda have found this course of action much more appealing than abandoning the narratives they have long grown to embrace. It, in many ways, is much easier to simply keep rationalizing one's present outlook by repackaging it in ways that *feel* fresh than to force oneself to consider *actually* fresh ideas that might challenge everything that seems to define one's ambitions and social value. And as younger generations of working-class people in the same culturally privileged intersectional spaces have come into their respective intellectual journeys, so too have many of their members found their own newfangled justifications for self-centeredness. The trend has continued, and the rationale is broadly the same. But it comes from a place of desperate clinging to a belief in capitalism as an idea, and in the pseudo free market it offers as the only ally the working person has left in a world of dwindling economic autonomy.[63] But as has been stated many times thus far in this book, it truly is capitalism itself, and not just a perverse version of it like many on the right claim, that has been responsible for many of the woes shared by the entire working class. In the following chapter, the specifics of this reality are laid out.

8

Systemic Deadfalls

In 2016, the year of Donald Trump's election, the gross domestic product (GDP) in the United States was nearing the twenty trillion mark. Two years later, it had crossed that threshold. Also over that course of time, unemployment rates in America dropped to—and remained hovering around—just under 4 percent.[1] It has been said as of this writing that there are not enough people to fill all the new jobs arriving on the market.[2] Scads of liberal and neoliberal economic writings throughout the years have rushed to highlight the fact that ever since the boom of industry in the early 1800s, average earnings in the United States have skyrocketed.[3] Innovation, technological advancement, scientific discovery, automation of various services, average income, GDP, job offerings, and so on are all various factors often cited as evidence for the veracity of the claim that capitalism, despite all its shortcomings, still lifts all boats. Yes, the rich are getting richer, but also, the claim goes, are the poor.[4]

Why, then, does working-class unrest continue to cycle back around and resurge in new forms every new generation, as this book has thus far demonstrated?[5] How can numbers on the page appear to tell a story of success and wealth in the United States while real flesh-and-blood working people continue to feel financially forgotten and left behind? Are these numbers lying?

The answer to this question is *mostly* no—while it is true that numbers and statistics can be manipulated at times for nefarious reasons, most of the time the data that fuels the numbers listed earlier is correct and merely presents a surface-level summation of where the economy is as a whole. *This* is the problem, in that a surface-level measurement of a country's overall and general economic condition is poised to lose sight of the very real lived-in daily realities of the average working person who has no connection to Wall Street. The numbers themselves aren't incorrect, but they are woefully lacking in context and controls for various life factors that often contribute to a person's overall well-being.

GDP, for instance, is itself an incredibly broad measurement of a given country's overall economic activity that mainly is measured via summarizing the monetary value of all finished corporate goods put into the market within a set time frame. In the United States, GDP is calculated and publicly shared both on a quarterly and on an annual basis. What this amounts to in application is a measurement, taken very seriously by policy makers and citizens alike, that is virtually only really accounting for how much *stuff* is put up for sale per year—it is not accounting for many other things that compound together to account for a person's everyday quality of life.[6]

This is because quality of life is a wholly *human* thing, and humanity exists way outside the lines that are drawn by an exclusively fiscal focus on the world. Psychology, for instance, as well as art, often gives deeper insight into the human condition than soulless numbers on a page ever could. While everyone's inner empiricist might genuinely have a knee-jerk reaction to such an observation, the reality still remains that while tangible funds to live with are indeed needed at the ground level of any viable existence, this should be seen as a means to an end rather than the end in and of itself.

The rhetoric of many self-fashioned realists and skeptics on the right increasingly leaves this notion behind, arguing instead that barely scraping by in one's finances should be seen as good enough, and that calling for things such as affordable means of learning, social acceptance for those who are often mistreated for being different, and other culturally concerned causes is essentially something that should be framed as infantile and mocked. But do we not all, at the end of the day, desire for relatively peaceful existences free of fear and antagonism? Of course, we do. While a world like that might not be the world we currently live in, that does not mean anyone calling to build that world is intrinsically wrong-headed or naïve. Abstract concepts such as romance, love, and comradery also factor into the emotional and mental well-being of individuals as they interact and share this world with each other. To make those interactions all the more understanding and lessen the chances of hate and mistreatment between fellow human beings is understandable and noble.

All of this transcends the confines of simply laboring to produce sellable junk for a company in exchange for the means of staying alive and taking care of one's family at the bare minimum. That process is for many people, again, a mere means to an end and not a fulfilling life's passion.

As such, many people work and toil in order to make their lives outside of work sustainable. But we must make no mistake that these lives outside of work are the lives most of us consider to be truly ours. The lives many of us live inside work conditions are lives characterized by varying degrees of put-on, servility to (often incompetent) superiors, and self-delusion. In order to get through our work days, we will often allow ourselves to buy into the company mission statement just enough to feel like our labor is making some sort of noble difference, and indeed, if the work we do is blue collar and necessary for things like energy, transportation, sanitation, and so on, then there is certainly some truth to that notion. But for an increasing number of people entering the workforce, the truly necessary jobs are largely unavailable, while busy work that has long been replaceable via automation (taking orders at restaurants, pressing buttons on elevators, selling products that already sell themselves in retail spaces, etc.) clings to life in an economy that continues to adopt technological advancement as a means of cutting costs and reducing the need to pay workers livable wages.

If someone reading this has the good fortune of working a job that is both truly secure and also genuinely enjoyable and/or connected to a major life passion, that person should recognize how lucky of a position that is to be in. For everyone else, work is merely what we must do to not starve.[7] Tying back in to the observation in Chapter 3 about how neoliberal hegemony has conditioned people to culturally attach value in personhood to how productive one is for a boss in the workforce, we must keep in mind that this cultural valuation of labor in workspaces as being tantamount to one's value as a complete human being is itself a fallacious distortion of the reality we all come home to at the end of the work week.[8] We know intuitively that our free time spent with loved ones and on recreational projects is the time when we can truly be ourselves and find the most tangible meaning for our lives. Yet, when asked upfront about how we view work, we are quick to attack the character of others who are not presently engaged in our collective concept of what "work" is: servility to a boss in a workspace that contributes directly to GDP. "Get a job" is a common refrain from one person who aims to attack another, with the implication being that the person not presently employed is lazy, incompetent, or not driven in life.

But it has been suggested that this is not the correct way to look at things, and that human beings should not feel shame for desiring a life free from the seemingly endless toil of renting one's own labor out to others in an attempt to possibly hold onto the more meaningful side of life found only in our free time. As wages continue to stagnate while cost of living continues to increase nationwide, that free time is becoming an ever-smaller aspect of our daily existence.[9] Is this the future we truly believe we deserve? Do we not all wish on some level that technological advancement would have our lives being *less* work-centric rather than more? Without compromising our capacity to indulge in the joys of life outside laborious, back-breaking servility to bosses?

Self-described "post-leftist" Bob Black, a prolific anarchist writer, once wrote in 1985 one of the most poignant essays on this topic wherein he declared a need for human beings to stop "working" in the colloquial, neoliberal sense and instead be "at play"—in other words, do work in fields and on projects that truly enrich their lives in a way that personally fulfills.[10] On whether or not workers actually already have the freedom to do this (as many right-libertarians and other "revolutionary" conservative types claim), Black stated the following in the essay:

Work makes a mockery of freedom. The official line is that we all have rights and live in a democracy. Other unfortunates who aren't free like we are have to live in police states. These victims obey orders or-else, no matter how arbitrary. The authorities keep them under regular surveillance. State bureaucrats control even the smaller details of everyday life. The officials who push them around are answerable only to the higher-ups, public or private. Either way, dissent and disobedience are punished. Informers report regularly to the authorities. All this is supposed to be a very bad thing. And so it is, although it is nothing but a description of the modern workplace. The liberals and conservatives and libertarians who lament totalitarianism are phonies and hypocrites. There is more freedom in any moderately de-Stalinized dictatorship than there is in the ordinary American workplace. You find the same sort of hierarchy and discipline in an office or factory as you do in a prison or a monastery. In fact, as Foucault and others have shown, prisons and factories came in at about the same time, and their operators consciously borrowed from each other's control techniques. A worker is a part-time slave. The boss says when to show up, when to leave, and what to do in the meantime. He tells you how much work to do and how fast. He is free to carry his control to humiliating extremes, regulating, if he feels like it, the clothes you wear or how often you go to the bathroom. With a few exceptions he can fire you for any reason, or no reason. He has you spied on by snitches and supervisors; he amasses a dossier on every employee. Talking back is called "insubordination," just as if a worker is a naughty child, and it not only gets you fired, it disqualifies you for unemployment compensation.[11]

In Black's view, "work" is a cultural concept that gives undue nobility to the idea of being servile to others for the purpose of fueling nationwide and international goals that only the corporatist class can truly benefit from. We are told, of course, that the benefits of rich people staying successful *are* felt by us in the form of even more technological and scientific innovation, or more product choices in the retail world, and therefore everyone, the working class included, wins. But it should be noted that on the first point, scientific innovation is almost always funded directly to the proper research facilities by either government initiatives or very specific private enterprise projects. The idea that the innovation that leads to the coolest new tech or medical breakthroughs is somehow a result of the capitalistic market being allowed to exploit workers is therefore remarkably unsubstantiated. Yet, it is the narrative we are sold: we must endure the anxiety, stress, physical and mental fatigue, and so on of working jobs we hate because the system could not possibly function any other way, and it would be selfish to demand that it even try. Thus, Black goes further:

> The demeaning system of domination I've described rules over half the waking hours of a majority of women and the vast majority of men for decades, for most of their lifespans. For certain purposes it's not too misleading to call our system democracy or capitalism or—better still—industrialism, but its real names are factory fascism and office oligarchy. Anybody who says these people are "free" is lying or stupid. You are what you do. If you do boring, stupid monotonous work, chances are you'll end up boring, stupid and monotonous.[12]

Remaining in servitude of GDP is not in the best interest of working people. This claim is not made lightly, and it is not simply due to what this chapter has put forth so far regarding the moral and philosophical angle of what life "should" be about. There is a much more empirical means of demonstrating that GDP fails to truly account for how well-off everyday working people truly are: cite alternative statistics that paint a much closer, accurate picture of everyday working-class life.

Returning to the earlier posited point about most workers not finding fulfillment in their jobs, the data backs up the claim. According to the most recent Gallup polls, only 13 percent of *all* workers feel satisfied with or engaged in their jobs worldwide.[13] In America, it isn't much better with barely over 30 percent claiming the same.[14] As for work itself being tied up with personal value, UC Berkeley researchers have demonstrated on the psychological side of things that being in a lifelong state of unemployment (which is on the rise, despite the supposedly low unemployment numbers cited at the top of the chapter)[15] has been shown to manifest as a sense of demoralization and ever-present malaise, negatively affecting a person's sense of self-worth and sanity.[16] In 2010, German researchers found that all of these negative thoughts and feelings that result from either extended unemployment or unfulfilling employment can compound in such a way that happiness may never recover, leaving emotional scars on people that are even more damaging than is the case with depression felt with permanent injuries or deaths of spouses.[17]

Work in many fields today is increasingly becoming a masquerade—something we feel we must do in order to earn our places in society despite many of us realizing that what we are often asked to do amounts to vacuous busy work. The late, great anthropologist David Graeber once wrote on the findings of his research regarding these sorts of jobs that they amount to "a form of paid employment that is so completely pointless, unnecessary, or pernicious that even the employee cannot justify its existence," adding however that "as part of the conditions of employment, the employee feels obliged to pretend that this is not the case."[18] In short, many of us who are still employed today increasingly realize that the work we do amounts to little, yet we also know that our societal surroundings still operate as if one must work for a boss in order to walk with self-respect and earn an "honest living." Therefore, the masquerade continues in spite of the growing disillusionment with the system from within. Fear of shame and being ostracized by the rest of society often plays a role in stifling the outcry.

What of unemployment itself? Is it not dropping, as cited at the top of the chapter? Yes and no. It is true that the official unemployment numbers are dropping, but unemployment numbers do not actually measure how many individuals are out of work. Let that point be stated again: official unemployment numbers are *not* accounting for the total number of unemployed people. Instead, these numbers account for how many unemployed people are still actively seeking employment in the workforce. This is very different from saying that the total number of people who cannot find work is actually decreasing—that number, as it turns out, might actually be growing. Since the year 2000, over five million manufacturing workers have lost their jobs.[19] Over 80 percent of those job losses were due to automation making the human element of that labor irrelevant.[20] Around 73 percent of all manufacturing jobs are occupied by men, and this job loss in that particular field has resulted in one in six working-age men now being completely gone from the workforce—one of the highest rates of this occurrence in the entire world.[21]

Of these displaced manufacturing workers, nearly 45 percent of them have remained unemployed ever since, unable to apply the skills they worked and studied for to any new job opportunities.[22] So yes, new jobs are indeed popping up, and there often aren't enough people to fill them, but this is because the current batch of displaced workers either live in a completely different part of the country or do not have the means of learning a brand new skill necessary to enter these new jobs. In other words, the market innovates for the purposes of producing newer, high-demand goods and services, which adds to GDP, but it does not always account for all of the people whose jobs are lost in this innovation's wake. And this leads to an incongruency between what the numbers on the page suggest and what real-life workers face in their daily lives. In America in 2018, a shocking 40 percent of the entire population did not have enough extra income or savings to cover an emergency $400 life expense.[23] That is not the mark of a workforce rolling in wealth and opportunity. Yet, appeals to the rise of new (unfilled and undertrained) jobs and GDP continue to be the main talking points in favor of how capitalism is wonderful, and whatever problems working people face must not be innate to the system itself. This is the kind of missing the wood for the trees that can only happen when the economic emphasis on measuring the quality of life drowns out everything else that makes us fulfilled human beings.

But isn't it still true, one might argue, that even with all of this incongruency and inability to lift most workers out of base-level financial sustainability, the current system still yet serves as the best foil to absolute poverty worldwide we have yet devised? After all, the World Bank seems pretty confident in its declaration that poverty is indeed decreasing everywhere.

Well, let us once again realize what was put forth at the top of this chapter: while the numbers themselves are usually correct, how they are used sometimes misses the reality for most everyday people living outside the world of neoliberal back-patting. For instance, when it comes to the poverty statistic, what the numbers are claimed to measure can be interpreted in different ways in order to fit different narratives. In the case of the World Bank numbers, what constitutes "poverty" has been changed over time to better fit the narrative that poverty itself has been globally reduced thanks to neoliberal fiscal policy.

The poverty line, as it is colloquially known, is supposed to mark the point at which an adult person's daily income becomes enough for said person to meet all of his or her daily needs. This threshold has historically been calculated by each nation for itself, but in 1990, economist Martin Ravallion, at the time director of the research department at the World Bank, argued for the first-ever standardized and centralized global poverty line to be adopted into the entity's policy vernacular. Ravallion determined this new line by highlighting the fact that a grouping of the world's poorest countries all had respective poverty lines hovering somewhere at or around one dollar per day. Therefore, "a dollar a day" became the standard line whenever a policy-informed individual would define and discuss poverty. In the year 2000, the World Bank utilized this definition in its world development report to declare the following:

The ongoing increase in population levels means that the absolute number of those living on $1 per day or less continues to increase. The worldwide total rose from 1.2 billion in 1987 to 1.5 billion today and, if recent trends persist, will reach 1.9 billion by 2015.[24]

This declaration was alarming, yet it seemed incontrovertible. But only four years later, Ravallion seemed to have changed his tune. In a 2004 report written by him and another World Bank fellow entitled "How Have the World's Poorest Fared since the Early 1980s?" Ravallion proclaimed that

While poverty has been increasing steadily for some two centuries, the introduction of free-market policies actually reduced the number of impoverished people by 400 million between 1981 and 2001.[25]

But wait a second—even taking into account the global rise in poverty up to 1981 claimed by the paper, what happened to the dire *continued* increase of poverty-stricken people well into the late 1990s accounted for just four years prior in the World Bank's world development report? Well, this shift in how the numbers were being read came about thanks to some slight tweaking that the World Bank chose to do regarding the specifics of the dollar per day poverty threshold. That threshold, originally at $1.02, was moved up just five cents to $1.08 by the World Bank. This might have been done to account for inflation, one might rightly assume. However, the real reason this was done was to adjust for changes in *purchasing power* of the US dollar, which was *not* the same thing as accounting for the inflation that had also occurred between the time the initial poverty line was established and this later shift.[26] As journalist Jason Hickel makes clear, the shift of the poverty line from $1.02 per day to $1.08 per day in 2004 was just the World Bank moving the valuation of the dollar's purchasing power parity (PPP) from the 1985 standard to the 1993 standard.[27] Since PPP does not update at the same rate of inflation, this actually *lowered* the real value of the daily income of the impoverished. What this meant in effect was the global poverty line had become tethered to purchasing power rather than to real-world income value of everyday people.[28] The poverty threshold as well had therefore been lowered, and 400 million people who had still counted as impoverished the day before immediately became reclassified as technically above the poverty line.[29]

This slight tweak made all the difference, where suddenly, a change by a fraction of a dollar based on PPP (a change that would likely not be noticed by many people at all), warped the measurement of impoverished people, rendering it significantly inaccurate. This was done again in 2008, when the poverty line was changed to $1.25, making it appear that 316 million more people were suddenly lifted out of economic hardship.[30] Both of these arbitrarily altered poverty thresholds, while seemingly innocuous at first blush, artificially took the posited global poverty number all-told from 1.9 billion down to 1.4 billion with a mere flick of the pen, suggesting that, when taking into account that relative poverty rates are still increasing and the only "decreases" were due to fancy number-fudging, the world actually has close to 50 percent *more* desperately poor people in it today than the new numbers suggest.[31] Much like with the so-called unemployment numbers, when new arbitrary standards are introduced to omit real flesh-and-blood people from statistical accounting, the context-free numbers on their own fail to truly represent the reality.

Now, even if the more typically right-libertarian and fiscally conservative approach were taken when analyzing all of this, the implications drawn would still actually be somewhat unsatisfactory. One of the defining pillars of these revolutionary spaces on the right is unwavering skepticism of globalized, centralized, or otherwise standardized policy. Here, the World Bank is demonstrating exactly that kind of approach, and it is arguably correct in this instance for skepticism of it to indeed be in play. Remember that even the initial global poverty line suggested by Ravallion, arguably as empirical as a global poverty line could be, is still not able to account for each country's own localized understanding of what "poverty" really means and feels like to live in.

The poorest countries in the world were observed as hovering around $1 a day in their own nationally determined poverty thresholds, and therefore, the global standard was set. But there are a few problems with this approach, namely, the fact that as a foundation for what poverty really is in the broadest sense, comparing $1 a day in these spaces to $1 a day in a country like the United States does not reap the same result for what it is like to live in a person's skin in both places—prices are different, priorities are different, economies are run by different policies, and so on. Studies have shown, even when conducted by the World Bank itself, that children living under $1 a day across the world can still have radically different qualities of life related to their health and lifespan depending on *which* countries they are living in.[32] The income might be the same on paper, but everything else is still largely conditional to the country's other elements, including how its government is run, and how the country in question arrives at *its* measurement for poverty. Indeed, in many of these poorest countries, the numbers claiming to demonstrate the $1 daily poverty line are put forth by bureaucrats and the corresponding data is often lacking. We just don't know what else is contributing to the overall poor quality of life seen in these spaces.

Every other individual country determines its own standards for its poverty line by taking all of these aforementioned country- and region-specific factors into account, which leads to discrepancies often when comparing national poverty lines of a given country's own standards to their international World Bank equivalents. For instance, while the local data in Sri Lanka, directly surveying real people on-the-ground, showed that 35 percent of the population lived below the national poverty line in 1990, the World Bank data that same year seemed to indicate that the number of destitute Sri Lanka citizens was just 4 percent.[33] As these standardized numbers continue to remain apparently low, the actual localized unrest and lowered quality of life gets swept under the rug. As recently as 2008, it was reported that the youth in Sri Lanka were choosing to join the military—not because were truly free to choose this path for their own personal fulfillment, but because, in many cases, it was the only viable means they could see for escaping the poverty that was crippling them.[34] All of this while the global reading for Sri Lankan population living under the poverty line would come out less than two years later as still being in the single-digit percentages.[35]

Yet another problem with the narrative about global reduced poverty, in addition to the lowering of the global poverty threshold as well as the loss of nuance present in the standardized approach, is the fact that even the most recent poverty line postulated by the World Bank, currently $1.90 per day, is not arguably anything we should be celebrating or accepting as a good enough base level on which to declare a person no longer impoverished.[36] This line might have begun with the point at which the poorest countries in the world declare their citizens are no longer in a state of "absolute poverty," but thinking in terms of actual daily livability, especially in the West, is less than $2 per day truly anything that we can consider is singlehandedly able to help a person stay alive and afloat for long?

According to a different statistic, one that actually *does* take more life factors of people into account (unlike GDP, unemployment numbers, and the World Bank's poverty line), the answer is no. The US Department of Agriculture has calculated that the *bare minimum* for sufficient food intake in this country would have to be $5 per day—$3.10 more than what the World Bank currently considers worthy of celebrating and being no longer poor.[37] And that is before one takes into account things like housing, personal hygiene, appropriate clothing for job interviews, office supplies for preparing resumes and doing paperwork (if one gets hired by said job), and transportation to-and-from work. Meaning that in real-world dollars, the apparent major drop in poverty cited by the World Bank does not even begin to account for the needs of actual people who might be above the poverty line but who are many, many dollars away from managing to survive in the economic system as it currently is designed to work.

In other countries, it isn't much better when the current $1.90 threshold is taken at its word—in India, for instance, children living at just above that threshold still have a 60 percent chance of ending up malnourished.[38] In Niger, infants of households in that same "out of poverty" daily income have mortality rates three times that of the worldwide norm.[39] The reality is that for people to actually be out of "poverty" in the sense that you or I mean when we use the term, daily income would have to be more than what the World Bank threshold claims. In fact, significantly more. In 2006, economist Dr. Peter Edward of Newcastle University argued for an "ethical poverty line" that would require minimum daily income of people worldwide to increase by nearly 4 percent before we would even be close to the actual livability.[40] Even then, a significant amount of daily needs would still need to be either provided outright or substantially subsidized by other means before the other aspects of manageable living, such as a house and a transportation to a job, could be consistently maintained. Hickel has reached similar estimations, saying that an actual viable daily minimum for people globally would have to be around $7.40, which increases the actual number of impoverished world citizens to around six times the number World Bank's numbers postulate (a number growing steadily since the 1980s).[41]

The problems with the World Bank's claim of global poverty reduction still do not quite end there. Because that number does not control for country-by-country variation. In other words, it might be implicit in the numbers as presented that the number of people now living above the World Bank's claimed "poverty line" (itself dubiously named, as we can now see) has increased everywhere "free-market policies" have touched equally—after all, this is what that 2004 report made it sound like: free-market capitalism is lifting people out of poverty evenly worldwide.[42] However, this is not quite correct. Back to Dr. Edward and his ethical poverty line, that same paper also attempted to see what the *actual* reduction of poverty, if any, was occurring worldwide by using a new fixed amount of exactly one actual dollar per day income as the new threshold. Taking that into account, Edward demonstrated that, while the total number of people in the world living below a fixed level of $1 a day did seem to decrease by 85 million between 1993 and 2001 (a more meager number than implied by the World Bank number-fudging), *all* of that decrease occurred in China, with its isolated numbers showing that a total number of 108 million of its citizens crossed the $1 a day threshold in the same period of time.[43] Elsewhere, things either got worse (such as in sub-Saharan Africa where poverty increased "significantly") or remained virtually unchanged (with the average impoverished person's income only going up globally by four cents).[44]

In other words, if neoliberal policy and capitalistic enterprise truly "lifted all boats" for innate reasons, as opposed a given country's living conditions improving due to other, country-specific conditions, we should have at least seen the very meager increase that we did see happen in a more evenly spread out manner across the entire capitalistic world. Instead, we saw either no change at all or a worsening of income and living conditions for the poor everywhere else except in China—and it is debated whether or not China even serves as the best example of the best form capitalism can take.

What all of this amounts to is that as a metric for how intrinsically good capitalism and neoliberal policy at large is, the World Bank statistic is found rather hollow upon further scrutiny. And as to whether or not capitalism truly lifts all boats, that also seems to be a matter of interpretation. While it is true that nations as entities have gradually gotten less violent and more wealthy on the whole, specific economies have offered varying degrees of economic so-called success for everyday working people that haven't always followed the global trend. What's more, the poorest people in most of these supposedly liberated capitalist countries haven't seen much tangible difference in their living conditions and overall quality of life for the whole of their time under capitalist influence. Despite what the surface-level numbers may claim, the daily realities of most working and poor people in most countries that claim to operate under capitalism are still not tangibly helped by it. To claim that the very meager improvements we have seen in certain cases like China and India certainly would not have happened without neoliberal influence is similar to the religious zealot who might claim that a successful businessman would have surely not found his success had it not been for prayer. The trends go the way that they go regardless due to more immediately surrounding conditions and circumstances, and the ideological rationale rushes to the front of the parade that is already in procession to claim its place as bandmaster.

Of course, there are certain metrics that seem to be much more useful for determining the actual state of daily existence for real-life people in real-life localized circumstances. There are even instances of these metrics improving their accuracy even more by adjusting their methods and focus to better account for things like wealth disparity between the wealthiest members of a society and said society's majority of working people. One such instance involves the Human Development Index (HDI), which was already a far better barometer for the state of tangible quality of life around the world because it took into account the domestic uniqueness of each country it measured. But even that was not quite enough for some of the researchers involved in the HDI's reports, and so, even more nuance was applied later on.

In its simplest form, the HDI is still very useful, as it is a composite index of education, life expectancy, and per capita income indicators in any given country as a means of ranking said country along for tiers of human wellness and development. The higher each of these three indicators is in a given year, the higher the country will rank against other countries being judged on these same merits. No single poverty line is in play, here: each country's status on each of these plains is determined independently and then the countries are compared.

However, HDI researchers went one step further in 2010 and introduced an even deeper layer to their work in the Inequality-Adjusted Human Development Index (IHDI).[45] This newer index chose to de-emphasize things like arbitrarily determined "quality of goods" and net wealth per capita of the country as a whole (i.e., GDP equivalent measurements), which resulted in certain so-called wealthy country rankings dropping in their positions along the index compared to what their equivalent rankings were on the simple HDI. It was made clear from the researchers involved that the IHDI was "the actual level of human development accounting for inequality," while the simple HDI, by contrast, "can be viewed as an index of 'potential' human development (or the maximum IHDI that could be achieved if there were no inequality)."[46] In short, while HDI is still useful in the broad strokes, it is idealistic and not as empirically correct as the IHDI. Why is it that these researchers can be very upfront about this and further develop their methods of measurement to account for it, while in the case of things like GDP and World Bank poverty statistics, all sense of nuance or accuracy seems almost entirely unimportant?

In any case, the difference is indeed tangible and very real when looking at the impact that applying nuance to the index makes. As of 2018, the simple HDI ranks the United States at thirteenth out of nearly sixty total countries collected in the data.[47] But when adjusted for inequality and taking real income and quality of life for most citizens into account, the United States drops down to the twenty-fifth rank.[48] This is a perfect snapshot of how much of a difference it makes when one dives deeper than surface-level reports and takes real-world conditions of everyday working people into account.

The reason for this significant drop in ranking once GDP is cut out of consideration is simple: most working-class Americans are in much direr financial and health straits than the pro-neoliberal narrative lets on. As we look deeper at specific studies focusing on the three main barometers considered by the HDI, the harsh reality becomes all the clearer. According to recent studies by the Commonwealth Fund, of the eleven top wealthiest nations by GDP, the United States is ranked the very worst regarding quality, affordability, and accessibility of health care for the majority of its citizens.[49] Out of forty countries analyzed by Pearson in 2014 regarding average cognitive skills and educational attainment for citizens, the United States ranked at fourteen.[50] Current average life expectancy in America is age eighty-one for women, and age seventy-six for men (once again, demonstrating that men get hit especially hard by working-class strife), bringing the country as a whole to a ranking of thirty-first on the World Health Organization's list in 2016.[51] With all of this lack of ubiquitous access across the board to these elements of life that can make or break a person's intellectual growth, emotional resolve, and overall health, is it really any wonder why so many people in the States feel so disenfranchised with the status quo?

These conditions, it should not be taken lightly, *radicalize* people.[52] They would radicalize anyone. And in fact, many working-class people who fall outside the intersectionally privileged areas of the populist rationale spectrum oftentimes become radicalized in a way that aligns them much more innately with the socialists and anarchist of old. It is these spaces, striking differences can be found with their right-wing equivalents. For one thing, minorities are far more represented in the populist working-class left.[53] For another, the ages of activists in these groups are far more diverse and varied than the earlier-cited statistics in this book of libertarian and conservative populist groups.[54] This is not only because members of minorities are more likely to see through any political narrative that assumes the present economic system is essentially egalitarian by nature (something virtually all economically conservative narratives must claim in order to present capitalism as the best possible system to advocate for), but also because, comparatively speaking, the answers provided by populist left literature offer more substance and courses of real action that can be engaged in well into a given activist's later years.

The right-libertarian movement often likes to cite its majority youth membership as something to brag about, as if this is somehow proof positive that it is doing something right. But the age demographic never substantially changes, meaning that the young, white men that start in this movement do not tend to grow old in it—they move on from it. Why? Because as the book has pointed out more than once by now, the worker unrest with the system itself returns every generation and takes yet another form. Because the answers provided by liberal and neoliberal populism do not offer anything more substantial than any other mainstream variant of the same basic narrative of "capitalism is good." But capitalism continues to not be good in its various realities implemented around the world—at least, for most. The elites, the arbiters of the liberal narrative since the 1830s, do benefit from the system as it exists. But once again, if a particular demographic amidst the working class has a limited view of what forms oppression can truly take, it becomes easier for that demographic (in this case, white working-class men) to be swayed in favor of a more digestible narrative—one in which the system that has historically promised success through hard work and triumph through wealth can continue to be perceived as an ally and remain unquestioned, even while its more flamboyant claims obscure the uglier reality residing underneath. A reality that is inconvenient to acknowledge. A reality that, if true, would suggest that capitalism is not the end point, and is instead a transitional state that has long worn out its utility.

* * *

I still remember the first time I heard the term "neoliberalism." At the time, I was still a self-identified right-libertarian and I truly believed that capitalism was the natural, unadulterated state of human markets. In my mind, capitalism was around from the very first moment sapiens invented the concept of mutual exchange. This was, of course, before I realized the actual history of its inception, as laid out earlier in the book.[55] Yet this default position, in which someone who is pro-free markets truly believes that capitalism is a naturally occurring process rather than a man-made economic system, is common among self-described conservatives and right-libertarians. To me, "neoliberalism" was nothing more than a pejorative directed at "true" free-market advocates like myself and did not accurately depict what my philosophy was all about. Then, I found out that libertarianism had been co-opted from socialists, and my wheels began to turn.[56]

As Chapter 5 demonstrated, John Locke, the father of classical liberalism, told us that oneself and one's labor are the innate rights human beings possess.[57] Neoliberalism, by contrast, tells us that our labor is in and of itself worthless without a direct connection to niches, cliques, marketing, and pre-established concepts of identity.[58] Political self-branding, complete with the need to virtue signal via loudly declared identity politics, is yet another symptom of this ailment—a symptom that all of us, regardless our politics, are enslaved by. When the anti-SJW crowd began to form its own unbending identity and narrative on the Internet, and its adherents complained ad nauseam about the SJWs and their unbending identity, the irony was initially missed. Largely because many of these online personalities originally came out of the so-called skeptic community, which implied that many of them were critical thinkers who would self-reflect and consider all evidence before taking a position on a given issue—social issues included. Therefore, it was assumed that they couldn't *possibly* have a politically charged bias. And yet, that assumption turned out to be untrue in many cases, and even the YouTube skeptics who emerged from this community as quasi-celebrities representing the movement of "rationality" had to ultimately resort to forming sterile, easily acceptable identities that appealed to beliefs their audience members already held in order to maintain said audience and make rent.[59] Enter Lauren Southern, Stefan Molyneux, et al. as delineated earlier in this book, and all the redressed nationalism and fascism they and their colleagues would go on to normalize in the broader populist conservative conversation.[60] It led to deadly outcomes, such as with the Charlottesville Unite the Right rally in 2017 and the New Zealand mosque shootings in 2019, in which once-moderate conservatives who became revolutionary in spirit fell down the rabbit holes carved out by these easily accessible online voices.[61]

What kind of system demands conformity to pre-existing expectations in order to live? What kind of system forces the less skilled among its citizens to undertake back-breaking work day and night for the sheer purpose of barely surviving, hand-to-mouth? Is this truly the system that supposedly encourages innovation, freedom of expression, and choice? Yes—if you are lucky enough to belong to specific demographics of people. This cold reality is justified, as demonstrated in the prior chapters as well, by the claim that there is no other possible way to successfully run a market. Through selfishness, we will have an externality of altruistic end result. Supposedly.

But here is yet another contradiction: if capitalism, both as it exists today and as it was when first formulated by the economic elites in the, truly is only a step removed from some organic, naturally occurring system of freely behaving people, then why does it prescribe self-interest as the most effective primary mover when we have scientific evidence to highly suggest the opposite is true in organic groups? Returning to Matt Ridley and his observations highlighted back in Chapter 3, the desire and need to work together is the much more demonstrable natural state of human beings due to how we evolved to work together for survival purposes. His summation of this phenomenon delineates a reality that transcends geographic space: "this is not some parochial Western tradition. It is a bias shared by the whole species. . . . Consciously or implicitly, we all share a belief in pursuing the greater good. We praise selflessness and decry selfishness."[62] Furthermore, why is it not doing more to *actually* raise people out of poverty, as demonstrated earlier in this chapter? Why can it only claim to do these things? If the capitalism of today were truly a perverted version of "real" capitalism like the liberal apologists of all stripes argue, why is there no clear evidence that *any* form of it, even elsewhere in the world free of American policy and regulation, can tangibly make the poor less so? Why must the fudging of numbers and a disingenuous focus on something like GDP rather than the IHDI be the only way the narrative of capitalism's greatness is maintained?

The implication here is that these imprecise methods and obfuscated narratives are called upon to support capitalism because capitalism cannot actually support itself on its own merits. It is an implication that seems to hold quite a bit of water once the initial claimed evidence of capitalism's effectiveness is peeled back and explored past. The oversimplified rhetorical exercise of arguing for a hands-off approach to economic management 100 percent of the time only lends itself to exploitation by powerful entities who will perpetuate the status quo and keep wealth inequality alive. Because there is such a thing as good regulation, and there is such a thing as bad regulation. Making a distinction between good and bad regulation, for instance, as opposed to the economically conservative distinction of more versus less regulation, allows for far more nuance and case-by-case dissection of the sorts of rigged injustices that harm the working class at large. Right-libertarians and conservatives often point out (correctly) that bad regulations resulting from government–corporate collusion can do everything from monopolize a market to restrict tangible worker mobility. Yet, when minority-specific limitations result from this same process, for instance, and good regulations are proposed to counteract the bad (and preserve a truly equitable recognition of civil freedoms), these same people suddenly tend to argue that the market as it already exists is too finely tuned to meddle with and therefore, any regulation is bad regulation simply because said regulation happens at the hands of the government.[63] Instead, they argue, help the marginalized by giving them access to more chances to become capitalists themselves.[64] Essentially, the argument is to fix capitalism's problems with more capitalism. But as law professor Mehrsa Baradaran notes, "the benefits of capitalism always accrue to the owners of the capital, not to the people living in enterprise zones or promise zones."[65] Even those who could benefit from becoming capitalists statistically never will become capitalists. So, the promise of capitalistic enterprise, especially for the historically marginalized, is essentially fantasy—yet another means of pacifying the masses in place making any fundamental systemic changes. It is the conservative equivalent of the welfare program—an illusion meant to warm the hearts and tame the tempers of those who need to feel justified in not budging a single inch in a manner that will truly count for the next generation.

But the original libertarians and anarchists in the socialist tradition understood that the point was not to be anti-government altogether but to instead remain skeptical of all forms of power structures that could not demonstrably justify themselves. It is not the case that all government involvement is wrong. Instead, it is the case that any government involvement that aims to benefit the elite and hinder the common man is what should be fought against. By recasting good regulation as "no regulation" and bad regulation as "regulation of any kind," modern right-libertarianism and conservative anarchism have stripped the entire working-class compass from its northward sense. In its place, a false sense of direction has been offered that blurs the lines between elitist and worker, focusing the antagonism on abstract cultural concepts rather than tangible economic ones and pitting workers against each other via hindering identity politics.

Seeing past this fog, once set up intentionally by elitists and counter-revolutionary insurgents and ultimately cascaded into organic feedback loops self-maintained by honest-yet-unaware pseudo-revolutionaries, requires first and foremost a willingness to consider the information that exists outside the echo chamber. Yes, hegemony is a real thing. Yes, many conservative populists, just like their liberal counterparts, seem to have fallen victim to it. No, they do not often write about or seem to fully understand the concept. Why? Because a Marxist identified it and coined the term for it. And Marxists are anti-freedom and evil, according to every right-of-center publication that has any influence whatsoever. So, how can one escape the false consciousness that has now organically taken over in these spaces when the tools and vocabulary needed to even wrap one's head around all of the involved elements are kept far out of reach? The simple answer is that, as long as no footwork is done by one's own accord, one cannot. And in most cases, this is exactly what happens. The well-meaning conservative activist, who goes populist and becomes a revolutionary, ends up missing half of the information he needs before he can actually make any informed judgment about the system he claims to oppose. Because he is an anti-political populist; a right-wing Jacobin. He has a frontier of antagonism shared in common with every other conservative variant he is liable to cross paths with. And the Marxist, the person who can explain to him everything he seeks to understand, is his *Other*. Communication breaks down before it can even begin, words like "capitalism," "socialism," "liberalism," and "libertarianism" take opposing meanings, and potential working-class allies prematurely mark themselves as enemies.

And the machine rages on, unchanging, for yet another generation.

Part III

How Privileged Populism Prevails

(Modern Analyses)

When Ideology Meets Reality

At the outset of this book, the question was posed: "what is freedom?" All-encompassing freedom for all was named as the most ubiquitously embraced version of the answer.[1] But what does that look like in the real world? How does the language and philosophy of "liberty," the apparent representative of this kind of freedom, manifest throughout our daily interactions, conversations, and political habits? In Chapter 5, a more Kantian realist approach was pitted against a contrastingly Hegelian approach at proposing mechanisms for achieving this liberty for everyday people. The Kantian view, in which all we should bother investing our energy in is what can already be demonstrated, is only part of the story behind neoliberal hegemony's stranglehold on the public consciousness. Another way through which this capitalist realist mindset takes shape is through the overly intellectualized philosophical debate between morality and realism. The aforementioned "facts don't care about your feelings" mantra overviewed in Chapter 7 stems in part from the philosophical idea that one must choose either moral consideration or empirical certainty whenever coming up against a given social problem.[2]

The shortcoming of this viewpoint is that these philosophical debates are in some sense meant to be abstract entanglements of ideas that take place on a different plain from where real-world, in-the-moment conflicts are harming real people in real crises. Yes, the results of these discussions can find appropriate application to these problems, but they are not definitive answers to the problems in and of themselves. Epistemological considerations about any given topic, in which a person is asked why she thinks she knows something, can find utility in personal growth and interpersonal interaction, but they won't singlehandedly solve a real-world crisis being experienced by the person. Much more needs to happen so these philosophical discussions can become tangible actions and mechanisms for betterment of life.

Yet, those who adhere to scientism in their faux-empirical thinking would like the rest of us to think that if a realist "wins" (another concept out-of-step with what real philosophy is supposed to be about) the philosophical debate of the day, then the realist perspective on the topic in question should trump any other ways of thinking about it from that day forward. Yet, oftentimes the realist perspective itself isn't even resting upon empirically unshakable ground. Instead, all that truly needs to be demonstrated, in the Kantian tradition, is that what appears to be known already is more important than what else could potentially be knowable. This is not truly scientific in approach because it could logically choose to stop caring about inquiry into a given subject or problem the moment an *adequate*, if not necessarily an empirically demonstrated, explanation is given. In application, that is what a Kantian-style materialist application of philosophy stands to potentially look like if in the wrong hands. Many of the anti-political populist types, as Chapters 2 and 3 have demonstrated them to be, are the sorts of people who apply the realist approach in this way when already convinced of their own correctness. These sorts of populists also being the types we find in the conservative populist movements we have been examining throughout this text means that it should come as no surprise to us that the libertarians and red-pilled rightists are among the chief offenders of this fallacious approach at "logic" and "reason" at the point in time we find them supporting Trump and being soft on the Alt-Right. The more fringe elements of this fake empiricism masquerade (such as the claims that "race" is a biological reality, that IQ is also genetically predetermined, and therefore IQ is locked at certain levels depending on one's perceived race)[3] might have once been too far on the outskirts of the populist rationale spectrum for the more typical anti-political populists of the conservative working class to take seriously, but as economic entropy has spread and more and more people have begun to break their backs under late capitalism's weight, these once-deplorable fringe actors now seem more than ever like brothers in solidarity. There is literally nowhere else to turn for said solidarity, because the narrative most economic conservatives of every stripe have been sold is that anything to the left of neoliberal fiscal policy leads to gulags and mass murder.

Does America have a cultural history fundamentally entangled with racism? Yes. From the moment slavery ended, the economic elites and their State cronies took steps to, in effect, criminalize Black life. As neoliberalism, liberalism's most recent perversion, took hegemonic hold in the West, that effort evolved too. The war on drugs is an unabashedly racist policy initiative that continues to target and imprison people of color as a means of retaining their free labor remembering the aforementioned Reagan campaign against the drugs primarily consumed by people of color, as well as the framing of young Black men as "militants.").[4] It is abhorrent, but it is also systemic and historically tethered to the elite class's inability or unwillingness to part with its means of retaining profit and power. Everyday conservative working-class people, traditionally raised in a cultural environment that encourages celebration and emulation of that aforementioned profit and power retention, are typically not conscious of the underlying history.

Yes, America has a racist cultural history. But that history does not always and necessarily equate to consciously racist individuals. This is the most sinister element to right-wing populism's ability to shift the narrative and push well-meaning people simply ignorant of the issues along the populist rationale spectrum toward a unique kind of racism: it does so by conceding legitimate class-based unrest, offering up untrue prejudicial explanations, and counting on the demographically susceptible members of the right to take cues from their historically racist cultural surroundings and rationalize the narrative in an ill-fated attempt at finding answers for their class-based strife. It is still wrong and worthy of scorn, but it must also be understood for the unique manifestation of prejudice that it is. And that then can be seen taking the form of other forms of unique prejudice against any number of other types of *Others* within the same economic bracket—trans and/or non-binary people, gay people, immigrants of color, people of less common religious faiths, and so forth are all more and more frequently admonished by the uniquely prejudiced working-class right all in ways that ultimately amount to the same broad stroke perspective: "minority groups are shown specific favor, therefore, they must be gaming the system and not working as hard as I am."

Thus, together *all* versions of conservative populists stay—even when a certain subset of the larger group holds abhorrent views about their fellow humans. To these self-fashioned plebiscites, any potential brothers in arms are needed to stop the perceived enemy (i.e., their brand of manufactured antagonist), and anyone left of conservative *is* the enemy. Here is found manifested the kind of process described by social breakdown theorists, while simultaneously falling in line with the expectations set up by the Rydgrenian Ethnic Competition Hypothesis. While Rydgren has shown skepticism toward the former in the past,[5] my submission is that, by understanding the extreme populist process through the lens of something like the populist rationale spectrum, *both* ethnic competition and social breakdown hypotheses are demonstrable, synthesized, and compatible to give us a fuller, more three-dimensional grasp of what is happening in these spaces.

This is aided by a far less extreme but still relevantly highlighted aspect of this realist philosophy being subsumed into the populist rationale spectrum's most normalizing region for the populist right when it comes to neoliberal economic systems being seen as an inescapable constant. The larger debate on the question of "liberty" right now is indeed between the moralists and the realists, and the moralists hold that politics themselves should be seen as an applied ethics in the sense that political policy itself essentially determines which of our abstract moral principles see validation through law. Political philosophers in general are tasked in this conversation to determine what these words like "liberty," "freedom," and "equality" mean, and how to realize them in political spaces and action. At the end of this process, posit the moralists, we will have determined for our society what is moral and subsequently prescribe said morality, in a sense, through legislation. Thought experiments ensue to reach these conclusions, in which potentially negative externalities come alongside these freedoms being realized, thereby justifying the concept of legal restriction for moral reasons and challenging the thinker to reconsider her own concepts of morality, fairness, and equality on the frontier of liberty. Only once these moral avenues have been carved out and the prescriptions made by the philosophizing, claim the moralists, can the real world of political action and policy put workable ideas into play.

For very understandable reasons, the realists contrast this approach entirely and argue for something more immediate and less concerned with hypothetical moral policing. Instead, they say, the focus should be on things that simply liberate real people from their real constrained situations using means we already have at our disposal. The claim goes that the policies we implement in the real world really just amount to using mechanisms and systems that we already know exist, and therefore, it is within these limitations that our efforts for human liberty are best realized.

Unfortunately, thanks to the narrowing of liberal ideas and the distortion of revolutionary ones delineated in Part II of this book, the only real type of realism to gain significant traction in the public political conversation is the realism prescribed by post-1830 liberalism. This realism posits that the real quest of political philosophers is to take part in philosophy that already assumes at its outset the natural validity of liberal systems such as State collusion with owners of capital and, of course, capitalism itself.

The Industrial Revolution, the New Deal, the Keynesian golden age, and so forth all have with them in common an accompanying narrative aimed at keeping complacent the underinformed masses. But these times in particular also saw class divide spotlighted at the forefront of common people's minds. As a result, a kind of self-delusion can be seen kicking in that itself is not entirely separated from the anti-political populism delineated in Chapter 2. It is adjacent to this phenomenon and shares many of its qualities, including the knack for legitimizing untruths in the name of feeling a sense of faux-awareness.

Much like the deliberate counter-revolutionary insurgencies outlined earlier by Harcourt, this mass rationalization of circumstances exists at a place on the populist rationale spectrum that a vast number of people reside: the need to make sense of one's place in the grand order of things. This desire in and of itself is not sinister, but it can lead to self-delusion when the reality is at odds with said desire. This is where the uniqueness of the present counter-revolutionary insurgency lies—it is not in and of itself a counter-revolution any longer. It is instead a genuine revolutionary movement in attitude and belief; it simply isn't revolutionary in its ultimate endgame. This is by design, as we have been able to demonstrate in the previous section of the book, but the designers have long let go of the wheel and the train is now on autopilot. Its passengers are mostly truthful and earnest working-class activists, passionately declaring their support for "real" capitalism rather than what they see as a perversion of it in what they call "crony capitalism" or "corporatism." It doesn't matter to the passengers that its actual history proves capitalism to have never been a free market for workers, or that its initial proponents were misrepresenting the reality of its intent (as well as the motives of its detractors). All that matters is that the narrative all fits together, and the American Dream remains alive. After all, for all of the working-class people's hard work, a proportionate reward seems more than reasonable. Socialism and (historically actuated) anarchism, though the original war cry of the working class, call for the dismantling of the entire system, and along with it, any chance of the American Dream as it is presented today surviving. Neoliberalism, while not ideal (and simply the modern version of capitalism apologetics started in the 1830s by the newfangled, anti-worker classical liberals), preserves the American Dream and keeps the hope of one's hard work paying off within one's own lifetime alive.

The latter is a more appealing option, but it doesn't actually stand to solve the real problem that keeps limiting worker autonomy in markets. This is because in order to believe in the attainability of the American Dream, one must also believe that the capitalistic system itself is designed to lead workers there. As we have seen in our exploration of capitalism's actual history, that belief is not true. Therefore, "corporatism" and capitalism are the same thing in intent. The supposed true free market of "real" capitalism often touted by libertarians and other economically conservative ideologies has *never* existed inside of capitalism itself because capitalism was designed from the beginning to benefit capitalists (owners and manufacturers) and not workers. This is a fundamentally impassable impediment that can only be bypassed with a myth—and a myth is precisely what pro-capitalist actors vying for the ears of the working-class devised.[6] Now, that myth has become so imbued within the conversation that our aforementioned passengers accept it without much question. But as more and more people within the working class have begun to experience the limitations of what capitalism can offer (after all, artificial hierarchies can only give so much autonomy to people on the ground floor), more and more passengers have been exiting the train.

For instance, a good majority of minority demographics, who felt these limitations much earlier in capitalism's tenure than their predominantly white male counterparts, have already gotten off several stations ago when it comes to the unshaking belief in the American Dream's attainability within capitalist constructs. But only recently have white working-class Americans also begun to feel the same disillusionment to the point where existing neoliberal pacifications are no longer enough. Said pacifications once made them feel culturally in control of their daily lives longer than less privileged people. But in the face of more socially progressive activism and the liberation (e.g., the granting of social and cultural influence) for more and more minority groups, that once-assured sense of cultural influence and predictability for white Americans exclusively has become shaken. This cultural progressivism has aligned by happenstance alongside the growth of white male working-class economic dissatisfaction, and to the untrained eye, this correlation could be seen as a causal link.

Therefore, as the anti-political populism delineated in Chapter 2 takes hold in these demographics, the manufactured antagonists of Chapter 3 become more and more believable—especially when the aforementioned desire to keep believing in the American Dream remains strong despite the rise in lived-in reasons (e.g., the spread of poverty into white suburbia highlighted in Chapter 3, or the increasing unrest in blue-collar regions of middle America that remained largely ignored for decades) to let it go.[7]

In the brilliant 2016 case study of this very demographic we are discussing, *Strangers in Their Own Land*, sociologist Arlie Russell Hochschild identifies the aforementioned phenomenon of cultural panic as being a disruption of what she calls a "deep story" for white working-class Americans.[8] She further explains a deep story as "a feels-as-if story—it's the story feelings tell, in the language of symbols. It removes judgement. It removes fact. It tells us how things feel."[9] Thus, for the white working-class American, the deep story is a reachable American Dream. Neoliberal policy normalizes the system that promises to give it, and culturally isolating circumstances make said system and its promise easier to digest. Hochschild describes moving along this story as waiting in line with others who look and think like you—others with who you share a sense of solidarity with due to experiencing the same working-class hardships *alongside* of cultural wars that seem to tap into our evolved-in tribal and protectionist sensibilities.[10]

Hochschild continues:

Just over the brow of the hill is the American Dream, the goal of everyone waiting in line. Many in the back of the line are people of color—poor, young and old, mainly without college degrees. It's scary to look back; there are so many behind you, *and in principle you wish them well.* Still, you've waited a long time, worked hard, and the line is barely moving. *You deserve to move forward a little faster.* (emphasis mine)[11]

This is a key element to the mindset of most everyday working people who also happen to be "white, older, Christian, and predominantly male."[12] They were born into this demographic, and so it is the only perception of the world they are immediately familiar with. But they share the same economic hardships as any other demographic of working-class person. They feel just as entitled to the American Dream as anyone else. *They're farther ahead in line.* So close to achieving everything they feel they have earned with all of their hard work and economic strife. Economically speaking, they do not feel very privileged. Thus, they resent being told of their white male privilege when everything they have thus far in their own lives has been fought for through long hours and grueling work. It is an understandable perspective to have. But culturally speaking, people who look like them have had an historical leg up in social influence and trustworthiness. This is a fact. Such interpersonal auspiciousness has therefore granted them a sense of security and of being on-top of things—their world, while financially hard, is one they feel very comfortable in making predictions about and feeling at least ideologically secure in. That is also a fact. So close, it seems, to finally achieving everything promised to them. All of their hard work is about to pay off—and these pesky leftists are asking them to let the people behind them cut in line!

This is why the rationale of populist peoples can be successfully thought of as existing on a spectrum—yes, the older demographics still have their religiosity, but the younger people within the otherwise-matching demographical traits find their own rationale for their populism outside of religious fundamentalism, as pointed out earlier in the book. Nevertheless, both groups reside very closely to one another on the populist rationale spectrum, which means there are far more beliefs shared in common, and on a far more visibly relatable frontier, than is the contrary. On these areas of agreement, solidarity can still be found. Similarly, as these like-minded populist groups find their collective voice and shared sense of grief, and this grief continues to be maligned by voices on the left who put their focus on the cultural and historical privilege of white males while seeming to ignore or minimalize the economic *under*privilege felt by many within that demographic today, both young and old groups of white male working-class conservatives may see their shared deep stories be *pushed* along the populist rationale spectrum toward a more extremist perspective of the other side of the debate—all in light of feeling cast aside and misunderstood by those to the political left of them.

As demonstrated by the data laid out in the previous chapters regarding actual job loss versus perceived unemployment rate, working-class men in particular have indeed fallen onto some tangibly hard and psychologically distressing times resulting from working-class strain.[13] On a daily basis, 121 Americans commit suicide.[14] Of those 121, 93 are men.[15] Seven out of ten of *those* men are white males, and middle-aged.[16] All told, the yearly death toll within these demographics from suicide is nearly 45,000.[17] This does not in any way validate the paranoia of the conservative white working class about cultural erosion, nor does it prove the more extremist beliefs regarding an impending "replacement" of the white "race" (in fact, "race" isn't even a genetic reality in humans and is solely a socially invented concept),[18] but these demographics *are* genuinely suffering under the collapse of late capitalism just like everyone else in the working class at large, and allowing basic human compassion on this front to fall by the wayside as hyper-focus on intersectional privilege dominates every sphere of social discourse signals a perceived lack of understanding to this increasingly hopeless subgroup of the working poor. If we are to understand how organic populist unrest can fall back into self-contained feedback loops that merely stand to perpetuate the ignorance and fear already present in such spaces, we must take seriously the earlier scenario and the perspectives, however distorted they may be, that lead to these people's anti-political populism spreading into cultural discourse. Pushing the paranoid even deeper into their paranoia by missing the woods for the trees (e.g., focusing almost exclusively on localized prejudices at the expense of the all-encompassing classism everyone in the working class could find solidarity on) is in many ways giving the elitist class exactly what it needs to survive: more distraction and more working-class division.

Does this mean we should simply cease discussion on these aforementioned localized prejudices that pit working-class people against each other from the other end of the spectrum? No. Quite on the contrary, we should be leaning *into* discourse and debate about all of these issues. But this approach is unlike what has become increasingly the norm, leading into the resurgence and empowerment of right-wing extremism. Shout-down culture at places historically meant for critical discourse, such as college campuses and other public forums, is on the rise despite what certain voices on the left might claim to the contrary.

To step back and delineate this a bit more in context: in the years leading up to the Trump election and the resurgence of more widespread crypto-fascist sympathies, there was an understandable backlash on the general left (everyday liberals, progressives, and left-anarchists of varying stripes) to the early brewing discourse that served as a gateway of sorts to the kind of unabashedly strident faux-skepticism and rebelliousness— created in large part by the post–Cold War neoconservative intellectuals (such as the likes of Irving Kristol, Gertrude Himmelfarb, and, later on, Christopher Hitchens) who had themselves come from Trotskyism and cut their debating teeth on combatting hard-core Soviet Union apologists and other Marxist-Leninists to great effect.[19] These types of intellectuals who ended up fighting for the conservative side knew how to combat the more extreme strands of the left on their own turf, and as such had much more relevant insight into the dogmatic pitfalls of the left than could have ever been mustered by the Christian fundamentalist types mentioned previously, themselves being hamstrung much more obviously by dogma of their own.[20] This was due in large part to these former Trotskyists' holding onto their critical theory proclivities and diagnosing problems of their opponents' thinking through looking at origin points and "overarching structures" present within them; the New Atheist movement, informed very heavily by Hitchens's own critical skepticism and later serving itself as a gateway into the faux-skepticism of red-pilled young conservatism, was arguably an organic bifurcation from this larger neoconservative intellectual renaissance.[21]

The co-opting of the leftist struggle, beginning with the liberal policy pandering to socialist working-class demands in the late 1800s and early 1900s (Chapter 5), continuing on with the conscious hijacking of socialist labels like anarchist and libertarian by capitalist apologists in the mid-twentieth century (Chapter 6), and trending further, into the twenty-first century, with the post-1960s Trotskyist-inspired neoconservative intellectualism just discussed, has gone a long way toward making liberal economic policy and cultural conservatism something of a sexy counterculture that frames itself as the intellectual opponent of status-quo norms. While this book has laid out the history behind this usurping as a means of demonstrating that these supposed antiestablishment movements are grounded in falsehoods, we must keep in mind once again the sincerity with which many of said movements' adherents passionately argue. To them, they are part of a genuine counterculture that aims to tear down perceived threats to integral American principles—of the more unbelievable variety, "Western culture," a vague and ill-defined concept that claims superiority of geographical location over all else; while a more reasonable fear of loss involves concepts like free speech and open discourse.

This ease of acceptance of such a narrative, that a new breed of intellectual conservatives are the sole vanguards of American sustainability, has been aided in recent decades by the brand of New Anger held on the right and observed by Peter Wood in Chapter 2. Since 9/11 especially, there has been a shifting of priorities within the American spirit, particularly on the right, that ignores the importance of working-class solidarity and gives undue emphasis instead to an almost mythic concept of "America" as a monolithic embodiment of freedom itself. "Western culture," as a peripheral concept, therefore gets bolstered into serving as freedom's torch—challenge anything at all about its perceived truisms, and one is seen as the enemy. One is seen as an *Other*.

Unfortunately for the leftist resistance to this narrative, certain elements of it actually do hold some truth. Especially on the free speech issue, the red-pilled faux-intellectuals and the post-Trotskyist neoconservatives unite in a persuasive chorus in favor of allowing *all* voices to be heard in public spaces, even those who might be trying to hurt with their words. What is "freedom?" Freedom for all.[22] The only time this principle needs to be amended, of course, is when the freedoms of others are abused to harm or limit the freedoms of others. This is where leftist critics of the free speech wars on college campuses throw their hats into the ring and, more often than not, misunderstand the inner workings of the speech as violence debate. To better grasp how and why this misunderstanding occurs, we need to make clear what the speech as violence debate even is and how it connects to issues of both legal censorship of hate speech and the more recent cancel culture online and on college campuses.

In her book *Excitable Speech*, critical theorist and philosopher Judith Butler puts forth a compelling case for language itself as a weapon of sorts when used for certain ends and in different degrees.[23] Butler in her own work builds upon foundations already laid prior by J. L. Austin that distinguished between "illocutionary" and "perlocutionary" speech, with the former being speech that performs a direct and immediate action and the latter being speech that leads to later negative hurtful effects upon another.[24] In both bases, speech is seen itself as an action, and an action that can indeed cause measurable harm. The idea that violence in and of itself must exclusively mean something that literally draws blood from flesh is a colloquial and culturally specific postulation that does not have much supported evidence throughout human history at large. Violence as a broader, more all-encompassing term that includes physical violence but also describes verbal, emotional, and mental assault has long-held precedent in both recorded history and in our own common phrases' etymological geneses. Terms such as "that hurts my feelings," for instance, should be enough to demonstrate this.

Yet, for many, especially on the right, the idea that language can be violent is a radical one that might even stand to threaten one of the most sacred human freedoms: the freedom of speech. There might actually be some legitimacy to that fear, given the fact that advocacy for censorship of hate speech on college campuses that leads to controversial campus speakers being disinvited and course curriculums to be excised does seem to be on the rise within the political left.[25] But it is important to note that Butler herself, one of the primary voices responsible for giving credence to the language as violence stance in the modern conversation, does not advocate for giving the State censorship power over speech. Later in her book, Butler makes the case that giving the State the sole power to make a judgment call regarding what is or is not hate speech, and therefore, what is or is not worthy of forceful censorship by the law, sets a dangerous precedent.

> Considered as discriminatory action, hate speech is a matter for the courts to decide, and so "hate speech" is not deemed hateful or discriminatory until the courts decide that it is. There is no hate speech in the full sense of that term until and unless there is a court that decides that there is. Indeed, the petition to call something hate speech, and to argue that it is also conduct, efficacious in its effects, consequentially and significantly privative of rights and liberties, is not yet to have made the case. The case is made only when it is "decided." In this sense, it is the decision of the State, the sanctioned utterance of the State, which produces the act of hate speech.[26]

Butler argues here that in our culture, before any harmful speech can be legally pushed back against, it must first be established by the State as qualifying as "hate speech," which gives the State the power to pick and choose what it wills to be wrong speech or speech worthy of legally acting against. Butler sees this as sinister, further stating:

> Thus hate speech is produced by the law, and constitutes one of its most savory productions; it becomes the legal instrument through which to produce and further a discourse on race a sexuality under the rubric of combatting racism and sexism. By such a formulation, I do not mean to suggest that the law causes or incites hate speech, but only that the decision to select which of the various acts of speech will be covered under the rubric of hate speech will be decided by the courts. Thus, the rubric is a legal norm to be augmented or restricted by the judiciary in the ways that it deems fit. This last impresses me as particularly important considering that hate speech arguments have been invoked against minority groups, that is, in those contexts in which homosexuality is rendered graphic (Mapplethorpe) or verbally explicit (the U.S. military) and those in which African-American vernacular, especially in rap music, recirculates the terms of social injury and is thereby held responsible for such terms. Those efforts at

regulation are inadvertently strengthened by the enhanced power of the State to enforce the distinctions between publicly protected and unprotected speech.[27]

In other words, from the moment that we grant the State the power to determine what counts as censor-worthy language, we allow for the likelihood that the next conversation surrounding what is or isn't harmful speech could very well lead to the censorship being applied to the marginalized—the very people the initial cry for government involvement in speech regulation was meant to protect. The reason for this is because regulatory arms of governments do not discriminate based upon cultural and historical context; they merely act on behalf of those who compel them to do so for whatever reason they may have. The reasons could be noble or sinister, and the outcome would still appear like the same action on paper: a government choosing to limit speech or behavior through regulatory means. Butler lamented that through this process, "the State not only constrains speech, but in the very act of constraining, produces legally consequential speech."[28] She also wisely observed as early as 1997 that the negative implications of all of this were "underestimated in the writings that favor hate speech legislation."[29]

This sort of cautionary rhetoric surrounding speech regulation, especially coming from someone who herself advocates the position that certain language *can* be injurious, makes two points: first, it demonstrates that it is indeed possible to hold the view that speech can be violent without advocating for State censorship, and second, it shows that leftists have historically been unwavering free speech advocates—something else the co-opted right-wing narrative has attempted to revise. The modern conversation on the right consists of voices who claim to stand for free speech, as opposed to those leftists, who it is posited want to silence their opponents rather than allow them to be combatted in the free exchange of ideas. But we have already demonstrated that at least one dominant leftist voice has stood on the right side of the free speech issue in Judith Butler. Another leftist voice who does the same is Noam Chomsky, who when asked at a speaking event his opinion on silencing hate speech, especially in the context of government censorship or omission of hate literature, said the following:

> Well, I'm against it. I don't think the State should have the power to decide what people think and say. I don't want the State to have that power. It's bad to have people running around with hate literature, but the way to [combat it] is not to give power to some more dangerous entity like the State. What you have to do is get to the people that [the hate mongers] are reaching.[30]

In another instance in which he was asked to address more specifically the free speech on college campuses issue, Chomsky reiterated his views and applied them to this form of campus censorship:

> I think we should really have open platforms in universities. If the students don't like something that's being said, they can stay away. But we should recognize that's a very minor part of it. The major part is the closing off of options for people who are critical, on the dissenting side, of the overwhelming consensus at the

university. . . . Up until about ten years ago, if I was giving a talk on the Middle-East at my own university, I would have to have police protection. There were times the police would insist on walking me back to my car because of information they'd picked up about threats. . . . There were meetings that were literally broken up by hecklers. But nobody ever protested that. I didn't, either. It's when students begin to veer in that direction on the other [dissenting] side that the protests begin. Now, I'm not defending what they're doing, but we should put it in context. The context is that preventing speech that is critical of the major consensus is never protested.[31]

Notice the nuance, here. Chomsky is just as unabashedly in favor of free speech as the next free speech advocate, but he isn't losing sight of the real reason why total free speech matters: to expose, protest, and rhetorically defeat the oppressive status quo. This angle of the debate is often lost by those on the right who claim to advocate free and open exchange of ideas. They will often advocate for the voices of extremists, but simultaneously move to discredit or misrepresent the leftist opposition to the topics in question. When former Breitbart editor Milo Yiannopoulos publicly deadnamed a trans high school student during a speech of his at University of Wisconsin-Milwaukee in 2016 (i.e., he called her by the name she was given at birth rather than the name she now has in attempt to "expose" her as the supposedly opposite gender), he was arguably using his freedom to speak as a means of limiting her freedom to not be harassed by countless strangers.[32] Was this not something worthy of scorning in the great ideas debate stage? And yet, the free speech advocates on the right who supported Yiannopoulos never bothered to call him out.[33] They simply continued to advocate that he have access to the platform to speak and behave as he pleased; they never saw said platform as an opportunity to engage him in any real debate or contest his many extreme and generalized claims against trans people, women, his fellow gay people, and all forms of liberals and leftists.[34]

In total, while the claim was to allow for a platform on which real debate and conversation could be allowed, no such debate ever took place. Yiannopoulos simply appeared at various venues, unchallenged, and free to say whatever he liked. The story was much the same for various other so-called free speech advocates on the right who continued to say horrible and outlandish things about marginalized people—everyone from Molyneux and Southern to Yiannopoulos himself. It became a worthy question after a time: Was this really about these public figures on the right fighting for the right to free debate? Or was it more about giving these figures the right to spout ignorant and harmful claims about marginalized groups without challenge? If it was in fact the latter, then the spirit of what they were fighting for aligned much more with the oppressive agenda feared by Butler and Chomsky than anything else. Certainly, it was not being done at the hands of a State, but it was still being done on behalf of influential public figures who had their own political agendas to promote. It wasn't so much free speech advocacy across the board as it was advocacy for speech favoritism. This was helped along by the accompanying "us vs. them" quality of much of the rhetoric that both sides brought in tow. Leftists were painted as "special snowflakes" who didn't care about free discourse, while the right-leaning figures who took to these forums continued to not actually engage in any real debate. These spaces became echo chambers for right-wing ideology that presented itself as a centrist reason.[35]

Still, there was an intellectual consistency present on the right in these discussions about free platforms that could be respected, and it was often not mirrored on the left—especially in spaces such as college campuses and other public forums. Many naysayers on the left have tried to downplay this culture of taking platforms away from invited speakers at universities as being overblown, but there is actually good reason to doubt those claims. In 2018, *The Washington Post* printed an article claiming that the campus free speech issue was "a myth," and that it was in fact young people who stood by free discourse the most.[36] Likewise, *Vox* contributor Matthew Yglesias wrote a similarly minded article bearing the promise that "support for free speech is rising," and that said support was "higher among liberals and college students."[37] Those articles were both citing from the same source, and that source was being presented incorrectly as if it accounted for a specific demographic being discussed: college students.

The source in question was the General Social Survey (GSS), itself a very respected source for opinion data. But the opinion data cited in this case, regarding attitudes within certain demographics on the free speech issue, accounted for much too broad a demographic to accurately represent college student attitudes specifically. The GSS data stated, fairly, that the people most likely to support free speech fell into the age range of eighteen to thirty-four.[38] That is encouraging news, but not all eighteen to thirty-four-year-olds are college students.[39] In fact, many are not, with the latest data suggesting that the vast majority of college students today do not even enter college until over age twenty-five.[40] Furthermore, the GSS also did not sample people in that age group who were residents of "institutions and group quarters."[41] This means that most college students would have been already excluded from the survey from the start due to them living in dorms.[42]

What's more is that the way in which the question about speaker support was posed in the GSS survey aimed to ask if people would support the views of noble public dissenters speaking out against oppressive establishment—that is, the same thing Chomsky made a point to clarify in his own answer that students are already aligned with. Of course, young people are going to be more likely to agree to support the speech of people they already agree with; the challenge comes when a person is asked if he or she will stand in principle for the speaking rights of those with whom they vehemently disagree. The GSS survey arguably did not give that opportunity to its participants.[43]

There is, however, a more representative sampling of specifically student opinion on free speech on campus in the form of a Gallup/Knight Foundation study from 2017 that showed roughly 70 percent of students wanted an open learning environment on campus that did not restrict offensive speech.[44] The aforementioned opinion pieces from the mainstream news outlets arguing against free speech on college campuses being a problem cited this study as another example that they were correct. However, the position was never that the shout-down culture on campus had become the majority opinion; only that it was real and on the rise. Looking at the 2017 results, the Gallup/Knight study showed that nearly 30 percent of college students *did* want to prohibit certain kinds of speech on campuses.[45] Comparing that result to the previous year, that position had risen by around 8 percent.[46] Conversely, the position that free and open debate should happen on college campuses had *fallen* by that same amount between 2016 and 2017.[47] This data suggests that there is in fact a rising trend on college campuses to shout down, disinvite, or otherwise limit controversial speech as opposed to engage with it and shine a light on its shortcomings. The latter course of action would certainly go a long way toward weakening the related anti-political claims by the extremists on the right, while the former has simply gone on to give it validation.

There are no critics more cutting of this sliver of the left than other leftists, however. Angela Nagle, a leftist herself who is critical of what she refers to as "Tumblr-liberals" (referring to the online forum Tumblr often associated with the left) and the "identitarian privilege-checking left," cites how the more casually anti-politically correct wing of the Alt-Right was in many ways carved out online in the forums of 4chan, a rival site to Tumblr, in response to the ultrasensitivity and identitarian populism present in the extreme leftist wing of the Internet.[48] The "divisions within the broad 'left,'" writes Nagle in her book *Kill All Normies*, "became more prominent than ever" leading up to and immediately following the Trump election in 2016, but Nagle argues that this was merely a culmination of many years of imprecise attempts to bust through the oppression of cultural normativity.[49] Issues of gender conformity and a newfound freedom to express oneself free of the culturally assumed binary meant that, especially online in spaces like Tumblr, a certain sliver of the left went all out and began to amplify its brand of "ultra-sensitive" identitarianism that contrasted to 4chan's "shocking irreverence," meaning that neither side was ever going to see eye to eye and it was only natural that they would see themselves as their own respective *Others*.[50]

Presented at first as a culture of tongue-in-cheek memes meant to troll and irritate the ultrasensitive section of the online left, the 4chan component of what became the current amalgamated Alt-Right was ultimately subsumed into the movement under the guise of anti-political solidarity being found regarding issues of free speech. Mike Wendling, author of *Alt-Right: From 4chan to the White House*, states the following about that process:

> And yet they found traction as their online efforts melded with the current fever-pitch of anti-elitism, and found a willing audience in a concentrated generational backlash against young men. These foot soldiers feel aggrieved by the success of feminism and the progress made by ethnic minorities, and have also felt rising anxiety as former certainties about race, sexuality and gender crumble. At the same time, some are puzzled and scared—as are many people the more traditional right as well as the left—by the censorious atmosphere of many university campuses today, a confusing, sometimes barely comprehensible minefield of trigger warnings, privilege checking, safe spaces, and complicated sexual politics. For the alt-right, all of those fall under the umbrella of one of the ideas they loathe the most: political correctness.[51]

Thus, the right-wing revolutionary members of 4chan (and its offshoot, 8chan), calling themselves "Kekistanis," moved along the populist rationale spectrum and into the Alt-Right proper as it solidified into the amalgamation of various fringe right identitarian groups the world came to know it as. It is arguable that had the left itself not been as divided as it was at the time due to it also combatting its own identitarian strand, this process might not have been as easily accomplished.[52] The biggest obstacle to overcome about the specific anxiety that got filtered into the Alt-Right was the fact that base-level opposition to extreme political correctness that serves as conversation stoppers was relatable and saw overlap across various political sub-spheres. This made it more difficult in the beginning to tell apart a moderate conservative from a budding extremist at first glance.

Nevertheless, mindful leftists continued to speak out about what they saw as a detriment to their own cause in the Tumblr-liberals and other faux-progressives that seemed more concerned with outward appearances and avoidance of hurt feelings than with genuine social justice. Returning again to Mark Fisher, it should be noted that he was one of the most tempered and thoughtful critics of this sliver of the left in his own writings. Fisher wrote an explosive critical essay in which he pointed out that the left could not fight for the broadly agreed-upon causes if it stayed divided, culminating his message in the following observation:

> "Left-wing" Twitter can often be a miserable, dispiriting zone. Earlier this year, there were some high-profile twitterstorms, in which particular left-identifying figures were "called out" and condemned. What these figures had said was sometimes objectionable; but nevertheless, the way in which they were personally vilified and hounded left a horrible residue: the stench of bad conscience and witch-hunting moralism. The reason I didn't speak out on any of these incidents, I'm ashamed to say, was fear. The bullies were in another part of the playground. I didn't want to attract their attention to me.[53]

But once he did speak out, Fisher did indeed receive all the hateful scorn he dreaded having to endure. A Marxist and advocate of equitable social justice, Fisher being accused of racism, misogyny, and other awful things was quite baseless.[54] But because he had dared to, in the words of Nagle, "touch on any of the Tumblr left's key sensitivities," Fisher would receive a "deluge of personal and vindictive mass abuse" for "years afterwards."[55]

So, why *was* this happening? The right-wing answer, "leftism is a brain disorder" (or some variant of that sentiment), doesn't quite offer the detail and connections needed to adequately satisfy that question, especially since we have established by now that not all leftists share the proclivity for censorship held by the Tumblr left, and that said proclivity has caused an internal rift within the left. But Nagle offers a compelling potential answer, namely that "the key driving force" behind the left's online call-out culture "is about creating scarcity in an environment in which virtue is the currency that can make or break the career or social success of an online user in this milieu, the counterforce of which was the anonymous underworld from which the right-wing trolling cultures emerged."[56]

Recalling what we have already established about neoliberalism from earlier in this book, this does make sense—in a culture that has long tethered personal value to how much a human being can behave like a good or currency in and of himself, it does stand to reason that when clicks and likes can translate to real-world monetary value for survival, one would gravitate toward carrying the personal capital belief system into the new online frontier where it can find new life and further application. Nobody is immune to the machine, even those on the left who claim to have a better understanding of all its moving parts. Thus, much like how the conservative and libertarian public figures found their "skepticism" niche to seek rent in their own way, it could be argued that the Tumblr left found its niche to be a virtue. A growing sense of empathy is a sign of maturity, and the left strives to mature. But at what point does deep-rooted empathy cross over into aesthetic virtue? Perhaps when the preconceived commerce introduced in Chapter 3 cannot be successfully applied to the online world, and therefore that world is deemed at some subconscious level as needing to be artificially engineered to fit into the existing concepts of human value. We are trained by neoliberal hegemony to think scarcity signifies value—even in non-economic spaces. Therefore, a scarcity of virtue in the leftist online world might have felt necessary as a means of demonstrating importance.

But as this book has alluded to more than once previously, "virtue signaling," in the colloquial understanding of the term, is fairly ubiquitous and doesn't just occur within groups that see virtue itself as a literal currency (like the Tumblr left). Self-validation in place of real empathic action, while arguably present in this area of the online- and college-dominated left, is also something the worst actors on the right are guilty of, and to a lesser degree, we all display this tendency on one level or another as we aim to find our comfort zones as the social creatures that we are.

Therefore, to truly peg why the Tumblr leftist, or the stereotypical social justice warrior, doesn't make the impact she thinks she is making, we have to reach deeper than merely understanding what motivates her. Certainly, this neoliberalized urge to find a sense of purpose through scarce virtue might be the driving force, but what dictates the *color* of the rhetoric itself and specific stated aims that are meant to represent that virtue?

Zero Books editor Douglass Lane has argued that the SJW fails not specifically because she isn't sincere in wanting to help, but because she is operating on the false assumption that political result follows from culture rather than from institutions.[57] This means that, much like the postmodernist philosophers of the 1970s, many SJWs focus almost all of their analysis of what drives human action onto ideas instead of systems. The critical theorists, on the other hand, try to analyze how both ideas *and* systems of class divide and hierarchy work in tandem with one another to perpetuate hegemony. This is why it isn't unusual to see self-described Marxists and neo-Marxists having intellectual skirmishes with both postmodernists on the outside as well as SJW leftists within their own broader socialist circle. SJW activism tends to therefore drive exclusively toward changing socially entrenched ideas first instead of institutional operations; when policy is indeed approached, it is only done so for the purposes of hurrying the reform of an idea upon society in a forceful manner.

This approach fails because society's own discourse is merely a series of feedback loops, such as the organic false consciousness brought on by neoliberal hegemony that Part Two of this book examined. Trying to use discourse against itself to wake a society up from a long-entrenched norm, all without better context or information having already been made available to the people within these feedback loops, falls short of the goal. Social change usually comes from material, tangible change first in which some new access to information is ensured or a new, tactile experience has been opened up to enough people at a time to shift the tide in a given feedback loop's established expectations.

Based on the most commonly observable actions and rhetoric attributed to the label, the SJW seems to see the world not as a system of interrelated power dynamics between individuals, collectives, laws, institutions, and hegemonic narratives, but instead as a wide-open space comprising of individual people whose actions can simply be shifted by changing the ideas residing in their minds.[58] Ironically, this is not too far away from how conservatives, libertarians, and liberal "centrists" also view the world and the people in it. This might also explain why that the extremists in both the Tumblr left and the populist right have fallen into identitarianism and neoliberal preconceived commerce in their activist spaces.[59] This also means that the SJW approach at changing society for the better is to go after the ideas themselves and/or the people deemed to hold those ideas. If a mind cannot be changed in this way, then the next thing to do is to silence the voice that gives life to it. This is why de-platforming, shouting down, and calling out are often observed as being the primary tactics of leftists who hold this perspective of the world.[60]

But none of this means that *all* leftists see the world this way—quite the contrary. It also wouldn't be fair to claim that these tactics represent the full raison d'être of any one of the SJW activists in question—they are, after all, individuals with multifaceted viewpoints on many aspects of life and their activism should not be seen as the example of the whole person. In this way, it is important to realize that the concept of the SJW, especially as the right has gone on to caricaturize it, does not really exist. Yet, the behaviors (and the potentially detrimental effects they draw) *do* exist, and so to ignore them completely would be disingenuous. Nevertheless, putting a hyper-focus on this aspect of the working-class political discussion without conceding the far greater danger present on the extreme right is something that should be met with scorn and suspicion. Unfortunately, this is almost always what is done on even the most mainstream and moderate conservative platforms. It stems, once again, from the fiscally induced desperate need to find solidarity and grow numbers on the right at all costs—even if it means keeping company with and turning a blind eye toward some of the worst publicly visible actors the political right has seen in decades.

* * *

Perhaps the better way to approach this whole conversation about the working-class rightists feeling like their freedom of speech and expression is threatened isn't to solely point fingers at so-called SJWs along with them (though it was important that we at least attempted to understand that phenomenon), but instead to determine how to better cultivate a positive utilization of the opportunities free speech provides across the entire working class, regardless of political proclivity. Much of the anti-political Jacobinism and New Anger that forms on the working-class right in the first place comes from a feeling of genuine distrust toward anything outside the perceived norm, as Part One of this book delineated. The working-class right's broad frontier of antagonism comprises manufactured boogeymen, of course, but if the genuine cry for open exchange of ideas that this same crowd exudes is to be put to real use, then the activism we see in revolutionary spaces should bring about, in the words of Douglass Lane, "*material* change" rather than stay in the abstract realm of ideas alone.[61]

Going back to our distinction between Hegelian and Kantian analysis of perception from Chapter 5, we already understand that Hegel had a different take on reality from Kant, with the latter being considered more materialist and the former idealist. Yet, Marx devised his historical materialism largely using Hegel's dialectic as its rationale. To Marx, the dialectic was needed to explain how so many contradictory things can come together to form narratives, but he still proposed that all manner of meaningful life aspects are determined first by their applied realities and material conditions rather than by intention or value. In other words, what we think of something has merit, but these perspectives are still brought about in some way or another by our material realities. This does not directly contradict Hegel, as his idealism was still posited as one that can be historically informed, which isn't quite the same thing as the idealism of those typically seen as being completely opposed to materialism.[62] Rather, Hegel's concept of the thing as we experience it leans on recognizing the historical process of ingraining certain ideas into our minds that can then be tethered to material things we experience. In Marx's words:

> Men make their own history, but they do not make it as they please; they do not make it under self-selected circumstances, but under circumstances existing already, given and transmitted from the past. The tradition of all dead generations weighs like a nightmare on the brains of the living. And just as they seem to be occupied with revolutionizing themselves and things, creating something that did not exist before, precisely in such epochs of revolutionary crisis they anxiously conjure up the spirits of the past to their service, borrowing from them names, battle slogans, and costumes in order to present this new scene in world history in time-honored disguise and borrowed language.[63]

A common objection to this line of thinking amounts to essentially conflating historical materialism with a kind of hard-line determinism that is incompatible with any concept of free will whatsoever, thereby framing it as fatalistic and overly philosophical. But a fairer interpretation of historical materialism would be to see it as being more in line with *compatible* determinism in which causal effects are not denied, yet autonomy of thinking people is still recognized as being capable of existing *within* the confines set in place by one's material circumstances.

To better explain what this looks like in action, let us return once more to the idea of hegemony and how it led to the organic feedback loops of false consciousness in which misguided populism now thrives.

In their book *Manufacturing Consent*, Noam Chomsky and Edward S. Herman described what they called the propaganda model, the mechanism by which the mass media perpetuates hegemony on behalf of the neoliberal capitalistic system that benefits the elite.[64] Once again, we see overlap between the anti-political populists on the working-class right and the old school socialists and anarchists on the working-class left. Both camps recognize something is amiss with their daily existences, but they come to very different conclusions as to what the cause of this malaise is. The right-wing populists of today are a less sophisticated version of their predecessors, but the right-of-center activist types have arguably never completely gotten it right because they have always still fallen under the shadow of neoliberal hegemony, just like every other mainstream political group. This means that what makes the right-wing populists stand out as revolutionaries amounts to a surface-level rebelliousness that does not ultimately call for true revolution. They will say they are against tyranny, but they will only actively fight the government while allowing private corporate tyranny to continue. They claim to want liberty, yet they often partake in the culture wars of their day, falling victim to prejudice and bigotry of other people they don't understand. Even the right-libertarians, who claim to at least tolerate other lifestyles and minorities they may not personally agree with, have recently trended more and more toward the same behavior as their alt-light counterparts and kept company with nationalists and crypto-fascists for the sake of economically facing solidarity.[65] If the Tumblr leftist's pitfall is trusting that policy follows from culture, then the right-wing populist's equivalent sin is believing that economic freedom trumps all other forms of human liberation. Yet, on the populist left, such pitfalls are usually already avoided because reverence for cultural analysis is already so present in the leftist wheelhouse. Chomsky and Herman, for instance, identified in their work not only the economic oppression of working people, but the cultural oppression as well by way of mainstream media conditioning. An important work, acknowledges Lane, but one that ultimately came down on the same side as the liberal and neoliberal sentiment when it came to its take on free speech: that free speech advocacy begins and ends with just opening up the forum and leaving it at that.[66]

It is arguable that this way of thinking about free speech is only part of the whole picture. Yes, as we have established, it is important to make sure a free and open forum is made available, and it is detrimental to the cause or utility of free speech to be selective in who speaks and who responds. But this on its own does not tackle the greater fear that now plagues spaces like online communities and public debate stages: Are we informed enough to use free speech responsibly, or can misinformation be spread just as quickly and take hold of minds just as assuredly as the truth? If the second case is true, then is simply opening up the forum to any and all voices without any additional mindfulness really going to get us anywhere? Will the misguided populists operating off of false information simply fade away over time as the truth "wins out" through some quasi-magical appeal to principle and nobility? Does it really work like that?

If one were being intellectually honest, the answer to that question would likely reside somewhere between an outright "no" and a highly conditional "maybe." The sheer fact that populism has been so easily manipulated into hate most recently, and that this process happened largely due to confirmation bias, cognitive dissonance, and misinformation appealing to existing prejudice, should demonstrate why. Not only did this process happen, but it largely happened through the open forum known as the Internet, where everyone being free to voice their perspectives across various social media platforms has often been celebrated as being the pinnacle of freedom and connectivity. But without any ubiquitous sense of *how* to process information in a way that gets to the truth, anyone can claim to be critically thinking when in reality he could simply be propagandizing or self-deluding.

What is the answer, then? Censorship? No, for all of the prior reasons given. But should there be some kind of minor regulation or limitation put on the Internet? Not necessarily. Because things being as they are currently in this system, the person ultimately determining how to regulate the online conversations is still going to be either a corporate head or a politician—minor or no, regulation of the many at the hands of the few is still not true democracy, and therefore presents far greater risks than benefits.

But to assume these are the only options is to ourselves fall into the hypnosis of neoliberal hegemony and capitalist realism. Much like the leftist SJW assuming that value must come from scarcity, we too might assume that "control" of information must bring with it implications of power dynamics and divide between haves and have-nots. But taking a step away from the machine, at least conceptually, we find they we would be wrong to make this assumption. Control of information is currently not democratic because we do not currently live in a society whose driving system is designed to allow for direct democratic control of anything. It is designed instead for exclusive ownership of the means to produce and control goods, information, and creativity at the hands of a select few. But just because we cannot imagine a dynamic in which we democratically control information in the *current* system does not mean that such a dynamic should not be something we strive for—remember the Kantian thing as it is versus the Hegelian thing that can be known.[67]

As Lane points out, the term "manufacturing consent," which Chomsky and Herman used for their book's title, was not coined by them originally.[68] Rather, it was political journalist Walter Lippman who came up with the phrase in *his* book *Public Opinion*.[69] There, Lippman argued *for* manufacturing consent—just manufacturing consent from within the working-class rather than from without.[70] Foucault's concept of power coming through discourse of knowledge comes into play once again as we return to our understanding in Chapter 3 of neoliberalism as a replacement for democratically discerned cultural value. Lippman took a similar approach to his understanding of "power," in that to him, power came through *how* information itself came to the people. Or, to put it another way, Lippman felt that consent was *always* going to be manufactured within systems of power—this was something he saw as inevitable.[71] The issue for him wasn't whether or not expression and information could be "free" or "open" in the colloquial sense, but instead through what means expression and information was going to be inevitably filtered.

Lippman wrote,

> without some form of censorship, propaganda in the strict sense of the word is impossible. In order to conduct a propaganda there must be some barrier between the public and the event. . . . For while people who have direct access can misconceive what they see, no one else can decide how they shall misconceive it, unless he can decide where they shall look, and at what.[72]

This led Lippman to articulate how propaganda itself can hide behind the idea of limited information for the sake of privacy—not that privacy itself isn't important, but that privacy as a concept can often stack up to the point where passed along information has already been filtered through so many personal limited perspectives that it isn't always reliable, instead putting up "barriers" between the information and the receiver.[73] Lippman also cautioned that privacy can also be misapplied in areas of public benefit, stating:

> Privacy is insisted upon at all kinds of places in the area of what is called public affairs. It is often very illuminating, therefore, to ask yourself how you got at the facts on which you base your opinion. Who actually saw, heard, felt, counted, named the thing, about which you have your opinion? Was it the man who told you, or the man who told him, or someone still further removed? How much was he permitted to see? When he informs you that France thinks this and that, what part of France did he watch? How was he able to watch it? Where was he when he watched it? What Frenchman was he permitted to talk to, what newspapers did he read, and where did they learn what they say? You can ask yourself these questions, but you can rarely answer them. They will remind you, however, of the distance which often separates your public opinion from the event with which it deals. And the reminder itself is a protection.[74]

The initial knee-jerk response to this quote today might be to argue that since the Internet, these various degrees of removal from the source are no longer a problem. Yet, look around: propaganda still prevails, consent is still being manufactured, and the Internet is now the prime arbiter of *mis*information to that end. Even in the realms of the "alternative media," which claims to be free of elitist interest. To Lippman's point, just because the information is now freer and more open than ever does not mitigate the problem of how this information is being filtered into public opinion and by what means. At the intersection between cultural ideas and material reality, Lippman finds his analysis, arguing that in all democratic societies, there is always a struggle between the idea of liberty and the material reality of control. Therefore, control is sought through perpetuation of perceived norms upon with cultural identity can adhere. In this way, ideas and material reality present themselves as either coterminous or even indistinguishable, and the general consensus of public opinion operates as such.

Lippman wrote "that the manufacture of consent is capable of great refinements no one, I think, denies," conceding again its power.[75] But what he came to see as its seeming inevitability arrived through observing democracy itself. In his words:

> The creation of consent is not a new art. It is a very old one which was supposed to have died out with the appearance of democracy. But it has not died out. It has, in fact, improved enormously in technic, because it is now based on analysis rather than on rule of thumb. And so, as a result of psychological research, coupled with the modern means of communication, the practice of democracy has turned a corner. A revolution is taking place, infinitely more significant than any shifting of economic power.[76]

Now, take a moment to apply this observation to the modern world of information conveyance via the Internet. This *should* make it easier than ever to cut through misinformation and find the objective truth. But in reality, as long as misinformation can appear like analysis and critical thinking, it does not need to actually be those things. The aforementioned pseudo-skeptics on YouTube, with video titles like "[opponent name here] gets DESTROYED by FACTS and LOGIC!," allow their own approach at false scarcity (in this case, the value is found in how logical they are) to show through and take advantage of the neoliberalized public opinion. The Internet is an ideal vehicle for such distortions of reality because it too can filter information and, if used for evil, obfuscate necessary context, history, and methodology in order to present a certain narrative that benefits the presenter of said information. The system of power that is currently dictating that information be filtered in this way is the present economic system we live under—actually existing capitalism.[77] The system of power that *could* be dictating how the Internet filters information instead is on of direct democratic control over the marketplace at the hands of working people.

But, according to Lippman (himself a socialist for a time, despite his later ironic influence on neoliberal policy), we are simply not there yet.[78] The general populace has not yet trained itself to epistemologically unpack the very culture it has been bred from. Society is far too complex, and even its smartest inhabitants (e.g., the public intellectuals, the teachers, the scientists) are still yet part of the bewildered masses, whose opinions and actions amount to what Lippman called, borrowing a phrase from English surgeon and social psychologist Wilfred Trotter, the "instinct of the herd."[79] To trust that this herd will have the wisdom to properly filter information for itself without first reconfiguring the very system that bewilders it in the first place is counterintuitive and naïve. Yet, the liberal (and neoliberal) concept of what it means to be a free speech advocate promotes that very approach. It is great to promote free and open forums, but that cannot and should not be seen as enough on its own if the end goal is for the working-class to find liberation through information and communication. More is needed. Just like the SJWs on the left need not solely focus on ideas over policy, no activist of any stripe should see free expression as the end goal for the liberation process—it is merely the midway point.

Beyond it, there lies an even more necessary goal: the escape from the hegemonized feedback loops that improperly filter information based on preconceptions present in a given group. In order to get past the organic false consciousness that has resulted from said hegemony, material change needs to be sought—to systems, institutions, and power relations that are presently taken for granted in our society.

Lippman observed that because this process had not yet taken place, and these systems and power dynamics went on unchallenged, certain innate limitations would remain part of the filtering process. It isn't just one dynamic that can affect behavior and access to information; one informs the other. "The size of a man's income," Lippman wrote, "has considerable effect on his access to the world beyond his neighborhood. With money he can overcome almost every tangible obstacle of communication . . . but men's ideas determine how that income shall be spent, and that in turn affects in the long run the amount of income they will have."[80] In place of the real environments these members of the bewildered masses reside, Lippman argued, they imagine pseudo-environments as a way to compensate for their inability to comprehend the full picture. To employ previously established terminology, Lippman's herd is unable to outthink the hegemony that dictates the daily existence of its members and see the "world outside."[81] Therefore, a mental image is conceptualized, itself partially informed by the hegemonic surroundings, in order for the herd's inhabitants (us) to cope and function. In Lippman's words, people "live in the same world, but they think and feel in different ones."[82]

Therefore, in order for a given democratic society to be both truly democratic but also empowered through information rather than propagandized, material change needs to be underway before "free speech" can truly be utilized in a way that is actually liberating. Pathways out of the present machine need to be laid, proposes Lane, by way of educational institutions and practices that are designed to circumvent the present system rather than march to its drumbeat, public policies that strengthen, rather than pacify, the citizenry, and economic opportunities that empower working people to truly be autonomous and have control over their own trajectories through life.[83] Only then can we expect our own Foucauldian power system of communication to be well-informed enough to democratically favor truth over ideology and filter information for ourselves accordingly.

But none of these things can ever actually happen in this society if the working class continues to divide itself along lines of misinformed and misguided anti-political populism. The irony is that, in the broad strokes, the pseudo-revolutionaries on the right and the socialists and anarchists on the left seem to want the same outcome: liberation for working people (i.e., the "freedom for all" outlined in the beginning chapters of the book).[84] But the hegemonic haze has long hung in the air, and the confused vocabulary each camp is left with only further entrenches the existing prejudices. As we strive to better ourselves and escape our own respective pseudo-environments *a la* Lippman's terminology, it is still quite easy to veer off course into an extremist rabbit hole. The populist rationale spectrum is treacherous, and the institutions that maintain the status quo are still in place. But beyond that, as was alluded to earlier, there are those in the skeptic world who appeal to the sense of intellectualism in all of us who seem to offer a way out, after all—but without the need to fundamentally change the system in the ways suggested earlier. The following chapter will focus a bit more on how the growing mass appeal of these figures and attitudes only further aggravate the problem of neoliberal hegemony and unwitting false consciousness. In these figures, privileged populist appeals to revolutionary sentiment without substance have found their most compelling tools for self-perpetuation yet.

Ignorance as Intellectualism

Confirmation Bias in the Lecture Hall

On April 19, 2019, at the Sony Centre in Toronto, Canada, clinical psychology professor Jordan B. Peterson (a capitalism supporter) and the aforementioned Marxist philosopher Slavoj Žižek held a public event now referred to as "The Peterson-Žižek Debate," but whose official title was "Happiness: Capitalism vs. Marxism."[1] The debate itself surrounded the question of whether or not capitalism was actually the best economic system best geared toward human happiness and freedom, and if Marxism could provide deeper insight regarding said system's shortcomings to that end. As a means of preparing for this debate, Žižek researched Dr. Peterson's prior work and found himself aligning with him on the issue of the SJW left's disinvitation proclivity (examined in the previous chapter).[2] However, it is arguable that Žižek stands against hyper-political correctness for very different reasons from Dr. Peterson, as the former is concerned with systemic revolution while the latter has made a career out of questioning challenges to hierarchical systems. Nevertheless, the two men found common ground on this front, which set the tone for what turned out to be a much more agreeable discussion that perhaps either side's fan base was hoping for.[3]

However, one area in which both men decidedly did *not* agree was on the topic of Marxism itself, and whether or not it held anything in common with the sort of postmodernist thinking that arguably lead to the Tumblr left's counterintuitive crusade against free forums. During the conversation, Žižek took particular contest with Peterson's tendency to label this crowd as "post-modern neo-Marxist" in its ideology, as well as his claim that the Frankfurt School, Žižek's intellectual heritage, was somehow responsible for conspiring to spread postmodernism across academia like a poison designed to shut down reverence for empiricism and debate.[4] "Where are these 'post-modern neo-Marxists?'" He beckoned his opponent. "What you describe as 'post-modern neo-Marxism,' where is, really, the Marxist element in it? . . . Do you see in them—in political correctness, and so on—any genuine will to change society? I don't see it. I think it's a hyper-moralization, which is a silent admission of defeat."[5] Peterson had no adequate response in that he was not able to name any Marxists who also adhered to postmodernism in the way he claimed.[6]

By making this distinction between the postmodernist and the Marxist, Žižek pointed out the same pitfalls in the Tumblr leftist thinking that this book has laid out in the previous chapter. He also demonstrated by doing this that not all leftists think the way that critics like Peterson claim, and that in fact it is likely only a small sliver of the left that behaves in these extreme ways. This blow to the anti-leftist narrative was successfully dealt with, thanks in large part to Žižek's diligence in researching and understanding his opponent's positions prior to sitting down with him. By contrast, Peterson's self-admitted preparation for debating Žižek was to simply reread *The Communist Manifesto* for the first time since his youth, revealing both at once that Peterson hadn't as good a grasp of Marxism as his rhetoric would indicate, and that he also did not seem to bother understanding the specific modern take on Marxism that Žižek offered in his writings.[7]

None of this boded well for Peterson, whose fan base is largely made up of the same young, white, and male demographic that vulgar libertarianism and other anti-political conservative groups also attract.[8] Another quality this fan base seems to possess is one of a perceived victimhood. Many of Peterson's fans view the modern world as one that threatens a natural order of things in which the male dominance over females is merely an organic occurrence that stands to keep chaos (embodied as female archetypes across human history, culture, and stories) in check through order (embodied as masculine archetypes across the same set of shared human elements)—this comes from Peterson himself, whose own adherence to the belief that Jungian archetypes should be taken quite literally is arguably the springboard for many of the postulations he has made throughout his career about male-female dynamics that have been perceived as sexist and misogynistic by his harshest critics.[9]

Remember last chapter's observation of how the strain of the current economic system can push more and more working-class people back into radical headspaces. Remember also from Part II of this book how that radicalization can be distracted from actual solutions and instead ingratiate these groups through appeals to their already-held beliefs into fighting to maintain the existing status quo. In other words, the demographics most likely to buy into a narrative that declares their viewpoint already correct while still appealing to their revolutionary working-class spirit are arguably the same demographics willing to buy into the sort of explanations for their unhappiness offered by the likes of Peterson. Historically privileged from a cultural standpoint, white men are primed to react much more harshly than other demographics to cultural shifts that can potentially bring about humiliation, threats to intellectual dominance, and radical upheavals of hierarchical social structures that they have been at the top of for generations. Conversely, economic underprivilege, something the entire working class has suffered from for just as long, *is* something white men can relate to across racial and gender lines. So, this victimhood that the particular cluster of white male conservatives and center-rightists views itself as being a part of it as the very least half-true, with genuine appeals to financial woes and worker strife often being the evidence this group gives for why they are *not* privileged, and why it is seen as such a personal affront when those accusations are thrown their way.[10]

Of course, if one takes the concept of intersectional privilege seriously and realizes that such a concept is in fact based on data, it becomes harder to claim that the concept of white male privilege is negated simply because financial privilege is something most white males in the working class do not possess.[11] The reality is much more nuanced than that, and we can see many instances throughout history of portions of culturally dominant groups finding overlap with the economically underprivileged. Nevertheless, this is why the narrative offered by the likes of public intellectuals who lean right like Peterson is so appealing to this demographic in particular: it recognizes and pays reverence to the financial plights said demographic endures while still celebrating the cultural dominance it is also beginning to see slip through its fingers—all without explicitly stating that there is any pre-existing cultural privilege to uphold. Peterson once infamously declared that "the idea that women were oppressed throughout history is an appalling theory."[12] Despite the fact that we can demonstrate that this is patently false, and that women, especially in Western history, were absolutely systemically limited in what resources and freedoms they had access to compared to their male counterparts, this is the sort of thinking that seems to appeal to Peterson's most loyal fans. Once again, if someone who presents himself as very smart and intellectual is essentially confirming one's pre-existing bias, then that serves as all the validation one needs to not step outside one's echo chamber and attempt to learn about contrasting perspectives on the world.

One critic of Peterson's, social philosopher Grant Maxwell, puts it thusly:

The men who are attracted to Peterson's ideas seem to have a profound sense that their dominant role in society is coming to an end, and that feminist postmodernism is the primary agent of this loss of privileged status. This grievance is not news to anyone who pays attention to politics, as it is this very sense of loss of an imagined golden age that largely seems to have motivated Trump voters. But the deeper register of this insight is that postmodernism has, in fact, constituted a kind of death—a death of the modern—and an end of the certainty and privilege that men–especially straight white men—have experienced in the era currently coming to a close.[13]

Paying attention to the general rhetoric coming from Peterson as well as his fans, this viewpoint is implicit yet never outright declared, opting instead for a seemingly sincere appeal to its own rogues gallery of manufactured *Others* in an attempt to scapegoat its own insecurity. But looking at the facts this book has laid out thus far about how capitalistic economic systems in crisis have always historically behaved, it becomes even more difficult to embrace Peterson's version of things as the truth when so much of his own cultural diagnosis seems devoid of the same kind of empiricism he claims to require of his intellectual opponents. Again, much of Peterson's perspective on the world springs from his very literal interpretation of Jungian analysis of human behavior's connection to folkloric archetypes. On the topic of chaos versus order, it becomes clear that Peterson really does believe that this symbolism is acted out in reality as a means of realizing some kind of natural and moral order. Here he is in his book *12 Rules for Life: An Antidote to Chaos* laying it all out:

Chaos is . . . what extends, eternally and without limit, beyond the boundaries of all states, all ideas, and all disciplines. . . . It's the foreigner, the stranger, the member of another gang, the rustle in the bushes . . . the hidden anger of your mother. . . . Chaos is symbolically associated with the feminine . . . . Order, by contrast, is explored territory. That's the hundreds-of-millions-of-years-old hierarchy of place, position, and authority. That's the structure of society. It's the structure provided by biology, too. . . . It's the flag of the nation. . . . It's the greatness of tradition, the rows of desks in the school classroom, the trains that leave on time . . . . In the domain of order, things behave as God intended.[14]

Whether or not Peterson himself intends it, this abstract way of framing the world lends itself quite easily to the sort of pushing along the populist rationale spectrum toward nationalism and fascism that this book is concerned with unpacking. For it isn't difficult for anyone of fair mind to see how calls for strong men to create order, just as nature's God intends, and for society to remain hierarchical so that its fundamental structure be preserved in the form of tradition, authority, and totemism (i.e., revering flags), can be easily exploited by the most extremist right-wing actors in the political sphere. But once again, in order for this sort of extremism to thrive in organic feedback loops of misguided disillusion and appeal to a more general audience as well, there must also be aspects to the narrative in question that contain kernels of relatable truth. Is this the case with Peterson's declarations about political correctness gone awry? As we have seen in the prior chapter, as well as Žižek's cultural grievances held in common, the answer is most certainly yes. As the financial strife all working-class people endure also demonstrates, the desperation one can feel in these economically strained spaces of existence aides in obscuring the line between misguided Jacobinistic populism and outright fascistic appeals to the worst underlying prejudices that conservative intellectualism has historically not been very apt at unmasking.[15]

In summation, how does one act on that revolutionary itch still present in the conservative wing of the working class without posing any real challenge to the actual oppressors? Well, by pinning the label of "oppressor" on something else that can serve as a scapegoat, of course. In this case, the "post-modern neo-Marxists" identified by Peterson, or political correctness and "SJWs" more broadly, serve as Peterson's *Others* perfectly. This does not mean every person in these conservative populist spaces is consciously misdirecting the anger; it merely means that the organic feedback loops of false consciousness that have formed over the course of neoliberal hegemony's slow but sure takeover tend to lead to this sort of thinking when the revolutionary desire takes hold in spaces devoid of the full picture regarding what is actually going on. Capitalism, as exemplified in Peterson's position in his aforementioned debate with Žižek, is seen as a liberating force rather than an oppressive one in these spaces because the surface-level narrative has been accepted in lieu of the objective reality. "The free market" as an idea promises liberty, despite capitalism in application always being exploitative and needlessly limiting to working people.

Peterson in his debate with Žižek denied this, arguing that while capitalism *is* hierarchical, this simply exemplifies how natural and good it is, appealing again to his belief in natural order.[16] Somewhat infamously, Peterson has made the argument that because hierarchy is observable within *some* communities of other animals, hierarchy within human society must therefore also be natural—and therefore good. The latter point can be easily discarded, seeing as how arguing that something being natural should equate to it also being morally desirable is a long-documented logical fallacy that does not stand on its own without contextual circumstance being taken into account.[17] The first point, that hierarchy's presence in some corners of nature suggests hierarchy in human culture is likewise natural, is also faulty, given the fact that one species seeming to have organically arrived at hierarchy does not on its own prove that our species has necessarily done the same—when it comes to how capitalism operates, as this book has already demonstrated, this is certainly not the case.[18] Capitalism has been artificially engineered by elites to benefit them through imposed mechanisms such as division of labor, primitive accumulation, and State-corporate collusion. To claim that capitalism cannot be exploitative because its hierarchical structure is somehow naturally occurring is to deny the empiricism Peterson so valiantly claims to revere.

But Peterson, much like many of his fellows in the group of specific public intellectuals that has come to be known as the Intellectual Dark Web, will often claim that he is merely being misunderstood or misinterpreted whenever his critics point out the incendiary implications of his vague and abstract rhetoric. When he speaks of the importance of masculinity as symbiotic to chaos, for instance, he may not actually be saying that masculinity is superior to femininity; merely that both are needed in order to maintain the natural rhythm of things. Regardless, even taking those exceptions into account, Peterson's prescribed natural order still yet sees masculine order being a corrective force against feminine chaos, which cannot help but lead his readers and listeners into a mindset that favors masculinity over femininity, framing the former as strong and the latter as weak.

In opinion magazine *Current Affairs*, editor Nathan J. Robinson offered up his own reasonable frustration with Peterson's slippery approach to both his initial arguments and his responses to criticism:

> If you try to suggest that he has justified patriarchy, he will tell you that when he refers to the "symbolically masculine" he *does* not mean "men." But it's usually unclear what he does mean, and any attempt to figure it out will be met with a barrage of yet more jargon. (What, for example, are we to make of his interpretation of *The Simpsons*, which stresses the importance of having a cruel bully around to keep the soft effeminate kids from taking over: "Without Nelson, King of the Bullies, the school would soon be overrun by resentful, touchy Milhouses, narcissistic, intellectual Martin Princes, soft, chocolate-gorging German children, and infantile Ralph Wiggums. Muntz is a corrective . . ." An endorsement of bullying the weak, surely? But Peterson would deny it.)[19]

Another aspect to Peterson's appeal, as well as the appeal of the right-leaning public intellectual at large, is once again the ability to appear objective and empirical even if the reality does not live up to that promise. As the previous few chapters have briefly discussed, the appeal to the newer, younger generation of rightists comes from the ability to shed the religious and/or emotionally charged image previously held by conservatives of old in lieu of what appears to be a sleeker appeal to cutting logic, reason, and evidence free of religiosity or emotional baggage. The aforementioned "skeptic" community online that grew out of New Atheism, which itself was largely informed by the ex-Trotskyist neoconservatism of Christopher Hitchens, vividly exemplifies this attitude and approach.[20] Even those adjacent to it, such as "facts don't care about your feelings" poster boy and conservative talk show host Ben Shapiro or, yes, Peterson himself, exude similar sentiments regarding logic and empiricism's importance—as well as science's need to be sterile and free from human emotion, which brings with it implicit the idea that empathy itself should be seen as a weakness.

Peterson's own shoot to stardom was largely due to this appeal. When Bill C-16 was put forth by the Canadian government in June 2017, gender identity was added to the existing list of protected classes of persons legally protected from discrimination.[21] While a reasonable amendment to an existing law, Dr. Peterson, a professor at the University of Toronto, questioned the application of the law and argued that it would force people by law to use preferred gender pronouns under threat of arrest. During a senate hearing concerning the bill prior to its implementation, Dr. Peterson was present and voiced the following concern:

> I oppose discrimination against gender identity and gender expression—that's not the point. The point is the specifics of the legislation that surrounds it and the insistence that people have to use compelled speech. That's what I'm objecting to. I've dealt with all sorts of people in my life. People who don't fit in in all sorts of different ways. I'm not a discriminatory person . . . but I think this legislation is reprehensible and I do not believe for a moment that it will do what it intends to do.[22]

Yet, these supposed specifics of the bill that would lead to compelled speech (and therefore pose a threat to free speech itself) were in fact nowhere to be found, and Peterson's claims have been shown time and again to be unfounded.[23] For one thing, the bill was more of a formality than anything, as it officially added gender identity and expression to the *federal* human rights code in Canada despite most of the individual *provinces* of the country already having passed their own equivalent anti-discriminatory laws years prior.[24] This meant that if the bill's actions truly could have resulted in literal criminalization of misgendering trans people, those effects would have already been seen in the provinces the equivalent laws were already in place. Since no such travesty ever occurred in said provinces, Peterson's claim seems considerably unfounded. Even if we wanted to be generous and claim that Dr. Peterson was referring more specifically to how gender expression was also added to Canada's criminal code by the bill, this also does not back up his claim that something as common as misgendering someone would be seen as a criminal act. The criminal code in question protects specific categories of persons, including color, age, sexual orientation, sex, and now gender identity, from extreme acts such as genocide and public, coordinated hate campaigns against individuals—none of which are even close to the equivalent of unintentionally calling a trans person by a pronoun they may not prefer.[25]

Yet, despite his clear misunderstanding of Bill C-16's limitations, Jordan Peterson's publicly visible outcry against what he misrepresented as a discriminatory legal measure against speech itself landed him many supporters online from the aforementioned 4chan crowd and its adjacent intellectual spaces. Suddenly, yet another academic figure peddling ignorance as intellectualism was upheld as the epitome of rationality, reason, and empiricism—all because he already agreed with the social views of many of those who became his most ardent fans.

Something else Peterson's work holds in common with others like him on the right-leaning intellectual stage is a newfound reverence for the writings of Friedrich Nietzsche. This adoration has spilled into the Alt-Right circles as well, with particular appreciation being hoisted upon Nietzsche's supposed concept of the Übermensch as a Superman-like figure. For the lost boys who flock to the revolutionary right for a sense of purpose, identity, and strength, this concept is quite attractive: a person who by sheer virtue of his own innate abilities can rise up and prove himself superior to others around him, even in the face of adversary. There is just one problem with this concept: it doesn't actually exist in Nietzsche's work. This misunderstanding is wide in its reach and seems to stem from the Thomas Common translation of Nietzsche's work, where "Übermensch" is literally translated as "Superman." The problem with this is that such a translation is not literal and takes much liberty when considering how the term "super" is taken in most English-speaking cultures. Nietzsche's other translator, Kaufmann, would go on to revise this initial translation into a much more accurate representation in English of what Nietzsche was actually trying to convey. Kaufmann once stated of Common that he "must have understood little German and even less English" for such a translation to be so botched.

The more accurate Kaufmann translation of the word "Übermensch" is not "Superman," but is instead "Overman." Why does this distinction matter? Because of the English connotations we tend to take from the word "over" versus the word "super." "Super" carries with it an expectation of carrying human characteristics to an extreme level—think alpha male attitudes, complete with chest-beating and bravado—while the word "over" implies the process of *overcoming* and transcending these same human characteristics. These are entirely mutually exclusive interpretations—one implies that human characteristics as we know them now are good and should be heightened, while the other frames human characteristics as we know them now to be full of shortcomings we must grow beyond.

Nietzsche himself laid out how his readers were to interpret his use of the term, as well. It is not even open for debate, considering that he himself, writing as his alter ego Zarathustra, stated the following context for it:

> I teach you the Overman. Man is something that shall be overcome. What have you done to overcome him? All beings so far have created something beyond themselves; and do you want to be the ebb of this great flood or even go back to the beasts rather than overcome man? What is the ape to man? A laughingstock or a painful embarrassment. And the man shall be just that for the Overman: a laughingstock or a painful embarrassment.[26]

By Nietzsche's own reasoning, a Superman is as close to the antithesis of an Übermensch as a person can possibly be. The more weighed down by his present humanity a man is, the more of an Üntermensch he becomes and the less capable he is of transcending his shortcomings and letting go to achieve greater things. In practice this means that if one truly wishes to understand and heed Nietzsche's words, one should strive to be *less* mensch rather than more mensch—the less mensch we are, the closer we are to being true Overmen—people who have transcended our human shortcomings and been greater in spite of them.

Peterson, along with others in the IDW (itself a grouping that went on to increasingly rub elbows with more extreme faux-intellectual conservatism like that of Molyneux and Southern), appeals instead to the Superman concept in which digging in one's heels and not apologizing for one's present state is what should be celebrated—no compromise, and no apologies. This has proven especially enticing to the white, male, and conservative demographic within the working class because once again he offered an answer to working-class woes that was devoid of the call to retrain one's own perception of the system itself that still culturally pacified the intersectionally privileged. In short, Peterson's brand of intellectualism tells conservative young men what they already want to hear rather than what they might *need* to hear in order to truly rise above their present economic circumstances. All the while, this approach at public intellectualism frames existing ignorance of the world outside's true nuance as a reasonable kind of centrism that contrasts appealingly to the seeming extremism of the SJW left. In reality, presenting social ignorance as noble to a group of people who stand to benefit from preserving their remaining privilege merely aids and abets the extremists on the right who rationalize such preservation by any means necessary. The end result can sometimes amount to once-centrist-identifying young men who fit into this demographic falling into white nationalism, as we saw occur with the Chris Cantwell crowd, initially identifying as libertarian, ultimately playing a significant role in the Unite the Right white supremacist rally in Charlottesville, VA.[27]

Two major forms of normalizing disingenuous faux-centrist narratives feature prominently in intellectualized discussion as presented to the general public at large, and not just a particular pocket of the right. One such form is a presentation of the "middle class" as an economic category in which most people of all walks of life can find common experience and outlook. This assists the narrative that the neoliberalized masses hold the normal, reasonable perspective due to their supposed common experience shared by the majority of the populace. The other form is the concept of the political moderate also being representative of the so-called normal and reasonable position.

Let us look at the idea of the middle class first. The middle class does indeed exist as an oft-cited economic category, as well as a cultural concept. In this way, it allows many working people, themselves still being exploited by the hierarchical dynamics of the system they live in, to identify with certain petty bourgeois figures who still retain enough overlap with their own daily outlook to warrant a feeling of solidarity with them. Additionally, the American Dream drive to believe in ubiquitously attainable success means that many working people's aspirations to become petty bourgeois figures themselves, such as famous actors living in million-dollar homes, lessens the sense of distance between them and these rich figures they admire. The other cultural function the middle-class concept serves is to give these types of working people a reason to look down on other working-class members and see them as something removed from their own experience. The significantly destitute, it is often presented, are not in the same position as the majority of everybody else, meaning that "everybody else," the middle class, are still benefitting from the system as it currently exists. Anthropologist Aaron Fox points out that this language of "middle class" as a culturally powerful concept arrived on the tongues of everyday working Americans in the wake of "America's post-war class compromise," arguing that this was "pervasive language" brought on by said compromise, and that what most people initially meant by "middle class" was simply "working people."[28]

Nevertheless, the distinction between working-class and some vague cultural concept of a class above that, the middle class, has now taken hold as a cultural concept and affects our self-perception. This divides workers, and it also paints a story of a multitiered economic existence in which the inhabitants of each tier can rise from the tier below through old-fashioned hard work and perseverance. This comes across as fairer and less exploitative, but it glosses over the colder reality, which is that in terms of applied access to fundamental economic opportunity in life, there truly are only two classes: the working class and the capitalists.

This is because capitalists, in the applied historical definition, are the people who exclusively hold access to all the various forms of natural and artificial commons: manufacturing technology, production companies, corporations, houses to rent, and so forth. They then use all of this property they have private dominance over to turn a profit by demanding everyone else pay them for its use. This profit becomes capital: profit that accrues more profit. This profit, after a while, is no longer gained through the capitalist's own labor, because he is ultimately able to use the labor of others to bring in his particular private property's returns—while keeping most of said returns for himself and only giving back small portions of it to his laborers, dividing *that* small portion up further in various ways among those in his employ.

By contrast, everybody else, regardless of specific economic bracket, lacks this same access to the same means of accruing capital for themselves, meaning that everyone in this camp, destitute or not, must sell their own labor to the capitalists in order to be financially stable. In application, these are two very distinct ways of life, and this is why the working class, as it was first defined, is seen as encompassing every working person who does not have open access to commons. Looking at things from this position of objectively observable application of one's economic autonomy (or lack thereof), the need to include a concept such as the middle class when determining the validity of solidarity with one another seems needless. Yet it serves as a cultural function to perpetuate working-class divide and cement the idea of a rational, everyday majority as being the norm, not in any real danger of economic destitution. It mutes the alarms and imposes a false lack of urgency. Of course, it presents the capitalist system as one in which everyone is equivalent to everyone else, and the only thing keeping someone away from being a capitalist herself is her own ambition.

False equivalency is also employed as a means of normalizing the most extremist position in a debate, consciously or otherwise. Here we find the second form of narrative normalization. When both sides of a debate are framed as equally extreme, the true extremists can equivocate their viewpoints against the viewpoints of those who stand diametrically (and often justifiably) opposed to them. Through this lack of precision we arrive at terms like the "alt-left," an ill-defined neologism brought about by people on the right simply for the purpose of muddying the waters and giving off the appearance of equal extremism being present in both left and right populist spaces. But the "alt-left," much like "cultural Marxism," is not something that we can trace back to a single meaning or use that is clear and descriptive of a specific group or philosophy. It is instead loosely thrown about by those who wish to appear as "reasonable" and centrist. After all, the assumption is often that the most reasonable position between two extremes must be right in the middle. But is this conventional wisdom actually based on anything substantive?

Something else that often gets assumed is that dictionary definitions of words somehow fully embody the words themselves and all of their cultural and historical meaning. That is simply not true; dictionary definitions of words often simply represent the most current consensus of the colloquial understandings of said words. Or, in the observational words of author Sheldon Richman, "dictionaries are descriptive, not prescriptive."[29] This can often lose sight of significant nuance and actual utility of a term when attempting to understand its place in a larger cultural conversation. In the case of "centrist," this is certainly the case. The dictionary definition of this term describes it as being more or less a synonym for someone who holds moderate political views. But the most up-to-date research in the social sciences reveals that centrism, in actual application, amounts to one of two broad approaches: either a conscious rejection of perceived bias in an attempt at fair consideration of opposing views, or a specialized approach to navigating the inputs and outputs of three-dimensional political decision-making. This second application of centrist thinking is a bit more complicated, so, we will attempt to unpack it. Let us look at an example of how the input-output process can affect—and be affected by—a person's political ideology.

If a fascist, to make our example extreme and obvious, wanted to reason for himself why his reality is what it is, his input processes of gathering initial information about what he observed would work toward filtering said information through a fascist lens. If the fascist already has a proclivity to view the world a certain way, then his confirmation bias is in play. If he is someone who has not yet become a fascist but ultimately will, it could be that this process will occur due to the individual's availability heuristics responding to limited access to all of the necessary information before a confident stance can be drawn.[30] In either case, the input dimension is dictating what information is being subsumed into the worldview of the person in question (the process dimension), as well as how that information is affecting further behaviors (the output dimension).

This process can occur across all ideologies, and when centrists take part in it, it often takes on the appearance of the first layer of centrist action listed earlier (i.e., merely avoiding conscious bias) while having the long-term effect of actualizing the second, more three-dimensional process of ideological formation. This is still ideological, though it might feign the appearance of a process that bucks ideology. The centrist would simply use, for instance, a conventionally socialist explanation for something while then arguing for perhaps a more conservative solution to the problem. The input for information would still have a narrow entryway, but somewhere in the second dimension, the processing of that information, a conscious drive for appearing reasonable and open to "both sides" of the issue, leads the ideological centrist to pull his professed position from a little bit of everything so that he will not appear biased. As a result, the third dimension of the centrist's decision-making process might look nothing like the first dimension of initial informational input, but in its own way, this will have been precisely the point and therefore still every bit as ideological as either of the extreme sides the centrist claims to be superior to.

This ideological approach at centrism, known in the scholarship as radical centrism, is in reality what most self-professed centrists are subscribing to—wittingly or otherwise.[31] This delineation traces back some decades, with several scholars independently arriving at similar understandings of what self-professed ideological centrism really amounts to. In his 1976 book *The Radical Center*, sociologist Donald Warren described the disillusioned and radicalized middle American (i.e., the demographic primed for cultivation into the anti-political populists examined in this book).[32] Just a few years later in 1980, Marilyn Ferguson observed of ideological centrism the following:

> [It can be] described as a kind of Radical Center. It is not neutral, not middle-of-the-road, but a view of the whole road. From this vantage point, we can see that various schools of thought on any one issue—political or otherwise—include valuable contributions along with error and exaggeration.[33]

In other words, "centrism" as a political stance fancies itself superior to other ideologies simply because its own ideology chooses to pick and choose what it likes from everyone else in order to present itself as having transcended the innate shortcomings of the comparatively limited viewpoints of those around it. The origins for this reside in a non-empirical approach at collage politics—what can be objectively demonstrated is not as important as what can appear unbiased and holistic. It is a kind of woo—a new age political mindset that is more in love with its own claims of superiority than with what is actually true. In the 1990s, the flavor of radical centrism being peddled to the public as rational was the so-called Third Way liberal politics of Bill Clinton. But it was still neoliberalism.

So, where does the more contemporary assumption come from postulating that political centrism is simply the same thing as being moderate? From a much smaller yet more recently cited wing of the sociological scholarship that ignores the more deeply rooted historical and cultural genesis of the concept of centrism and instead favors the sterile dictionary definition of the term. This arguably revisionist approach to explaining centrism saw most recent mainstream publication in the 2008 Oliver H. Woshinsky book *Explaining Politics*, in which the author described political centrists as "moderates who place themselves at the center of the traditional Left-Right spectrum of political ideas."[34] This definition is more convenient for people who essentially continue to equivocate extremists who wish to oppress with responders who wish to push back against the oppression.[35]

This care and attention to the peaks and valleys of the complex reality of the situation matters not, it seems, to those who have already decided that their already-existing biases and prejudices are valid and who select which public intellectuals to prescribe to as a means of keeping their echo chambers intact. Even classical liberalism itself, in its most unadulterated, earliest form, is arguably not being properly conveyed by this crowd despite claims of adherence to it becoming nearly ubiquitous across the conservative revolutionary spectrum by this point. Locke's view on the commons in relation to property restrictions, for instance? Nowhere to be found within these scads of supposedly classical liberal crusaders. Instead, modern right-libertarians now fight for a world that embodies the very antithesis of Locke's vision; a world in which the idea of private property as a natural right is central to their belief system. Followed to its logical conclusion, say the most extreme among them, the concept of property rights makes it perfectly moral to build border walls around nations and excise undesirables.

It is within these problematic rhetorical corners that right-libertarians and other conservative faux-revolutionaries paint themselves into where fascism and nationalism have been able to thrive, and this is a major reason why extremists like the Alt-Right have been able to frame their ideas as mainstream in right-leaning circles that fancy themselves to be revolutionary. The result is a convoluted hodgepodge of vaguely anti-status quo-sounding rhetoric that proposes bad solutions to misidentified problems—all of which have no superior alternative explanations in mainstream libertarian discourse due to modern libertarianism's own worship of neoliberal economies.

One need only examine the words of right-libertarian intellectual Hans-Hermann Hoppe, and his belief that classically liberal societies should be free to throw out all who might disagree with established dogma, to see that this aforementioned crypto-fascistic idea on borders and cultural preservation is not an outlier position in the liberty movement. To be fair to Hoppe, he does not call himself Alt-Right. But despite this, he holds much sway in the most extreme wings of anarcho-capitalism where libertarianism and the Alt-Right overlap—thanks largely to his views on property and borders. Because of this, Hoppe has been called "perhaps the single most influential libertarian philosopher of the Alt-Right movement."[36] One white supremacy watchdog journal had this to say on Hoppe's influence in these spaces:

> To be clear, Hoppe does not identify as alt-right, but runs in the same circles as prominent white nationalists. His popularity among fringe Anarcho-Capitalists—or AnCaps—has resulted in a plethora of memes, sometimes depicting Hoppe as Pepe the Frog, and often bearing the slogan "Hippity Hoppity, Get Off My Property."[37]

But this is not meant to simply glance over a few accusations removed from Hoppe's literature itself. In fact, let us allow Hoppe to explain his positions in his own words, so as to avoid misrepresentation. Here he is in his book *Democracy—The God That Failed*:

> There can be no tolerance toward democrats and communists in a libertarian social order. They will have to be physically separated and expelled from society. Likewise, in a covenant founded for the purpose of protecting family and kin, there can be no tolerance toward those habitually promoting lifestyles incompatible with this goal. They—the advocates of alternative, non-family and kin-centered lifestyles such as, for instance, individual hedonism, parasitism, nature-environment worship,

homosexuality, or communism—will have to be physically removed from society, too, if one is to maintain a libertarian order.[38]

Well, then. It is certainly good to encounter someone who doesn't mince words about where he stands! But here is the really interesting part: Hoppe claims that he is not arguing from a place of homophobia. Frankly, I am willing to take him at his word for that—he is perhaps not consciously homophobic. Indeed, it doesn't take conscious homophobia to explain positions like these; ignorance of the recent scholarship dealing with culturally aligned topics such as these is seemingly somewhat common in the economically conservative conversation. After all, neoliberalism lends itself quite well to the drowning out of anything of value in human culture that doesn't involve capitalistic obsession with profit and efficiency. Here is Hoppe again better qualifying why gay people specifically are just too seemingly inefficient for the growth of a libertarian nation:

> In March of 2004, during a 75-minute lecture in my Money and Banking class on time preference, interest, and capital, I presented numerous examples designed to illustrate the concept of time preference (or in the terminology of the sociologist Edward Banfield of "present- and future-orientation"). As one brief example, I referred to homosexuals as a group which, because they typically do not have children, tend to have a higher degree of time preference and are more present-oriented. I also noted—as have many other scholars—that J.M Keynes, whose economic theories were the subject of some upcoming lectures, had been a homosexual and that this might be useful to know when considering his short-run economic policy recommendation and his famous dictum "in the long run we are all dead."[39]

So, Hoppe believes that gay people have a different "time preference" than straights, and therefore, their active social participation seemingly isn't conducive to social or economic growth.[40] An argument that would be provocative and interesting if it weren't demonstrably false. Many gay people adopt, and many straight people choose to never procreate. Hoppe is found here representing "homosexuals" almost like quaint exhibits of discordant humans one can observe behind glass, completely removed from the reality one can find through reading any number of studies on the subject of gay parenting. The entire passage quoted above stirred up controversy, yet it could have been rendered self-evidently superfluous to the man himself had the sociological conversation been brought into the fold regarding right-libertarianism's focus, and his adorning and impressionable fans could have been spared the harmful misrepresentation of gay people's contribution to society that had been inflicted upon them, there. Having kids *might* affect one's long-term perspective in one's personal life, but being philanthropic and forward-thinking on a large scale about one's society (or one's fellow inhabitants within said society) does not require parenthood or fertility. There is in fact an entire movement of politically active people on the left who call themselves "progressive" explicitly *because* they want society and humanity to progress. Many of these progressives are, contrary to Hoppe's predictions, long-term-planning homosexuals. Hoppe might not consciously hate gay people, but he certainly seems to view them as fundamentally different from their straight counterparts. Which means he doesn't grasp the basic empirical bedrock of human genetics upon which we can comfortably declare that we *are* all essentially the same. Any differences in motivation or perspective from person to person are far more nurture than nature, and Hoppe's apparent inability to step outside of his capital gains echo chamber blinds him to that fact.

But we must also take heed of the other undesirables Hoppe lists in the first quoted passage from *Democracy*: communists, and even *Democrats,* are too out of line for him, warranting societal exclusion. Yet again, as long as it is *presented* as empirical, many readers and onlookers will take an opinion like this one as *being* empirical. This is one of many examples of how socially conservative positions have been injected back into the modern conservative, so-called skeptical discussion, and in the case of one Hoppe fan who went on to become a white nationalist, Cristopher Cantwell, the idea of physical removal became a meme that was shared by himself and his followers ad nauseam. Helicopters lifting undesirables out of an ideal anarcho-capitalist utopia was a jokingly suggested tactic against "SJWs" and "fake libertarians" who stood up for legal protections for everyone.[41] This meme was making reference to how the brutal right-wing Chilean dictator Augusto Pinochet disposed of thousands of people he didn't like, oftentimes dropping bound innocent people from helicopters over the open ocean to drown in agony.[42] But since he had (with the help of the US government) overthrown a *communist* country, then that was seemingly a good enough rationale to celebrate him, even if only in jest—"all socialists are totalitarian and against liberty," after all.

More disturbing was how Hoppe's own promotion of physical removal in mainstream right-libertarian spaces seemed to be where much of the libertarian and anarcho-capitalist community was saying the Pinochet apologetics among his fans were originating from, as many of these helicopter memes depicted Hoppe himself as being part of the death flights.[43] Kevin Carson has pointed out that "there are a lot of self-described AnCaps on the right who are very authoritarian and just won't admit it . . . the helicopter types, the Chris Cantwell types, the self-described 'anarcho-Pinochetists.'"[44] Carson continues: "They are a group of people that, as capitalism collapses, we may very well end up having to fight. They're already marching in places like Charlottesville because they see the collapse of the system they identify with as some kind of conspiracy that has been engineered against them by so-called 'social justice warriors.'"[45]

One article from a prominent libertarian publication stated during this rise in violent sentiment that "all it takes is a Hoppe, skip and a jump for those who are joking online about throwing communists from helicopters to justify their actions," and noting that "a growing wave of libertarians and anarcho-capitalists are finding themselves drawn to the world of anti-communist rhetoric, which extends to the nth degree. So, is commie killing a justified response to the violation of the non-aggression principle, or is this simply lunacy concocted to ideologically discriminate?"[46]

Hoppe himself would continue to platform right-wing extremism as a respectable form of libertarianism even after the Alt-Right had formed into a tangibly fascist movement, speaking at his Property and Freedom Society's 2017 conference to declare that libertarianism *should* appeal to frustrated, "disadvantaged" whites, arguing that all libertarians "could learn something in this respect from the Alt-Right."[47] He went further, validating the sense of victimhood the white men in these spaces feel by arguing that "ruling elite" had been engaging in a "systemic culture war" in which minority groups are pitted against whites.[48] The real crisis isn't economic hierarchy, says Hoppe, but is rather due to minorities getting a bunch of privilege to oppress others with:

> A new victimology has been proclaimed and promoted. Women—and in particular, single mothers—blacks, browns, Latinos, homosexuals, lesbians, bi, and transsexuals have been awarded victim status and accorded legal privileges through nondiscrimination or affirmative action decrees, as well. Most recently, such privileges have been expanded also to foreign national immigrants, whether legal or illegal, insofar as they fall into one of the just mentioned categories or as members of non-Christian religions—such as Islam, for instance.[49]

"For instance." Of course. We can be sure that Islam was just a random example Hoppe pulled from his memory banks with no tactical intent whatsoever.

So, as we can see here, the frontier of antagonism outlined in Part I is on full display, appealing to the culturally privileged yet fearful areas of the populist rationale spectrum where neoliberal hegemony has become so prevalent as to make Hoppe's explanations for the crisis appear more believable than they should.

Hoppe also said elsewhere in the speech that property rights and closed borders were the core of libertarian ideology, admitting that the so-called real, noble libertarianism he promoted was born "in Rothbard's living room," and accusing the other libertarians (i.e., the libertarians who still adhere to the initial passions that fueled the likes of Déjacque and Proudhan) of being "plain ignorant of human psychology and sociology" and "devoid of any common sense," invoking of course the same tactics as Rand and Rothbard at their worst by accusing another party of being the non-empirical one while ignoring the empirical evidence that actually disproves one's own narrative.[50]

Toward the end of the speech, Hoppe called for the abolition of "all affirmative action and nondiscrimination laws and regulations" on the grounds that they are "blatant violations of the principle of the equality before the law." He also argued for shutting down all "university departments for black, Latino, women, genderqueer studies and so forth" before recommending that the police render social justice advocates "beaten into submission."[51] As a libertarian, Hoppe seemed to be directly contradicting the idea of skepticism toward State power and use of force. Finally, he called for the elimination of "all welfare parasites and bums" by way of eliminating all social programs designed to assist this impoverished "underclass" whose problems—including unemployment, alcoholism, child abuse, and "female-headed households"—Hoppe blamed on their own supposed poor judgment and lack of control.[52]

Hoppe may be among the most extreme examples, but he is certainly not alone in holding some positions that, while giving credence to fascist ideals, are not in and of themselves entirely incompatible with the newfangled language of "liberty" adhered to by many on the revolutionary right today. Among the blind spots couched within modern vulgar libertarianism and the revolutionary right at large is the appeal to "freedom" without any prescription on how said freedom should be best utilized to beget more freedom for even more people. The reductionist one-size-fits-all appeal to principles over a willingness to qualify specific positions on specific freedom issues for different groups of people lends itself terribly well toward situations like those highlighted over the course of this section of the book where a fight for free speech may simply result in a bigoted screed going unchallenged on a one-man stage, or an appeal to across-the-board freedom in the economy may result in the freedom for bosses to exploit rather than the freedom for workers to thrive. Yes, in the more extreme cases as late capitalism continues to close in the walls, a certain pocket of the white conservative working class might equate a fight against tyranny to their own misperceived victimhood at the hands of minority groups gaining more access to the ever-dwindling economic opportunities to support oneself and feel like a valid human being.

Cantwell in particular would later go on to be front-and-center at the infamous Unite the Right rally, promoting in news interviews a form of anarchism laced with white nationalism. The frontier of antagonism had certainly reached Cantwell's corner of the so-called liberty movement. How this happened had a lot to do with how libertarianism at large had already become drastically capitalistic in the West ever since its aforementioned collusion with laissez-faire economics in the mid-twentieth century, as Hoppe himself had corroborated, and how that in itself lent faux-legitimacy to the white working-class ignorance (and their subsequent wooing into fascistic narratives) cited earlier.[53]

We can take on right-libertarianism's growing problems with communism and democracy one at a time. First, it is integral to remember, as cited earlier in this book, that most on the right, vulgar libertarians included, fundamentally mischaracterize socialism in order to subsume it into the broader frontier of antagonism they have cultivated. It isn't so much that libertarianism itself (i.e., anti-authoritarianism), when divorced from its present conservative bedfellows, is innately contrary to communists' own end game for society—after all, the first self-described libertarians in the political sense were French anarcho-socialists, as we have previously established—it more has to do with the fact that right-wing depictions of communism tend to conflate the most egregious examples of its failures at the State level with the moral and anti-authoritarian writings of Karl Marx; the former is like a low-hanging fruit, as anyone can observe the regime of a Joseph Stalin and judge it to be immoral and an affront to human rights, and the latter is very complex and highly debated even among scholars who generally agree with it. To boil down "communism" (and, by extension, all other possible variations of socialist) into something that advocates for tyranny and loss of human individuality across the board is to not only fall short of the nuance, but to promote sloppy thinking as reasoned scholarship—to promote ignorance as intellectualism, much like in the case of the Intellectual Dark Web.

Returning to what historian Lucien van der Walt had articulated, the ruling class comprises two major types of elite and not just one: the economic elites and the cultural elites, both of whom work through the State to reach their goals.[54] The cultural elites with power can much more easily overlap with the culturally privileged within the working class and spin narratives of victimhood and impending revolution from an elitist perspective, and said narratives can themselves be born out of the organic hegemonic feedback loops long-entrenched in these spaces. Hoppe and Peterson and their ilk may genuinely not be pushing a consciously harmful narrative, and they may be truthful in their positions of wanting liberation through their suggested means, but the empirical reality simply does not align with their positions, and if nobody challenges those sorts of economically linked and culturally confounded claims by the likes of Hoppe and Peterson (and why would they in a thought movement that genuinely believes in neoliberal ideology?), then it becomes harder to dispute the more obviously nationalistic argumentation that gets seemingly logically connected to them with much rhetorical aplomb.

Which brings us to the next major problem with modern right-libertarianism: its growing disdain for the democratic process. This particular sticking point of modern libertarian rhetoric is one that presents itself at first as quite reasonable—it is easy to see how simple majority rule can senselessly perpetuate injustice for far longer than it should ever have lingered. But herein lies the problem: not all forms of democracy amount to majority rule, but much of the modern conservative rhetoric paints this as being the case. Ayn Rand famously declared once that the greatest minority is the individual, and the belief that democracy always amounts to majority tyranny has prevailed in much of intellectual conservatism since. We can also see an apparent majority rule limitation at work in America regarding various important civil rights issues over the centuries. After all, it was the majoritarian democratic process that kept the legalization of things such as the female vote away well into the twentieth century, and gay marriage from gaining serious political attention even into the early twenty-first century. Not to mention that the democratic process needed majority rule in order to finally abolish slavery, one of the most objectively demonstrable human rights violations in history, through a constitutional amendment.

On the other hand, that same democratic process is also what made all the difference in the end, and without it, gay marriage may never have been legalized under any non-democratic government model. It is a complex issue, and different forms of democracy have been conceptualized over the years. One moral appeal for an alternative to straight democracy was the original concept of America as being a constitutional republic with democratic elements. This way, in theory, certain basic protections for all citizens can and should be recognized outside of the majority rule dynamic. But as we have seen, that has not always been the reality. But there is also a distinction that is increasingly being made between majoritarian democracy and consensus democracy, with the latter appealing to a relevant, research-based consensus on a given issue trumping simple majority appeal while still retaining broadly democratic elements and function. This is achieved by taking into account as wide a range of opinions on a given issue as possible and then forming a legislative consensus based on corroborated data. Such a system has been successfully implemented in places like Sweden, Belgium, Denmark, and elsewhere. But figures like Hoppe, who are growing in popularity in the right-libertarian movement, don't seem to want even that. Suffice it to say however that a utopia where removal of one's fellow humans on ideological grounds, backed by an ill-defined concept of property rights and a reductionist criticism of the democratic process, is nothing like the liberated world actual classical liberals or libertarians of old envisioned. It is also true that various forms of direct democracy could in fact one day lead to successful anarchistic market, which many of the right-libertarians claim they essentially want.[55] To dismiss fully the prospect of democratic elements to social order is therefore rather contradictory for this wing of rightists if their convictions are to be taken seriously.

Despite this contradiction, more and more self-described libertarians in America are rallying behind the idea that closed borders amount to classical liberal policy. Amusing? Yes. But also dangerous. Dangerous because of the normalizing process such rhetoric unjustly throws nationalistic concepts into, and because of the undue vindication it gives the scared and lost boys of a context-starved working-class demographic, who themselves hold views that come from a place of emotional toil and reactionaryism rather than reasoned empiricism. When the limitations of capitalistic enterprise are run up against by this new generation of American Dream–believing aspirants, the cognitive dissonance that results serves as a ripe breeding ground for wrong-headed explanations and whole cloth boogeymen. It cannot *possibly* be that neoliberalism breeds unhealthy expectations and monetizes every aspect of the human condition, say the vulgar libertarian heroes of these impressionable young would-be revolutionaries, nor can it be that capitalism itself is systemically unsound; it *must* be instead, therefore, something else.

That something else is up for grabs depending on what type of libertarian one talks to, but "the State," as conveyed by most in the liberty movement as a monolithic bad guy entity completely devoid of nuance, is not the answer in this case. Yes, it is indeed the most common named culprit for why working-class people can't get a break, but, as previously demonstrated in this book, only in the context where isolated objections about market failures are in need of addressing. The typical narrative offered by (once again, typically well-meaning) right-libertarian spokespeople is that whenever the otherwise-perfect economic system known as capitalism fails to deliver the American Dream to hopeful hard workers, it's the government's fault for interfering with its pesky regulations and anti-worker collusion with business owners (even though the business owners often make the first move in this sort of arrangement, only the government is ever typically blamed). This position makes implicit in its very connective tissue the claim that capitalism itself would be entire pro-worker without the government element. In order for that claim to be true, however, capitalism as an economic system must be demonstrated as being pro-worker by design. Unfortunately, as shown elsewhere in this work, that is not what the historical record shows—quite the opposite.[56] Nevertheless, with the government collusion element removed from the equation, capitalism itself is still praised by much of modern libertarianism as the best system we could possibly hope for in order for hardworking people to best benefit from the fruits of their own labor. Since that is not what we see happening, and since quality of life is demonstrably going down, even within market arenas more devoid of government tampering than others, there still remains a question: why?

The answer, for anyone who has bothered to look at the actual history behind capitalism's creation, is simple: capitalism is *not* pro-worker. It never has been. It was designed to perpetuate class divides that were already present under feudalism before it, and it has a built-in system of hierarchy that aims to reinforce divide-and-conquer systems of supposed "efficiency," such as division of labor, primitive accumulation, and artificial revoking of access to the commons.[57] But since pro-capitalist working-class rightists don't want to believe that, their movements' official platforms lack any satisfactory explanation to the ever-growing question: why can working people not succeed in a supposedly free market despite their hardest efforts and highest discipline? For generations, this was a question only non-privileged demographics within the working class bothered to ask. Now, white working-class people are starting to feel the weight as late capitalism continues its death rattle into the twenty-first century. But for this stripe of working-class laborer, more likely to get roped in by the empty promises of faux-revolutionary conservatism than most, they still want their revolution while also craving for the American Dream to remain attainable. Thus, to right-libertarianism and the other varieties of revolutionary conservatism they go, and from there, even more rightward, but with no solidified answer to the question of why capitalism still fails even when it is working exactly as designed. Since the system itself cannot possibly be the problem in their minds, treachery must be afoot elsewhere—from the outside! Something other than the system itself, whose promises of fame and fortune rest upon its authenticity being maintained. The Hegel dialectic would also be helpful in these instances since it demonstrates through its concern with both internal and external contradiction that nothing has a primarily external cause, and that everything is informed by its internal qualities first and foremost. Once this is understood, fascism is rendered conceptually untenable.

Yet, the fear of socialist insight in these spaces leads most occupying them to never get anywhere close to concepts like historical materialism, cultural hegemony, or the dialectic, meaning that the outside threat hypothesis still wins out in the minds of these hopeful entrepreneurs and CEOs of tomorrow, willing to ride the gears of the present machine to its top for their own sense of accomplishment and value, unwilling to dismantle said machine altogether. Within that thought process, advocacy of closed borders and the belief in a threat of "cultural erosion" (itself another dog whistle for the aforementioned white genocide conspiracy theory) can gain support quite organically. From there, those who are primed for all-out fascist thinking by such a point need only a slight push to fall into it headlong.

New Spins on Old, Misguided Hatreds

In July 2017, a speech was given by Jeff Deist, director of the right-libertarian *Mises Institute* in Auburn, Alabama, entitled "For a New Libertarian."[1] In the speech, Deist prescribed a new united front approach to spreading so-called libertarianism moving forward. In order to succeed, Deist argued, libertarians need to resist the direction the world is moving in, where "states are shifting from national to supra-national," and wherein "globalism in effect means more centralized control by an emerging cartel of allied states like the EU (and their NGO accomplices)."[2] This rhetoric would later be compared by critics of Deist to the conspiratorial screeds of libertarian-turned-right-wing extremist Alex Jones, what with his use of terms like "globalism" and what could be interpreted as an allusion to the ever-elusively defined New World Order. But instead of blindly joining that chorus, let us read further before passing judgment.

Here is Mr. Deist's main argument from the speech, where he closes by summarizing all of his prior thoughts:

> I'm sure all of us would fight for our physical persons if we were attacked, or for our families if they were attacked. We might fight for close friends, too. And perhaps even our neighbors. In fact we might like to think we would physically defend a total stranger in some circumstances, for example an old woman being attacked and robbed. And we probably would fight for our towns and communities if they were physically invaded by an outside force, even though we don't personally know all of the people in our towns and communities.[3]

So far things already seem a bit needlessly wrapped up in the anti-political Jacobinistic antagonism delineated in Part I of the book, but perhaps Deist will surprise us if we read elsewhere in the speech as a whole.

> We might fight for property too, maybe not as fiercely. We certainly would protect our homes, but that's because of the people inside. How about cars? Would you physically tangle with an armed robber who was driving away in your car? Or would you let him go, and not risk death or injury, just to save your car? How about your wallet? How about someone stealing 40% of your income, as many governments do? Would you take up arms to prevent this? We probably wouldn't fight for bitcoin, or net neutrality, or a capital gains tax hike, by the way. How about an abstraction, like fighting for "your country" or freedom or your religion.[4]

Deist here is starting to veer the speech into a direction of protectionism that, according to libertarian critic of Deist Apollo Slater, cannot help but demand "central planning."[5] Slater stated about the speech that it was "a reminder that statism will always threaten to infect the liberty movement."[6]

The speech goes on to make many other alarming statements, such as: "nationalism is on the rise in Europe. . . . We should seize on this," and arguing that it is silly and "utopian" for libertarians to "give up" on their "ethnic or nationalist or cultural alliances."[7]

It isn't so much that Deist personally thinks this way so much as it is that he seems to will it upon the rest of his movement as the be-all, end-all approach to successfully liberating those deserving of liberation. As Slater points out in his analysis, the deserving ones seem to be exclusively "white Europeans."[8] Regardless of Deist's own intentions with his word choices, it is terribly clear that many of the proto-fascistic extremists who find overlap with modern right-libertarianism can find validation in such broad language that doesn't seem to account for their means of infiltration.

But Deist isn't finished, capping things off with the following:

This is where things get more tenuous. Many people have and will fight for such abstractions. But if you ask soldiers they'll tell you that in the heat of battle they're really fighting for their mates, to protect the men in their units—and to fulfill a personal sense of duty. In other words, blood and soil and God and nation still matter to people. Libertarians ignore this at the risk of irrelevance.[9]

There is a lot to unpack, here, but we can start with the obvious: "blood and soil" is an old Nazi term that was designed to rile up ethnic and geographic pride within the German population. It is therefore both fascistic and nationalistic in its most recent historical context. The term *does* originate a little earlier in Germany than when the Nazis specifically picked it up for their own propaganda, but even in its earliest documented usage, it was still nationalistic in its sentiments. This means that when Jeff Deist chose of his own free will to use this term in his speech, he was either completely ignorant of its origins and just so happened to use it by coincidence, or he used the term in spite of its historical stigma for some reason. Either way, it understandably stirred up controversy with people who did know of the term's origins, and it was seen by them as yet another example of the conservative liberty movement's willingness to cozy up to anyone and everyone to the right of them as a means of strategy against the claimed great Satan of socialism.

Beyond that, however, the speech also demonstrates a link between the concept of private property (sloppily conflated with personal property, per the typical conservative gallop) as a natural right, and the concept of closed national borders as a natural extension of said right. It also appears to assume moral superiority in a person's caring only about the things that immediately concern him. Sure, Deist throws the hypothetical altruist a bone by citing how it is natural and moral to defend a neighbor, or other "strangers" within one's own community, but he is very careful not to leave the confines of nearby geographical surroundings when making this illustration. As for people outside one's own community? Those people are the "invaders" in Deist's scenario. So much of this rhetoric amounts to celebration of selfishness, distrust of multiculturalism, and at the very least could be interpreted as possible extremist dog whistling. For myself, still hanging onto the broader label of "libertarian" at the time but having long been disillusioned with the right-libertarian variation's continuing rightward momentum in the cultural space, Deist's speech was the last straw. I could no longer excuse the shortsightedness.

This newfound outward display of nationalistic favoritism was really a culmination of the past century's long and tangled history of libertarian ideological shifting. As Canadian historian Quinn Slobodian records, neoliberalism hit a schism that helped cement Rothbardian right-libertarianism as a legitimate school of economic thought in the wake of "the egalitarian challenge of the 1960s," leading to some key libertarian figures willingly going the way of cultural empathy and the others willingly going the way of economics-first.[10] And as time went on, many others sharing the moniker of "libertarian" jarringly began to publicly shift into a different philosophical stance altogether—one of hard nationalism, ethnocentrism, and rhetorical elements sympathetic to xenophobia. This was no longer the movement I had so enthusiastically joined the better part of a decade prior; rather than continue to promulgate the positive benefits of personal liberation and "free trade of ideas," these new right-libertarians had instead allowed their circle to become something of a haven for some incredibly destructive perspectives that were seeming to become more aligned with crypto-fascistic sentiment by the week.

But the groundwork had already been laid across all of the interrelated conservative movements that saw themselves as revolutionary. From the vulgar libertarians to the online skeptics to the 4chan alt-lighters to the run-of-the-mill working-class Republicans, it had become okay, and even rational, to hate. The frustration with the limits of late capitalism and the disillusionment with the neoliberal narrative had finally caught up to the most privileged pocket of the working class, but that frustration and disillusionment had fallen down a rabbit hole that misdirected the anger toward other members of the working class rather than toward the elite corporate class or the systemic foundations. Any chance of being exposed to the more nuanced truth of the matter had been closed off years prior behind a steady influx of anti-socialist propaganda that ultimately became genuinely believed by those peddling it. The only thing left to do was to continue being angry with only half of the puzzle available. In 2020, during the thick of the presidential election, former Trump staffer and podcast host Steve Bannon called for the beheading of Dr. Anthony Fauci, the pandemic expert who was part of Trump's Covid-19 task force but who was beginning to publicly question Trump's approach to handling the pandemic.[11] Bannon justified this call by comparing the action to the public hanging of the Tories in Pennsylvania in 1788, likening Fauci and other anti-Trump public actors as traitors to their country.[12] Bannon stated, "that's how you win the revolution. No one wants to talk about it, but revolution isn't some sort of garden party, right? It's civil war."[13]

As was previously covered, this incomplete view of the world proved the perfect breeding ground for more and more extremist rhetoric to slip by and gain influence. Tap into the populist unrest, perpetuate the ignorance of what is really going on, offer up a perceived representative on behalf of the plight, and then make it so the thought of losing this ally (in this case, Trump) equals the end of the chance for one's socioeconomic situation to be helped, and the desperation sets in. It can even lead to a former government official calling for the public unlawful execution of a dissenting voice to the fake populist leader.

Indeed, it culminated on the ground level into a tangible pathway for many impressionable white men that led from revolutionary conservativism to extremist nationalism—what Matt Lewis of *The Daily Beast* called the libertarian-to-Alt-Right-pipeline.[14] The sex appeal of the faux-intellectualism of the online skeptics who shared the conservative viewpoint on issues like immigration and certain minority rights (this movement as a whole is presently rife with transphobia hiding behind scientism, for instance) helped validate existing cultural biases present in these other aforementioned groups and ultimately led to violent action on behalf of the true believers who felt like *their* revolution was nigh.

One case of this was the deadly New Zealand Christchurch mosque shooting in March 2019, where the gunman cited the "Great Replacement" version of the white genocide conspiracy theory popularized by Southern as his motivation for the murders, even going so far as to title his manifesto after it.[15] He saw himself as an "identitarian," something Southern and others in her circle were citing as a positive example of evidence-based libertarian activism leading up to the attack.[16] There was even record of him having been corresponding with a key leader in the identitarian movement, Martin Sellner, being invited to Sellner's abode for coffee quite close in time to the attack, indicating even further ideological conditioning could have been happening beyond the initially recognized influence of the Great Replacement conspiracy theory.[17]

Another instance of this was when a far-right militia group plotted the following year to kidnap Democratic governor of Michigan Gretchen Whitmer and take her to another State to carry out a citizen-led "trial" to punish her for her perceived socialist, traitorous actions against her citizens.[18]

Yet another case of right-wing violence being carried out by revolutionary-minded Trump supporters was when that same year a Trump sticker-spangled caravan of cars swarmed a Biden campaign bus and tried to run it off the road.[19] Trump himself made light of the situation, joking at a campaign rally after the news broke that the caravan was simply welcoming the Biden bus, "protecting" it because his supporters are "nice." The remark led to an eruption of laughter from many of his supporters in the audience.[20] Biden, despite his radical centrist policy proposals, grounded in typical capitalist apparatus, was dishonestly called a "socialist" by Trump during the whole reelection campaign who would lead the economy to Marxism if elected.[21]

Among the more obvious examples of this specific line of thinking turning violent was, of course, the Unite the Right rally in Charlottesville, VA, that took place in August of 2017—only one month after the Jeff Deist speech cemented right-libertarianism as at least willing to utilize fascist terminology—and resulted in the murder of activist Heather Heyer at the hands of a white nationalist when he rammed his car into a crowd of peaceful protestors.[22] When asked to condemn these actions, Trump infamously dodged the request, instead positing the claim that there were "good people on both sides" of that conflict in Charlottesville. Three years later, during his reelection campaign and his first presidential debate with his opponent Joe Biden, Trump was asked once again by moderator Chris Wallace to condemn right-wing terrorism and white nationalism carried out in his name. This time, Trump stunned even more people with his message to right-wing extremists: "stand back . . . and standby."[23]

The 2017 rally in Charlottesville itself was billed and advertised as a broadly conservative event meant to unite all stripes of revolutionaries in the conservative movement at large—including red-pilled conservatives, right-libertarians, and neoconservatives. Calls to join the rally went around the circles I still occupied at the time as a libertarian, and people I knew (or thought I knew) seemed interested in attending. Just a year prior, I could not have imagined any of these people defending the actions at Charlottesville, but before my very eyes, people I either had connections with or knew directly proceeded to bend over backward for weeks afterward attempting to depict Heyer's murderer as an innocent, peaceful protestor fearful for his life and acting in self-defense. It was disgusting, but it was also an indicator of just how far the rot had spread in the movement I once thought stood above ideological viciousness. The left-libertarianism of Proudhon and Bakunin would not have stood for such ideological poison gaining such a foothold, but the colloquial view of what it now means to be a libertarian invokes the specter of Rothbardian right-libertarianism almost exclusively thanks to that form of libertarianism managing to take over almost all of the prominent public visibility that historically socialist libertarianism more broadly used to hold.[24]

The culmination of everything we have looked at thus far, from the language of "replacement" to the presentation of ignorance as intellectualism to the manufacturing of *Others* to accommodate said ignorance, could be seen on full display that day in Charlottesville. "You will not replace us!" yelled the angry mob, itself consisting of not just white nationalists, but also of right-libertarians, red-pilled alt-lighters, and other forms of privileged revolutionary.[25] "Blood and soil!" was also a regular chant on display, mere weeks after an influential libertarian think-tank had seemingly revived the phrase for a mainstream conservative application.[26]

Many of the marchers, much like all of the privileged revolutionaries of focus in this book, seemed to genuinely believe that what they were doing was fighting a clear and present threat of tyranny. The mythical SJW variant of the *Other* was seen as more real and imminent than capitalistic oppression, despite all of the evidence of the latter significantly outweighing the spangled and vague evidence of the former. Narratives, appealing to the deep feels-as-if stories of these intersectionally privileged pockets of the white working class, had gone on to win out over objective facts while simultaneously presenting themselves as if they *were* the objective facts.[27] Returning to Dr. Roderick Long, his observation of how these faux-revolutionary conservative mindsets, leading all the way up to fascism itself, always seem to exist at this seemingly oxymoronic crossroads between elitism and working-class strife is quite synthesizing for us when we take into account also the previously cited observations of power relations of Poulantzas and Paxton:

> Fascism differs from old-style conservatism in embracing an ideal of industrial progress directed by managerial technocrats, as well as adopting a populist stance of championing the "little guy" against elites—remember the folksiness.

If fascism's technocratic tendencies appear to conflict with its anti-rationalist tendencies, well, in the words of proto-fascist Moeller van den Bruck, "we must be strong enough to live in contradictions." Some of the difference between fascism and the older conservatism may be due to the advances won by [the liberals]. The progress of liberalism and of industry had the effect of shifting wealth, at least in part, from the traditional aristocracy to new private hands, thus creating new private interest groups with the ability to operate as political entrepreneurs; hence, perhaps, the tendency toward the emergence of a plutocratic class nominally outside the traditional state apparatus. Likewise, the progress of democracy meant that plutocracy could hope to triumph only by donning the populist guise; hence the paradox of an elitist movement marching forward under the banner of anti-elitism. . . . Hence fascism's odd fusion of privilege and folksiness; one might call it a movement that thinks like Halliburton and talks like George W. Bush.[28]

This process had been helped along through seemingly corroborating narratives coming from adjacent thought movements with similar worldviews such as the online skeptic community and the Intellectual Dark Web, helping to sell the illusion that it was intelligent and empirical to take these stances. Much of this rebellious, countercultural attitude found by this point in right-wing faux-revolutionary circles was itself co-opted from leftism, as were many of the terminologies and labels used, such as "libertarian," "anarchist," and "revolution."[29] All of *that* had occurred in an effort to simply maintain the status quo as it currently exists so as to keep neoliberal policy (and its subsequent elitist favoritism) alive.

Following this chain of events back to the origin point, the greatest irony on display was that these right-wing revolutionaries were ultimately fighting for a revolution of privilege, and the world they hoped to build was in actuality a world already in existence which stood only to benefit the most elite of economic classes and the most privileged of demographics—in other words, a world that had no interest in real revolution of any kind. These supposed revolutionaries were fighting for what in effect stood to amount to a counter-revolution after all.

As for how many of these privileged revolutionaries then fell into full-blown nationalism and fascism from there, well, that was by design on behalf of the Alt-Right masterminds, who knew they would need to swoop in and exploit all of the ignorance and populist unrest brewing within the culturally privileged pockets of the economically underprivileged working class—not unlike the other instances of right-wing extremism co-opting working-class populism cited earlier in this book, marking yet another case where the cycle of worker dissatisfaction with capitalism came back around in yet another generation, with that generation being particularly lacking in the vocabulary and historical knowledge to adequately dodge this new spin on the old con of faux-intellectual racism.[30]

This particular effort had been going on since at least 2009, when Alt-Right founder Richard Spencer's *Alternative Right* publication began gaining disdain from other conservatives in the less visible, non-mainstream conservative press. That year, an article appeared in *The American Conservative* written by Clark Stooksbury describing Spencer's movement in which Stooksbury simply stated "no thanks."[31] Then, in 2010,

E. D. Kain of *True/Slant* warned that "this is white nationalism, folks, dressed up in faux-intellectuaism."[32] Likewise, after interviewing Spencer that same year, Tim Mak of *FrumForum* declared that Spencer's new brand of extreme conservatives were "going to be white nationalists, but, by God, they're going to be a little fancy about it," concluding that the resurrected race realism and nationalism apologetics found in Spencer's ideology should be "locked in a padded room."[33] Also in 2010, Richard Spencer teamed up with aforementioned right-libertarian academic Hans-Hermann Hoppe to speak at Hoppe's Property and Freedom Society and promote the "alternative right" as a growing positive phenomenon of intellectual resurgence within conservatism.[34]

With that exposure, Spencer had already begun to reach across the populist rationale spectrum and hook in the more impressionable among the populist conservatives who were looking for answers and not finding them in the conservative circles at the time, which were all primarily influenced by neoliberal economic narratives. This willingness to jettison prior forms of conservatism and adhere to a supposedly empirical brand of intellectualism, Spencer was also weaving common threads between his movement and the growing online skeptic community, itself beginning to take on a more anti-SJW, anti-feminist tone. All of this made for an apparently more advanced form of conservatism—one that could leave religion behind and be "scientific."[35] But as *National Review* columnist Ross Douthat would come to lament, "if you dislike the religious right, wait until you meet the post-religious right."[36]

Thus, the organic neoliberal feedback loops that grew out of the hegemony of a century of liberal elitism pandering to workers and obscuring the reality of the exploitative nature of capitalism finally began to break down. But with a lack of real alternatives to the given system offered up by any mainstream political group, the most extreme among the right-wing ideologues were able to woo over many working-class populists on the right who felt underserved by their existing political camps. The privileged revolutionaries of varying stripes found solidarity in hate.[37]

Only three years after the Charlottesville march, these revolutionaries brought to fruition what had been a long-gestating desire for what in their minds felt like a genuinely revolutionary breaking point, even more extreme than what was seen in 2017. On January 6, 2021, when the US Congress was set to make official the democratic election of Joseph R. Biden, Jr. as the forty-sixth president, Trump, the *caudillo*-styled leader himself, held a rally right up the road from the Capitol building in which he urged his supporters to be on the lookout for whether or not then–vice president Mike Pence would prove his "loyalty" by rejecting the legitimacy of the election. The implication of Trump's words, though not explicitly stated, was that *this* was the moment he had been asking his supporters to "standby" for. That *this* was the moment when their revolutionary urge might finally reach its moment to be let loose. indeed, Trump's personal lawyer Rudi Giuliani was also in attendance at this rally, and he stated that the supporters there needed to prepare for a "trial by combat" against what had been presented by the administration for months by this point (without any corroborated evidence) as a fraudulent election unfairly rigged to throw Trump out of office illegitimately.[38]

Once it was clear that Pence was indeed not going to undermine the democratic nature of the Biden election, Trump took to social media to declare that Pence "lacked the courage" to do what must be done, which was all the most rabid among his revolutionary-minded populist supporters needed to justify their subsequent march on the Capitol. They gathered by the thousands and stormed the building, ramming down doors and overpowering capital building security, all in the name of their perceived revolution. When asked by reporters who arrived on the scene amidst the chaos why they were doing this, the responses from many of the marchers that day were all essentially the same. One woman declared, "this is the revolution," while another marcher simply answered, "1776."[39] The marches quickly dissolved into a collective mob, and when they breached security and stormed the building, they began chanting revolutionary mantras like "1776! 1776! 1776!" and "This is our house! This is our house!"[40] Ultimately, after hours of Trump doing nothing, Mike Pence from a safe location finally had to make the call to dispatch the National Guard in order to stop the mob from taking their attempted coup any further.

So, what made this event not a true revolution? Why is it that certain acts throughout history that aesthetically present very similarly have indeed been deemed true revolutions in favor of democracy, while this example from the right-wing populists has been called an affront to that same democracy? Wouldn't the people always act in their own best interest in a case like this? Of course, if one has been reading this book linearly up to this point, the reasons why this attempted revolution was of a faux quality are going to be numerous and obvious. The historical distortion of public understanding of what real libertarianism was, the revisionist reframing of revolutionary rhetoric to serve status quo systems like capitalism, the means by which the Trump presidency built its campaign on tapping into already-existing populist unrest, and so on, all play into our understanding of why the march on DC in January of 2021 was not legitimate. But if any real headway is to be made toward retrieving the working-class spirit from these populists on the right, many of whom may still hold genuinely revolutionary ideals and who may yet be reached with the more nuanced reality laid out across these pages, there should at least be a good-faith effort made toward understanding how to go about radical behavior in order to bring about real change rather than to simply fall victim to the same hate-mongering that has undone the right. Therefore, the final portion of this chapter will aim to do precisely that.

* * *

When the streets of the Los Angeles neighborhood Watts exploded with riots and civilian rebellion against law enforcement for six days straight in August of 1965, the world sat up and took notice. It all started one afternoon when a highway patrolman decided to pull over a car with a suspected drunk driver at the wheel. When the car's passenger offered to take over for the driver (both the driver and passenger were Black), the police officer refused and ordered the car impounded. Passerby on the street started gathering around in defense of the men in the car, arguing that the policeman's behavior was out of line. This was not the first time that cops had been witnessed abusing their power against minorities in this area; for months prior, a string of police brutality incidents had veered the entire community into great distrust and anger toward the local police force, so this particular incident with the car was simply the last straw. Before long, people were actively trying to stop the patrolman from going through with the deed of towing the car, and rocks started to be thrown. The officer fought back, calling for backup, and the Watts riots began.

By the end of the six-day stretch, over 1,000 people were injured, 34 were confirmed dead, and millions of dollars' worth of damage had happened.[41] Hospitals were full, as were the jails, and the entire community was consumed by apparent chaos.

However, this was political violence with a very clear point: the Black community had been brutalized by the State militia in the form of the police in their neighborhoods for too long, and enough was finally enough. Despite the initial seemingly disastrous immediate effects, the Watts Rebellion quickly became seen as, according to journalist Mary McMahon, "sobering for Californians and Americans in general, illustrating the extremely volatile mood in urban black neighborhoods and setting the stage for the coming years of the civil rights struggle."[42]

This demonstrates that sometimes, when properly aimed and uniformly precise in purpose, political violence can, and does, indeed bring about public awareness of very real issues of oppression. As the previous chapter highlighted, confusing the hatred of the oppressors with the pushback of the oppressed (and their allies) can often pass as a reasonable, centrist position. But in the end, it is equivocating two very different stances with completely different rationales. The Alt-Right and AntiFa, for example, are not two sides of the same coin. One group stands to oppress others while the other group stands to go to extreme lengths to stop the oppressors who struck first. Whether or not one chooses to agree with AntiFa's methods is beside the point; AntiFa's actions are not done with the intention of excising whole demographics of people to appease extreme anti-political paranoia, which means that AntiFa is objectively not the same animal as the Alt-Right. It also doesn't hurt to be aware of the fact that AntiFa has existed for much longer in history and has always stood by the consistent message of fighting back against fascism in whatever form it takes, from the Nazis all the way to the Alt-Right.

Having said this, the intent of a group, movement, or person may not be as clear when the tactics become harder to distinguish from those of the oppressors. On June 29, 2019, an Alt-Right group known as the Proud Boys (once again originating in right-libertarian circles) came up against a group of AntiFa protestors in Portland, OR. The clash itself was not that unusual, of course, but something that made it more notable was that this was an instance where AntiFa, the movement motivated by a fight against hate and senseless violence, was itself the arbiter of senseless violence. Andy Ngo, a journalist for center-right political publication *Quillette*, was beaten bloody by AntiFa members to the point of needing hospitalization.[43] Ngo was not there in support of the Alt-Right, as he is Asian-American and gay and therefore a potential target of right-wing extremism himself. Yet within the chaos of the larger scuffle, he nevertheless became marked as an enemy due to his more moderate conservatism and was promptly assaulted.

The immediately visible problem with this is that all it does is add fuel to the narrative that socialism, and "the left" as a whole entity, is violent by nature, since AntiFa often displays clear affiliation with both. Second, it also means that potential working-class solidarity against the oppressive classes gets pushed even further back into the shadows as people yet again pick political sides and draw lines across ideological grounds, missing the wood for the trees. What is more problematic, however, is that Andy Ngo was a non-combatant, meaning that tactically and morally, things become needlessly gray in situations like these to both others within the left and the general neoliberalized public. Ngo, understandably shaken and offended by the attack, went on to tell the press that AntiFa represents "extremists, violent communists and anarchists" who are "actually agitating for a revolution."[44] If anyone can look at that sort of mainstream coverage and think that genuine working-class revolution comes out appearing reasonable, that person's faculties might be in need of assessment. Calling upon Douglass Lane once again, he argues that this sort of tactical approach of shooting first without any grasp of degrees or context is a mistake for anyone who really cares about changing the system for the better.[45] Because all it does is give cause for the masses to listen to the narrative of the neoliberal elite and disregard the cries for change from the anarchists and socialists who historically have the intellectual high ground. Instances such as the aforementioned apologetics on behalf of Heather Heyer's murderer, while demonstrably incorrect, unfortunately become further legitimized when real cases of uncalled for extremism from leftist protestors turn needlessly violent against the wrong people.

So, what should the response be? Well, the aforementioned faux-centrists call, of course, for a reasonable amount of law and order as a means of culling "both sides," yet again perpetuating the incorrect narrative that being politically moderate is somehow the only reasonable and empirical position one can take in these matters—another affront to ever actually getting any real change to the status quo underway. It's also a means of wrapping a veneer of apparent normalization around something that has historically always leaned toward authoritarianism.[46] The politics behind typical law and order campaigns, points out Carl Freedman in his book *The Age of Nixon*, can be seen as aligning with a tension between innately opposed concepts: restraint and power.[47] Law carries with it a promise of restraining the power over others we might have as citizens, but also that the State itself stands to implement over all of us. The problem here is that in order for law to truly act justly as promised, cites Lane, a certain amount of disorder must be expected.[48] To paraphrase William Blackstone, better it is for ten guilty men to go free than for even one innocent person to be unjustly executed. Likewise, if order is what we truly want, then the law itself cannot always be just, since our present system currently operates at its smoothest when the law is bent and certain skirtings of on-the-books provisions are unchallenged.[49] In other words, "order" in our present reality is in practice a synonym for "business as usual." Ideologically, then, the actual implication of all familiar law and order campaigns is that in any given instance, only one of these things will be abided by—historically, order almost always wins out over law.

When George Wallace, the forty-fifth governor of Alabama, ran for president in 1968 as a so-called moderate, law and order-independent candidate, for example, he was actually running to preserve what he saw as the order of his own voter base's preferred way of things (appealing to that base's feels-as-if stories in the vein of those identified by Hochschild in Chapter 9).[50] What he was running *against* amounted to the new reality being built thanks to the strides taken by the civil rights movement—something that would ultimately be embedded in the law.[51] At the outset of any appeal to the preservation of an older order like this, the law is initially cited as something noble that chaotic ruffians (i.e., *Others*) are aiming to tear down.[52] But once the new legal reality is established and it includes more freedoms for those same ruffians, suddenly the narrative changes and order alone is clung to while the law is reframed as oppressive and in need of changing. This explains somewhat how right-wing faux-revolutionary movements can depict themselves so successfully as genuinely revolutionary—they too have a bone to pick with the present laws! But only when said laws also happen to be getting in the way of established privilege of varying kinds.

Of course, when order wins out over law in principle, the reality of law after this is often a corrupt one that legalizes the re-establishment of privilege (either culturally or economically) in which the legal rights of certain groups of people are overshadowed by a perceived moderate norm that is presented as the reasonable state of affairs to fight for. When Donald Trump promised in his 2016 presidential campaign to make America "great again," he was appealing to this process on the cultural level. When he took office, he implemented the process on the economic level, giving the elite class further kickbacks and cementing the business-as-usual state of affairs. His ideal order became the law, but his prior appeals for order before he had the means to realize it were *against* the then-present law, helping it appear revolutionary to his misguided working-class supporters. Therefore, "law and order" is an illusory concept that pits two contradictory concepts against one another while presenting itself as a just marriage between the two. This of course is true even if things are flipped and the more noble actors are the ones challenging the present legal reality. Across the board, using force to stop behavior that is perceived as delinquency by the present powers can often lead to greater resistance to said force and greater amounts of disorder. Law enforcement, by definition, is force. Therefore, enforcing the law does not lead to order unless it becomes entirely oppressive, at which point it is unjust and thus no longer truly the ideal of what law is supposed to represent.

This is true both conceptually for societies in general and practically in the immediate moment. This is why law enforcement itself will often take a non-interventionist approach when trying to maintain "order" at public protest events, argues Lane.[53] Getting more involved than absolutely necessary stands to potentially escalate the tension and make things more extreme and potentially violent—even if a certain amount of smaller-scale unlawfulness has to take place in the meantime. For much of the left, though, the understanding of "order" and a just form of the law as contradictory concepts is already established. Therefore, this kind of disorder that law enforcement wants to avoid is sometimes exactly what the leftist protestors are after because it has the potential to shake things up in a way that could potentially be positive; it could help divorce order from the law in the minds of onlookers.

But if those leftists truly want to utilize violence and disorder as a means of bringing about positive social change, warns Lane, they need to remember the history of radical unrest and how it has often led to very morally confused results when not executed as part of an ongoing, organized, and morally consistent charge.[54] Žižek, for instance, has delineated a difference between what he sees as radical violence and impotent violence, with the former being of the tactical sort described above while the latter amounts to outbursts of short-term, purely reactionary rage.[55] How to tell the difference? Well, violence is often the thing that brings about initial systemic change historically, but it is equally true that once a new power structure has been established, violence is no longer the primary means by which oppressors maintain their control domestically.[56] Instead, it is hegemony, as we have seen throughout the course of this book, that takes the front seat in this regard. Through cultural conditioning, the given status quo retains its influence.

The violence we see happening at the hands of police officers against Black men, or the violent language regularly hurled at socially oppressed groups by Donald Trump and his sycophantic supporters, *is* a clear example of active perpetuation of oppression. However, this sort of violence amounts to the impotent sort described by Žižek in that, since its only concern is to maintain an idea of existing law and order, it never really becomes radical.[57] It isn't trying to move anything forward. This fact in itself can often expose impotent violent authoritarianism for the empty vessel it truly is. It might be argued, therefore, then since the status quo now seems to be turning to more violent means of maintaining its grip, it is becoming desperate in the face of late capitalism's usefulness (and, by extension, neoliberal hegemony's soundness) having finally run its course.

By this same token, the protestors can also fall into the trap of exuding impotent violence rather than tactical and organized violence—though they do not need to, as their violence stands to bring about something new rather than simply maintain an existing state of affairs. This is why it is put forth here that the assault of Andy Ngo, and any other instance in which leftist revolutionaries find themselves harming non-combatants and getting no positive results from it, cannot qualify as anything other than senseless and needless violence. The AntiFa members who do this sort of thing are not trying to cause change in that moment; they justify their actions as amounting to a kind of conceptual self-defense.[58] This is not radical, and therefore, its results aren't, either. It is purely reactionary, which makes those behind the act harder to distinguish from their right-wing enemies than ever.[59]

This is a state of things arguably predicted by Gramsci when he mused that "the crisis consists precisely in the fact that the old is dying and the new cannot be born; in this interregnum a great variety of morbid symptoms appear."[60] As we have been able to see thus far, the privileged revolutionaries this book aims to understand can themselves be seen as one of those morbid symptoms. But if the radicals of the left wish to rise above becoming a symptom as well, they need to make sure that whatever violence does arise amidst their protests and riots has a real point beyond their own selfish, reactionary whims in the moment. It needs to truly aim to usher in a new order of things—one that truly will operate differently from the one we currently inhabit. That means being the bigger people and not resorting to the same sort of mindless hate and anger displayed by the extremists they fight on the right.

Fortunately, despite the narratives to portray things otherwise, much of the left *does* engage in this more tactical way and avoids the aforementioned pitfalls. But the sliver of the left that presently demonstrates a lack of focus in its own violent protests ends up validating the most extreme narratives coming from the right that frames all leftists as mindless, imprecise assailants driven by a love of disorder rather than a desire for humanistic change. The Watts Rebellion took aim at specific oppressive forces; the most extreme leftist members of AntiFa take aim at whoever is in the way in the given moment. But leftist working-class revolt more generally does remain deliberate and focused in its outcry, meaning that it is important for anyone observing from the sidelines to remain skeptical of the right's narrative that everyone on the left is simply a violent reactionary. This narrative remains one of the most effective bait-and-switches left in the extreme right's arsenal, as it appeals to a general audience while also serving as a potential entry point for budding conservative radicals. Heeding the evidence in spite of this narrative is still necessary for any real skepticism to win out.

What does this evidence reveal? That most political violence seen today in America is indeed of the right-wing, not left-wing, variety. According to the Anti-Defamation League, every single death at the hands of political terrorism in the year 2018 was at the hands of some variant of right-wing extremist.[61] More specifically, 78 percent of total domestic extremist-related murders were carried out by white supremacists,

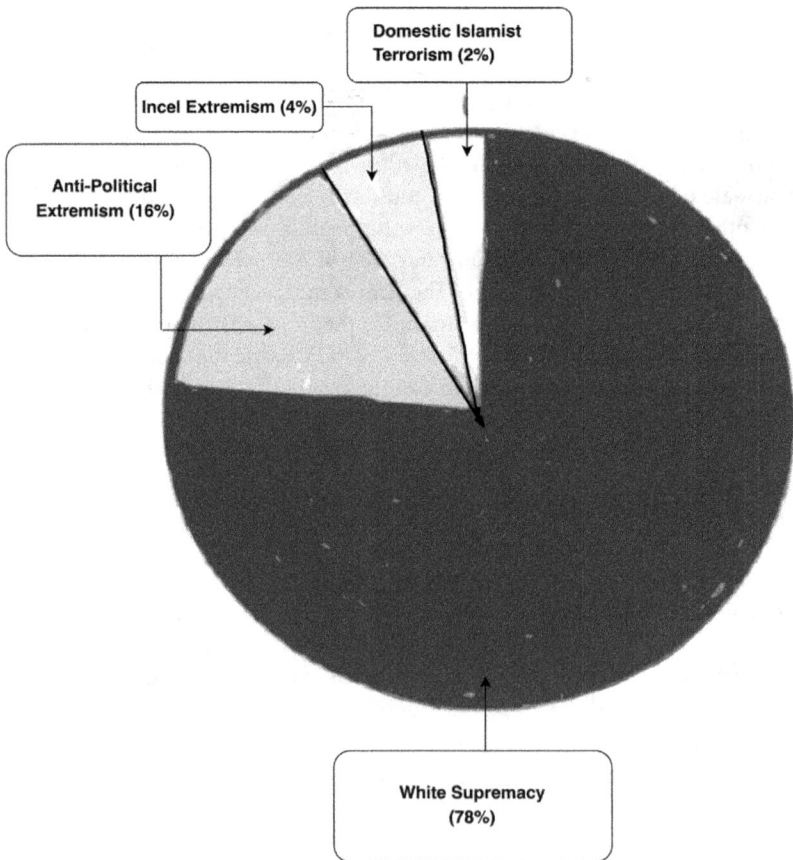

Figure 11.1 By percentage, recorded ideological motivations between all domestic terrorist acts in the United States for the year 2018. Source: Anti-Defamation League.

16 percent by Jacobinistic anti-political right-wingers (see Chapter 2), 4 percent by self-described "incels" (involuntary celibates), and 2 percent by domestic Islamist extremism[62] (Figure 11.1). According to the Center for Strategic and International Studies, similar data has been gathered, showing that the overwhelming majority of these deaths happened at the hands of both white supremacists and anti-government extremists, including militias and "sovereign citizen" groups.[63] Furthermore, the Center for Investigative Reporting found in a near-decade-long investigation that from the year 2008 to the year 2017, 178 of the domestic terror incidents were right-wing (roughly 91 percent) while only 19 were left-wing in ideological motivation (around 9 percent).[64]

These data points remain consistent across the board regardless of which institution is interpreting the data itself. It should be plainly visible when looking at these numbers that in spite of all the cries from the right of oppression and violence at the hands of leftists, the reality is that it is the right-wingers, and not the socialists, who are doing the killing and silencing. To claim that the split between violent extremists on both sides is somehow equal in any capacity is to commit an obvious and shameful false equivalency fallacy. The aforementioned march on the Capitol in 2021 could also be seen as indeed a domestic, right-wing act of terrorism. After all, several people were indeed killed, and the sentiment behind the attempted coup was made obvious by all those involved on the day.

Thus, we have seen the data, explored the history, untangled the rationale, and delineated the mindsets, systems, and events that have resulted in the privileged revolutionaries on the right and their movements within the working-class. While one volume alone surely will not be enough to fully understand every facet of the phenomenon this book chose to take on as its subject, it is certainly the case that this specific kind of focus on these lesser-explored areas of radical history and how they tangled with the right wing as capitalism gained its hegemonic footing is worthy of putting to paper. It is the author's hope that further sojourning down this particular path will continue in academic writing moving forward as even more scholars and laypeople alike take interest in populism and its implications for the future of society at large. How can it potentially be veered to be more conducive for positive change for all? How can the existing elements in play in the populist conversation, even on the right, possibly lead to *actual* liberation for working people?

Conclusion

Redirecting the Revolutionary Urge

On the morning of Saturday, November 7, 2020, after nearly a week of extended vote counting, and in the midst of the most devastating pandemic in memory, Joseph R. Biden, Jr. was elected the forty-sixth president of the United States. In his victory, a sense of renewed hope for healing across the country brightly coruscated. Elements of this win were historic, including the overall number of total votes, as well as the fact that Biden's vice-presidential pick, Kamala Harris, was both the first woman and the first woman of color to ever be elected to that office. In their victory speeches, both Harris and Biden spoke of being true representatives for all Americans, including those in the minority groups the previous president had done much work to harm and hinder. None of that should be taken away from the election outcome, and all of its best and most truthful promises should be infinitely lauded. Yet, it remained a telling aspect of the election that Biden did not win against his opponent by the supposed landslide most of the mainstream polls were predicting. He won by enough of a margin to pull off the popular vote and electoral college, but pulling back to see the overall voter turnout, it was still strikingly and darkly obvious that about seventy million people still would have wanted to see Donald Trump have a second presidential term. According to the Pew Research Center, only 46 percent of Biden voters "strongly supported" him, while 66 percent of Trump supporters strongly supported him.[1]

As such, the Biden victory in many ways was much more of a vote in favor of compassion and empathy for one's fellow Americans than it was a sign of universal excitement about Biden in and of himself. The margin between Biden and Trump was narrow enough in several swing States that Trump was legally able to demand recounts and vote audits in those instances, and in the face of Trump's loss he remained a fake populist to the end, framing his legal challenges as a push by a populist outsider against a corrupt system of elites attempting to jettison him out of the driver's seat. Several Trump supporters took to social media and ran with this framing of the situation. One such supporter tweeted, "Throw out every illegal vote and do a recount. Really not that difficult."[2] Another stated the following screed: "once upon a time, the media existed to defend the common man. . . . Now journalists gaslight and censor the people to protect the establishment. Citizens are saying they had their votes stolen. TELL THE TRUTH."[3]

This rhetoric once again demonstrated that the anti-elitist, revolutionary content of the character of right-wing populism was still fully alight, and that the figure of the moment it had chosen to look to as its representative, Trump, was still successfully peddling his faux-populism to his base. This is why it was so easy for the January 6, 2021, march on the Capitol building to quickly snowball into the outright coup attempt that it became: that sense of the need for revolutionary change and action still remains across all of the working class, even those on the right who are historically misguided. If a real effort to redirect that urge is not undertaken, then a similar situation is inevitable in the future.

This still-present outcry of populist dissatisfaction with the system on behalf of working-class conservatives, alongside the fact that Biden's win was not as monumental as expected, lends credence to the claim that quickly became prominent in more leftist journalistic circles that the establishment Democrats had still ultimately failed to tap into the populist narrative and dare to truly understand and speak to the working poor.[4] After all, Biden was not exactly the most radical of candidates, and stood to merely bring the country back to its neoliberal state prior to Trump's arrival; he did not symbolize any significant change to the economic status quo beyond how it operated prior to 2017. Nevertheless, neoliberalism is markedly better than fascism for anyone who understands the danger the latter poses to democracy at large, and for this reason alone it should be celebrated that Biden earned his victory over Trump. But that cannot be where the effort to pull the country back to solidarity ends.

If this notion about the votes being more anti-Trump than pro-Biden is indeed the case, and if the business-as-usual capitalist system under Biden proceeds to ultimately continue exploiting workers, then the country still faces a very real risk of another Trump-like candidate coming along in the future and possibly veering the country back toward fascism all over again. Properly parsing out and understanding the conditions that led to that situation in the first place is therefore an invaluable step toward avoiding that particular recycling of history. This book has attempted to play its part in better refining that understanding. But moving forward, how can the most earnest elements of the conservative working class be reached before the populist rationale spectrum process begins to take hold and misdirect their anguish?

In the views of this book and its author, the answer to that question is to solidify a newfangled approach at populist solidarity that takes elements from both of organic populism's origin points—classical socialism and radical liberalism—while also managing to be neither of those things in total in order to best respond to the present-day plights working people now face in the twenty-first century.

Original, revolutionary libertarianism, as it is described in this book, must be understood *not* as the present-day libertarianism touted by the right, but as a long-lost sentiment of the socialist left that is by now centuries deceased—a lofty ideal far away from realization. It is not the wish of the author for the reader to take away from this work the idea that these pages condone or promulgate a simple revival of something so outdated, nor that all modern conservatives who tout "libertarianism" themselves have any modern socialist underlying potential. Rather, the prospect for moving forward should be more focused on finding what common threads there are across the entire working class, fashion a new rhetoric that redirects the revolutionary urge into something more realistic and achievable, but can retain rhetorical elements of the aforementioned classical schools of thought.

In the present world we live in, there is no realistic direct path toward the type of early socialism the broadly individualist anarchists like Proudhon and Bakunin defined as the logical (or even the desirable) next step for the afflicted and aggrieved working-class revolutionary. What is much more attainable, useful, and necessary for working people in the present political moment is something much more along the lines of an economic policy shift informed by the most politically viable offshoot of socialist thought in applied practice to date: social democracy. Indeed, an election, policy, or structure that would have immediate and real-world effects for working people, realigning the country to a market model that allows for checks, balances, and reforms inspired by something like the New Deal, but going much further toward true worker representation and minus that model's most egregious aforementioned shortcomings, is the most fathomable and graspable next step. That is a reality that the author neither disputes nor discourages.

Why, then, does this book concern itself with retaining this so-called revolutionary urge within working people, even on the right, when the pitfalls of such thinking have been put up on full display for the entirety of its length? Is revolutionary libertarianism the panacea to solve all the plights currently pushing conservative populists into their extremist proclivities? The answer to that question is decisively no. What this book has aimed to do is simply educate the anti-political populists of the right to not only the alternative ideological pathways they can access but also of how their revolutionary itch can still be scratched without needing to fully regress into the forgotten annals of their present ideology. From there, this urge for revolutionary change can perhaps be redirected and revised into something compatible with the aforementioned social democracy-infused policies that stand to salvage worker independence in the future.

But, one may wonder, is it not contradictory to claim that both a revolutionary, historically libertarian ideal and a revised, more grounded form of socially Democratic governance can complement one another? Not if one is to take seriously the reality of many leftist voices today who consider themselves to be both libertarian and socialist in equal measure. Noam Chomsky, the late David Graeber, Kevin Carson, Gary Chartier, Sheldon Richman, Rodrick Long and so on have all at various points referred to themselves as both socialist and libertarian—these are not long-dead figures in the pro-worker movement whose ideas have not been applied for centuries. These are voices whose influences are very much in play today, and they manage to argue in favor of the same variant of realistic economic future structural direction that was suggested earlier. They know, much like this author does, that the only realistic option for immediate next steps on this front would have to utilize the more compassionate elements of governance to standardize the approach to economic stability in a way that would necessarily require a certain amount of hierarchy and State oversight to remain in play. This does not mean, however, that a longer endgame envisioning an even further liberated reality cannot coexist with such a roadmap.

This is where I must push back to any possible speculation that I somehow believe that modern right-libertarians ubiquitously possess the makings of modern leftists underneath their veneers. I do not. What I do believe, however, is that the common ancestry found within the revolutionary urge at large is such that it is possible to redirect the desire for self-liberation, whatever form it takes, into a newer version of left-libertarianism and/or radical liberalism that is mindful of the tangled history of these movements without being beholden to them. The aforementioned list of influential writers on the left who don the label "libertarian socialist" stand to be evidence of this newer tradition already existing and thriving (and therefore being a valid interpretation). Those on the revolutionary right who have genuinely abhorrent views about their fellow human beings fueling their participation in right-wing populism are (1) not likely to benefit from the suggested ideological pivoting suggested in the forthcoming pages, and (2) not the revolutionary rightists being spoken of in this context, anyway. This is strictly a suggestion of how the most earnest forms of right-wing populism could (but not necessarily will) pivot into a better form of itself utilizing its common revolutionary ancestry with organic populist movements as a springboard.

It is my hope that throughout the preceding pages, a common thread of sincerity within most working-class members of the revolutionary right was prevalent. As such, it is safe to assume that, while misguided, the drive that brings many people on the right into these privileged revolutionary spaces is genuine and the desire for true liberation from oppressive forces and systems inspired. The book has spent a good portion of its total length aiming to drive the point home that the false consciousness observed within these aforementioned spaces is organically occurring and that the feedback loops informed by long-ingrained hegemonic propaganda are simply blinding the vast majority of these actors to the more complex reality.

Taking all of this into account, it stands to reason that what this book should do in its final stretch of argumentation is attempt to offer this brand of sincere-yet-misguided rightists some potential means of exodus from neoliberal hegemony rather than simply castigate them with no subsequent promulgations for a way forward. There are indeed ways of reaching similar systemic and economic outcomes to what the right-libertarians, alt-lighters, and other right-wing revolutionaries already claim to seek—ways that are actually grounded in a proper historical understanding of capitalism, socialism, and liberalism.

After all, it is the stance of this book that a major contributing factor to the rise of the faux-revolutionary right has been the fact that few alternatives to the neoliberal way of viewing the world ever reach the ear of the conservative working class. Keeping that in mind, the attempt will be made in the following pages to at least begin a journey down a path conducive to forward motion of truly liberating ideas in the truest, most historically literate sense—without falling into the trap of trapsing over long-abandoned ground. In order to do that, we must first summarize a list of key takeaways from the overall project this book undertook.

Following are some specific discerned facts pertaining to the main thesis of the book, accompanied by their summaries. It is upon these conclusions we can then build.

Revolutionary Rightists Are Largely Unwitting Players in a Larger Hegemonic Game

While it is true that certain actors in all of this, predominantly the conscious leaders of groups like the Alt-Right as well as certain elitist figures who promote culturally aligned narratives, have intentionally infiltrated the revolutionary rhetoric of the right, it is equally, if not more so, the case that the vast majority of both working-class and petty bourgeois actors who perpetuate the myths that have kept the capitalist status quo alive have been doing so precisely because of the growing populist worker unrest, not in spite of it.

Something more than merely an academic interest in the Trump election compelled me to write about this topic. In fact, as touched upon at the very start, it was the particular vantage point I had during that time that lent itself so well to my own understanding of the movement I was in at the time in right-libertarianism. As I grappled with the reality of Donald Trump's rise to power (and the baffling apologetics surrounding it), I began to see it as a symptom of a larger issue rather than an isolated instance of temporary collective insanity. I realized that the narrative I had initially subscribed to myself of neoliberalism as a social good was beginning to find its limits. Those limits, as it turns out, do not boil down to a simple black-and-white dichotomy of left versus right, since much of what excites the left about human emancipation has over the centuries slowly found new forms inside of the more anti-political rhetoric on the right, as well.

As the book has laid out, this can lead many well-meaning and honest people into following that revolutionary rhetoric, at its outset shared by both the more radical areas of the left *and* the right, toward the latter direction. The only differentiating factor between whether a potential revolutionary might go left or right in his politics is how much prior knowledge of actual revolutionary history said individual has been exposed to prior to his radicalization. If a person comes into his political knowledge only aware of the nearly ubiquitous neoliberal version of economic theory, then his radicalization will still necessarily have to adhere, at least initially, to an interpretation of the world that is more anti-political Jacobin than it is socialist, antiestablishment Jacobin.[5] The same broadly identifiable grievances with exhausted State power and worker limitation will still be present, but what potential foils to those problems will even be visible, much less considered, will be severely limited. Ironically, this form of Jacobinism gives rise to the very thing the conservative Jacobins claim to be against, with Kropotkin recognizing it as being ideologically coterminous with an oppressive government, once describing "the hierarchical, centralized, Jacobin, anti-libertarian principles of the State" as being entangled with the everyday concept of perceived justice.[6]

The cultural hegemony in play as a means of perpetuating the status quo that oppresses all workers is something many on the right still remain unaware of—in part because even the term "hegemony" originates from a political perspective that all stripes of conservative and neoliberal are told to fear and distrust: Marxism. But it remains undeniable that Marxist analysis of economic systems in crisis, and the cultural tactics used to artificially keep said systems alive in the face of such crisis, is still the most empirically sound and applicable means of ontologically understanding the how and why behind the prevailing of oppressive governmental apparatus. Despite this, most self-identified conservatives and right-wingers remain unwilling to trust in such analysis as an intellectual convoy for their own rebellious curiosities.

Realizing this, anyone who cares to mitigate this issue of misguided populism on the right should, in this author's view, approach debate with this crowd from a place of empathy and context. Minds will never fully be changed across the board, yet more de-radicalization from the right will occur if the right radicals in question are aware that their own plights are truly understood and somewhat shared with the rest of the working class—even those on the left who are often generalized and demonized by narratives on the right, which leads us to our next key conclusion:

Many Revolutionaries on the Right Have Legitimate Initial Class-Based Grievances

We are increasingly occupying an age of politics in which existing political labels mean less than perhaps they ever have before, and in which expert projections regarding expected political trends have been turned upside down. An age in which one's self-described philosophical allegiances could directly contradict one's actions and yet seemingly never be prodigious enough to sink reputations or serve as a wake-up call for the sane. An age of confused and angry plebiscites (made up predominantly of white males who lean politically right) who go on to poison the wells of their own movements with toxic ideology—or tolerance of said ideology—based on the bolstering of an irrational and contradictory fear that something vital about US culture would be lost if more ubiquitous freedom were gained for *all* people.[7]

But what caused said bolstering? Unlike the worst strains of conservatism of yesteryear, which admittedly bears striking similarity on the surface, this modern populist conservatism is one whose origin point isn't seemingly grounded in malicious prejudice and is instead initially borne out of real class-based strife and then subsequently infiltrated and distorted. As we have already established, the Alt-Right was not the first cause. It was a symptom. A fringe political movement, fronted by a publicly visible racist and nationalist in the figure of Richard Spencer, would not have on its own had the influence and the numbers of direct adherents necessary to pull off such a feat. As this book has argued, something more organic and elusive has played a role: honest ignorance in the face of neoliberalism's hegemonic cultural influence. But that in and of itself does not negate the initial sense of unrest that the conservative working class feels. Indeed, it is the same sense of unrest felt by everyone in the working class, regardless of political affiliation. By ignoring that reality, many leftist critics of right-wing populism have arguably missed the fact that beyond surface-level rhetorical divides, the origin point for both right and left working-class populism is the same. It begins with the lived-in reality of most working people, all of whom feel the effects of late capitalism reaching its limitations.

In Chapter 9, we looked at the data regarding how many of the workers most heavily affected by late capitalist shift have indeed been men,[8] and how many of the jobs these men have been displaced from are located in regions of the country often left behind by Democrats and subsequently more prone to political and economic conservativism.[9] In fact, even Democratic strategists themselves were aware of this fact, with one particular strategist, Andrew Levinson, arguing back in 2013 that "many white workers today do not simply live in different neighborhoods from the relatively affluent but in entirely different geographic areas." Levinson further opined that many of these forgotten workers "reside in three distinct locations: the rust belt, small towns, and the urban fringe. We see these areas as we drive past them but, since they no longer sit next to giant automobile factories and steel mills, our eyes do not immediately process them as 'working-class' communities."[10]

While this does not excuse the hate and ignorance that then follow, it is still necessary to recognize that being displaced by a system of increasing automation and increasing disregard for flesh-and-blood human workers' livelihoods in lieu of maximized profits (which is, as has been demonstrated, what said system was designed to prioritize from the beginning) would radicalize anyone. But without any sense that the self-described "progressives" in the policy-making region of the country (note: the liberal elitist takeover and subsequent empty pandering are outlined in Chapters 5 and 6) actually had the answers or cared to legitimately change things for the better for working people, that left these already conservative-leaning regions and demographics wide open to alternative explanations and proposed solutions for the hard times being felt.[11]

Those hard times bring with them resentment that, out of ignorance to larger forces in play, can then be exploited and channeled into sinister patterns of thought.[12] Remember the "feels-as-if" stories delineated by Arlie Hochschild in Chapter 9 and the subsequent feeling of being robbed of what one has earned with one's hard work when additional measures are taken to try and include minority groups in more employment pools and welfare initiatives.[13] And law professor Joan C. Williams corroborates this observation with her own work, stating that "whites from different classes are racist in quite different ways," and pointing out that the racism seen in much of the working-class white conservatism of today comes from a place of belief that non-whites in the same economic class were simply not earning the same living by cheating the system in some way and not sharing the same noble work ethic as everyone else.[14] This unique form of prejudice, not necessarily grounded in textbook racism, has been further corroborated in other research, including a study as far back as 1997 by Roel W. Meertiens and Thomas F. Pettigrew in *Public Opinion Quarterly* that demonstrated just how long-brewing much of this misguided resentment has been.[15] In a case study of white working-class prejudice in Canarsie, Brooklyn, sociologist Jonathan Rieder interviewed various residents who exuded the same sentiment—one housewife in particular who stated outright that the perceived prejudice seen from the outside is "really a class problem," further opining that "I don't care about the color of a person if they're nice people."[16]

The resentment instead came from, according to Rieder, a seeming lack of reverence on behalf of certain groups outside of the predominantly white conservative working-class communities for hard work and frugalness, with "flashy cars, booze," and so forth being "all they cared about," with the "they" in question amounting to non-white working-class people seen as taking the perceived easy way out of the back-breaking work everyone else was suffering under.[17] This led Rieder to conclude that "beneath the surface of apparently racial judgements was the ineluctable reality of class cultures in conflict."[18] And after several generations of this perspective not being adequately addressed or contextualized, it is easier to see how the extremism much of the more radicalized right wing demonstrates today could have slithered its way into the minds of those kept in the ideological dark.

Is this still racism? Of course it is. It should be condemned. But as was argued previously in Chapter 9, we still must strive to understand the fact that it is systemic racism, and not individual initial racist beliefs, that plays the larger role in perpetuating the myth of the "lazy" or "undeserving" minority within the white conservative working class. A person belonging to this demographic can genuinely not hold personal beliefs in racial superiority while simultaneously buying into culturally ingrained assumptions that indirectly inform other beliefs and actions that themselves are more immediately induced by systemically confounded problems of class struggle.[19]

This broader theme of needing to have earned one's opportunities in life via the fruit of one's own labor is also recurring, and it is a sentiment that working-class socialists also have historically held dear, once again demonstrating the common ancestry between both perspectives. Likewise, the broader anarchist tradition from the very beginning has been skeptical of the opportunities for said self-sufficiency to be robbed through oppressive means, both in the private sector and by way of centralized State force, and this naturally leads to the kind of logical populism that sparked the fire for the rightists as well, with anarchist historian Larry Gambone noting that

A populist orientation requires that one search for all the various beliefs and activities that are of a general libertarian and social nature found among ordinary people. These would consist of any form of decentralism, direct democracy, regionalism, opposition to government and regulation, all forms of voluntary association, free exchange and mutual aid.[20]

Being able to recognize this common revolutionary spirit across the entire working class, and tap into the areas of overlapping grievance, is key for moving out of our present state of divided, obfuscated antagonism toward one another while the elitist forces that primarily benefit from an unchanging system remain untouched. The first step toward de-radicalization of the still yet reachable areas of the revolutionary right should be through recognition of the seriousness of their class-related plights and the process of looking past the surface-level misguided prejudice prior to any conversation surrounding the merits of their ideology. Such ideology is a Gramscian symptom of a genuine set of problems that simply manifest differently through the privileged revolutionary's limited yet sincere perspective.

Anarcho-communist writer Logan Marie Glitterbomb concurs, arguing that counter-recruitment is something anti-fascist activists should be housing in their arsenal of tactics in order reach the people in the right-wing working class who are indeed still reachable:

Counter-recruitment is not necessarily about converting someone to your point of view, but rather refocusing their aim from those most marginalized in society towards those actually responsible for oppression. In other words, it's not about turning people into socialists, anarchists, libertarians, or whatever, but rather it's about making them realize that immigrants, anti-police brutality activists, people of color, etc. are not their enemy. This does not mean that counter-recruitment never succeeds in converting someone politically, just that even if it doesn't that doesn't mean it's a failure.[21]

Glitterbomb is right—even if the end result is that a revolutionary rightist is rendered only less so after being forced to acknowledge the more nuanced reality of the system he lives in, that is still leaving him in a better place than he was found. It is as simple as knowing the difference between talking at someone versus talking with someone, and if that someone in question feels heard and understood, the ideological differences take a back seat to the problem that solidarity can form around: stymied individual autonomy. The fight to liberate everyday working people as a means of retrieving that autonomy is what birthed the broadly libertarian project to begin with. Neglecting to partake in the effort to help the Jacobinistic, anti-political populists see that reality is to simply leave the existing narrative gaps open for further neoliberal distortion, or, worse, right-wing infiltration. Not only is this approach good praxis, it is also simply the correct thing to do in the name of valuing truth over ideology.

The fascism and nationalism that have managed to find new life within the pseudo-intellectual spaces of these revolutionary rightist movements has found a good deal of its success by counting on one assumed axiom of neoliberal dogma never being overturned, even in supposedly socially liberal and progressive spaces: the belief that for society to function, someone (or some group) must always come out the victor over others in a struggle for dominance or demonstrated superiority.[22] This measure of "success" prematurely poisons any further conversation about freedom or liberation working-class people could ever have with each other toward truly liberating ends. Such a measure has been postulated as an unshakeable truth far longer than its utility has necessitated, and a ubiquitous reassessment of its veracity may very well stand to bring about a type of working-class solidarity viable enough to render hierarchical thinking as rightly worthy of the annals of outdated doctrine.

Liberalism Is a Narrowed, Elitist, Multi-Stage Distortion of Its Former Self

Liberalism in its earliest form was derived from Enlightenment-era scholars' application of Natural Law Theory to the problems of their time dealing with human limitation versus liberation. Out of that tradition came some of the most prominent concepts of humanity the Western world still identifies itself with today, liberalism chief among them. But as this book has laid out, that initial spark of promise for true human liberation that liberalism's earliest adopters championed barely lasted into the following century, with so-called classical liberal economists adopting a more narrowed, elitist perspective on issues such as access to the commons, division of labor, and property rights.[23] In *Liberalism: A Counter-History*, Domenico Losurdo argues that while in its initial state the term "liberal" was a noun, by the time talk of a "liberal party" emerged in the year 1818 in the writings of Benjamin Constant, the term had shifted to an adjective.[24] It is therefore some point between liberalism's inception as a humanistic concept and its application as a quality of political policy that may serve as its first key distortion. Indeed, as Domenico illustrates with cutting commentary and historical precision throughout his book, it is as a State policy that "liberalism" found its footing in oppression and tyranny, both domestically and in foreign relations, on behalf of the elite classes that hid behind its promise of civilizing freedom. Even by the time we get to the writings of the thinkers typically considered to be classically liberal by today's standards, the rot has already begun and the narrative already shifted.

That shifting, of course, continued into the twentieth century when neoliberalism, the latest form of liberal distortion, took hold of the Western mind en masse with its promise of further liberation for working-class people—but this, too, was merely a means of exasperating the problem and keeping the artificial hierarchical structure of the market buttressed long after average everyday working people would have stood for it had it not contained the same pseudo-Lockean rhetoric of its predecessor. But what remains constant throughout this entire distortion process is the appeal to individual autonomy as a means of liberating the person for his or her own pursuit of purpose. In the wake of neoliberal policy's exhausted effects, fewer and fewer people have that purpose.[25] In its place we have collectively been sold a farcical imitation: pride in humanity as a commodity.[26] But even that is now reaching its limits of utility, and so, liberalism is left rendered a shell of what it once promised to be, with no viable alternative in sight for most people in the West who simply trust in the mainstream narratives for answers. On the right, especially, the socialistic and anarchistic alternatives are seen as frightening and dangerous, and yet, it is ironically from that tradition that even the right-wing populists' revolutionary passion originates.

Modern Right-Wing Revolutionary Sentiment Shares Common Ancestry with Socialism

Whether it be the modern right-libertarians, the red-pilled right, the alt-light, or even the 4chan and 8chan posters and their Qanon true believers, all of these variants of revolutionary rightists who have not yet fallen all the way into outright fascism and nationalism all share the common and understandable class-induced populist unrest outlined earlier. That unrest, and the purported quest and goals for mitigating it, is grounded in socialist origins in both rhetoric and prescription. This history, though tangled, has been inescapably laid out previously in Chapter 6 of this book. However, it is important to note that even socialist revolutionary sentiment has an earlier origin: original liberalism. The liberalism of John Locke and Adam Smith, not the liberalism of Frédéric Bastiat and his contemporaries. By Bastiat's time, liberalism was no longer a noun but an adjective—his was the economic tradition of the French Liberal School, and it aimed to serve as the place of intellectual elites, as Dr. Stephanie Mudge's history of liberal tradition was previously shown to unveil.[27]

Taking into account how liberalism's shift into an elitist adjective coincided with the boom of industry and the rising threat to Polanyi's identified manufacturing class, one could surmise that perhaps the libertarian socialists of the likes of Proudhon and Déjacque rose up as a response to this shift in liberalism's intellectual interpretation. These early libertarians still advocated for the same pro-liberty principles liberalism claimed to embody, yet in the face of the Industrial Revolution and the subsequent enclosures and other limitations the State imposed on workers, the liberals had forsaken their philosophical charge. New advocates for historically liberal principles were needed to fight for tangible worker liberation, not just empty appeasement through disingenuous policy, and the differentiating name, "libertarian," helped set these new pro-worker intellectuals apart from the old.

In this sense, the modern right revolutionaries aren't wrong to say that there is classical liberal tradition in their philosophy's makeup. But for any of their bifurcations, particularly the modern libertarians, to claim that socialism is somehow the exact opposite of what they advocate is to grossly misrepresent and limit socialism while simultaneously adding unearned credibility to the concept that liberalism's distorted forms are somehow innocent of the responsibility for the current state of economic affairs. The reality is that if these revolutionaries on the right truly want to systemically change things in a way that is favorable to their ideal vision of truly liberated markets (and, subsequently, the people operating within them), then their against-the-system rhetoric and spirit must be reconciled with its true historical origins—this is the only means by which the fully contextualized picture for how and why the system they claim to distrust truly operates.

* * *

Keeping these key conclusions in mind, is there indeed a way of reconciling these two worlds that have been forcibly divorced by capitalistic revisionists—the liberal and the socialist? Even upon the initial split, things were heated, with Proudhon infamously telling Bastiat upon hearing his version of liberalism:

> Your intelligence is asleep, or rather it has never been awake. You are a man for whom logic does not exist. You do not hear anything, you do not understand anything. You are without philosophy, without science, without humanity. Your ability to reason, like your ability to pay attention and make comparisons, is zero. Scientifically, Mr. Bastiat, you are a dead man.[28]

Yet, Proudhon's frustration with the new post-industry liberal gallop he was witnessing is well met, here. We have seen what it ultimately led to, with the present neoliberal state of affairs holding a stranglehold on nearly every facet of Western economic and social thoroughfare, confounding the truth with a sweeping narrative tinged with capitalist apologetics and calls for unjustifiable hierarchy in the name of claimed human freedom. In the face of this, however, more working people than ever are feeling the strain. The Lockean liberal spirit is still present. How do we go about reconciling the historical vision with the present reality?

Isolating and identifying the initial version of liberalism before it became an adjective, in Losurdo's words, is arguably the first step. Fortunately, much work toward that end has already been done by Gary Chartier, who in his book *Flourishing Lives* parses "liberalism" into three distinct forms: classical, modern, and radical.[29] For Chartier, the question isn't about whether or not liberalism is still a viable revolutionary philosophy, but whether or not the *type* of liberalism we presently engage in is the best form it can take for kindling free and rewarding lives for all people. He lays out what the original form of liberalism (i.e., liberalism the noun) looked like as follows:

> Liberalism originally emerged as, among other things (i) a deepening of the Western religious emphasis on the distinct and irreplaceable value of the particular person; (ii) an outgrowth of the Reformation's rejection of institutional authority and increasing, if hesitant, recognition of the value and inescapability of private judgement; (iii) a response to the recognition, in light especially of the Wars of Religion, that using force, and especially state power, to impose a vision of the good could not but prove a source of destructive and interminable conflict; (iv) an acknowledgement of the potential of market freedom to create and disseminate vast wealth; (v) an increasing awareness of the indefensibility of royal power, linked, arguably, with an attempted reassertion of the integrity and independence of institutions monarchs had sought to supplant; and (vi) a generalization of the attitude embodied in the increasingly successful project of modern science, an attitude rooted in appreciation for open-ended inquiry and for the rational criticism of existing assumptions.[30]

What Chartier is describing here is not so dissimilar from the earliest socialist principles, broadly speaking. Even the Marxists, different from the anarchists, still stated from the start their displeasure with centralized State control over all aspects of working-class people's lives and prospects. Marx and Engels mourned in *The Communist Manifesto*:

> The bourgeoisie keeps more and more doing away with the scattered state of the population, of the means of production, and of property. It has agglomerated production, and has concentrated property in a few hands. The necessary consequence of this was political centralization. Independent, or but loosely connected provinces, with separate interests, laws, governments and systems of taxation, became lumped together into one nation, with one government, one code of laws, one national class-interest.[31]

While centralization under vested interest bourgeoisie rule troubled Marx, the growth of industry and technological advancement themselves were actually celebrated by himself and Engels in their manifesto, wondrously soliloquizing, "what earlier century had even a presentiment that such productive forces slumbered in the lap of social labour?"[32] The distinction for Marx and Engels was that the praise and financial returns should go to the workers themselves, the proletariat class, and not the bourgeoisie class (i.e., the capitalists and their State cronies), which was reaping all of the benefits and subsequently making all the rules. Once again, our aforementioned realignment model of economic structure, informed by social democracy, offers a means of achieving a near future much farther removed from that reality than the system we live in currently.

Hold that summation of the state of things up next to the similar chastising of hierarchical social and economic structure documented in this book as being exuded by the anarchists from the same era, and it appears that both major camps of emergent socialist thought broadly agreed that artificial human limitation was bad, and on what parties were mainly responsible for those limitations.[33] This is a similar outlook to that of the earliest liberal thinkers as demonstrated earlier by Chartier. That earliest form of liberalism, full of grand egalitarian ideas, arguably never truly took shape in the way it was imagined, while modern liberalism also has failed to realize the promise. Chartier therefore argues for this third form of liberalism, radical liberalism, as he calls it, to implement the original liberal ideal via appealing to and taking more seriously the anarchistic interpretation of human liberation, effectively merging with it. Originally conceptualized liberalism, observes Chartier, "sought to provide a bulwark against arbitrary power—as exercised initially by kings and later by their parliamentary successors *and* as delegated to governments' aristocratic and corporate cronies."[34] It is this observation of natural law liberalism's earliest incarnation's intentions that leads Chartier to therefore declare that despite more common Natural Law theorists often being "inclined to embrace heteronormativity, to reject sexual liberation, and to endorse communitarian politics," his contention is that "its most visible representatives have also been willing to accept relatively strong protections for freedom of speech and some version of Mill's Harm Principle," meaning that radical liberalism through the purest Natural Law Theory lens is actually a *rejection* of such aforementioned normative conformity and rather something that has "sought to protect diversity" in the spirit of true individual liberation.[35]

Chartier sums up these thoughts by stating: "if the defining commitments of the political left are to the rejection of *exclusion, subordination, deprivation, militarism,* and *imperialism,* then natural law liberalism qualifies as a position of the left."[36] In other words, the truest form of liberal idealism is neither classical liberalism nor neoliberalism, but rather a liberalism that takes seriously natural law and holds reverence for anarchism's overlapping concern for human freedom outside of economic constraints—what Chartier dubs "radical liberalism."[37] In this way, it is indeed possible to salvage some elements (while revising others) of the revolutionary sentiment found in common both on the left and on the right in our populist working-class present by recognizing the shared principles between the earliest posited goals of both liberalism and socialism. The divide between these camps is derived from liberalism's transformation into an adjective—in application, liberalism's turn away from humanistic philosophy and toward disingenuous descriptions of politicized elitist policy—and not from some inherent, irreconcilable difference between liberalism itself and classical socialist tradition.[38] On the contrary, the two can be seen as coterminous.

But this then brings us to another point of potential confusion. The reader may recall the brief overview of the apparent differences between Kantian and Hegelian approaches to the concept of knowable reality and alignment of actionable goals accordingly.[39] The reader might also remember that it was this author's conclusion that a conducive path forward for would-be revolutionary populists is to side with Hegel and interpret knowable reality as something beyond what we can already objectively demonstrate as a means of inducing positive forward-thinking and imagination regarding our systemic future. But it has long been a point of debate as to whether or not Hegelian philosophy is even compatible with a reverence for the validity of natural law. Karl Popper is one of the most prominent philosophical critics of Hegel on these grounds, claiming that Hegel advances an "ethical and juridical positivism, the doctrine that what is, is good, since there can be no standards but existing standards; it is the doctrine that might is right."[40] Further, even though Hegel was known to use the term "natural law" in his writing, most predominantly in his essay *The Scientific Ways of Treating Natural Law*, scholar H. B. Acton argued that Hegel's use of the term must have been done ironically since Hegel's ethical world of *Sittlichkeit* seems devoid of the concept of self-evidence.[41]

On the other side of the debate, scholars such as Thom Brooks have contended that Hegel more than fits with the natural law approach, with Brooks specifically positing that Hegel "satisfies all but one of the four general features of natural law," which Brooks outlines as follows: (i) that we can distinguish between "law" and "true law"; (ii) that we make said distinction in the interest of justice; (iii) that the term "true law" posits the existence of universal rights; and (iv) that the standard of justice is something external to the law.[42] Following these criteria, Brooks therefore argues that Hegel does indeed advocate a theory of law compatible with Natural Law Theory. But it is equally the case that Hegel is also an advocate of a theory of *morality* on the same grounds, seeing as how he claims to have discovered objective moral realities based around the concept of will.[43]

Returning to the earlier-cited Hegelian concept of the thing as it exists for us versus the thing as it exists outside of interpretation and experience, Hegel describes how and why one can still identify universal natural rights within that distinction:

It may be infuriating to know that one has a right and then be denied it on the grounds that it cannot be proved. But the right which I have must also be a posited right: I must be able to describe it and prove it, and a right which has being in itself cannot be recognized by society until it has also been posited.[44]

In other words, while we might indeed have universal natural rights, we still must bring them into the present perception in order to make them applicable and tangibly real in a way that will have actual effect in our lives. We must bring these rights (the thing as it is) into the realm of visibility within society (the thing as we experience it) in order to benefit from them. Interpreting Hegel in this way means that Chartier's aforementioned radical liberalism is still applicable through a Hegelian lens, provided we allow for our own understanding of what such radical liberalism looks like in our lived-in reality to shift and adapt situationally much like Hegel's own description of natural law did in his work.

To be certain, Hegel's is a body of work much too dense, complex, and idiosyncratic to do full justice within the limited capacity in which this book has visited it; thus, it must be made clear that the author does not intend for this passage alone to be seen as a fully bolstered argument for the case for the validity of Hegelian natural law. Instead, it is merely intended to demonstrate that the ability to apply a Hegelian perspective to the prospect of achievable systemic futures from within our present socioeconomic system is indeed possible, even when considering the project of salvaging the common populist proclivity found in both the classical socialist and earliest liberal traditions—*a la* Chartier and his radical liberalism.

Hegel wrote that "self-consciousness exists in itself and for itself, in that, and by the fact that it exists for another self-consciousness; that is to say, it *is* only by being acknowledged or 'recognized.'"[45] To that end, it is useful to keep in mind that we can always attempt to transcend our present situation as all revolutionaries wish to do, but only if we remain mindful of the fact that norms are intersubjective, or "recognitive," in Hegel's sense, might that quest reach its triumph.

* * *

Throughout this book, I have described the broad revolutionary mindset as existing on a plain of perception I refer to as the populist rationale spectrum. This is to say that the various forms of revolutionary populism now seen cropping up across the working class reside in an initial sentiment broadly shared in common regardless of political leanings: a sentiment informed by the initial liberalism that served as the precursor to both socialism and what became known as classical liberalism—and a sentiment standing to be rescued and redefined for a modern state of affairs by the aforementioned radical liberalism. From this common intellectual ancestor, it is possible to veer in either the direction of radicalism and leftist anarchism or in the direction of neoliberalism and faux-revolutionary conservatism. The common threads that cause these two schools of thought to appear similar in both surface-level rhetoric and ethical origin have been laid out in various ways over the course of the preceding chapters. While I have been rightly critical of the most toxic and sinister elements of the extreme rightists in the movements examined in this book, I would also like to think I have been quite fair when striving to understand how the process of shifting from mere rebellious conservatism into these more extremist mindsets originates.

Being able to comprehend this process by understanding the present hegemonic circumstances, as well as the tangled history of appropriation of prior terms and distortion of philosophies, is a necessary step for potentially curtailing said process from continuing into yet another generation. As has been shown, worker unrest and subsequent desire for revolt against oppression is cyclical and has cropped up again and again in slightly different forms for generations, now. Yet this latest populist outcry is unique in many ways, thanks in large part to the role neoliberal hegemony has played in obfuscating the clarity surrounding what has precisely been the producer of the latest economic crisis in the modern West. While it has not been unique in its observations, it is my hope that this book will stand apart from many similar volumes in its particular synthesis of the data and presentation of the history so as to function as a useful means of praxis for reaching and redirecting the revolutionary urge still present in many people on the right who consider themselves radicals but lack the vocabulary or perspective to yet grasp the fullness of their socioeconomic situation. If even one mind can be changed by the arguments laid out within these pages, then the effort will have been entirely worthwhile.

Another scholar who has suggested the existence of a radical form of liberalism we should aspire to, Jason Byas, has explained said need through a working-class lens as follows:

> Liberalism in general, I think, is about this positive sum, natural harmony of interests, but part of why [modern] liberalism in various shades looks silly to people is because it ignores a lot of the very real aspects of domination and conflict that isn't social life—that is why you often see "liberalism" and "radicalism" kind of expressed as antonyms, because radicalism is seeing the deep conflicts in life, the deep dominations that are structuring our world, while liberalism seems to be papering over that.[46]

Urbinati's reasoning for being more skeptical of populism's positive utility counts on democracy as predating liberalism, in her words, and therefore being predisposed to majoritarian faux-representative appeal rather than truly representative appeal.[47] However, if the truest and earliest forms of liberalism are in fact this initial liberalism that inspired Jacobinism, itself the earliest precursor to populism, then such declarations are demonstrably incorrect. Urbinati's claims that populism as a whole is essentially "illiberal democracy" can still be applied to our analysis, however, if limited to *rightward-leaning* populism more specifically.[48] As this book has noted, the systemic economic oppression of our present system in something every working-class person feels to one degree or another, with increasing despair more prevalent than ever within historically culturally privileged corners of the working class. Also, as noted, this radicalizes these demographics just as much as it does any other—modern visible liberalism, often represented as the political voice of the working-class person while in actuality only serving to perpetuate the benefits of the elite (a trend begun as early as the aforementioned shift of liberalism from a noun to an adjective and the welfare policies of Otto von Bismarck),[49] is seen as insincere by a growing number. Especially on the working-class right, where viable alternatives to liberalism have remained shunned and misrepresented, is this the case. Properly understanding and somewhat empathizing with this perspective as a means of helping truly liberate others from it is something that arguably anyone on the left who truly cares about liberation from our present system should strive for.

Make no mistake, however: this book's main mission is not to outright convert anyone to a particular political proclivity; rather, it is simply intended to successfully build a convincing argument (or set of arguments) calling into question the prevailing narrative concerning the claimed diametrically opposed natures of liberalism and socialism, contest the claimed synonymous nature of capitalism and free markets, and demonstrate how the much more complex history behind these assumptions ties into not only the present economic crisis but the various stripes of conservative populist responses to said crisis. One need not fully arrive at the same conclusion the book itself does concerning the utility or viable future of the revolutionary project in order to still benefit from the realizations that stand to be made through reading it—realizations about how empty certain claimed axioms about capitalist policy truly are, or about how complex and interwoven the relationship really is between liberalism, conservatism, and anarchism. What at the very least might be gained from reading this work is a better grasp on just how alike *all* facets of the working class truly are and, likewise, how uniform in result the elite class's own ventures appear.

The revolutionary sentiment is therefore, when put into practical action, not a fight between right and left but is rather a fight against the above from the below. Working-class solidarity is needed under such circumstances, but properly contextualized perspective has long been missing from that prospect. To truly unpack populism as it exists on the right and carry it successfully into the new, revised form it *could* take, it must be rescued from privilege in all its forms—economic, cultural, and ethical.

Acknowledgments

As is the case with any undertaking such as this, the strongest elements of this book cannot be fully claimed by just myself. Meanwhile, I will gladly take complete responsibility for any of its shortcomings.

This project was not something I anticipated. A few short years ago I would have laughed at the suggestion that such a thing as the 2016 presidential election (and all the right-wing populist extremism that made it possible) could even happen. At the time of said election, I was taking part in a seminar at Columbia University all about the anthropological study of the phenomenon of populist movements. The fortuitousness of the timing wasn't lost on any of us participants, including the professor leading the course, who rightly pointed out that the most successful campaigns of the 2016 election cycle had been at least somewhat populist, whether they had fed off arguably positive energy (e.g., the Sanders campaign) or tapped into a festering negativity by giving it a unifying face and voice (e.g., Trump).

That professor who ran the seminar was Dr. Claudio Lomnitz, who I would continue to correspond with long after I had left Columbia and whose own interest in studying populism from an anthropological perspective truly inspired me and planted the seed for what has ultimately become this project. I am greatly indebted to the resources, literature, and insightful discussion he provided in that seminar space, for much of it became the foundation of the first part of the book, in which unpacking the phenomenon of populism as an organic logic takes center stage.

I am also thankful to all of my other professors and academic mentors along the way, too numerous to name, who played their parts in helping me think critically and question the narratives that carry society through its many vacant postulations and obfuscated annals. My intellectual journey thus far would not have arrived at this place without all of their wisdom, patience, and compassion.

Thanks to all of the people who were willing to grant their time and insight on the working manuscript in various capacities, key among them being the following individuals.

Thanks to Dr. Gary Chartier, who was a great source of encouragement in the final stretch of the manuscript, and who also helped me get a better grasp on the language surrounding the divide between left- and right-libertarianism as it appears throughout the book. Thanks to Dr. Christopher Gunderson of Howard University, the person who pushed me early on to unabashedly utilize the rich Marxist scholarship already in print tackling the populist issue. In addition, Dr. Gunderson helped the manuscript's preface find its voice so as to better represent the book's overarching quest to define and understand revolutionary unrest for a broader set of readers than it originally exuded. Thanks to Dr. Lomnitz once again, who was able to provide insight regarding who the target audience of the book should be. Thanks to Nathaniel Owen, founder of *Being Libertarian* and fellow skeptic of right-libertarianism's ideological hold, who helped significantly with the passage in the book focusing on the new right's misaimed reverence for Friedrich Nietzsche. Thanks to Dr. Adam Payne, who played a role in helping me better synthesize my positions on the topics covered in this book through many a stimulating intellectual conversation. Thanks to Dave Stagner, my wise sage of a friend who shares my lament for the state of the liberty movement today and whose decades of insight from an on-the-ground activist's perspective proved invaluable in my determining how I was going to convey the arguments in a way that would reach the intended audience without appearing patronizing.

To my other friends who put up with my endless rants on the various topics surrounding the manuscript: you know who you are, and I deeply appreciate your patience as I thought out loud on more occasions than you probably would have preferred at times.

Special thanks to my family for supporting me during this reclusive time of my life as I wrote this manuscript alongside surviving a pandemic lockdown and laying out plans for my next academic ventures. I am always humbled by just how much you always believe in me no matter what form my madness takes. To my other loved ones who kept me going through the final stretch of this project while I juggled unexpected life shakeups: you already know how much you matter, but I am declaring it to be the case here.

Special thanks to Olivia Dellow, Nayiri Kendir, Tomasz Hoskins, and everyone else at Bloomsbury and I.B. Tauris for believing in this book. The process of composing a proposal, sending it out, and hoping for someone out there in the publishing circuit to grasp the value of a manuscript in ten pages or less, especially after one has put years of work into a given project, is not taken lightly. The fact that the potential here was not only seen but was also enthusiastically supported is not soon forgotten. Thanks to my peer reviewers who guided the final manuscript revisions and provided invaluable perspectives on its effectiveness.

This book will certainly be richer because of the loving care it has seen from everyone involved in all their varying ways, including the list of people given earlier, and I could not be more grateful for and humbled by the generosity of their time whenever and wherever they were able to give it.

Notes

Introduction

1 According to the Pew Research Center.
2 Fareed Zakaria, "Why Trump Won." 2017, CNN. Retrieved from http://www.cnn.com /2017/07/31/opinions/why-trump-won-zakaria/index.html
3 Michael Lind, "Donald Trump: The Perfect Populist." 2016, *Politico*. Retrieved from http://www.politico.com/magazine/story/2016/03/donald-trump-the-perfect-populist -213697.
4 Gary Rivlin, "America's Poverty Tax: How the Working Poor Get Stiffed." 2011, *The Daily Beast*. Retrieved from http://www.thedailybeast.com/americas-poverty-tax-how -the-working-poor-get-stiffed.
5 This is something Poulantzas had previously identified as class system fragmentation, in which facets of the working class would get syphoned off via different means induced by the state and/or capitalism in order that class divide itself be rendered less knowable and thus action against it be less palatable.
6 This is not to outright discredit the idea that fascism still infiltrates as a means of gaining hegemonic influence. In fact, it is essentially undeniable that the Alt-Right itself was yet another means of doing this. But had it not been able to work in tandem with the already-existing hegemony provided by centuries of liberal (and decades of neoliberal) apologetics, the Alt-Right itself would not have been as tolerated within the conservative populism of the early twenty-first century as it ultimately was. This isn't to say that successful infiltration, rather just mere toleration and normalization, hasn't happened of late—as we were warned by the post-left anarchists like Bob Black and Lawrence Jarach, the anarchist movement more broadly has indeed been penetrated in the more individualist wings by the "national anarchism" bifurcation. This in its own way has played a part in the more intellectualized normalization when it comes to the prevailing of nationalist myths among the youth who should otherwise know better, and this will be touched upon briefly in Chapter 9.
7 The etymological origins of the term trace back as far as Engels in his "Letter to Mehring," in which he described the ideology of the ruling class as having been embedded within the subordinate class.
8 William Mazzarella, "The Anthropology of Populism: Beyond the Liberal Sentiment." *Annual Review of Anthropology*. 2019. 48 (2013), 45–60.
9 Nicos Poulantzas, *Fascism and Dictatorship: The Third International and the Problem of Fascism*, Trans. Judith White. London and New York: Verso, 2019 [1974], p. 143.
10 Arthur Joel Katz, "Has America Lived Up to Its Declaration?" 2011, *Patch*. Retrieved from http://patch.com/pennsylvania/hellertown/has-america-lived-up-to-its-declar ation.
11 George Monbiot, "Neoliberalism—The Ideology at the Root of All Our Problems." 2016, *The Guardian*. Retrieved from http://www.theguardian.com/books/2016/apr/15/ neoliberalism-ideology-problem-george-monbiot.

12 Henry Heller, *A Marxist History of Capitalism*. Abingdon-on-Thames: Routledge, 2018, p. 9.
13 This distortion of terms and narrowing of focus for liberalism at large is closely examined in Chapter 5 and, to some extent as it relates to liberalism's connections to socialism, in Chapter 6.
14 This is loosely the thesis of several newer books, such as Enzo Traverso's *The New Faces of Fascism* (Verso, 2019), but I find such explanations contrived and unconvincing because they do not take into account the more organic aspects of populist unrest that lead to the breakdown of the cut-and-dry base/power structure dynamic and the promulgation of something far more nuanced and multilayered. This is another reason why the work of Poulantzas has proven far more compelling and prescriptive for me as I have overviewed the data and formed this book's thesis. Essentially, fascism doesn't have a "new face" but is instead exactly what it has always been—working-class desperation simply carves out room for more lenience toward it when the more culturally privileged subgroups of said class are part of the conversation.
15 This refers to Antonio Gramsci's concept of hegemony, arguably one of the most integral elements to anti-capitalist dissection of propagandized cultural norms, and unsurprisingly yet another Marxist-coined anthropological analysis tool that is often completely absent in liberal and conservative social science literature despite its incredible scholarly utility.
16 I say "supposed" because Locke holds more broadly liberal ideas about commons, ownership, and the purpose of work, which makes him less like the subsequent classical liberals of the 1800s and more like the all-encompassing tradition of liberalism described by Noam Chomsky as including anarchism at the time. These differences are explored in more detail in Chapter 5.
17 See Part III of the book.
18 The idea that as a heated political discussion progresses, it becomes inevitable that someone or something will eventually be compared to Adolf Hitler or the Nazis, regardless of the original topic.
19 Poulantzas, *Fascism and Dictatorship*, p. 57.
20 Hannah Arendt, *The Origins of Totalitarianism*, Revised ed. Boston: Houghton Mifflin Harcourt, 1976, p. 460.
21 This is a point that has been made by Matthew B. Crawford, author of *Shop Class as Soulcraft: An Inquiry into the Value of Work*. New York: Penguin Press, 2009.

Chapter 1

1 *Being Libertarian* official Facebook page stats.
2 Site stats, privy to the author during his time there as editor.
3 Ibid.
4 Interview with author, conducted in late 2015.
5 Conversation with author in 2016.
6 Chase Rachels, "Fascism Is a Step towards Liberty." 2018, *Radical Capitalist*. Retrieved from http://www.radicalcapitalist.org/2018/04/10/fascism-is-a-step-towards-liberty/.
7 Ibid.
8 Ibid.
9 Ibid.

10 Ibid.
11 Hoppe will be dealt with later on in the book—in Part III.
12 *Liberty Hangout* Facebook page stats.
13 T. J. Roberts, "For a Peaceful Society, Privatize Everything and Abolish the State." 2018, *Liberty Hangout*. Retrieved from http://www.libertyhangout.org/2018/05/pe aceful-society-privatize-everything-abolish-the-state/.
14 Ibid.
15 Ibid.
16 Interview with author, conducted in 2017.
17 Official Libertarian Party Policies and Agenda.
18 Ibid.
19 Conversation with author in 2017.
20 This is explained in Chapter 6.
21 This is elaborated on in Chapter 6.
22 Discussion with author art CPAC 2017.
23 Ibid.
24 Ibid.
25 Ibid.
26 Hubert Davis, "Twitter Suspends White Nationalist Stefan Molyneux." 2020, *Screen Rant*. Retrieved from http://screenrant.com/twitter-suspends-stefan-molyneux/.
27 Read the following chapters for a full delineation of just how this occurs.
28 Ibid.
29 Personal correspondence with author.
30 Ibid.

Chapter 2

1 Ernesto Laclau, *On Populist Reason*. London and New York: Verso, 2005, p. ix.
2 Ibid., pp. 157–64.
3 Ibid., p. 3.
4 Ibid., p. 81.
5 Cole Edick, "Contemporary Challenges in the Study of Populism: A Workshop on Ideational Approaches." 2019, *Items: Insights from the Social Sciences*. Retrieved from http://items.ssrc.org/democracy-papers/contemporary-challenges-in-the-study-of-p opulism-a-workshop-on-ideational-approaches/#:~:text=The%20ideational%20app roach%20defines%20populism%20as%20a%20%E2%80%9Cthincentered,ideas%20ce ntered%20on%20this%20simple%20contrasting%20of%20groups.
6 Cas Mudde and Cristobal Rovira Kaltwasser, *Populism: A Very Short Introduction*. Oxford: Oxford University Press, 2017, p. 6.
7 James Ferguson, *The Anti-Politics Machine*. Minneapolis and London: University of Minnesota Press, 1994.
8 Ibid., pp. 8–9, 62.
9 Ibid., p. 194.
10 Ibid., p. 198.
11 Ibid.
12 Nadia Urbinati, *Me the People: How Populism Transforms Democracy*. Cambridge and London: Harvard University Press, 2019, p. 201.

13 Read Chapter 6 for a deeper dissection of just what is precisely going on, here, and why these groups and their labels have gotten muddled and confused over the centuries. The chapter will also identify the issues where these movements still find overlapping principles today, and how these positions can be made distinct from the more haphazard anti-politics of the populist right.

14 This is more fully explored in Chapter 3.

15 J. Glynos and A. Mondon, "The Political Logic of Populist Hype: The Case of Right-Wing Populism's 'Meteoric Rise' and Its relation to the Status Quo." 2016, *Populismus Working Paper Series* 4. Retrieved from http://www.populismus.gr/wpcontent/uploads/2016/12/WP4-glynos-mondon-final-upload.pdf.

16 Nicholas Confessore, "Cambridge Analytica and Facebook: The Scandal and the Fallout So Far." 2018, *The New York Times*. Retrieved from http://www.nytimes.com/2018/04/04/us/politics/cambridge-analytica-scandal-fallout.html.

17 Jacquie Lee, George Petras, et al., "Exit Polls—By the Numbers: Trump Capitalizes on Voter Dissatisfaction." 2016, *USA Today*. Retrieved from http://www.usatoday.com/story/news/politics/elections/2016/2016/11/09/exit-polls-numbers-trump-capitalizing-dissatisfaction/93500118/.

18 National Election Pool Survey by Edison Research. George Petras, Mitchell Thorson, *USA Today*.

19 Ibid.

20 Peter J. Boyer, "Donald Trump: King of Deregulation." 2017, *The Weekly Standard*. Retrieved from http://www.weeklystandard.com/donald-trump-king-of-deregulation/article/2010141.

21 Janelle Ross, "Who Really Supports Donald Trump, Ted Cruz, Ben Carson, Marco Rubio and Jeb Bush—In 5 Charts." 2016, *The Washington Post*. Retrieved from http://www.washingtonpost.com/news/the-fix/wp/2015/12/15/who-really-supports-donald-trump-ted-cruz-ben-carson-marco-rubio-and-jeb-bush-in-5-charts/?noredirect=on&utm_term=.b5af4b05ccb6.

22 Michael Pollard and Joshua Mendelsohn, "RAND Kicks Off 2016 Presidential Election Panel Survey." 2016, *RAND Corporation*. Retrieved from http://www.rand.org/blog/2016/01/rand-kicks-off-2016-presidential-election-panel-survey.html.

23 Peter Wood, *A Bee in the Mouth: Anger in America Now*. New York: Encounter Books, 2006, p. 30.

24 Ibid., pp. 29–30.

25 In a sequence from *Get Me Roger Stone*, a clip from the dramatized adaptation of the 2000 presidential election *Recount* is featured that depicts the infamous "Brooks Brothers riot" when the recount of the votes in Florida was stopped due to angry and violent protests at Miami-Dade County at the hands of the Bush-backed recount committee. Roger Stone was a participant in the actual riots, and he is depicted in the documentary as taking credit for initiating them.

26 Wood, *A Bee in the Mouth*, p. 31.

27 Ibid.

28 This shift from political to cultural, as well as distrusting to outright paranoid, is better explored in Chapter 3 when hyper-skepticism within anti-political populist thinking is demonstrated.

29 Wood, *A Bee in the Mouth*.

30 This perspective was also likely stoked by the emergence of what became colloquially known as "the 9/11 Republican" after the September 11, 2001, terror attacks. Many more people ended up identifying as conservative at least in part due to the perceived

need to support America's supposed retaliation for the attacks that became the Iraq invasion. That amounted to historically Democratic voters choosing to vote Republican in 2004 since it was Bush's war, and for many, this bolstered the collective conservative identity as being on the "right" side of American sovereignty. Therefore, attacks on/neglect for American conservatism in general became misrepresented in the minds of traditional conservatives as tantamount to attacking American freedom itself.

31 Laclau, *On Populist Reason*, p. 157.
32 Ibid., pp. 157–9.
33 Bob F. Brockley, "Debunking 'Horseshoe Theory.'" 2019, *Medium*. Retrieved from http://www.medium.com/@pplswar/debunking-horseshoe-theory-31c558b8d51c.
34 Specifically, radical centrism is unpacked and argued against in Chapter 10.
35 Brockley, "Debunking 'Horseshoe Theory'".
36 See Fleck, "Trump the Caudillo: Tapping into Already-Existing Populist Unrest," from Jack David Eller (Ed.), *The Anthropology of Donald Trump*, Abington-on-Thames: Routledge, 2021.
37 Further elaborated on in Chapters 5 and 6.
38 Noah Berlatsky, "Let's Put an End to 'Horseshoe Theory' Once and For All." 2018, *Pacific Standard*. Retrieved from http://www.psmag.com/social-justice/an-end-to -horseshoe-theory.
39 Mazzarella.
40 Dinorah Azpuru, Mary Fran T. Malone, Orlando J. Perez, "American Caudillo: The Rise of Strongmen Politics in the United States and Latin America." 2017, *Paper Prepared for Delivery at the 2017 Conference at the Latin American Political Science Association, ALACIP, Montevideo, Uruguay.*
41 Ibid.
42 Ibid.
43 Ibid.
44 Ibid.
45 Ibid.
46 Ibid.
47 David Vicker, "Germany's Red-Brown Coalition ('Querfront')." 2018, *Dialog International*. Retrieved from http://www.dialoginternational.com/dialog_internat ional/2018/06/germanys-red-brown-coalition-querfront.html.
48 Jonathan Haidt, "How Common Threats Can Make Common (Political) Ground." 2012, *TED*. Retrieved from http://www.ted.com/talks/jonathan_haidt_how_common _threats_can_make_common_political_ground.
49 Graham Jesse and Haidt, "Moral Foundations Theory: The Pragmatic Validity of Moral Pluralism." *Advances in Experimental Social Psychology*. 47 (2013), 55–130.
50 The folksiness of fascism is further elaborated on in Chapters 3, 5, and 11, in which the related writings of Robert O. Paxton and Roderick T. Long are quoted.
51 Many texts on the subject seem to credit modern populism's origins to more recent times overlook the importance of Jacobinism for setting the true stage.
52 Taken from notes from Dr. Lomnitz's "Anthropology of Populism" seminar at Columbia University in the fall of 2016, in which the author was a participant.
53 Alexandra Sims and Andrew Buncombe, "Who Voted for Donald Trump? Mostly White Men and Women, Voting Data Reveals." 2016, *The Independent*. Retrieved from http://www.independent.co.uk/news/world/americas/us-elections/who-voted-for -donald-trump-white-men-and-women-most-responsible-for-new-president-elect voting-data-a7407996.html.

54 Nicholas Carnes and Noam Lupu, "It's Time to Bust the Myth: Most Trump Voters Were Not Working Class." 2017, *The Washington Post*. Retrieved from http://www .washingtonpost.com/news/monkey-cage/wp/2017/06/05/its-time-to-bust-the-myt h-most-trump-voters-were-not-working-class/?noredirect=on&utm_term=.069fe2c 8897c.

55 John B. Judis, *The Populist Explosion: How the Great Recession Transformed American and European Politics*. New York: Columbia University Press, 2016, pp. 71–3.

56 "Here's a Timeline of Every Time Donald Trump Ran for President." 2015, *TVGuideNews*. Retrieved from http://www.tvguide.com/news/donald-trump-pres idential-campaign-timeline/.

57 Alec Tyson and Shiva Maniam, "Behind Trump's Victory: Divisions by Race, Gender, and Education." 2016, *Pew Research Center*.

58 Urbinati, *Democracy Disfigured: Opinion, Truth, and the People*. Cambridge and London: Harvard University Press, 2014, p. 167.

59 Urbinati, *Me the People*, p. 121.

60 Laclau, *On Populist Reason*, p. 209.

61 This book explores how "identity-tethered" can and does corrupt into "identitarian" in Chapters 9–11.

Chapter 3

1 Ryszad Kapuscinski, *The Other*. London and New York: Verso, 2008, pp. 79–80.

2 Ibid., pp. 80–1.

3 Matt Ridley, *The Origins of Virtue*. New York: Viking, 1996, p. 38.

4 Ibid.

5 George Zipf, *Human Behavior and the Principle of Least Effort: An Introduction to Human Ecology*. Boston: Addison-Wesley Publishing, 1949.

6 Robert O. Paxton, *The Anatomy of Fascism*. New York: Vintage, 2004.

7 Ibid., pp. 4–5.

8 Ibid., p. 5.

9 George Williams most famously edited a book titled simply *Group Selection* in 1971 containing the leading biologists' most relevant papers from the previous decade, including by his colleague William Hamilton, on the topic. These collected works were considered at the time to collectively be enough of a consensus to safely put to bed group selection explanations for natural selection and march forward in evolutionary sciences grounding all further scholarship firmly in gene-centric view.

10 Ibid.

11 Ibid.

12 Ibid.

13 Ibid.

14 Robert Sapolsky, lecture on behavioral evolution, "Behavioral Evolution II," held on April 2, 2010, at Stanford University.

15 Ibid.

16 Ibid.

17 David Sloan Wilson and Edward O. Wilson, "Evolution: Survival of the Selfless." *New Scientist*. 196, 2628 (2007), 42–6.

18 Ridley, *The Origins of Virtue*, p. 38.

19 Stefano Fella and Carlo Ruzza, *Reinventing the Italian Right: Territorial Politics, Populism, and Posy-Fascism*. Abington-on-Thames: Routledge, 2009, p. 215.

20 Daniel Cox, Rachel Lienesch, Robert P. Jones, PhD "Beyond Economics: Fears of Cultural Displacement Pushed the White Working Class to Trump." 2017, *The Public Religion Research Institute*. Retrieved from http://www.prri.org/research/white-working-class-attitudes-economy-trade-immigration-election-donald-trump/.

21 Emma Green. "It Was Cultural Anxiety That Drove White, Working-Class Voters to Trump." 2017, *The Atlantic*. Retrieved from http://www.theatlantic.com/politics/archive/2017/05/white-working-class-trump-cultural-anxiety/525771/.

22 Kimberlé Crenshaw, "Demarginalizing the Demographics of Race and Sex: A Black Feminist Critique of Antidiscrimination Doctrine, Feminist Theory and Antiracist Politics." *University of Chicago Legal Forum*. 1 (1989), 139–67.

23 Shannon Ridgway, "Oppression Olympics: The Games We Shouldn't Be Playing." 2012, *Everyday Feminism*. Retrieved from http://everydayfeminism.com/2012/11/oppression-olympics/.

24 What is meant by "identitarian" is the sentiment shared by the Alt-Right and the nationalist movements elsewhere in Europe that has revived the racist myth of white genocide, which Chapter 5 will demonstrate plays into why closed-border rhetoric is becoming so popular even among libertarians in America, who oxymoronically claim they are for freedom and anarchism.

25 Cox, Jones, et al., "In Search of Libertarians in America." 2013, *Public Religion Research Institute*. Retrieved from http://www.prri.org/research/2013-american-values-survey/.

26 According to the US Census.

27 "Is Populism Good for American Democracy?" 2017, *Templeton*. Retrieved from http://templetonhonorscollege.com/blog/2017/01/13/populism-good-american-democracy.

28 Michelle Chen, "Why Are American's Suburbs Becoming Poorer?" 2017, *The Nation*. Retrieved from http://www.thenation.com/article/why-are-americas-suburbs-becoming-poorer/.

29 This is something that will be explored in greater depth in Chapter 8. There, the oft-cited data that claims to prove that the whole world is getting richer is unpacked and examined to see how much realworld, daily effect it actually amounts to for most people.

30 Chen, "Why Are American's Suburbs Becoming Poorer?"

31 Scott W. Allard, *Places in Need: The Changing Geography of Poverty*. New York: The Russell Sage Foundation, 2017.

32 Chen, "Why Are American's Suburbs Becoming Poorer?"

33 Mikhail Bakunin, "Man, Society, and Freedom." From *Bakunin on Anarchy: A New Selection of Writings Nearly All Published for the First Time in English by the Founder of the World Anarchist Movement*, Trans. and Ed. Sam Dolgoff. New York: Alfred A. Knopf, 1972.

34 Clifford Geertz, *The Interpretation of Cultures*. New York: Basic Books, 1973 [1972], p. 49.

35 Hervé Varenne, Ray McDermott, et al., *Successful Failure: The School America Builds*. Boulder: Westview Press, 1998, p. 132.

36 Co-authored with Thomas Luckmann.

37 Michel de Certeau, *The Practice of Everyday Life*. Berkeley, Los Angeles, and London: University of California Press, 1984.

38 Wendy Brown, *Undoing the Demos: Neoliberalism's Stealth Revolution*. New York: Zone Books, 2015, p. 176.

39 Ibid., pp. 134–5.

40 Mark Manson, "The American Dream is Killing Us." 2016, *MarkManson.net*. Retrieved from http://markmanson.net/american-dream.

41 This phenomenon is known as "cognitive dissonance," and it often leads to discomfort and even violent reactions when a person's entrenched worldview is contradicted by contrary evidence. Taking this into consideration, there are few worldviews more entrenched in the human psyche than the false belief in capitalism as the sole giver of innovation, progress, and opportunity.

42 Cox and Jones, "In Search of Libertarians in America."

43 Slavoj Zizek, quoted from his film *The Pervert's Guide to Ideology*, directed by Sophie Fiennes and distributed in 2012 by Zeitgeist Films and P Guide Productions.

44 Johannes Fabian, *Time and the Other: How Anthropology Makes Its Object*. New York: Columbia University Press, 2014 [1983].

45 In addition, the entire third part of the book further connects the conflicts of Chapter 5 to the specific manifestations that amount to both the Alt-Right and their less-sharply barbed intellectual bedfellows in the red-pilled "alt-light."

46 Peter Schrag, *Paradise Lost: California's Experience, America's Future*. New York: The New Press, 1998, p. 10.

47 Ibid.

48 Ibid.

49 Daniel Pipes, *Conspiracy: How the Paranoid Style Flourishes and Where It Comes From*. New York: Simon and Schuster, 1997, p. 147.

50 Ibid., p. 1.

51 See Chapter 4.

52 Gail Collins, "Trump Makes His Birther Lie Worse." 2016, *The New York Times*. Retrieved from: http://www.nytimes.com/2016/09/17/opinion/trump-makes-his-birther-lie-worse.html.

53 Ibid.

54 Derby, p. 205.

55 Lomnitz.

56 "Donald Trump: Mexico Will Pay for the Wall, '100%.'" 2016, *BBC News*. Retrieved from: http://www.bbc.com/news/election-us-2016-37241284.

57 Darius Rubics, "Donald Trump Introduces New Muslim/Refugee Badges..." 2016, *News Examiner*. Retrieved from: http://newsexaminer.net/politics/donald-trump-introduces-refugee-muslim-badges/.

58 Slavoj Zizek, "The Need to Traverse the Fantasy." 2015, *In These Times*. Retrieved from: http://inthesetimes.com/article/18722/Slavoj-Zizek-on-Syria-refugees-Eurocentrism-Western-Values-Lacan-Islam.

59 Eric Hoffer, *The True Believer*. New York: Harper & Row, 1951, pp. 52–3.

60 Crenshaw, "Demarginalizing the Demographics of Race and Sex."

61 This is explored more in depth in van der Walt's book *Black Flame: The Revolutionary Class Politics of Anarchism and Syndicalism, Counter-Power Vol. I*.

62 More of this to be explored in the following section of the book.

63 Chris Hedges, *America: The Farewell Tour*. New York: Simon & Schuster, 2018, pp. 88–9.

64 Paxton, *The Anatomy of Fascism*, p. 119.

65 Ibid.

66 Ibid.
67 Poulantzas, *Fascism and Dictatorship*, p. 72.
68 Ibid.

Chapter 4

1 Ibid.
2 Antonio Gramsci, *Selections from the Prison Notebooks*. New York: International Publishers Co., 1974, p. 224.
3 Ibid.
4 Thomas Cahill, *Sailing the Wine-Dark Sea: Why the Greeks Matter*. New York: Anchor, 2004, p. 47.
5 Ibid.
6 For a deep dive into these specific strategies of the producers inflicted upon the consumers, I highly recommend a read of Chomsky and Herman's *Manufacturing Consent*, which makes the case pretty solidly for how this process is without a doubt happening, therefore permeating hegemonic propaganda into virtually every facet of everyday life.
7 Gramsci, *Selections from the Prison Notebooks*.
8 See Chapter 3.
9 Poulantzas, *Fascism and Dictatorship*, p. xiv.
10 Vincent Navarro, "Why Left Wing Populism Is Not Enough." 2019, *CounterPunch*. Retrieved from http://www.counterpunch.org/2019/04/26/why-left-wing-populism -is-not-enough/.
11 Poulantzas, *Fascism and Dictatorship*, pp. 73–5.
12 Ibid., pp. 72–3.
13 Ibid., p. 87.
14 Ibid.
15 Ibid., p. 78.
16 Ibid., p. 144.
17 Ibid., p. xiv.
18 Ibid.
19 Urbinati, *Democracy Disfigured*, Ibid.
20 Chapter 5 breaks down how liberalism began as a genuinely pro-worker school of thought and then began to narrow into pro-elitist apologetics fashioned to still appear in favor of liberation for the common man; Chapter 6 explains, among other things, how capitalism as an economic system was designed for the purposes of exploiting workers and the closing of access to the true abilities to benefit from one's own labor for the working class.
21 Judis, *The Populist Explosion*, p. 88.
22 Poulantzas, *Fascism and Dictatorship*, pp. 114–15.
23 Ibid.
24 Ibid.
25 Ibid.
26 The Editors of Encyclopaedia Britannica, "Italian Popular Party." 2012, *Encyclopaedia Britannica*. Retrieved from http://www.britannica.com/topic/Italian-Popular-Party.
27 Poulantzas, *Fascism and Dictatorship*, p. 115.

28 The Editors of Encyclopaedia Britannica, Ibid.

29 Poulantzas, *Fascism and Dictatorship*, p. 168.

30 Mark Jones, *Founding Weimar: Violence and the German Revolution*. Cambridge: Cambridge University Press, 2016, p. 183.

31 Poulantzas, *Fascism and Dictatorship*.

32 William L. Shirer, *The Rise and Fall of the Third Reich: A History of Nazi Germany*. New York: Simon & Schuster, 2011, p. 55.

33 Sebastian Haffner, *Defying Hitler*. London: Picador, 2000, pp. 30–1, 33.

34 Konrad Heiden, *Der Fuehrer: Hitler's Rise to Power*. Boston: Houghton Mifflin Company, 1944, pp. 21–2.

35 Samuel W. Mitcham, Jr., *Why Hitler? The Genesis of the Nazi Reich*. Westport: Praeger, 1996, pp. 34–5.

36 Shirer, *The Rise and Fall of the Third Reich*, p. 33.

37 Poulantzas, *Fascism and Dictatorship*.

38 Ibid., pp. 168–9.

39 Ibid., p. 169.

40 Ibid.

41 Ibid.

42 Vicker, "Germany's Red-Brown Coalition ('Querfront')."

43 Uwe Backes, *Politischer Extremismus in Demokratischen Verfassungsstaaten*. Wiesbaden: Springer, 1989, pp. 251–2.

44 Berlatsky, "Let's Put an End to 'Horseshoe Theory' Once and for All."

45 The precursor to the National Socialists was the German Workers Party, itself formed in 1919 alongside the Spartacists as just another pro-worker group fighting for revolution that would later become disillusioned in the wake of liberal, unsubstantial economic policy that kept the ruling class in power.

46 Poulantzas, *Fascism and Dictatorship*, p. 89.

47 Ibid.

48 Zizek, "The Need to Traverse the Fantasy."

49 Jens Rydgren, *Movements of Exclusion: Radical Right-Wing Populism in the Western World*. Hauppauge: Nova Science Publishers, 2005.

50 Ruth Patrick and Rydgren, "Voting for the Radical Right in Swedish Municipalities: Social Marginality and Ethnic Competition." *Scandinavian Political Studies*. 34, 3 (2011), 202–25.

51 Judis, *The Populist Explosion*, p. 96.

52 Stephen Castles, "The Guest Worker in Western Europe—An Obituary." *The International Migration Review*. 20, 4 (1986), 761–78.

53 Ibid.

54 Judis, *The Populist Explosion*, Ibid.

55 Ibid.

56 Chapters 5 and 6 outline how neoliberal policy does not deliver on the larger promise of liberalism, and Chapter 8 demonstrates how surface-level growth does not account for the everyday realities of many working people who continue to see less and less return for their labor within these hierarchical market spaces.

57 Judis, *The Populist Explosion*, p. 89.

58 John Sides and Jack Citrin, "European Opinions about Immigration: The Role of Identities, Interests and Information." *British Journal of Political Science*. 37 (2007), 477–504.

59 Judis, *The Populist Explosion*, Ibid.

60 Urbinati, *Me the People*, p. 201.
61 Urbinati, *Democracy Disfigured*, Ibid.
62 See Chapter 5.
63 Denise Mann, "Skin Color Affects Ability to Empathize with Pain." 2010, *CNN Health*. Retrieved from http://www.cnn.com/2010/HEALTH/05/27/race.empathy/index.html.
64 Rydgren, *Movements of Exclusion*, p. vii.
65 Ibid.
66 Ibid.
67 Shane Burley, *Fascism Today: What It Is and How to End It*. Oakland: AK Press, 2017, p. 75.
68 Kenneth Houston, "The Importance of Postmodernism in the Post-Truth Age." 2018, *Areo*. Retrieved from http://areomagazine.com/2018/04/15/the-necessity-of-postmodernism-in-the-post-truth-age/.
69 Burley, *Fascism Today*.
70 It is certainly true that Neo-Marxists were the founders of the Frankfurt School, but as Lois Tyson explains on p. 53 of *Critical Theory Today: A User-Friendly Guide*, Marxist theory is but one approach among many within critical theory at large, and many non-Marxists still benefit from applying Marx's observations and ideas to their own work, considering the significant foundation he laid for sociocultural criticism at large. Doing so does not, of course, necessitate that they themselves subscribe to Marxism wholesale.
71 Burley, *Fascism Today*.
72 Frederic Spotts, *Hitler and the Power of Aesthetics*. Woodstock: Overlook Press, 2002, pp. 18, 24.
73 Urbinati, *Democracy Disfigured*.
74 The original populist approach was Jacobinistic rather than technocratic, making it more susceptible to propagandizing. For more details on this, refer back to Chapter 3.
75 See Chapter 9.
76 Keith Preston, *El Salvador: A War by Proxy*. London: Black House Publishing, 2013, p. 70.
77 Ibid., p. 1.
78 Ibid., p. 51.
79 Ibid., p. 124.
80 Elisabeth Jean Wood, *Insurgent Collective Action and Civil War in El Salvador*. Cambridge: Cambridge University Press, 2003, pp. 1–4, 14–15.
81 Ibid.
82 Preston, *El Salvador*, p. 70.
83 According to the CIA World Factbook.
84 Raymond Bonner, *Weakness and Deceit: U.S. Policy and El Salvador*. New York: Times Books, 1984, pp. 256–60.
85 Judis, *The Populist Explosion*, p. 93.
86 Ibid., pp. 93–4.
87 James Shields, *The Extreme Right in France: From Petain to Le Pen*. Abingdon-on-Thames: Routledge, 2007, p. 195.
88 Judis, *The Populist Explosion*, p. 141.
89 Shields, *The Extreme Right in France*, p. 183.
90 Ibid., p. 174.
91 Urbinati, *Democracy Disfigured*.

92 Judis, *The Populist Explosion*, p. 143.
93 Ibid.
94 See Chapter 5.
95 Ian Haney López, *Dog Whistle Politics: How Coded Racial Appeals Have Reinvented Racism and Wrecked the Middle Class*. Oxford: Oxford University Press, 2014, p. 4.
96 Ibid., pp. 35–6.
97 Ibid.
98 See Chapter 3 for a reacquaintance with the concept of homophily.
99 ACLU, "The War on Marijuana in Black and White: Billions of Dollars Wasted on Racially Biased Arrests." Retrieved from http://www.aclu.org/issues/mass-incarcer ation/smart-justice/war-marijuana-black-and-white?redirect=billions-dollars-wasted -racially-biased-arrests.
100 Jefferey Fagan, *Second Supplemental Report of Jeffrey Fagan, Ph.D.* at 11 tbl.3, Floyd v. City of New York, 2013 US Dist. LEXIS 68790 (S.D.N.Y. 2013) (08 Civ. 01034 (SAS)) (hereinafter Fagan).
101 US Census Bureau, Census (2010).
102 Fagan at 35 tbl.15.
103 Robert Reich, "The Middle Class & Economic Issues." Presented on November 22, 1994, before the Democratic Leadership Council.
104 Ibid.

Chapter 5

1 Adam Smith, *The Wealth of Nations*. Book IV, Chapter II. 1776.
2 See Chapter 3.
3 This is explored further in Chapter 6 when we unpack the historical use of the term "libertarian" by socialist and anarchist thinkers to describe a sentiment beyond what mere liberalism was accounting for—even in its classical form.
4 Kevin Carson, *Studies in Mutualist Political Economy*. Charleston: BookSurge Publishing, 2007, p. 116.
5 Dan Sullivan, "Are You A Real Libertarian, or a ROYAL Libertarian?" 1998. Retrieved from http://www.cooperativeindividualism.org/sullivan-dan_are-you-a-real-liberta rian-or-a-royal-libertarian-1998.html.
6 John Locke, *Second Treatise*, Chapter V. Retrieved from http://www.constitution.org/jl /2ndtr05.htm.
7 Ibid.
8 Ibid.
9 Ibid.
10 Ibid.
11 Wood, *A Bee in the Mouth*, p. 29.
12 Poulantzas, *Fascism and Dictatorship*, p. 144.
13 Savannah Smith, "Journalist Lauren Southern Detained by Italians for Blocking a Boat of Refugees." *The Goldwater*. Retrieved from http://thegoldwater.com/news/2879-J ournalist-Lauren-Southern-Detained-By-Italians-For-Blocking-A-Boat-Of-Refugees.
14 Cyrus Engineer, "'Put on a Bronzer, Get in a Dingy': Kay Burley Forced to Stop Canadian's Anti-Immigration Rant." *Express*. Retrieved from http://www.express.co .uk/news/uk/706308/sky-news-lauren-southern-kay-burley.

15 Lizzie Dearden, "Generation Identity: Far-Right Group Sending UK Recruits to Military-Style Training Camps in Europe." 2017, *The Independent*. Retrieved from http://www.independent.co.uk/news/uk/home-news/generation-identity-far-right-gro up-training-camps-europe-uk-recruits-military-white-nationalist-a8046641.html.

16 Lauren Southern, "The Great Replacement." Retrieved from http://www.youtube.com/ watch?v=OTDmsmN43NA.

17 Ibid.

18 Ibid.

19 "Renaud Camus Convicted of Provoking Hatred Against Muslims." *L'Express*. Retrieved from http://www.lexpress.fr/actualite/societe/renaud-camus-condamne-po ur-provocation-a-la-haine-contre-les-musulmans_1507772.html.

20 Southern, "The Great Replacement."

21 "Migrants in the UK: An Overview." 2017, *The Migration Observatory at the University of Oxford*. Retrieved from http://www.migrationobservatory.ox.ac.uk/resources/brie fings/migrants-in-the-uk-an-overview/#kp1.

22 Ibid.

23 Judis, *The Populist Explosion*, p. 96.

24 Hans-Georg Betz, *Radical Right-Wing Populism in Western Europe*. London: Palgrave Macmillan, 1994, pp. 73–4.

25 Drum, "Here's Why Libertarians Are Mostly Men." 2015, *Mother Jones*. Retrieved from http://www.motherjones.com/kevin-drum/2015/06/heres-why-libertarians-are -mostly-men/.

26 Stefan Molyneux, quoted from his film, *The 100 Year March: A Philosopher in Poland*, directed and self-distributed by Molyneux.

27 Ibid.

28 Ibid.

29 Ibid.

30 Benjamin Lee, "Why We Fight: Understanding the Counter-Jihad Movement." *Religion Compass*. 10, 10 (2016), 257–65.

31 Nasar Meer, "Racialization and Religion: Race, Culture and Difference in the Study of Antisemitism and Islamophobia." *Ethnic and Racial Studies*. 36, 3 (2013), 385–98.

32 Southern, "The Great Replacement."

33 Mark Fisher, *Capitalist Realism: Is There No Alternative?* Washington: Zero Books, 2009, p. 13.

34 Stephanie L. Mudge, *Leftism Reinvented: Western Parties from Socialism to Neoliberalism*. Cambridge and London: Harvard University Press, 2018, p. 69.

35 Ibid.

36 The next chapter will dive deep into the how and why of this process, explaining the need for socialism as a distinct identity and comparing the differences between 1800s liberalism and 1800s socialism.

37 Roderick T. Long, "They Saw It Coming: The Nineteenth Century Libertarian Critique of Fascism." 2012 [2005]. *Center for a Stateless Society*. Retrieved from http://www.c4ss .org/content/15126.

38 Milton Friedman, *Capitalism and Freedom*. Chicago: University of Chicago Press, 1962; 40th Anniversary Ed. 2002, p.117.

39 G. Rao, "Familiarity Does Not Breed Contempt: Diversity, Discrimination and Generosity in Delhi Schools." *Harvard*, Working Paper; last updated 1/10/2018. Retrieved from http://scholar.harvard.edu/rao/publications/familiarity-does-not- breed-contempt-diversity-discrimination-and-generosity-delhi.

40   Scott Page, *The Difference: How the Power of Diversity Creates Better Groups, Firms, Schools, and Societies.* Princeton: Princeton University Press, 2008.

41   Ibid., p. 137.

42   Ibid., p. 75.

43   Ibid.

44   Victoria Pitts-Taylor, *The Brain's Body: Neuroscience and Corporeal Politics.* Durham; London: Duke University Press, 2016, pp. 36–9.

45   Friedman, *Capitalism and Freedom*, p. 117.

46   Ibid.

47   Ibid.

48   Ronnie Citron-Fink, "Don't Let Politicians Pollute the EPA." 2017, *Moms Clean Air Force*. Retrieved from http://www.momscleanairforce.org/life-before-epa/.

49   EPA, "40th Anniversary of the Clean Air Act." 2010. Retrieved from http://www.epa.gov/clean-air-act-overview/40th-anniversary-clean-air-act.

50   Murray Rothbard, "Confiscation and the Homestead Principle." *Libertarian Forum.* 1, 6 (1969), 3–4.

51   "On the 'Miracle of Chile' and Pinochet." *InsightSur.* Retrieved from http://insightsur.com/2012/04/23/on-the-miracle-of-chile-and-pinochet/.

52   David Harvey, *A Brief History of Neoliberalism.* Oxford: Oxford University Press, 2005, p. 9.

53   Ibid., pp. 8–9.

54   It is also arguable that Friedman himself, to his credit, was aware of this need for context and pragmatism and was never actually against it, seeing as how he dedicated an entire chapter of his book *Money Mischief* (Harcourt, 1992) to the issues in Chile, arguing that its recession was inevitable due to "changes in the prices of oil and copper" (p. 239), but also pointing out that Chile's pegging of its peso to the American dollar led to needless inflation of costs relative to average Chilean wages at the time.

55   Harvey, *A Brief History of Neoliberalism*, p. 59.

56   Ibid., p. 60.

57   The University of Manchester, "Rail Privatisation is 'Great Train Robbery,' finds CERSC Report." 2013. Retrieved from http://www.manchester.ac.uk/discover/news/rail-privatisation-is-great-train-robbery-finds-cresc-report/.

58   "Train Fares: UK Rail Passengers Face Biggest Rise for Five Years." 2017, *The Guardian*. Retrieved from http://www.theguardian.com/money/2017/dec/05/rail-fares-rise-ticket-prices.

59   "Rail Fare Rises: Commuters 'Priced Off' UK Trains, Union Says." 2018, *BBC News*. Retrieved from http://www.bbc.com/news/uk-42536159.

60   And, according to certain groups of neoliberal scholars and pundits, they still are. America's economy as of 2018 appeared to be "booming," according to Anne Sraders of *The Street*, a Wall Street lip service publication. And "the mixed economy" was supposedly the reason why. What tends to be cited in these instances is the GDP of a given country's economy. Chapter 8 explains why this is not a good barometer for quality of life for most working people. The article in question, "What Is a Mixed Economy? Pros, Cons and Examples in 2018," was retrieved from http://www.thestreet.com/markets/what-is-a-mixed-economy-14728913.

61   Robert Dahl and Charles Lindblom, *Politics, Economy, and Welfare: Planning and Politico-Economic Systems Resolved Into Basic Social Processes.* New York: Harper, 1953.

62 Robin Shepherd, "So, How Many did Communism Kill?" 2013, *The Commentator*. Retrieved from http://www.thecommentator.com/article/4230/so_how_many_did_co mmunism_kill.

63 Benjamin R. Tucker, *Socialism: What It Is*. 1884. Retrieved from http://www.panarchy. org/tucker/socialism.html.

64 Noam Chomsky makes a very compelling case for not just the Soviets' propaganda being responsible for the mischaracterization of socialism, but also US government propaganda playing a part during its country's red scare periods. An instance of him making this argument can be found here: http://www.youtube.com/watch?v=yQsc eZ9skQI.

65 Wenfang Tang, *Populist Authoritarianism: Chinese Political Culture and Regime Sustainability*. Oxford: Oxford University Press, 2016, p. 6.

66 Although there would later be a falling out between Mao and the Marxist-Leninists of the Soviet Union after they declared that the Chinese revolution was merely an agrarian one and that China was a civilization not industrialized enough to be a location for "true" revolution in the Marxist understanding of the conditions that must be present to make revolution occur. Mao went on to claim that it was in fact the Soviets who were deviating from Marxism and that his version of communism was bringing socialism back around to its true roots. In reality, neither Marxist-Leninism nor Marxist-Leninist-Maoism looked anything like the socialism of Marx in practice, seeing as how both were severely statist and totalitarian.

67 The economists in question, collectively dubbed the Austrian School, were pro-capitalism in their definitions, and saw true capitalism as more or less synonymous with completely free markets and saw both as positive manifestations. The negative connotation of runaway free markets leading to unsustainability did not come from them, but rather from other scholars who observed the atrocities and exploitation of workers under capitalist systems throughout history. Because of the Austrian School's conflation of "markets" and "capitalism," however, alongside said school's influence on economic literature, the public opinion of capitalism came to shift into the version it holds even today, wherein free trade is often blamed for worker exploitation and monopoly rather than the real cause: state deregulation of, and collusion with, hierarchical businesses for the purposes of perpetuating a modern equivalent of feudalism to benefit the elite classes of society.

68 Harvey, *A Brief History of Neoliberalism*, p. 88.

69 Preston, *El Salvador*, p. 50.

70 Harvey, *A Brief History of Neoliberalism*.

71 Preston, *El Salvador*, p. 51.

72 Jeffrey Khan, "Ronald Reagan Launched His Political Career Using the Berkeley Campus as a Target." 2004, *UC Berkeley News*. Retrieved from http://www.berkeley. edu/news/media/releases/2004/06/08_reagan.shtml.

73 Frantz Fanon, *The Wretched of the Earth*, Trans. Richard Filcox. New York: Grove Press, 2004 [1961], p. 55.

74 Fisher, *Capitalist Realism*, p. 29.

75 Ibid., pp. 4–6.

76 Cullen Roache, "Common Myths About Keynesian Economics." 2015, *Pragmatic Capitalism*. Retrieved from http://www.pragcap.com/myths-keynesian-economics/

77 Harvey, *A Brief History of Neoliberalism*.

78 Laclau, *On Populist Reason*, p. 72.

79 Ibid., p. 73.

80 Ibid., p. 74.
81 See Chapter 2.
82 Slavoj Zizek, *Less Than Nothing: Hegel and the Shadow of Dialectical Materialism*. London and New York: Verso, 2012.
83 Alexander Davidson, "Consumer Patternicity: Investigating the Influence of Abstract Mindsets on Personal Need for Structure." *Advances in Consumer Research*. 42 (2014), 781–2.
84 Slavoj Zizek, *Interrogating the Real*. New York: Continuum, 2005, p. 262.
85 Fisher, *Capitalist Realism*, pp. 16–20.
86 My counterargument to this conclusion is that other knowable forms of applied classical liberal concepts do indeed exist outside the reductionist confines of present vulgar libertarian and conservative rhetoric. I explore later (in the conclusion of this book) what those forms might look like through a combination of broad classically liberal concepts regarding human interaction and classical anarchist (i.e., socialist) economic systems that would bypass and render unnecessary the present hierarchical structures of actually existing capitalism.
87 More specific examples of what I am talking about are presented in Chapter 8, where capitalism itself is laid bare as the antithesis to the historically libertarian ideals it supposedly upholds.
88 Robert W. McChesney, Introduction. From Chomsky, *Profit Over People: Neoliberalism and Global Order*. New York, Toronto, and London: Seven Stories Press, 1999, p. 15.
89 Rydgren, *Movements of Exclusion*, p. 15.
90 Peter Frase, *Four Futures: Life after Capitalism*. London and New York: Verso, 2016, pp. 3, 12–13.
91 Ibid.

Chapter 6

1 Matt Lewis, "The Insidious Libertarian-to-Alt-Right-Pipeline." 2017, *The Daily Beast*. Retrieved from http://www.thedailybeast.com/the-insidious-libertarian-to-alt-right -pipeline.
2 Notice how almost every prominent libertarian thinker who misrepresents socialism as a "statist" ideology also uses the terms "libertarian" and "classical liberalism" completely interchangeably—as if they are one and the same, and always have been. One of the most recent examples of this occurring in print can be found in the article "Libertarianism and Classical Liberalism: A Short Introduction" by George Mason University economist Daniel B. Klein, in which he introduces neither classical liberalism nor libertarianism, but instead plays apologetics for neoliberal, pro-status quo "shifting" rather than meaningful systemic change. The article can be found at the following web address: http://fee.org/articles/libertarianism-and-classical-liberal ism-a-short-introduction/.
3 Joseph Déjacque, letter to Proudhon, "Of the Human-Being Male and Female." 1857. *(Translation mine)*.
4 Ibid.
5 Ibid.
6 Ibid.

7 Ibid.
8 Ibid.
9 Gaetano Manfredonia, *La chanson anarchiste en France des origines à 1914*. Paris: L'Harmattan, 1997, pp. 82–94.
10 Frederic Bastiat, *The Law*. Auburn: The Ludwig von Mises Institute, 2007, pp. 15–18.
11 Long, "They Saw It Coming."
12 Mudge, *Leftism Reinvented*, p. 75.
13 Karl Polanyi, *The Great Transformation: The Political and Economic Origins of Our Time*. Boston: Beacon Press, 1957; 2001, p. 143.
14 Ibid., pp. 142–3.
15 "The National Archives Learning Curve | Victorian Britain | Caring Nation." 2008, *Learningcurve.gov.uk*. Retrieved from http://www.learningcurve.gov.uk/victorianbrit ain/caring/default.htm.
16 Amy R. Caldwell, John Beeler, et al., *Sources of Western History*, 2nd ed. Boston and New York: Bedford/St. Martin's Press, 2011, p. 369.
17 Polanyi, *The Great Transformation*, pp. 142–3.
18 Jacob Field, *Is Capitalism Working?: A Primer for the 21st Century*. London and New York: Thames and Hudson, 2018, p. 22.
19 Frase, *Four Futures*, p. 15.
20 Harvey, from his podcast *David Harvey's Anti-Capitalist Chronicles*, episode "Erosion of Consumer Choices," April 25, 2019. Retrieved from http://www.overcast.fm/ +PbDX3eyRE.
21 Polanyi, *The Great Transformation*, pp. 142–3.
22 Carson, *Studies in Mutualist Political Economy*, p. 118.
23 Harvey, *A Brief History of Neoliberalism*.
24 Karl Marx and Friedrich Engels, *Capital*, vol. 1, vol. 35 of Marx and Engels *Collected Works*. New York: International Publishers, 1996, p. 704.
25 Carson, *Studies in Mutualist Political Economy*, p. 159.
26 Field, *Is Capitalism Working?* p. 32.
27 Ibid.
28 Carson, *Studies in Mutualist Political Economy*, pp. 118–24.
29 Bastiat, *The Law*, p. 17.
30 Ibid., pp. 17, 19–20.
31 K. Carson, *The Homebrew Industrial Revolution: A Low-Overhead Manifesto*. Charleston: BookSurge Publishing, 2010, p.2.
32 Marx and Engels, *Collected Works*, Ibid.
33 Jean Maitron, *Le mouvement anarchiste en France*, Gallimard, coll., 1992.
34 Mudge, *Leftism Reinvented*, p. 69.
35 Ibid., p. 70.
36 Ibid., p. 72.
37 Johanna Bockman, *Markets in the Name of Socialism: The Left-Wing Origins of Neoliberalism*. Stanford: Stanford University Press, 2011.
38 Friedrich Darmstaedter, *Bismarck and the Creation of the Second Reich*. Piscataway: Transaction Publishers, 2008, pp. xiv, xvii.
39 Sheldon Richman, "Mutual Aid Societies." Delivered at the Foundation for Economic Education in 2009 and retrieved from http://www.youtube.com/watch?v=6lReWpkn0 dU.
40 Ibid.
41 Bockman, *Markets in the Name of Socialism*, p. 21.

42 This also demonstrates beyond much doubt that the apparent discrepancy between marginal utility and the labor theory of value was largely overblown and presented as a false dichotomy by the extremists on both sides of that particular debate for over a century—market socialists have long been capable of recognizing the validity of both labor theory and marginal utility, at least as far back as Leon Walras.

43 Bockman, *Markets in the Name of Socialism*.

44 "Socialists Again Ousted by New York Assembly," September 22, 1920. *Minnesota Daily Star,* p. 1.

45 For a definition of "degenerated workers state," see Chapter 7.

46 Chomsky, *Profits Over People*, p. 24.

47 Daniel Soyer, "Jewish Socialism in the United States, 1920–1948." *My Jewish Learning*. Retrieved from http://www.myjewishlearning.com/article/jewish-socialism-in-the-u nited-states-1920-1948/.

48 Poulantzas, *Fascism and Dictatorship*.

49 Ibid.

50 Harold L. Cole and Lee E. Ohanian, "New Deal Policies and the Persistence of the Great Depression: A General Equilibrium Analysis." 2004, *Journal of Political Economy*. Retrieved from http://www.jstor.org/stable/10.1086/421169?seq=1#metada ta_info_tab_contents.

51 Ibid.

52 Ibid.

53 Jim Powell, "How FDR's New Deal Harmed Millions of Poor People." 2003, *Cato Institute*. Retrieved from http://www.cato.org/publications/commentary/how-fdrs-ne w-deal-harmed-millions-poor-people.

54 Poulantzas, *Political Power and Social Class*. New York and London: Verso, 1975, p. 301.

55 Rhonda Levine, *Class Struggle and the New Deal: Industrial Labor, Industrial Capital, and the State*. Lawrence: University Press of Kansas, 1988.

56 Preston, *El Salvador*.

57 Paul Avrich, *Anarchist Voices: An Oral History of Anarchism in America*. Oakland: AK Press, 2005, pp. 471–2.

58 See Chapter 3.

59 Peter Marshall, *Demanding the Impossible: A History of Anarchism*. London: Harper, 1993, p. 558.

60 See the beginning of this chapter.

61 Pyotr Kropotkin, *Mutual Aid: A Factor of Evolution*. London: Freedom Press, 2009.

62 See Chapter 5.

63 According to Stanford University Data of Federal Income Tax Brackets and Maximum Tax Rates: 1950–80.

64 According to The Brookings Institution.

65 Geoffrey Pike, "70% Tax Rates Won't Bring Back the 1950s." *Libertarian Investments*. Retrieved from http://www.libertarianinvestments.com/2019/01/12/70-tax-rates-won t-bring-back-the-1950s/.

66 Ibid.

67 Mark Schmitt, "The 70% Marginal Tax Rate Is Only the Beginning of a Fair System." 2019, *Vox*. Retrieved from http://www.vox.com/polyarchy/2019/1/11/18178515/70 -marginal-tax-rate-ocasio-cortez.

68 Bockman, *Markets in the Name of Socialism*, p. 58.

69 Jason Stanley, *How Fascism Works: The Politics of Us and Them*. New York: Random House, 2018, p. 25.

70 Poulantzas, *Fascism and Dictatorship*, p. 144.

71 "Kronstadt 1921: The End of the Bolshevik Myth." 2008, *Anarchist Writers*. Retrieved from http://anarchism.pageabode.com/anarcho/kronstadt-1921-the-end-of-the-bolshevik-myth.

72 Paul Kengor, *The Politically Incorrect Guide to Communism*. Washington, DC: Regnery Publishing, pp. 115–18, 143, 172.

73 Bernard E. Harcourt, *The Counterrevolution: How Our Government Went to War Against Its Own Citizens*. New York: Basic Books, 2018.

74 More on this found in Chapters 9 and 10.

75 See Chapter 4.

76 This interpretation has most visibly been pointed out by historians Kevin M. Kruse, Joseph Crespino, and Matthew Lassiter, with the title "suburban strategy" being coined by Lassiter.

77 Julian E. Zelizer. *Governing America: The Revival of Political* History. Princeton: Princeton University Press, 2012, p. 69.

78 Ibid.

79 Angela Nagle, *Kill All Normies: Online Culture Wars from 4chan and Tumblr to Trump and the Alt-Right*. Washington: Zero Books, 2017, p. 41.

80 Chapter 9 deep dives into what political voices on the right are actually describing with the "social justice warrior" label as well as what seems to motivate that particular pocket of leftists that seem to hold counterintuitive views on how to go about their activism.

81 Richman, "Libertarian Left: Free Market Anti-Capitalism, the Unknown Ideal." 2011, *The American Conservative*. Retrieved from http://www.theamericanconservative.com/articles/libertarian-left.

82 Clarence B. Carson, "Capitalism: Yes and No." 1985, *The Freeman*. Retrieved from http://www.fee.org/articles/capitalism-yes-and-no/.

83 Ibid.

84 Richard Vedder, "Statistical Malfeasance and Interpreting Economic Phenomena." *The Review of Austrian Economics*. 10, 2 (1997), 77–90.

85 Bryan Caplan, "Why I Am Not an Austrian Economist." 1997, *George Mason University*. Retrieved from http://www.econfaculty.gmu.edu/bcaplan/whyaust.htm.

86 K. Carson, "Austrian and Marxist Theories of Monetary Capital: A Mutualist Synthesis." 2016, *The Anarchist Library*. Retrieved from http://theanarchistlibrary.org/library/kevin-carson-austrian-and-marxist-theories-of-monopoly-capital.

87 Roderick T. Long, "What the Hell is Praxeology?" *Praxeology.net*. Retrieved from http://www.praxeology.net/praxeo.htm.

88 Murray Rothbard, "Praxeology: The Methodology of Austrian Economics." 2012 [1976], *Mises.org*. Retrieved from http://www.mises.org/library/praxeology-methodology-austrian-economics.

89 Ibid.

90 Ibid.

91 See Chapter 3.

92 See the following chapter.

93 Rothbard, "Praxeology."

94 Ibid.

95 Ibid.

96 Long, "What the Hell Is Praxeology?"
97 One such example is how anthropology now partakes in the multidisciplinary study of an academically delineated stage of existence on Earth we are currently inhabiting known as the Anthropocene. The idea that all of the complex and imposed interactions between humans, animals, and their shared ecological surroundings play a part in the shifting status of our present-day existence, and therefore all relevant fields must come together and integrate their findings to best understand it.
98 The author recognizes that Rothbard's literature has in some cases been embraced by left-market anarchists, and that it is arguable that perhaps Rothbard himself held such leanings at different points in his career. However, the point of this chapter is to demonstrate the fact that Rothbard made a conscious decision, whatever the motivation, to usurp socialist and anarchist terminology for the purposes of reframing them as in support of capitalism—a completely untrue framing at the time. Whether one chooses to salvage aspects of Rothbard's more leftist-compatible concepts or not is beside the point that Rothbard's actions played a key role in the ongoing distortion of actual libertarian ideals.
99 Murray Rothbard, *The Betrayal of the American Right*. Auburn: The Ludwig von Mises Institute, 2007, p. 83.
100 Ibid.
101 Ibid.
102 Ibid.
103 Murray Rothbard, "Are Libertarians Anarchists?" 1970, *Lew Rockwell*. Retrieved from http://www.lewrockwell.com/1970/01/murray-n-rothbard/are-libertarians-anarchists/.
104 Ibid.
105 Quinn Slobodian, "Anti-'68ers and the Racist-Libertarian Alliance: How a Schism among Austrian School Neoliberals Helped Spawn the Alt-Right." 2019, *Cultural Politics*. Retrieved from http://www.academia.edu/39530020/Anti-68ers_and_th e_Racist-Libertarian_Alliance_How_a_Schism_among_Austrian_School_Neoliberal s_Helped_Spawn_the_Alt_Right?fbclid=IwAR3jJ9b4REIVAC5hmkknCloYpEL4z-w8 495Aczva4HxU70QwLyyfh_cmaRc.
106 Rothbard, "Homestead Principle."
107 Karl Hess, *Dear America*. New York: Morrow, 1975, pp. 3, 5.

Chapter 7

1 Chris Hedges, *American Fascists: The Christian Right and the War on America*. New York and London: The Free Press, 2006, p. 27.
2 Barbara Parker and Christy Macy, "Secular Humanism, the Hatch Amendment, and Public Education." *People for the American Way*, Washington, DC, 1985, p. 8.
3 Amelia Hill, "The Quarterlife Crisis: Young, Insecure and Depressed." 2011, *The Guardian*. Retrieved from http://www.theguardian.com/society/2011/may/05/quarterl ife-crisis-young-insecure-depressed.
4 Joseph Pearce, "Science versus Scientism." 2016, *Intellectual Takeout*. Retrieved from http://http://www.intellectualtakeout.org/blog/science-versus-scientism.
5 Elliot Gulliver-Needham, "Adam Smith to Richard Spencer: Why Libertarians Turn to the Alt-Right." 2018, *Medium*. Retrieved from http://www.medium.com/@elliotgulliv erneedham/why-libertarians-are-embracing-fascism-5a9747a44db9.

6 See Chapter 5.

7 Atticus Goldfinch, "Actually, Facts Do Care About Your Feelings." 2016, *The Buckley Club*. Retrieved from http://thebuckleyclub.com/actually-facts-do-care-about-your-feelings-dc4d7b0bcb5c.

8 Emma Grey Ellis, "The Alt-Right Doesn't Need to be Visible to Succeed." 2018, *Wired*. Retrieved from http://www.wired.com/story/alt-right-doesnt-need-visible-to-succe ed/.

9 George Hawley, "The Demography of the Alt-Right." 2018, *Institute for Family Studies*. Retrieved from http://ifstudies.org/blog/the-demography-of-the-alt-right.

10 See Chapter 3.

11 Nick Gillespie, quoted by *Angry White Men*. Retrieved from http://www.angrywhit emen.org/2017/10/15/hans-hermann-hoppe-sings-the-alt-rights-praises-at-the-2017-property-freedom-society-conference/.

12 Ibid.

13 Jonathan Haidt, *The Righteous Mind: Why Good People are Divided by Politics and Religion*. New York: Pantheon, p. 231.

14 See Chapters 5 and 6.

15 Nancy MacLean, *Democracy in Chains: The Deep History of the Radical Right's Stealth Plan for America*. New York: Penguin Books, 2017, p. 53.

16 Ibid.

17 Ibid., pp. 1–4, 131.

18 Ibid., pp. 36, 50, 53, 108.

19 See Chapter 4.

20 Chapter 9 goes into more detail regarding unwittingly oppressive mindsets on behalf of working-class white people who simply feel like their time has come and their place in line for the American Dream is organic and earned.

21 Jenny Che, "Here Are the 10 Cities with the Longest Work Weeks." 2017 [2015], *Huffington Post*. Retrieved from http://www.huffingtonpost.com/2015/03/18/cities-lo ngest-work-weeks_n_6894118.html.

22 Andrew O'Hehir, "White Panic, White Denial: The Racial Prehistory of the McKinney Pool Party that White America Can't Let Go." 2015, *AlterNet*. Retrieved from http://www.alternet.org/2015/06/white-panic-white-denial-racial-prehistory-mckinney-p ool-party-white-america-cant-let-go/.

23 This is one of the main theses in George Gilder's book *Knowledge and Power*, in which "true" capitalism in Gilder's view necessarily transforms human self-interest into altruism out of the need to preserve one's business in a world of competition. But since no such world actually exists within capitalism, and the system has always been designed to eliminate competition and exploit workers from the very beginning, Gilder's call for "true" capitalism amounts to yet another vacuous screed for the ignorant.

24 Anne C. Heller, *Ayn Rand and the World She Made*. New York: Farrar, Straus, and Giroux, pp. 1–22.

25 Yes, it is true that universities would not have even been open to women at all by this time in Russian history had the revolution not occurred, but one good result does not, and should not, trump scads of bad results regarding other aspects of basic human rights and equality. Similar arguments have been made regarding Cuba's literacy rate going up after Castro and Guevara's bloody revolution led to the needless deaths of multitudes—and I am similarly baffled and disturbed in those cases. For a detailed accounting of the specifics of Guevara and Castro's list of victims, I recommend the online database *Cuba Archive*, located at http://www.cubaarchive.org.

26 Heller, *Ayn Rand and the World She Made*.
27 Frances Stonor Saunders, *The Cultural Cold War: The CIA and the World of Arts and Letters*. New York: The New Press, 2000, p. 14.
28 Carson, *Studies in Mutualist Political Economy*, pp. 298–9.
29 Ibid.
30 Leon Trotsky, *The Revolution Betrayed*. 1936. Retrieved from http://www.marxists.org/archive/trotsky/1936/revbet/revbetray.pdf.
31 Gary Chartier, *Anarchy and Legal Order: Law and Politics for a Stateless Society*. Cambridge: Cambridge University Press, 2012, p. 5.
32 Ibid.
33 Ayn Rand, *Capitalism: The Unknown Ideal*. New York: New American Library, 1967.
34 Ibid., p. i.
35 See Chapters 3 and 5.
36 Rand, interview with *Playboy*.
37 Ayn Rand, "What Can One Do?" *The Ayn Rand Letter*. 1, 7 (1971–6).
38 "What Is ARI's View on the Libertarian Movement?" *Ayn Rand Institute*. Retrieved from http://www.ari.aynrand.org/faq.
39 Ayn Rand, *The Virtue of Selfishness: A New Concept of Egoism*. New York: New American Library, 1967.
40 Rand quote. Retrieved from http://www.youtube.com/watch?time_continue=24&v=qL3ukTMo-0o.
41 See Chapter 3.
42 Rand, *Capitalism: The Unknown Ideal*, pp. 1–2.
43 Ibid.
44 Ibid., pp. 2, 7.
45 See Chapter 3.
46 Elliott Sober and D. Wilson, *Unto Others: The Evolution and Psychology of Unselfish Behavior*. Cambridge: Harvard University Press, 1999, pp. 329–33.
47 Rand, *The Virtue of Selfishness*.
48 Max Stirner, *The Ego and Its Own: The Case of the Individual Against Authority*. London and New York: Verso, 2014.
49 Paul Thomas, *Karl Marx and the Anarchists*. Abingdon-on-Thames: Routledge, 1985, p. 142.
50 Svein Olav Nyberg, "The Union of Egoists." *Non Serviam*. 12, 1 (2012), 13–14.
51 Rand, speaking through her *Atlas Shrugged* character John Galt in a contextualized section from Galt's speech, as featured in her book *For the New Intellectual*, p. 128.
52 Ibid.
53 Douglass Moggach, *The New Hegelians*. Cambridge: Cambridge University Press, 2006, p. 194.
54 Stirner, *The Ego and Its Own*, p. 248.
55 Roderick T. Long, *Reason and Value: Aristotle versus Ayn Rand*. Washington, DC: The Objectivist Center, 2000.
56 Ibid., p. 101.
57 Ibid., p. 5.
58 Ibid., p. 7.
59 Ibid., p. 49.
60 Ibid.
61 Ibid., p. 27.
62 Ibid., pp. 27–8.

63 Arlie Russell Hochschild, *Strangers in Their Own Land: Anger and Mourning on the American Right*. New York and London: The New Press, 2016, p. 151.

Chapter 8

1 According to the US Bureau of Labor Statistics.
2 Danielle Paquette, "2018's Challenge: Too Many Jobs, Not Enough Workers." 2017, *The Washington Post*. Retrieved from http://www.washingtonpost.com/news/wonk/wp/2017/12/28/2018s-challenge-too-many-jobs-not-enough-workers/?utm_term=.b9d880b8099e.
3 Deirdre McCloskey, "Why Does 1% of History have 99% of the Wealth?" 2014, *Learn Liberty*. Retrieved from http://www.learnliberty.org/videos/why-does-1-of-history-have-99-of-the-wealth/.
4 Aimee Picchi, "The Rich Get Richer, and the Poor Get…" 2016, *CBS News*. Retrieved from http://www.cbsnews.com/news/inequality-1-percent-99-percent-income-growth/.
5 See Chapters 4–6.
6 Andrew Yang, *The War on Normal People: The Truth About America's Disappearing Jobs and Why Universal Basic Income is Our Future*. New York and Boston: Hachette Books, 2018, p. 161.
7 Ibid., p. 66.
8 See Chapter 3.
9 Drew Desilver, "For Most U.S. Workers, Real Wages Have Barely Budged in Decades." 2018, *Pew Research Center*. Retrieved from http://www.pewresearch.org/fact-tank/2018/08/07/for-most-us-workers-real-wages-have-barely-budged-for-decades/.
10 Bob Black, "The Abolition of Work." 1985. Retrieved from http://deoxy.org/endwork.htm.
11 Ibid.
12 Ibid.
13 According to Gallup research in 2013.
14 Ibid.
15 Read further into Chapter 8 for details as to why this is in fact the case.
16 Yang, *The War on Normal People*, p. 66.
17 Ibid.
18 David Graeber, *Bullshit Jobs: A Theory*. New York: Simon and Schuster, 2018, pp. 9–10.
19 Yang, *The War on Normal People*, p. 41.
20 Federica Cocco, "Most US Manufacturing Jobs Lost to Technology, Not Trade." 2016, *Financial Times*. Retrieved from http://www.ft.com/content/dec677c0-b7e6-11e6-ba85-95d1533d9a62.
21 Derek Thompson, "The Missing Men." 2016, *The Atlantic*. Retrieved from http://www.theatlantic.com/business/archive/2016/06/the-missing-men/488858/.
22 According to the Manufacturers Alliance for Productivity and Innovation in 2013.
23 According to the Federal Reserve Board.
24 The World Bank, *Entering the 21st Century: World Development Report 1999/2000*. Oxford: Oxford University Press, 2000, p. 25.
25 Martin Ravallion and Shaonua Chen, "How Have the World's Poorest Fared Since the Early 1980s?" 2004, *The World Bank*. Retrieved from http://www.econ.worldbank.org/

external/default/main?pagePK=64165259&theSitePK=469382&piPK=64165421&m
enuPK=64166322&entityID=000112742_20040722172047.

26 Michael Schramm, Thomas Pogge, et al., *Absolute Poverty and Global Justice:
    Empirical Data, Moral Theories, and Initiatives*. Abington-on-Thames: Routledge,
    2009, pp. 25–6.

27 Jason Hickel, "Exposing the Great 'Poverty Reduction' Lie." 2014, *Al Jazeera*. Retrieved
    from http://www.aljazeera.com/indepth/opinion/2014/08/exposing-great-poverty-red
    uctio-201481211590729809.html.

28 Michael Roberts, "Bill Gates and 4bn in Poverty." 2017, *The Next Recession*. Retrieved
    from http://www.thenextrecession.wordpress.com/2017/04/05/bill-gates-and-4bn-in-
    poverty/amp/.

29 Hickel, "Exposing the Great 'Poverty Reduction' Lie."

30 Schramm and Pogge, *Absolute Poverty and Global Justice*.

31 Ibid.

32 A. Wagstaff, "Child Health on a Dollar a Day: Some Tentative Cross-Country
    Comparisons." *Social Science and Medicine*, 57, 9 (2003).

33 Hickel, "Exposing the Great 'Poverty Reduction' Lie."

34 "Sri Lankan Youth Join Military to Escape Poverty." 2008, *Daily Times (Pakistan)*.
    Retrieved from http://www.dailytimes.com.pk/default.asp?page=2008%5C07%5C18
    %5Cstory_18-7-2008_pg4_15.

35 According to the CIA World Factbook.

36 Roberts, "Bill Gates and 4bn in Poverty."

37 Ibid.

38 Ibid.

39 Ibid.

40 Ibid.

41 Jason Hickel, *The Divide: A Brief Guide to Global Inequality and Its Solutions*. London:
    Windmill Books, 2017.

42 Martin and Chen, "How Have the World's Poorest Fared Since the Early 1980s?"

43 Roberts, "Bill Gates and 4bn in Poverty."

44 Ibid.

45 HDI, "Inequality-Adjusted Human Development Index." 2010, *IHDI: Construction &
    Analysis*. Retrieved from http://www.ophi.org.uk/wp-content/uploads/IHDI-Primer-3
    -Mar-2011.pdf.

46 Ibid.

47 According to the Human Development Index 2018 report.

48 Ibid.

49 Eric C. Schneider, Dana O. Sarnak, et al., "Mirror, Mirror 2017: International
    Comparison Reflects Flaws and Opportunities for Better U.S. Health Care." 2017, *The
    Commonwealth Fund*. Retrieved from http://www.interactives.commonwealthfund.
    org/2017/july/mirror-mirror/.

50 According to Pearson in 2014.

51 According to the World Health Organization in 2016.

52 Rydgren, *Movements of Exclusion*, p. 27.

53 Shawn Gude and Michael A. McCarthy, "Democratic Socialists Want to Fight for
    Minority Rights, Not Suppress Them." 2018, *Jacobin*. Retrieved from http://www.
    jacobinmag.com/2018/08/democratic-socialism-minority-rights-friedersdorf-the-
    atlantic/.

54 Drum.

55 See Chapter 6.
56 Ibid.
57 See Chapter 5.
58 Ibid.
59 Nagle, *Kill All Normies*, pp. 45–6.
60 See Chapter 5.
61 These instances are detailed in Chapter 10.
62 Ridley, *The Origins of Virtue*, p. 38.
63 Mehrsa Baradaran, "The Real Roots of 'Black Capitalism.'" 2019, *New York Times*. Retrieved from http://www.nytimes.com/2019/03/31/opinion/nixon-capitalism-b lacks.html.
64 Ibid.
65 Ibid.

Chapter 9

1   See this book's introduction.
2   Goldfinch, "Actually, Facts Do Care About Your Feelings."
3   Eric Turkheimer, Kathryn Paige Harden, et al., "Charles Murray is Once Again Peddling Junk Science about Race and IQ." 2017, *Vox*. Retrieved from http://www.vox.com/the-big-idea/2017/5/18/15655638/charles-murray-race-iq-sam-harris-science-fr ee-speech.
4   Preston, *El Salvador*.
5   "What Is Social Breakdown Thesis?" 2017, *The Audiopedia*.
6   See Chapter 6.
7   Allard, *Places in Need*.
8   Hochschild, *Strangers in Their Own Land*, p. 135.
9   Ibid.
10 See Chapter 3.
11 Hochschild, *Strangers in Their Own Land*, p. 136.
12 Ibid.
13 See Chapter 8.
14 According to the American Association of Suicidology.
15 Ibid.
16 Ibid.
17 Ibid.
18 Joseph L. Graves, Jr., *The Race Myth: Why We Pretend Race Exists in America*. New York: Plume, 2005.
19 Nagle, *Kill All Normies*, p. 60.
20 Ibid.
21 Ibid.
22 See Introduction.
23 Judith Butler, *Excitable Speech: A Politics of the Performative*. Abington-on-Thames: Routledge, 1997.
24 Ibid., p. 3.
25 Michael Brockway, "Free Speech on Campus: Is It in Danger?" 2018, *Real Clear Policy*. Retrieved from http://www.realclearpolicy.com/video/2018/04/18/free_speech_on_ca mpus_is_it_in_danger.html#!.

26 Butler, *Excitable Speech*, p. 96.
27 Ibid., p. 97.
28 Ibid.
29 Ibid., p. 98.
30 Audio from Chomsky Q&A on banning hate literature. Retrieved from http://www
    .youtube.com/watch?v=ZPn2G3-o9dg.
31 Audio from interviewer question to Chomsky on student no platforming movement.
    Retrieved from http://www.youtube.com/watch?v=3MkjtXylEQE.
32 Brittney McNamara, "Milo Yiannopoulos Harassed a Transgender Student at Her
    School." 2016, *Teen Vogue*. Retrieved from http://www.teenvogue.com/story/milo
    -yiannopoulos-harassed-a-transgender-student-at-her-school.
33 Nagle, *Kill All Normies*, p. 64.
34 Ibid., pp. 64–5.
35 For a full dive into what this feigned moderate centrism actually amounts to, see the
    following chapter.
36 Jeffrey Adam Sachs, "The 'Campus Free Speech Crisis' is a Myth. Here Are the Facts."
    2018, *The Washington Post*. Retrieved from http://www.washingtonpost.com/news/
    monkey-cage/wp/2018/03/16/the-campus-free-speech-crisis-is-a-myth-here-are-the-f
    acts/?utm_term=.8b13b15b8ea1.
37 Matthew Yglesias, "Everything We Think About the Political Correctness Debate is
    Wrong." 2018, *Vox*. Retrieved from http://www.vox.com/policy-and-politics/2018/3
    /12/17100496/political-correctness-data.
38 According to the General Social Survey.
39 Brockway, "Free Speech on Campus."
40 According to U.S. News and World Report.
41 According to the General Social Survey.
42 Brockway, "Free Speech on Campus."
43 Ibid.
44 According to the Gallop/Knight Foundation.
45 Ibid.
46 Ibid.
47 Ibid.
48 Nagle, *Kill All Normies*, p. 75.
49 Ibid., p. 68.
50 Ibid.
51 Mike Wendling, *Alt-Right: From 4chan to the White House*. London: Pluto Press, 2018,
    pp. 3–4.
52 More on what the orchestrators of the Alt-Right aimed to do from the start in
    Chapter 11.
53 Mark Fisher, "Exiting the Vampire Castle." 2013, *Open Democracy*. Retrieved from
    http://www.opendemocracy.net/en/opendemocracyuk/exiting-vampire-castle/.
54 Nagle, *Kill All Normies*, p. 75.
55 Ibid.
56 Ibid., p. 76.
57 Douglass Lane, from his video essay "Can There be an Anti-SJW Left? (Part Two)."
    Retrieved from http://www.youtube.com/watch?v=GNtwHjWYoc0.
58 Ibid.
59 "Preconceived Commerce" was defined in Chapter 3.
60 Lane, "Anti-SJW Left."

61 Lane, from his 2019 video essay "YouTube Censorship, Noam Chomsky, and Other People's Politics." Retrieved from http://www.youtube.com/watch?v=mhgS9gOSvdE.

62 This is something Hegel demonstrates in his introduction of the Phenomenology, if one wishes to dig deeper.

63 Karl Marx, "The Eighteenth Brumaire of Louis Napoleon." 1852, *Die Revolution*. Retrieved from http://www.marx2mao.com/M&E/EBLB52.html.

64 Chomsky and Herman.

65 Gulliver-Needham, "Adam Smith to Richard Spencer."

66 Lane, "YouTube Censorship."

67 See the Kant vs. Hegel analysis from Chapter 5.

68 Lane, "YouTube Censorship."

69 Walter Lippman, *Public Opinion*. New York and London: The Free Press, 1922; 1997.

70 Ibid., p. 159.

71 Ibid.

72 Ibid., p. 28.

73 Ibid., p. 29.

74 Ibid.

75 Ibid. p. 159.

76 Ibid.

77 The reason why is because rent-seeking is a prime mover of dishonest content online. If clicks, likes, and Patreon money can help pay a content creator's way through life in a system as systemically uncaring of working-class struggle as this one, then said content creator is more likely to present whatever social or political narrative he feels he needs to in order to reach a particular audience.

78 Lane, "YouTube Censorship."

79 Lippman, *Public Opinion*, p. 34.

80 Ibid., p. 32.

81 Ibid., p. 13.

82 Ibid.

83 Lane, "YouTube Censorship."

84 See Introduction.

Chapter 10

1 The Zizek-Peterson Debate. Retrieved from http://www.youtube.com/watch?v=qsHJ 3LvUWTs.

2 Ibid.

3 Ibid.

4 Ibid.

5 Ibid.

6 Ibid.

7 Ibid.

8 Nellie Bowles, "Jordan Peterson: Custodian of the Patriarchy." 2018, *The New York Times*. Retrieved from http://www.nytimes.com/2018/05/18/style/jordan-peterson-12 -rules-for-life.html.

9 Grant Maxwell, "Why Are So Many Young Men Drawn to Jordan Peterson's Intellectual Misogyny?" 2018, *APA Online*. Retrieved from http://www.blog.apaonline

.org/2018/02/20/why-are-so-many-young-men-drawn-to-jordan-petersons-intelle
ctual-misogyny/.

10 See Chapter 9.

11 See Chapter 3.

12 Jason McBride, "The Pronoun Warrior." 2017, *Toronto Life*. Retrieved from http://
www.torontolife.com/city/u-t-professor-sparked-vicious-battle-gender-neutral-p
ronouns/.

13 Maxwell, "Why Are So Many Young."

14 Jordan B. Peterson, *12 Rules for Life: An Antidote to Chaos*. Toronto: Random House
Canada, 2018, pp. 35–7.

15 More on this repackaging of hate, and how it succeeds in these specific demographics,
explored in the following chapter.

16 The Zizek-Peterson debate.

17 This is known as the naturalistic fallacy, in which the person posing the argument
assumes at the outset that something being naturally occurring is the same thing as
it being morally good or beneficial. This is fallacious because in many cases, bucking
our nature as humans has been shown to be the beneficial and/or morally superior
decision (e.g., fast travel, modern medicine, or artificial insemination).

18 See Chapters 5, 6, and 8.

19 Nathan J. Robinson, "The Intellectual We Deserve." 2018, *Current Affairs*. Retrieved
from http://www.currentaffairs.org/2018/03/the-intellectual-we-deserve.

20 Nagle, *Kill All Normies*, p. 60.

21 The bill itself can be read at http://www.parl.ca/DocumentViewer/en/42-1/bill/C-16/
royal-assent.

22 Peterson, during hearing on Bill C-16, May 2017. Retrieved from http://www.youtube
.com/watch?v=KnIAAkSNtqo&t=2470s.

23 Brenda Cossman, "Bill C-16—No, It's Not About Criminalizing Pronoun Misuse."
2017, *University of Toronto*. Retrieved from http://www.sds.utoronto.ca/blog/bill-c-16
-no-its-not-about-criminalizing-pronoun-misuse/.

24 Ibid.

25 Ibid.

26 Friedrich Nietzsche, *Thus Spoke Zarathustra*. Trans. Walter Kaufmann. New York:
Modern Library, 1995, pp. 3–5.

27 More on this explored in the next chapter.

28 Aaron A. Fox, *Real Country: Music and Language in Working-Class Culture*. Durham:
Duke University Press, 2004, p. 32.

29 Richman, "Capitalism vs. the Free Market." Delivered at The Future of Freedom
Foundation on March 1, 2010 and retrieved from http://www.youtube.com/watch?r
eload=9&v=GSoxYGTCwRA.

30 Availability heuristics are mental shortcuts that need immediate examples that spring
to the mind of the person to connect dots and form schema. In other words, if all you
have ever seen as an example of a specific minority is a stereotype, any opinion you form
about that minority without further research will itself be stereotypical and incomplete.

31 It is also known as "centrist proper," "middle radicalism," "middle American
radicalism" depending on which scholar one appeals to on the subject. But these all
amount to the same descriptions of the same thing: a radical who chooses to appear
non-radical because he takes portions of every other ideology to form his own.

32 Donald L. Warren, *The Radical Center: Middle Americans and the Politics of
Alienation*. Notre Dame: University of Notre Dame Press, 1976.

33　Marylin Ferguson, *The Aquarian Conspiracy: Personal and Social Transformation in Our Time*. New York: Tarcher, 1980, pp. 228–9.

34　Oliver H. Woshinsky, *Explaining Politics: Culture, Institutions, and Political Behavior*. Abington-on-Thames: Routledge, 2008, p. 165.

35　However, there are reasonable critiques to be made of the left's extremists' actions despite their noble motivations, and that will be explored in Chapter 11.

36　Eyes on the Right, "Hans-Hermann Hoppe Sings the Alt-Right's Praises at the 2017 Property & Freedom Society Conference." 2017, *Angry White Men*. Retrieved from http://www.angrywhitemen.org/2017/10/15/hans-hermann-hoppe-sings-the-alt -rights-praises-at-the-2017-property-freedom-society-conference/.

37　Ibid.

38　Hans-Hermann Hoppe, *Democracy—The God That Failed: The Economics and Politics of Monarchy, Democracy, and Natural Order*. Piscataway: Transaction Publishers, 2001, p. 218.

39　Ibid., p. 206.

40　Ibid.

41　David Futrelle, "If Donald Trump Offers You a Helicopter Ride, Just Say No." 2016, *We Hunted the Mammoth*. Retrieved from http://www.wehuntedthemammoth.com/2016 /06/17/memeday-if-donald-trump-offers-you-a-free-helicopter-ride-say-no/.

42　"Ex Piloto de Pinochet Reconocio Que Lanzo Cuerpos Al Mar." 2001, *Emol.com*. Retrieved from http://www.emol.com/noticias/todas/2001/01/11/42929/ex-piloto-de-pinochet-reconocio-que-lanzo-cuerpos-al-mar.html.

43　David McManus, "Libertarianism, Helicopters, and Leftists." 2017, *Being Libertarian*. Retrieved from http://www.beinglibertarian.com/libertarianism-helicopters-leftists/.

44　Carson, interview with *Primo Nutmeg*, Oct. 2017.

45　Ibid.

46　McManus, "Libertarianism, Helicopters, and Leftists."

47　Hoppe, "Libertarianism and the Alt-Right." Delivered at the Property and Freedom Society Conference. 2017. Retrieved from http://www.youtube.com/watch?v=TICd CM4j7x8.

48　Ibid.

49　Ibid.

50　Ibid.

51　Ibid.

52　Ibid.

53　See Chapter 6.

54　Van der Walt.

55　One of the most theoretically sound, yet readable, volumes on these proposed alternative, direct democratic markets is *Alternatives to Capitalism: Proposals for a Democratic Economy* (Verso, 2016), written by Robin Hahnel and Erik Olin Wright.

56　See Chapters 5, 6, and 8.

57　Ibid.

Chapter 11

1　Jeff Deist, "For a New Libertarian." Delivered at the 2017 Mises University, and archived at http://www.mises.org/wire/new-libertarian.

2   Ibid.
3   Ibid.
4   Ibid.
5   Apollo Slater, "'Blood and Soil' Libertarianism: A Response to Jeff Deist." 2017, *ApolloSlater.com*. Retrieved from http://apolloslater.com/blood-and-soil-libertarianism-a-response-to-jeff-deist/.
6   Ibid.
7   Deist, "For a New Libertarian."
8   Slater, "'Blood and Soil' Libertarianism."
9   Deist, "For a New Libertarian.
10 Slobodian, "Anti-'68ers and the Racist-Libertarian Alliance."
11 Jon Jackson, "Steve Bannon Calls for the Beheading of Dr. Fauci on Podcast." 2020, *MSN*. Retrieved from http://www.msn.com/en-us/news/politics/steve-bannon-calls-for-the-beheading-of-dr-fauci-on-podcast/ar-BB1aJO9A.
12 The hanging was of two Quaker businessmen, Levi and Abraham Doan, who were found out by their fellow townspeople to have been in business with the British. The record of this event can be found at the following link: http://www.executedtoday.com/2018/09/24/1788-levi-and-abraham-doan-attainted-tories/.
13 Jackson, "Steve Bannon Calls for the Beheading."
14 Lewis, "The Insidious Libertarian-to-Alt-Right-Pipeline."
15 Kristen Gelineau, "New Zealand Mosque Shooter: A White Nationalist Seeking Revenge." 2019, *America: The Jesuit Review*. Retrieved from http://www.americamagazine.org/politics-society/2019/03/15/new-zealand-mosque-shooter-white-nationalist-seeking-revenge.
16 Southern, "The Great Replacement."
17 Jason Wilson, "Christchurch Shooter's Links to Austrian Far Right 'More Extensive Than Thought.'" 2019, *The Guardian*. Retrieved from http://www.theguardian.com/world/2019/may/16/christchurch-shooters-links-to-austrian-far-right-more-extensive-than-thought.
18 We know now more than ever that these militia members were far-right, as they were also revealed later to have been seen protesting at a Trump supporter–organized anti-lockdown rally aimed at standing against Covid-19 safety provisions implemented by the governor. Details of that can be found at the following resource: http://www.msn.com/en-us/news/us/members-of-michigan-militia-charged-with-plot-to-kidnap-whitmer-spotted-at-anti-lockdown-rallies-wapo/ar-BB1aBd0Y?item=spalink%253A20201030.97&ocid=uxbndlbing.
19 David Jackson and Kevin Johnson, "FBI Says It's Reviewing Biden Bus Swarmed by 'Trump Train' Caravan, Contrary to Trump Tweet." 2020, *USA Today*. Retrieved from http://www.msn.com/en-us/news/politics/fbi-says-its-reviewing-biden-bus-swarmed-by-trump-train-caravan-contrary-to-trump-tweet/ar-BB1aCuhO?ocid=uxbndlbing.
20 Nina Golgowski, "Trump Jokes His Supporters Were 'Protecting' Biden's Bus on Highway." 2020, *Huffington Post*. Retrieved from http://www.huffpost.com/entry/trump-jokes-about-biden-bus-swarm_n_5f9f0687c5b65662bcc83c9b.
21 Barry Eichengreen, "How Can Joe Biden Deal with Donald Trump's Obstruction in Transition?" 202, *The Guardian*. Retrieved from http://www.theguardian.com/business/2020/nov/09/joe-biden-deal-donald-trump-transition-president-elect.
22 Dominique Mosbergen and Andy Campbell, "Heather Heyer 'Murdered While Protesting Against Hate' In Charlottesville, Friends Say." 2017, *The Huffington Post*.

Retrieved from http://www.huffpost.com/entry/heather-heyer-charlottesville-victim_n_59902e7ee4b09071f69a41c0.

23 Courtney Subramanian and Jordan Culver, "Donald Trump Sidesteps Call to Condemn White Supremacists—and the Proud Boys Were 'Extremely Excited' About It." 2020, *USA Today*. Retrieved from http://www.usatoday.com/story/news/politics/elections/2020/09/29/trump-debate-white-supremacists-stand-back-stand-by/3583339001/.

24 See Chapter 6.

25 Southern, "The Great Replacement."

26 Deist, "For a New Libertarian."

27 Hochschild, *Strangers in Their Own Land*, p. 135.

28 Long, "Critique of Fascism."

29 See Chapters 5, 6, and 8.

30 E. D. Kain, "Richard Spencer and the Ugly White Nationalism of the Alternative Right." 2010, *True/Slant*. Retrieved from http://www.trueslant.com/erikkain/2010/03/13/richard-spencer-and-the-ugly-white-nationalism-of-the-alternative-right/.

31 Clark Stooksbury, "No Thanks." 2009, *The American Conservative*. Retrieved from http://www.amconmag.com/blog/2009/05/30/no-thanks/.

32 Kain, "Richard Spencer and the Ugly White."

33 Tim Mak, "The 'New' Racist Right." 2010, *FrumForum*. Retrieved from http://www.frumforum.com/the-new-racist-right.

34 PFS 2010. Footage found at http://www.vimeo.com/12598475—Note that the avatar of the commenter under the video, who sings the praises of Spencer, is of the anarcho-capitalist flag.

35 See Chapters 7 and 9 for further discussion of scientism.

36 Ross Douthat, Tweet from February 29, 2016.

37 Rydgren, *Movements of Exclusion*, p. 28.

38 See the final chapter.

39 Audio recordings from the day of, provided by NPR and retrieved from https://www.npr.org/2021/01/07/954324571/pro-trump-crowd-turns-into-violent-mob-breaches-u-s-capitol.

40 Ibid.

41 Mary McMahon, "What Was the Watts Rebellion?" 2019, *Wise Geek*. Retrieved from http:// www.wisegeek.com/what-was-the-watts-rebellion.htm.

42 Ibid.

43 Valerie Richardson, "Andy Ngo: Lack of Democratic Outrage Shows 'I'm the Wrong Type of Victim.'" 2019, *The Washington Times*. Retrieved from http://www.washingtontimes.com/news/2019/jul/9/andy-ngo-lack-democratic-outrage-shows-im-wrong-ty/.

44 Ibid.

45 Lane, from his 2019 video essay entitled "The Meaning of 'Law and Order' and the Limits of AntiFa." Retrieved from http://www.youtube.com/watch?v=CHLU-OEF5us.

46 Ibid.

47 Carl Freedman, *The Age of Nixon: A Study in Cultural Power*. Washington: Zero Books, 2012.

48 Lane, "Law and Order."

49 Ibid.

50 Hochschild, *Strangers in Their Own Land*.

51 H. W. Brands, *American Dreams: The United States since 1945*. New York: Penguin Press, 2010, p. 165.

52 Preston, *El Salvador*.

53 Lane, "Law and Order."
54 Ibid.
55 Zizek, "Some Politically Incorrect Reflections on Violence in France & Related Matters." 2005, *Lacan.com*. Retrieved from http://www.lacan.com/zizfrance.htm.
56 Ibid.
57 Lane, "Law and Order."
58 Ibid.
59 Ibid.
60 Gramsci, *Selections from the Prison Notebooks*, p. 276.
61 According to the ADL report, "Domestic Extremist-Related Killings in the U.S. by Perpetrator Affiliation, 2018." Retrieved from http://www.adl.org/media/12480/.
62 Ibid.
63 According the CSIS Report, "The Rise of Far-Right Extremism in the United States." Retrieved from http://www.csis.org/analysis/rise-far-right-extremism-united-states.
64 David Neiwert, "Home Is Where the Hate Is." 2017, *Type Investigations*. Retrieved from http://www.typeinvestigations.org/investigation/2017/06/22/home-hate/.

Conclusion

1 Pew Research Center.
2 Tweet retrieved from http://twitter.com/ksorbs/status/1325086195924291585.
3 Tweet retrieved from http://mobile.twitter.com/RealCandaceO/status/132475459 5248308225.
4 Eric Levitz, "Election Results: Biden Won, But the Democrats Lost." 2020, *NY Mag*. Retrieved from http://nymag.com/intelligencer/2020/11/2020-election-results-biden -won-democrats-senate-loss.html.
5 See Chapter 2.
6 Kropotkin, "Organized Vengeance Called 'Justice.'" Date unknown. Retrieved from http://www.theanarchistlibrary.org/library/petr-kropotkin-organised-vengeance-ca lled-justice.
7 Wood, *A Bee in the Mouth*.
8 Yang, *The War on Normal People*.
9 Hochschild, *Strangers in Their Own Land*, p. 135.
10 Andrew Levinson, *The White Working Class Today: Who They Are, How They Think and How Progressives Can Regain Their Support*. Lexington: Democratic Strategist Press, 2013, p. 52.
11 Rydgren, *Movements of Exclusion*, pp. 25–7.
12 Eric Kaufmann, *White Shift: Populism, Immigration, and the Future of White Majorities*. New York: Harry N. Abrams, 2019, p. 122.
13 Hochschild, *Strangers in Their Own Land*.
14 Joan C. Williams, *White Working Class: Overcoming Class Cluelessness in America*. Boston: Harvard Business Review Press, 2017, pp. 61–2.
15 Roel W. Meertiens and Thomas F. Pettigrew, "Is Subtle Prejudice Really Prejudice?" *Public Opinion Quarterly* 61 (1997), 54–71.
16 Jonathan Rieder, *Canarsie: The Jews and Italians of Brooklyn against Liberalism*. Cambridge: Harvard University Press, 1985, pp. 59, 60, 63.
17 Ibid.
18 Ibid.

19   Rydgren, *Movements of Exclusion*, p. 27.
20   Larry Gambone, "An Anarchist Strategy Discussion." 2004, *Mutualist.org*. Retrieved from http://www.mutualist.org/id13.html.
21   Logan Glitterbomb, "The Power of Counter-Recruitment." 2019, *Center for a Stateless Society*. Retrieved from http://www.c4ss.org/content/52091.
22   Jason Byas, interview with *Non Serviam*, 2019.
23   See Chapters 5 and 6.
24   Domenico Losurdo, *Liberalism: A Counter-History*, Trans. Gregory Elliott. New York and London: Verso, 2011, p. 241.
25   Urbinati argues that this loss of purpose in the old liberal sense of personal liberation within mutual community as a whole has also played a part in the shift toward individualism being seen as a fetishized selfishness in her book *The Tyranny of the Moderns*. Yale University Press, 2015.
26   See Chapter 3.
27   Mudge, *Leftism Reinvented*.
28   Charles George Roche, *Frederic Bastiat: A Man Alone*. New York: Arlington House, 1971, p. 153.
29   Gary Chartier, *Flourishing Lives: Exploring Natural Law Liberalism*. Cambridge: Cambridge University Press, 2019, p. 16.
30   Ibid.
31   Karl Marx and Friedrich Engels, *The Communist Manifesto*. London: Arcturus, 2018 [1848], pp. 32–3.
32   Ibid.
33   Recall Déjacque's letter to Proudhon in sourced in Chapter 6, Bakunin's essay on the individual quoted in Chapter 3, previous citation of Kropotkin's work on mutual aid, and so on.
34   Chartier, *Flourishing Lives*.
35   Ibid, pp. 16, 19.
36   Ibid, p. 28.
37   Ibid, p. 16.
38   Losurdo, *Liberalism: A Counter-History*.
39   See Chapter 5.
40   Karl R. Popper, *The Open Society and Its Enemies*. Princeton: Princeton University Press, 1966, p. 243.
41   H. B. Acton, in his introduction to Georg Wilhelm Friedrich Hegel, *Natural Law: The Scientific Ways of Treating Natural Law, Its Place in Moral Philosophy, and Its Relation to the Positive Sciences of Law*, Trans. T. M. Knox. Philadelphia: University of Pennsylvania Press, 1975, p. 16.
42   Thom Brooks, "Natural Law Internalism," from *Hegel's Philosophy of Right*, Ed. Thom Brooks. Malden: Wiley-Blackwell, 2012, p. 171.
43   Hegel, *Elements of the Philosophy of the Right*, Ed. Allen W. Wood and Hugh Barr Nisbet. Cambridge: Cambridge University Press, 1991.
44   Ibid., §222Z.
45   Hegel, *Phenomenology of Spirit*, Trans. A. V. Miller. Oxford: Clarendon Press, 1977 [1807], p. 229.
46   Byas, interview with *Non Serviam*.
47   Urbinati, *Me the People*, p. 11.
48   Ibid., p. 10.
49   Richman, "Mutual Aid Societies."

Bibliography

Allard, Scott W. 2017. *Places in Need: The Changing Geography of Poverty*. New York: The Russell Sage Foundation.

Arendt, Hannah. 1976. *The Origins of Totalitarianism* (Revised ed.). Boston: Houghton Mifflin Harcourt.

Avrich, Paul. 2005. *Anarchist Voices: An Oral History of Anarchism in America*. Oakland: AK Press.

Backes, Uwe. 1989. *Politischer Extremismus in Demokratischen Verfassungsstaaten*. Weisbaden: Springer.

Bakunin, Mikhail (Trans. Sam Dolgoff). 1972. *Bakunin on Anarchy: A New Selection of Writings Nearly All Published for the First Time in English by the Founder of the World Anarchist Movement*. New York: Alfred A. Knopf.

Bastiat, Frederic. 1850. *The Law*. Auburn: The Ludwig von Mises Institute, 2007.

Bockman, Joanna. 2011. *Markets in the Name of Socialism: The Left-Wing Origins of Neoliberalism*. Stanford: Stanford University Press.

Bonner, Raymond. 1984. *Weakness and Deceit: U.S. Policy and El Salvador*. New York: Times Books.

Brands, H.W. 2010. *American Dreams: The United States Since 1945*. New York: Penguin Press.

Brooks, Thom (Ed.). 2012. *Hegel's Philosophy of Right*. Malden: Wiley-Blackwell.

Brown, Wendy. 2015. *Undoing the Demos: Neoliberalism's Stealth Revolution*. New York: Zone Books.

Burley, Shane. 2017. *Fascism Today: What It Is and How to End It*. Oakland: AK Press.

Butler, Judith. 1997. *Excitable Speech: A Politics of the Performative*. Abingdon-on-Thames: Routledge.

Cahill, Thomas. 2004. *Sailing the Wine-Dark Sea: Why the Greeks Matter*. New York: Anchor.

Caldwell, Amy R. and John Beeler (Eds.). 2011. *Sources of Western History* (2nd Ed.). Boston and New York: Bedford/St. Martin's Press.

Carson, Kevin. 2007. *Studies in Mutualist Political Economy*. Charleston: Booksurge Publishing.

Carson, Kevin. 2010. *The Homebrew Industrial Revolution: A Low-Overhead Manifesto*. Charleston: Booksurge Publishing.

Certeau, Michel de. 2015 [1980]. *The Practice of Everyday Life*. Berkeley, Los Angeles, and London: University of California Press.

Chartier, Gary. 2012. *Anarchy and Legal Order: Law and Politics for a Stateless Society*. Cambridge: Cambridge University Press.

Chartier, Gary. 2019. *Flourishing Lives: Exploring Natural Law Liberalism*. Cambridge: Cambridge University Press.

Chomsky, Noam. 1999. *Profit Over People: Neoliberalism and Global Order*. New York, Toronto, and London: Seven Stories Press.

Chomsky, Noam and Edward S. Herman. 1988. *Manufacturing Consent: The Political Economy of the Mass Media*. New York: Pantheon Books.

Crawford, Matthew B. 2009. *Shop Class as Soulcraft: An Inquiry Into the Value of Work*. New York: Penguin Press.

Dahl, Robert and Charles Lindlom. 1953. *Politics, Economy, and Welfare: Planning and Politico-Economic Systems Resolved Into Basic Social Processes*. New York: Harper.

Darmstaedter, Friedrich. 2008. *Bismarck and the Creation of the Second Reich*. Piscataway: Transaction Publishers.

Fabian, Johannes. 2014 [1983]. *Time and the Other: How Anthropology Makes Its Object*. New York: Columbia University Press.

Fanon, Frantz (Trans. Richard Filcox). 2004 [1961]. *The Wretched of the Earth*. New York: Grove Press.

Fella, Stefano and Carlo Ruzza. 2009. *Reinventing the Italian Right: Territorial Politics, Populism, and Post-Fascism*. Abingdon-on-Thames: Routledge.

Ferguson, James. 2019. *The Anti-Politics Machine*. Minneapolis and London: University of Minnesota Press.

Ferguson, Marylin. 1980. *The Aquarian Conspiracy: Personal and Social Transformations in Our Time*. New York: Tarcher.

Field, Jacob. 2018. *Is Capitalism Working? A Primer for the 21st Century*. London and New York: Thames and Hudson.

Fisher, Mark. 2009. *Capitalist Realism: Is There No Alternative?* Washington: Zero Books.

Fox, Aaron A. 2004. *Real Country: Music and Language in Working-Class Culture*. Durham: Duke University Press.

Frase, Peter. 2016. *Life After Capitalism*. London and New York: Verso.

Freedman, Carl. 2012. *The Age of Nixon: A Study in Cultural Power*. Washington: Zero Books.

Friedman, Milton. 2002 [1962]. *Capitalism and Freedom*. Chicago: University of Chicago Press.

Friedman, Milton. 1992. *Money Mischief*. New York: Harcourt.

Geertz, Clifford. 1972. *The Interpretation of Cultures*. New York: Basic Books.

Gilder, George. 2013. *Knowledge and Power: The Information Theory of Capitalism and How it is Revolutionizing Our World*. Washington, DC: Regnery Publishing.

Graeber, David. 2018. *Bullshit Jobs: A Theory*. New York: Simon and Schuster.

Gramsci, Antonio. 1974. *Selections from the Prison Notebooks*. New York: International Publishers Co.

Graves, Jr., Joseph L. 2005. *The Race Myth: Why We Pretend Race Exists in America*. New York: Plume.

Haffner, Sebastian. 2000. *Defying Hitler*. London: Picador.

Hahnel, Robin and Erik Olin Wright. 2016. *Alternatives to Capitalism: Proposals for a Democratic Economy*. New York and London: Verso.

Haidt, Jonathan. 2012. *The Righteous Mind: Why Good People Are Divided by Politics and Religion*. New York: Pantheon.

Harcourt, Bernard E. 2018. *The Counterrevolution: How Our Government Went to War Against Its Own Citizens*. New York: Basic Books.

Harvey, David. 2005. *A Brief History of Neoliberalism*. Oxford: Oxford University Press.

Hedges, Chris. 2006. *American Fascists: The Christian Right and the War on America*. New York and London: The Free Press.

Hedges, Chris. 2018. *America: The Farewell Tour*. New York: Simon & Schuster.

Hegel, Georg Wilhelm Friedrich (Trans. A.V. Miller). 1977 [1807]. *Phenomenology of the Spirit*. Oxford: Clarendon Press.

Hegel, Georg Wilhelm Friedrich (Trans. T.M. Knox). 1975. *Natural Law: The Scientific Ways of Treating Natural Law, Its Place in Moral Philosophy, and Its Relation to the Positive Sciences of Law*. Philadelphia: University of Pennsylvania Press.

Hegel, Georg Wilhelm Friedrich (Trans. an Ed. Allen W. Wood and Hugh Barr Nisbet). 1991. *Elements of the Philosophy of the Right*. Cambridge: Cambridge University Press.

Heiden, Kondrad. 1944. *Der Fuehrer: Hitler's Rise to Power*. Boston: Houghton Mifflin Company.

Heller, Anne C. 2009. *Ayn Rand and the World She Made*. New York: Farrar, Strauss, and Giroux.

Heller, Henry. 2018. *A Marxist History of Capitalism*. Abingdon-on-Thames: Routledge.

Hess, Karl. 1975. *Dear America*. New York: Morrow.

Hickel, Jason. 2017. *The Divide: A Brief Guide to Global Inequality and Its Solutions*. London: Windmill Books.

Hochschild, Arlie Russell. 2016. *Strangers in Their Own Land: Anger and Mourning on the American Right*. New York: The New Press.

Hoffer, Eric. 1951. *The True Believer*. New York: Harper & Row.

Jones, Mark. 2016. *Founding Weimar: Violence and the German Revolution*. Cambridge: Cambridge University Press.

Judis, John B. 2016. *The Populist Explosion: How the Great Recession Transformed American and European Politics*. New York: Columbia University Press.

Kapuscinski, Ryszad. 2008. *The Other*. London and New York: Verso.

Kaufmann, Eric. 2019. *White Shift: Populism, Immigration, and the Future of White Majorities*. New York: Harry N. Abrams.

Kengor, Paul. 2017. *The Politically Incorrect Guide to Communism*. Washington, DC: Regnery Publishing.

Kropotkin, Pyotr. 2009 [1902]. *Mutual Aid: A Factor of Evolution*. London: Freedom Press.

Laclau, Ernesto. 2005. *On Populist Reason*. London and New York: Verso.

Levine, Rhonda. 1988. *Class Struggle and the New Deal: Industrial Labor, Industrial Capital, and the State*. Lawrence: University Press of Kansas.

Levinson, Andrew. 2013. *The White Working Class Today: Who They Are, How They Think and How Progressives Can Regain Their Support*. Lexington: Democratic Strategist Press.

Lippman, Walter. 1997 [1922]. *Public Opinion*. New York and London: The Free Press.

Locke, John. 1689. *Two Treatises of Government*. http://www.constitution.org/jl/2ndtr05.htm

Long, Roderick T. 2000. *Reason and Value: Aristotle versus Rand*. Washington, DC: The Objectivist Center.

Lopez, Ian Haney. 2014. *Dog Whistle Politics: How Coded Racial Appeals Have Reinvented Racism and Wrecked the Middle Class*. Oxford: Oxford University Press.

Losurdo, Domenico (Trans. Gregory Elliott). 2011. *Liberalism: A Counter-History*. New York and London: Verso.

MacLean, Nancy. 2017. *Democracy in Chains: The Deep History of the Radical Right's Stealth Plan for America*. New York: Penguin Books.

Manfredonia, Gaetano. 1997. *La Chanson Anarchiste en France des Origines à 1914*. Paris: L'Harmattan.

Marshall, Peter. 1993. *Demanding the Impossible: A History of Anarchism*. London: Harper.

Marx, Karl and Friederich Engels. 1996. *Marx and Engels Collected Works, Volume 35: Capital, Vol. 1: Production of Capital*. New York: International Publishers.

Marx, Karl and Friederich Engels. 2018 [1848]. *The Communist Manifesto*. London: Arcturus.

Mitcham, Jr., Samuel W. 1996. *Why Hitler? The Genesis of the Nazi Reich*. Westport: Praeger.

Moggach, Douglass. 2006. *The New Hegelians*. Cambridge: Cambridge University Press.

Mudde, Cas and Cristobal Rovira Kaltwasser. 2017. *Populism: A Very Short Introduction*. Oxford: Oxford University Press.

Mudge, Stephanie L. 2018. *Leftism Reinvented: Western Parties from Socialism to Neoliberalism*. Cambridge and London: Harvard University Press.

Nagle, Angela. 2017. *Kill All Normies: Online Culture Wars from 4Chan and Tumblr to Trump and the Alt-Right*. Washington: Zero Books.

Nietzsche, Friedrich (Trans. Walter Kaufmann). 1995. *Thus Spoke Zarathustra*. New York: Modern Library.

Page, Scott. 2008. *The Difference: How the Power of Diversity Creates Better Groups, Firms, Schools, and Societies*. Princeton: Princeton University Press.

Paxton, Robert O. 2004. *The Anatomy of Fascism*. New York: Vintage.

Pipes, Daniel. 1997. *Conspiracy: How the Paranoid Style Flourishes and Where It Comes From*. New York: Simon and Schuster.

Pitts-Taylor, Victoria. 2016. *The Brain's Body: Neuroscience and Corporeal Politics*. Durham and London: Duke University Press.

Polanyi, Karl. 2001 [1957]. *The Great Transformation: The Political and Economic Origins of Our Time*. Boston: Beacon Press.

Popper, Karl R. 1966. *The Open Society and Its Enemies*. Princeton: Princeton University Press.

Poulantzas, Nicos (Trans. Judith White). 2019 [1974]. *Fascism and Dictatorship: The Third International and the Problem of Fascism*. London and New York: Verso.

Poulantzas, Nicos. 1975. *Political Power and Social Class*. New York and London: Verso.

Preston, Keith. 2013. *El Salvador: A War by Proxy*. London: Black House Publishing.

Rand, Ayn. 1961. *For the New Intellectual*. New York : Random House.

Rand, Ayn. 1967a. *Capitalism: The Unknown Ideal*. New York: New American Library.

Rand, Ayn. 1967b. *The Virtue of Selfishness: A New Concept of Egoism*. New York: New American Library.

Ridley, Matt. 1996. *The Origins of Virtue*. New York: Viking.

Rieder, Jonathan. 1985. *Canarsie: The Jews and Italians of Brooklyn against Liberalism*. Cambridge and London: Harvard University Press.

Roche, Charles George. 1971. *Frederic Bastiat: A Man Alone*. New York: Arlington House.

Rothbard, Murray. 2007 . *The Betrayal of the American Right*. Auburn: Ludwig von Mises Institute.

Rydgren, Jens (Ed.). 2005. *Movements of Exclusion: Radical Right-Wing Populism in the Western World*. Hauppauge: Nova Science Publishers.

Saunders, Frances Stonor. 2000. *The Cultural Cold War: The CIA and the World of Arts and Letters*. New York: The New Press.

Schrag, Peter. 1998. *Paradise Lost: California's Experience, America's Future*. New York: The New Press.

Schramm, Michael and Thomas Pogge (Eds.). 2009. *Absolute Poverty and Global Justice: Empirical Data, Moral Theories, and Initiatives*. Abingdon-on-Thames: Routledge.

Shields, James. 2007. *The Extreme Right in France: From Petain to Le Pen*. Abingdon-on-Thames: Routledge.

Shirer, William L. 2011. *The Rise and Fall of the Third Reich: A History of Nazi Germany*. New York: Simon & Schuster.

Smith, Adam. 1776. *The Wealth of Nations*. N. P.

Spotts, Frederic. 2002. *Hitler and the Power of Aesthetics*. Woodstock: Overlook Press.

Stanley, Jason. 2018. *How Fascism Works: The Politics of Us and Them*. New York: Random House.

Stirner, Max. 2014 [1844]. *The Ego and Its Own: The Case of the Individual Against Authority*. London and New York: Verso.

Tang, Wenfang. 2016. *Populist Authoritarianism: Chinese Political Culture and Regime Sustainability*. Oxford: Oxford University Press.

Thomas, Paul. 1985. *Karl Marx and the Anarchists*. Abingdon-on-Thames: Routledge.

Traverso, Enzo. 2019. *The New Faces of Fascism*. London and New York: Verso.

Trotsky, Leon. 1936. *The Revolution Betrayed*. http://www.marxists.org/archive/trotsky/1936/revbet/revbetray.pdf.

Tyson, Lois. 2006. *Critical Theory Today: A User-Friendly Guide* (2nd Ed.). Abingdon-on-Thames: Routledge.

Urbinati, Nadia. 2014. *Democracy Disfigured: Opinion, Truth, and the People*. Cambridge and London: Harvard University Press.

Urbinati, Nadia. 2015. *The Tyranny of the Moderns*. New Haven: Yale University Press.

Urbinati, Nadia. 2019. *Me the People: How Populism Transforms Democracy*. Cambridge and London: Harvard University Press.

Varenne, Herve and Ray McDermott (Eds.). 1998. *Successful Failure: The School America Builds*. Boulder: Westview Press.

Walt, Lucien van der. 2009. *Black Flame: The Revolutionary Class Politics of Anarchism and Syndicalism*. Oakland: AK Press.

Warren, Donald L. 1976. *The Radical Center: Middle Americans and the Politics of Alienation*. Notre Dame: University of Notre Dame Press.

Wendling, Mike. 2018. *Alt-Right: From 4Chan to the White House*. London: Pluto Press.

Williams, George (Ed.). 2008 [1971]. *Group Selection*. Abingdon-on-Thames: Routledge.

Williams, Joan C. 2017. *White Working Class: Overcoming Class Cluelessness in America*. Boston: Harvard Business Review Press.

Wilson, David Sloan and Elliot Sober. 1999. *Unto Others: The Evolution and Psychology of Unselfish Behavior*. Cambridge and London: Harvard University Press.

Wood, Elisabeth Jean. 2003. *Insurgent Collective Action and Civil War in El Salvador*. Cambridge: Cambridge University Press.

Wood, Peter. 2006. *A Bee in the Mouth: Anger in America Now*. New York: Encounter Books.

Woshinsky, Oliver H. 2008. *Explaining Politics: Culture, Institutions, and Political Behavior*. Abington-on-Thames: Routledge.

Yang, Andrew. 2018. *The War on Normal People: The Truth About America's Disappearing Jobs and Why Universal Basic Income is Our Future*. New York and Boston: Hachette Books.

Zelizer, Julian E. 2012. *Governing America: The Revival of Political History*. Princeton: Princeton University Press.

Zipf, George. 1949. *Human Behavior and the Principle of Least Effort: An Introduction to Human Ecology*. Boston: Addison-Wesley Publishing.

Žizek, Slavoj. 2005. *Interrogating the Real*. New York: Continuum.

Žizek, Slavoj. 2012. *Less Than Nothing: Hegel and the Shadow of Dialectical Materialism*. London and New York: Verso.

About the Author

Micah J. Fleck is an anthropologist and neuro researcher whose writings cover various topics including the learning brain, gender, the development of political populism, and empathy as an evolutionary mechanism in group selection and human communities. He holds degrees from Columbia University and Harvard University and is currently senior writer and editor at *The Trans Muse Planet* and researcher and curriculum designer at MIDAS Multiple Intelligences Research, Inc. He is also the author of *Anthropology for Beginners* and a contributing author to the essay collection *The Anthropology of Donald Trump: Culture and the Exceptional Moment*.

Index

www.ingramcontent.com/pod-product-compliance
Lightning Source LLC
Chambersburg PA
CBHW060155280326
41932CB00012B/1766